THE J.T. FABER BOOK OF
TENNIS AND RACKETS

THE J.T. FABER BOOK OF
TENNIS AND RACKETS

Lord Aberdare

Quiller Press
London

First published in Great Britain in 2001 by
Quiller Press Limited
46 Lillie Road
London SW6 1TN

2 4 6 8 10 9 7 5 3 1

A CIP catalogue record for this title is available from the British Library

ISBN 1 899163 62 X

Printed and bound in Great Britain by
Butler & Tanner Ltd,
Frome and London

CONTENTS

FOREWORD

IT WAS WITH GREAT PLEASURE that I agreed to sponsor this completely new edition of Morys Aberdare's superb history of Tennis and Rackets. I am immensely proud that, in doing so, I continue my family's involvement not only with this publication but also with two games that have given me and so many of my friends a lifetime of enjoyment.

There may be other books available about these great games, but it seems to me that none are as well researched or as thorough as the current volume. I feel sure that it will come to be regarded as the definitive work on the subject, preserving for all time the long and illustrious history of the games.

Since the original text was published twenty years ago, a remarkable resurgence has taken place in both Tennis and Rackets, with new courts springing up all over the world and more players than ever before embracing the sports with renewed enthusiasm. These are truly exciting times for both games, and this is a very timely publication.

I have known Morys Aberdare since the 1930s when we learned the game of Rackets in the same courts at Winchester. Nobody is better qualified to take on a project as ambitious as this, and we are fortunate indeed that his ability to articulate his subject is as rich and extensive as his knowledge of it. We owe him a considerable debt of gratitude and I am delighted to be associated once again with an outstanding publication which I am certain will prove invaluable to sportsmen both now and well into the future.

JULIAN FABER

ACKNOWLEDGEMENTS

I MUST FIRST EXPRESS my gratitude to my editor Roddy Bloomfield. It was his idea to update my original book to cover the last twenty years of the twentieth century and it was he who arranged for Julian Faber to sponsor its production. I am extremely grateful to both of them. The huge task of co-ordinating a programme of updated information and illustration from every court in the world was underaken by Roddy Bloomfield with his usual enthusiasm. He depended on materials supplied by the clubs themselves and I am most grateful to all of those who helped him. Their names appear at the end of the book.

On the historical side, there have been three people who have made especially significant contributions to the literature of Tennis and I have made much use of their scholarly works – Roger Morgan, Heiner Gillmeister and Cees de Bondt.

For their help in reading, writing, correcting and suggesting in the Tennis section of the book, I am especially grateful to Chris Ronaldson, Julian Snow, Michael Garnett and Melvyn Pignon. In the Rackets section, I am enormously grateful to Norman Rosser in particular, and to Nigel Gordon and Peter Ashford. Others who have made important contributions to the book are Howard Angus, David Best, Richard Gray, David Hunn, Professor Nicholas Orme of Exeter University, Richard Gray, Bill Stephens and Michael Wolton.

An especially important contributor to the book as a whole, who deserves the highest praise, is Brigadier Andrew Myrtle. His overreaching knowledge of the administration of both games has been invaluable. He has also tackled the tedious job of assembling statistics of winners of the major competitions.

LORD ABERDARE

Fontainebleau.

Part I

Tennis

A ball game illustrated in the tomb of Beni Hassan.

HOW TENNIS BEGAN

GAMES OF BALL were just as much a part of ancient civilisations as they are of today's world. The earliest known illustration of a ball game comes from the ancient Egyptian tomb of Beni Hassan, built before 2000 BC, which depicts two women astride the backs of two other women, evidently playing ball. In another tomb, the shrine of Hathor in the Temple of Deir-er-Bahari, built about 1500 BC, the Pharaoh, Thotmes III, is shown holding a stick in one hand and a ball in the other. In the background are two other figures, probably priests, also holding balls.

Robert W. Henderson, formerly librarian at the New York Racquet and Tennis Club, is the greatest expert on the history of Tennis. In his authoritative book on the origin of ball games, *Ball, Bat and Bishop*, published in 1947, he has shown that such early ball games developed from religious ceremonies, often connected with the fertility celebrations of springtime. He suggests that the ball may originally have represented the most significant part of man – his head. It seems natural that a ball should have come into use early in man's history as a result of the innate urge to throw, hit or catch small round objects such as stones or apples. It is known that balls featured in certain rain-making ceremonies performed by women, and this could explain the illustration in the tomb of Beni Hassan.

In Islam similar religious rites are known to have existed, often involving large groups of contestants wielding sticks and stones and resembling a primitive form of hockey. In Persia games were played on horseback and are reminiscent of a form of polo, with large numbers of horsemen on either side.

Herodotus asserted that the Lydians originated ball games, and Polydorus Vergilius wrote a book of inventions in 1499 in which he said:

Dice, Tables, Tennis and Cards were found of the Lydians, a people of Asia, and begun not for any lucre or pleasure, but for a Common-wealth. For when the Countrey had great scarcenesse and want of Corn, insomuch that it was not able to suffice the people, they mitigated and swaged their hunger and scarcity by taking their meat moderately one day, and by applying such sports and pastimes the next day, to drive away the tediousnesse of their famine and hunger.

Ball games of a sort were part of the great civilisations of Greece and Rome. The Greeks were exponents of physical fitness and the ball played a part in their gymnastic exercises. Homer in the sixth book of the *Odyssey* relates how Nausicaa, daughter of Alcinous, the King of Phaeacia, goes to a river to do the family washing. While the clothes are drying she plays ball with her companions. One of the girls misses a catch and the ball falls into the river. The cries of the girls awaken Odysseus. Bajot in his *Eloge de la Paume* published in 1854 quotes Anne Lefèvre, later Dacier, who wrote on this episode:

Eustace (a twelfth-century bishop of Salonica) believes that it is the game of hephetinda *or* phennis, *in which you try to take each other by surprise; you make as if to throw the ball to one of the players, but you throw it to another who doesn't expect it. Sophocles wrote a drama on this Homeric subject which he called* pluntrias *and in which he showed Nausicaa playing this game. It was a great success. I wish it had survived so that we might see what art could make of such a subject. However, this game which Homer here describes, was common even among women.*

For their gymnastic ball games the Greeks used the word Sphairistike, borrowed by Major Walter Wingfield in 1873 for his game of lawn tennis. According to Hieronymus Mercurialis, author of *De Arte Gymnastica* published in 1572, the Greeks had at least four different ball games, which he labelled 'the little ball, the great ball, the hollow ball and the inflated ball'. The first three were of various sizes and were thrown from player to player as part of gymnastic exercises. The great ball was something like a medicine ball filled with sand.

The game with an inflated ball was called *episcyrum* and resembled a primitive form of rugby football. Two sides took part and evidently attempted to drive the ball through their opponents' defence to score a goal.

Mercurialis also identifies four Roman ball games according to the type of ball used – the *follis*, the *trigonalis*, the *paganica* and the *harpastum*. The *follis* was a large leather ball filled with air. It was propelled by the forearm, which was protected by an arm-guard (*bracciale*). An illustration shows it to be the game of Pallone, though it is very doubtful that this was really played by the Romans.

The term *trigonalis* suggests a threesome and the game seems to have involved three players probably positioned in the shape of a triangle. The ball was passed between them and the object was to prevent it from touching the ground. Evidently this led to considerable exertion as it was usually followed by a warm bath. The *paganica* was a country game played with a ball of skin stuffed with feathers. *Harpastum* seems to have resembled the Greek *episcyrum* using a leather ball.

These old Roman ball games are mentioned in contemporary writings but not in detail. Several references occur in Martial's *Epigrams*, in one to Atticus praising the merits of a good run rather than boxing, wrestling or ball games, he mentions all four of the games identified by Mercurialis.

'Neither *pila* [presumably *trigonalis*] nor *follis* nor *paganica* prepare you for a warm bath – nor striking at a dummy with a blunt sword. Don't twist your arms on the wrestling mat nor dash to seize the dusty *harpasta*.' (BOOK VII. 32). Later he lists all four balls:

'Pila Paganica. *This ball which swells with tightly pressed feathers is less flaccid than the* follis *and less compact than the* pila' [*presumably again* trigonalis] (BOOK XIV. 45)

'Pila Trigonalis. *If you know how to defeat me with your cunning left-handers, I am yours. You don't? You fool, give me back the ball*' (BOOK XIV. 46)

'Follis. *Go away young man; quiet old age suits me; it is fitting for boys to play with the* follis, *and for old men*' (BOOK XIV. 47)

'Harpasta. *These the pansy-boy, who enlarges his neck with wasted effort, swiftly seizes on the dusty ground of Antaeus*' (BOOK XIV. 48)

The game of Follis *as illustrated by Mercurialis.*

As in fives, it was clearly an advantage to play equally well with both hands. Martial writes of Menogenes: 'he will take the warm *trigonem* with either right or left hand.'

Certainly there were competitive ball games, played with hand and foot. Manilius writes in the first century AD:

Let Feasts unbend the Clowns, let Labour yield
To Sport and Mirth, and Pastime Crown the Field;
None give so sure, and none avoid the Fall
So well; or catch and turn the flying Ball.
To vigorous Stroak their active Arms command,
Or with their Foot supply the place of Hand,
Or when in Sport they shall the Ball divide
From Hand to Hand, and toss on every side;
Now throw the flying Globes, and now retain,
Or play them back upon themselves again.
Now back, now forward, round, and every way
O're all their Limbs the active Balls shall play,
As taught to know their meaning, and obey.

But they were normally associated with the Baths, where Petronius introduces Trimalchio to his readers:

Then all of a sudden we noticed a bald old fellow in a reddish shirt who was playing ball with some long-haired slave-boys. It wasn't the lads who made us stop and stare, though they were well worth a good look; it was the old boy their master. He had house-slippers on his feet and was doing things with a green ball. If a ball touched the ground, he wouldn't pick it up. A slave stood by with a bagful and handed out a new one to the players. And we observed another novelty. Two eunuchs were posted on opposite sides of the group. One held a silver jerry; the other counted the balls – not when they were in play, caught and hurled from hand to hand, but when they were missed.

We gaped a bit at these pomposities, but then Menelaus (Agamemnon's assistant) bustled up. 'That's the chap at whose table you're going to eat,' he said. 'In fact, you're at this moment watching the prelims of the dinner.'

No sooner had he got this information out than Trimalchio cracked his fingers. The eunuch with the jerry rushed up at the signal and held it out. Trimalchio went on playing as he relieved his bladder, then he called for a basin of water, dipped in his fingertips, and wiped them on the head of one of the young players.

Gianni Clerici in his magnificent book *500 Anni di Tennis* even suggests that the Romans played with a racket, and cites a passage from Ovid's *Ars Amatoria*. However, Ovid is surely referring to board games, resembling dice, draughts and backgammon, rather than to any ball game.

Galen, one of the pioneers of medicine writing in the second century AD, highly recommended exercise with the small ball. He considered it superior to other gymnastic exercises and listed several of its advantages such as relative safety, modest cost, little apparatus and no waiting. He pointed out that it was useful in exercising every part of the body, including the eyes, and was adaptable for all ages, and the weak as well as the strong. He recommended it to doctors for convalescent exercise.

Clearly at this point the ball was still mainly associated with gymnastic exercise and games had not yet been formalised. Galen was a good example of his own precepts, living to be 100 years old.

The first reference to a formal ball game occurs in a letter from Sidonius Apollinaris, a fifth-century Bishop of Clermont in Gaul, then overrun by the Visigoths.

Addressing Eriphius, he writes:

Tired at last of this long rest, we felt a desire to do something. Presently dividing ourselves into two companies, according to age, the first loudly called for a game of tennis, the others for a table and dice. I was the first to make a move for the tennis; for, as you know, I love it as much as my books. On the other hand, my brother Domicius, a man of great elegance and love of sport, got hold of some dice, rattled them, and rapped his dice-box as though he was sounding a trumpet to summon the players to him. As for us, we had a long game with the scholars, in order to refresh our limbs, numbed by a too long rest, by this healthy exercise. The noble Philimathius himself, as the Mantuan poet says, Ausus et ipse manu juvenum tentare laborem, constantly mingled with the tennis-players. He excelled at it when he was younger; but when he had been frequently hustled from the middle, where they stood upright, by the shock of some player running against him; when, at other times, going within the base, he could neither bar the way nor get out of the way of the ball, as it flew before him, or came upon him, and found a difficulty in recovering himself from his falls, being frequently overturned, he was the first to leave the game, panting and greatly heated. The exercise had caused his liver to swell, and he suffered a sharp pain. I stopped shortly afterwards, by way of charitably stopping at the same time as he, and thus relieving our brother from the annoyance of his fatigue.

With the spread of Christianity through Europe, many pagan buildings and pagan rituals were adapted to new use. Temples became churches, spring rites became Easter festivals and with them many ball games were translated. First in Spain, later in France, Easter festivals are known to have been associated with ball games of a primitive sort.

Early in the twelfth century at Auxerre in S.W. France, it was the custom on Easter Day for a ball to be handed to the Dean by a student priest. A procession entered the church and the ball was thrown from one person to another as they advanced up the aisle. Similar ball ceremonies existed at Auxerre in 1396 when the chapter issued an ordinance on the presentation of balls by new canons on the first Monday after Easter; and in 1412 another ordinance was issued limiting the size of the ball. It was not until 1538 that the old custom was finally abolished by order of an ecclesiastical court.

At Vienne, the Archbishop himself threw a ball into the midst of the congregation and some form of game was played.

In the thirteenth century at Nevers, the canons used to play at Easter and the bishop himself gave instructions for refreshment to be served to all members of the choir who took part.

These rituals had their critics. Jean Beleth, a theologian from Paris, disapproved of bishops and even archbishops taking part in these ball games at Christmas and Easter in the cloisters or episcopal palaces; he condemned them as pagan practices. This is the first mention of ball games being played in a cloister. William Durandus, Bishop of Meaux in 1326, quoted Beleth in support of his case against ball games; it is clear that they took place mainly in Meaux, Auxerre and Troyes.

To regulate the practice, several ecclesiastical councils issued edicts. Pierre de Colmien, Archbishop of Rouen in 1245, forbade priests to play. St Charles Borromeo, Archbishop of Milan, allowed only young priests in training to play. Jean de Longueville forbade his priests to play often in public, especially with laymen. Others acted as did the Council of Sens in 1485 and 'forbade all priests and all in holy orders to play tennis without shame in a shirt and in indecent undress'. An early illustration in the Bodleian Library shows just such an episode.

Until the last years of the twentieth century, the prevailing view was that the likely origin of Tennis lay in cloisters. The available evidence – the shape of the court and early references to, and illustrations of, the game being played in ecclesiastical circles – seemed to indicate that this was the case.

However, more light has been shed on the matter by Dr Heiner Gillmeister, a Chaucerian scholar and linguist, in his book *Tennis: A Cultural History*, first published in Germany in 1990, and also by Roger Morgan in *Tennis: The Development of the European Ball Game*, published in 1995. Gillmeister, who has meticulously studied evidence provided in contemporary literature and illustration, theorises that the origins of the game lie in medieval tournaments, especially the Pas d'Armes, in which knights on one side try to storm entry to a castle defended by the other side. He suggests that this knightly exercise was adapted by humbler folk into a game played in the open outside the walled city, which seems somewhat far-fetched to me.

Morgan takes a different view. He has unearthed a great many street games originating in Europe that included aspects of modern Tennis in their rules, such as scoring in 15s and the use of chases. This is in sympathy with Antonio Scaino da Salò, an Italian scholar who published the first-ever treatise on Tennis,

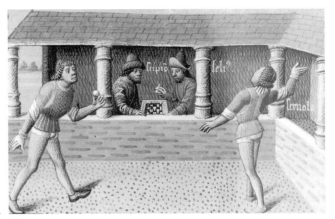

Tennis in a cloister.

Trattato del Giuoco della Palla, in 1555. Scaino writes of various different types of game, modified to suit the location of the court and the equipment of the player.

Morgan points to the unsuitability of the size and shape of a cloister and to instances of Tennis being played in church buildings despite the existence of a cloister. Evidence that the game spread from street to closed court and not the reverse may be seen in the need for adapting the old open-air rules. Chases, which in the original game were marked at the point where the ball was 'stopped', were not possible in the closed court. The rule was altered to marking a chase at the second bounce. The winning areas of the street game became the winning openings (dedans, grille, trou, lune) of the closed court. Such a transition seems far more credible than the reverse from closed court to the street, or indeed from Pas d'Armes.

Morgan suggests that the penthouse (which gives the court its cloister-like look) was of no significance in the early days and was in fact no more than the canopy providing shelter for shoppers in medieval streets. The association of the game with the church may have derived from the fact that ecclesiastical buildings provided walls and buttresses where the game could be played without interruption from pedestrians.

We are still left, however, with what Morgan describes as a 'tantalising gap from Greco/Roman times to the Middle Ages'. How did the Royal Tennis court of Henry II at the Louvre, described by Scaino in 1555, emerge from the multifarious forms of court elsewhere? Who decided on the positioning of the galleries and the penthouse? How did the tambour come to be inserted and why was the grille provided? It is tempting to think that there was a prototype somewhere and that these features formed part of an existing building, a castle perhaps, or an ecclesiastical building. Perhaps we shall never know.

Professor Nicholas Orme of Exeter University accepts the probable street origin of Tennis and that there were a great variety of rules depending on local geography. What is certain is that the game finally became well established when taken up by the aristocracy in the fifteenth and sixteenth centuries and more sophisticated courts began to be built for their use. I am indebted to Roger Morgan for allowing me to make use of his recent research into the drawings of Androuet du Cerceau, an eminent French architect of the sixteenth century. He was put on to this source of information by Cees de Bondt of the Dutch Real Tennis Association. Between 1545 and 1586, du Cerceau designed many châteaux, some of which included one or more Tennis courts. He was employed as a designer and architect by the royal family and received a pension from them for the last ten years of his life. His designs of Tennis courts differ from the known model at the Louvre. The penthouse is supported at intervals by pillars all around the court and there are no dedans, grille or tambour. Morgan refers to these courts as 'pillared galleries'. They occur in many of du Cerceau's designs and some possibly pre-date the Louvre court of 1555. Some were sited in moats and use the outer walls of the châteaux as the main walls of the courts. Existing turrets and buttresses were incorporated and this may be the origin of some of the unusual features of the Tennis court. Features differed from court to court. Just as the game in the street took various shapes according to the location, this seems to have been the case too with the development of closed courts.

Research work carried out in Italy by Cees de Bondt, covering the period 1450 to 1789, which I have been privileged to read, shows the existence of a considerable number of 'Pallacorda' courts built by the great aristocratic families of Italy, including Medici, Gonzaga, Este and the ecclesiastical princes in Rome. These varied in size and layout, becoming more standardised in the late sixteenth century.

The popularity of Tennis at this time in France is attested to by several contemporary witnesses. Jerome Lippomano, Venetian Ambassador to Henri III for three years from 1577, wrote that there were more than 1800 Tennis courts in Paris and at least a thousand écus (an ecu was three francs) were spent on the game every day. 'The French enjoy the game and play with marvellous grace and dexterity,' he said, and they 'eat four or five times a day without any rule or fixed hour. Little bread or fruit, a lot of meat and pastry.'

Francesco Gregory d'Ierni, who accompanied the Papal Legate, Alexandre de Medicis, Cardinal of Florence, to Paris in 1596, writes of '250 tennis courts, very beautiful and very well equipped, which they say, before the recent wars, gave employment to some 7000 people.' This figure may be an underestimate according to Thomas Plater in his *Description of Paris* in 1599. 'Some allege,' he writes, 'that there are about 1100 tennis courts in Paris; admittedly there are only half that number, but it is still a respectable figure.'

Another witness is Sir Robert Dallington, secretary to the English Ambassador to France, who wrote in 1598:

As for his exercises, there is danger but of one in France, and that is tennis play: this is dangerous (if used with too much violence) for the body: and (if followed with too much diligence) for the purse.

As for the exercise of Tennis play...it is more here used than in all Christendome besides; whereof may witnesse the infinite number of Tennis Courts throughout the land, insomuch as yee cannot finde that little Burgade, or towne in France, that hath not one or more of them. Here are, as you see, three-score in Orléans, and I know not how many hundred there be in Paris: but of this I am sure, that if there were in other places the like proportion, ye should have two Tennis Courts for every one Church through France. Methinks it also strange, how apt they be here to play well, that he would thinke they were borne with Rackets in their hands, even the children themselves manage them so well, and some of their women also, as we observed at Blois.

There is one great abuse in this exercise, that the Magistrates do suffer every poore Citizen and Artificer to play thereat, who spendeth that on the Holyday at Tennis, which he got the whole weeke for the keeping of his poore family. A thing more hurtful than our Ale-houses in England, though the one and the other be bad enough.

And of this I dare assure you, that of this sort of poore people, there be more Tennis Players in France, than Aledrinkers, or Malt-wormes (as they call them) with us.

The testimony of such people has to be believed. My conclusion is that the name *jeu de paume* was applied to innumerable variants of the game in the streets and the chateaux; some were played in the open, some in covered areas. They had their own versions of the rules depending on their location and were played by old and young, rich and poor. As Dr Gillmeister has pointed out, historians have concentrated their attention on the doings of the king and court and have overlooked the popularity of the game among the ordinary people of France and other countries in Europe.

WHY TENNIS?

Tennis was in origin a French game, known in its early days as *cache, jeu de bonde* and, eventually, *jeu de paume*. The first of these names is from the Northern French dialect of Picardy and was adopted into Scots at an early date, although it does not appear in a written source (in the form of *caich*) before the last decades of the fifteenth century. Picardian *cache* reappears in the fifteenth-century Dutch *kaetsspel*, the sixteenth-century *Katzball* and *Katzenspil* in German, and the Scots *caichepule*, found in 1526. James VI of Scotland (James I of England), advising his son Henry in 1598, recommended 'playing at the cache'. Why then did the English call it Tennis?

It is an intriguing question which has long puzzled historians. Many ingenious theories have been advanced, most of them unsatisfactory. One suggestion was that it was played five-a-side, making a total of ten players; another that it derived from *tenes bound*, an old Norman expression referring to the tendons or cords protecting the hand; another that it came from the Greek *phennis* or the Latin *teniludium* or *tenere* (to catch), or the German *Tenne* (a threshing floor), or even from the old Egyptian city of Tinnis, famous for its fabrics which may have been used to make Tennis balls. Another suggestion was that it derived from Tennois or Sennois in the Champagne district.

Most of these theories suffer from one great defect: they don't explain why a foreign word should have been used to describe a French game.

A plausible explanation seems to be that given by John Minshew in his *Guide into Tongues* published in 1617. He derives it from the French imperative of *tenir* (hold) – 'which word the Frenchmen, the only tennis players, use to speake when they strike the ball at tennis.' If French players used to call out *tenez* (i.e. hold or take heed) before each service, it could be that their English pupils came to call the game by this term.

That the English were not the only ones to choose this word for the name of the game is shown by a curious extract from the *Cronica di Firenze* by Donato Velluti, writing between 1367 and 1370, but referring back to an event in 1325.

> *Thomas of Lippaccio was an ecclesiastic endowed with a benefice on the other side of the mountains [i.e. beyond the Alps], beautiful in form, tall and courageous as a lion. He sold the benefice referred to and came over here [i.e. to Florence] for there had arrived 500 French courtiers that were the handsomest and finest set of people I ever saw, with plenty of money, all noblemen and great barons, among whom I saw one who was taller by a whole head and neck than any tall man, and his foot more than half an arm long. Almost all of them were killed at the defeat of Altopascio. He played all day with them at ball, and at this time was the beginning in these parts of playing at tenes.*

This suggests that the Italians, too, used *tenes* to describe what the French called *jeu de paume*, although later they came to call it in their own language *giuoco della corda*.

But what evidence is there that the French players did call out *tenez* before serving? The difficulty lies in the fact that such customs are not normally recorded by writers about a game. Consider, for example, the game of Rackets in which the marker calls out 'play' after each good stroke. This is certainly not recorded by writers on Rackets and should the custom cease a researcher 500 years hence would have great difficulty establishing its use.

However, the remarkable fact is that some evidence does exist that a warning cry was given before serving, although in Latin, the *lingua franca* of the day, rather than in French. The first of such evidence comes from the *Colloquies* of Erasmus. These were written as Latin exercises for his students in Paris and became a standard school textbook. He first published them in 1518, but added to them in later editions, including a section on sport in 1522.

The part on Tennis is in the form of a dialogue between Nicholas and Jerome. They draw lots for side and Nicholas wins the service. Before he serves Jerome says to him, 'Well, good luck. Serve the ball on to the penthouse. If anyone serves without warning, that service is not good.'* (*Qui miserit nihil praefatus frustra miserit*). Then Nicholas serves, calling out: *Hem, accipe igitur.* Later he serves again using the words *Rursus accipe pilam.* So it looks as if the server was required to give warning before serving and it seems likely that Erasmus uses the word *accipe* as a translation of the French *tenez*.

Antonio Scaino is unfortunately not very helpful on this particular subject, but at one point he refers to the duty of the captain of each side to call and reply at the beginning of the rally.

The vital key occurs in a Latin/French phrasebook written in 1580 by a Frenchman, Maturin Cordier, under the title *Commentarius Puerorum*, which includes a section on Tennis, '*Ludus Pilae Palmariae*'. The game is three-a-side with a pint of wine at stake. The players toss for sides in the modern manner by spinning a racket, the alternatives being *pluye* (rain, probably 'rough') and *beau temps* (fine, probably 'smooth'). The server calls out '*Tenez, j'y mets*' (look out, I'm serving), and this is translated: *Excipe: ecce mitto.* Here surely is the proof. *Excipe* or *accipe* is the translation of *tenez*, used by French players before serving.

Cordier goes on to confirm what Erasmus had written, that a word of warning was required before serving, although in this case he used the word *jouez* rather than *tenez*. One player says: '*Ton coup ne vault rien: car tu n'as pas dict, Jouez*' translated into Latin very similar to that of Erasmus – *frustra misisti: utpote nihil praefatus* (your service is not good because you didn't call 'play'). He defines *jouez* as a word uttered by the server and in his Latin translation uses *excipe*.

In the light of this sixteenth-century evidence, it seems almost certain that the server had under the rules to give a word of warning and that the word used in French was either *tenez* or *jouez*. *Tenez* would seem to be the earlier word and no doubt gave rise to its use to describe the game in England.

In the present Basque game of *rebot,* the server has

to warn his opponents either orally or by gesture that he is about to serve and his opponents have to acknowledge the warning. In the *Petit Manuel de la Longue Paume* by Edmond Collin, written in 1891, rule thirteen is: *On avertit chaque fois que l'on tire* (one gives warning each time one serves).

A much later writer, R. Frissart, in a curious pamphlet of 1641 entitled *Carmen de Ludo Pilae Reticulo*, dedicated to Cardinal Richelieu, illustrated the war between Louis XIII of France and Philip IV of Spain in terms of a Tennis match. They spin a racket for sides; the French king chooses smooth (rectos) and wins; so he serves crying out, '*Excipe.*' He uses the same *excipe* on several other occasions when he serves and so does the Spanish king when it is his turn to serve.

Gillmeister refers to a children's game called *tenee-ui* played in the Rhineland Palatinate and evidently developed from contact with French neighbours. A similar game is known in English-speaking countries as cat, and both games are played with a short wooden stick, tapering at both ends, rather than with a ball. In *tenee-ui* the server cries out *tennee* and the receiver replies *ui* suggesting the French *oui*.

A similar exchange of cries was observed in the Faroe Islands by Jens Christian Svabo, watching children playing a similar sort of game in 1781/2. In that case they called out *exebiti* or *exaksebiti* and the reply was *roti*. The first two words are clearly *excipite* or *accipite* and the reply is derived from *parati* (ready).

Gillmeister also calls in evidence a poem on the battle of Agincourt, describing the siege of Harfleur in terms of a Tennis match. There are three extant versions of this Middle English poem, but the two labelled the B-version and the C-version by Dr Gillmeister are of special interest. In these a big gun, before serving its 'ball', is heard to exclaim:

B. *Tenys seyde the grete gonne,*
   How felawes go we to game.
C. *Than sayd the greate gunne,*
   Holde felowes we go to game.

This evidence from the Agincourt poem is reinforced by a Shrewsbury clergyman in the 1420s, one John Audelay, calling back to memory Henry's feat of arms in another poem:

With tenes hold he ferd ham halle
With tenez! hold! he frightened them all

This certainly seems to suggest that Minshew was right in his etymology of the word and that *Tenez* or 'hold' was the normal word of warning before service.

---

*Translated by Craig R. Thompson, 1965.

KEEPING THE SCORE

ONE PRACTICE IN TENNIS that dates back to its very earliest days is scoring in points worth 15 each until a total of 60 is reached to win one game. The first mention of this scoring in 15s occurs in the Middle English poem on the Battle of Agincourt, mentioned in the previous chapter. Henry V, having laid siege to Harfleur, places his guns in position.

My gonnes schall lye upon this grene.
For they schall play with Harflete
A game at the tenys as y wene.

Other siege-engines are placed on a hill

To marke the chase whan they play well.

Three great guns are brought forward – London, Messyngere and Kynge's Daughter. London fires first:

'XV be fore' than sayd London, in same,
Hys ball foull fayre he gan throwe.

Messyngere fires next:

'XXX his myne' sayd Messyngere,
'I woll hit wyn if that I may.'

Kynge's Daughter fires the third shot:

The Kynge's Doughter sayd 'Harke how they play,
Helpe my madonys at this tyde.'
XLV, 'that nys no naye'.

The next evidence is contained in the Middle Dutch didactic treatise of 1431 *Dat Kaetspel Ghemoralizeert*, and the third in a poem written in 1439 by the French prince Charles d'Orléans while imprisoned in England:

J'ay tant joué avecques Aage
A la paulme que maintenant
J'ay quarante-cinq.

(I have played Tennis so much with Time that I am now 45).

Confirmation in Latin comes from Erasmus's *Colloquies* of 1552 during the game between Nicholas's side and Jerome's. Nicholas's side wins a love-game and the points are clearly described in Latin – *Quindecim, Triginta, Quadraginta quinque*. Modern usage of the word forty is merely a shortened version of the original forty-five. Even when Maturin Cordier wrote in 1580, it was not unusual to abbreviate the rather clumsy forty-five. In Latin it was *quadraginta quinque* and this, he tells us, was shortened to 'quadra' by the young.

In 1431, Jan van der Berghe in Holland had posed the question why 15s, but he could find no satisfactory answer. The first attempt at explanation was made by Antonio Scaino in 1555. He argued that there are three degrees of victory in each game:

1 The simple, when both players score points in the course of a game.
2 The double, what we now call a love-game.
3 The treble or furious, when one player reaches 40-love and his opponent wins the next five points and the game.

Who wouldn't be furious!

Betting was frequent in those days and the treble victory brought a triple reward to the backer. This being the finest achievement of all, Scaino reasoned that the 5 points necessary should be multiplied by the three degrees of treble victory to arrive at the magic number 15.

Scaino's typically medieval exposition is not very satisfactory. A more likely account is given by a French scholar, Jean Gosselin, writing in 1579 his *Déclaration de Deux Doubtes qui se trouvent en comptant dans le Jeu de Paume*. He confesses that he has found no previous authority on the subject and that the origin is buried in antiquity. He goes on to propound two theories of his own. The first is based on the fact that the number 60 often represented a complete whole in medieval times. A physical sign or sextant, the sixth part of a circle, consisted of 60 degrees; each degree was made up of 60 minutes, each minute of 60 seconds. It was natural therefore to take the figure 60 to represent a game, and the four points which made up the game were each worth 15 in consequence.

On the whole, this theory of Gosselin's seems to be the most satisfactory of any. Undoubtedly, in the Middle Ages the number 60 had a significance which it is now more usual to find attached to the number 100. It would be quite logical therefore to divide the game into four equal stages of 15. Gosselin's other theory was based on geometrical figures and is extremely complicated. It revolves around various measurements, particularly a *clima*, which is 60 feet in length and in breadth. Once again he finds the magical number 60 and proceeds to divide it up into four equal parts of 15.

More modern writers have propounded other theories. One ingenious theorist of 1885 pointed out that in French courts there are 14 chases marked on the floor. Thus, if the marker calls any number from 1 to 14, it means a chase. He suggests that the number 15 was therefore chosen for the first point won, so that there could be no confusion with a chase. This theory fails because there were no chases marked on the floor at the time when scoring by 15s was first used.

In 1913 A.E. Crawley advanced a theory based on the division of the clock into 60 minutes, made up of four quarters each of 15 minutes. In 1920 he added another based on the sexagesimal system of coinage in use in France in the fourteenth century. Both these ideas lend weight to Gosselin's theory of the segment: they are added proof of the medieval significance of the number 60 to denote a whole. From that point its division into four equal parts is a natural step.

The origin of the word deuce is fortunately simple. It was often the habit in France to call *à un* instead of 40, meaning that the player was within one stroke of winning a game. When both players reached 40, the rules required the winning of two consecutive points (advantage, game) and the score was called *à deux*. The old score *à un* has fallen into disuse, and *à deux* has developed into deuce in English.

More difficulties arise in tracing the origin of the term love to mean nothing in Tennis scoring. An unlikely theory, albeit ingenious, ascribes its derivation to a corruption of the French word *l'oeuf*, the egg. It is argued that the figure nought was familiarly known in France as an egg, in the same way that in this country a nought in cricket is called a duck's egg. However, there is no evidence to support this theory. Malcolm D. Whitman is probably nearer the mark when he argues

that the use of the word love to mean nothing is as old as the English language. He quotes a saying of the year 971, apparently from an entry in the *Oxford English Dictionary*: *ne for feu, ne for nanes mannes lufou* – the equivalent of the modern 'neither for love nor money'. Love is equivalent to nothing, also, in such phrases as 'a labour of love' and 'to play for love'. In Latin the world *gratis*, meaning literally for favours or for love, is used in English to mean for nothing.

The origin of the word service may lie in the ancient practice of having a servant to play the first stroke. Henry VIII employed a man in this capacity and in the ancient Italian game of *pallone a tripolino* delivered the service.

Another ancient aspect of Tennis, and one that has continued to give it a very special charm right up to the present day, is the chase, derived from the French *chasser*, to hunt or chase. The chase developed from the earliest Tennis of all: *longue paume*, which was *jeu de paume* played in the open. A large open space was required and often five players on either side would face each other across the cord or net. The ball was originally struck with the hand on the volley or at the first bounce and the players would seek to hit it as far as they possibly could. If one side failed to get the ball up, it made a chase – not at its second bounce as today, but at the point where it ceased to roll. The players would seek to stop it rolling as quickly as possible to reduce the length of the chase that they in turn would have to play for.

In such conditions, chases were marked by placing some object on the ground. In Erasmus's *Colloquies* it is clear that Nicholas and Jerome were playing *longue paume*. Erasmus uses the word *terminus* for chase – the point at which the ball ceases to roll. Nicholas says, 'Mark the chase with a shell or stone, or with your cap if you prefer.' And later, having made the chases, he remarks, 'We have two quite long chases.'

Most people associate Basque games with the *chistera*, the basket used in various games of *pelota* or *jai-alai*. In fact, the *chistera* dates from 1857, but the games played with the bare hand, the gloved hand and the bat date back to the origins of Tennis.

Rebot, one of the most ancient of these Basque games, incorporates the chase. Unlike most Basque games, *Rebot* is played by two teams across a centre line – very similar to *longue paume* except that both ends of the court are bounded by a wall. One side has a smaller area to defend than the other and the way of forcing a change of side is by making a chase – as in Tennis.

The chase is made at the point where the ball ceases

to roll or is stopped, and is made on the smaller side of the court only. It is marked by a branch or a small flag on that side. It is played for as in Tennis, when one side reaches 40 or there are two chases.

The two sides then change ends and the centre line is deemed to be at the point where the chase was made. This means that the opponents have an even smaller area between the new centre line and the back wall to make a better chase.

The first mention of a chase being scored at the second bounce is made by Juan Luis Vivès, a friend of Erasmus, who also wrote a Latin exercise book for students in dialogue form. He had studied in Paris, but came to England in 1522 where he lectured on philosophy at Corpus Christi College, Oxford. He received an allowance from Henry VIII and obviously knew Tennis well. He wrote his *Leges Ludi* in 1539, and one of his two characters explains that 'the ball, indeed, is either returned on the volley or at its first bounce. For on its second bounce it is dead and a mark is made where it struck the ground.'

An illustration of an early seventeenth-century court at Tübingen in Germany shows a marker holding a special object used to mark a chase before the development of chase lines.

Scaino explains that the making of a chase when the ball stops rolling is not appropriate for the game of *courte paume*, played in a court with a back wall. 'In the court game,' he writes, 'they insist on the chase being marked at the point where the ball hits the ground at its second bounce, this being the custom in almost the whole of Tuscany and, in my opinion, a very excellent custom, worthy to be accepted by valiant and esteemed players.'

The first known illustration showing chase lines marked on a court is an etching in *Grosser Herren Stands und Adelichen Haus-Vatters* by F.P. Florin, published in Nuremberg about 1719.

An early seventeenth-century court at Tübingen, showing the marker with his chase-marking equipment.

BASIC PRINCIPLES OF PLAY

To the uninitiated Tennis appears to be a very complicated game, but in reality – apart from the system of chases – it is not. Lawn tennis is derived from it and the two games have much in common. Both are played over a net and in either singles or doubles. Both require the ball to be returned either on the volley or after it has struck the ground once, although in Tennis it may rebound off the walls before striking the ground for a second time. Both are scored in games by points of 15, 30, 40, deuce and advantage; and in sets won by the first player to reach six games, although in Tennis the winning margin can be a single game, i.e. 6–5.

In Tennis, however, there are certain openings in the walls of the court that give the player who strikes a ball into them an outright point. These are the dedans, the grille and the winning gallery (see plan). The court has another feature, the tambour, off which the ball comes at an awkward angle, not easily anticipated.

Service at Tennis is always delivered from the dedans end; the ball has to bounce at least once on the penthouse, in between a line marked on it at the centre of the court and its join with the far end (hazard end) penthouse; another line on the back penthouse limits the distance it may roll round towards the grille. As in lawn tennis it is an advantage to serve and a player will seek to remain on the service side as long as possible.

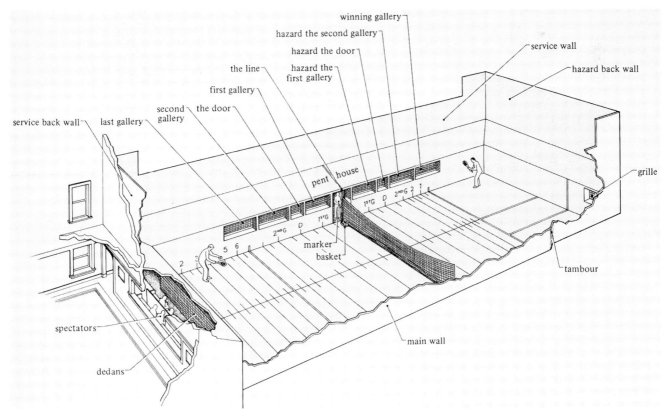

Plan of a Tennis court.

The only way the receiver can cross over and gain the service is by means of a chase.

A chase is made when a ball strikes the ground on its second bounce anywhere on the service side or on the receiver's (hazard) side between the net and the winning gallery. In most ball-games the ball would be 'dead'; at Tennis it makes a chase at the point on the floor where it bounces for the second time. Lines across the court enable the scorer ('marker') to record accurately the exact spot. A chase is also made if the ball enters any of the galleries – except, of course, the winning gallery. Each gallery has its own name (see plan).

The chase lines are numbered on the service side from the back wall at yard intervals from 1 to 6. Thereafter lines are drawn opposite the galleries and are described by the name of the appropriate gallery. On the hazard side there are only two yard chases after the second gallery; between them and the back wall no chase can be made. On both sides, the nearer the back wall the chase is made, the better it is for scoring purposes.

When a chase is made, neither side scores a point; the relevant chase (e.g. chase 2 – chase 5 – chase the last gallery) goes into cold storage for the time being. When there are two chase or when one player is within a point of winning a game, the players change ends and play off any outstanding chases. The player who made the chase now has to defend it; his opponent attacks it. To win the chase the attacker must make a better chase than the one being played. In other words he must ensure that every ball he plays will bounce on its second bounce between his opponent's back wall and the line of the chase being played. The defender will seek to return any such shot before its second bounce, but, if he judges that it will fall at a point worse than the chase being played, he will leave it and win the point.

The need to bring the ball sharply down off the back wall and thereby make a better chase is responsible for the typical cut shot of the Tennis player, not appropriate in the different conditions of lawn tennis.

One other difference in scoring between the two games can cause confusion. At lawn tennis the server's points are called first (e.g. 15–40); at Tennis, because service can change in the middle of a game, it is the winner of the last point whose score is called first.

DEVELOPMENT OF THE RACKET

Without doubt Tennis was first played with the bare hand – indeed it was known in its country of origin as *jeu de paume* (palm game). Anyone who has seen young Basques hitting a hard ball up against a '*fronton*' (the large front wall) will know the strength and skill that can be developed. However, it was not to be expected that everybody was tough enough for such painful sport, and gloves came into use. An excellent example is the Basque glove known as a *passaka*, used for an ancient game played in a *trinquet* – a form of court, developed from the hazard side of a Tennis court. Then followed wooden bats, *battoirs*, and eventually a *battoir* with a head strung with sheep gut – a primitive racket.

Chaucer's use of that word in his *Troilus and Criseyde* – when Troilus says, 'But kanstow playen raket, to and for, Nettle in, dok out, now this, now that Pandare?' – has led to theories that the racket was used earlier. Robert W. Henderson has asserted that Chaucer's 'racket' was in fact a game of dice, but Heiner Gillmeister, who has had several scholarly articles published on Chaucerian problem words, believes that Chaucer, to judge from the context, had in mind some form of Tennis, although whether 'raket' referred to the game itself or to some sort of implement we have at present no means of knowing.

The case of Margot has also been cited as evidence of an early use of the racket. About 1427, 'came to Paris a woman called Margot, rather young, from twenty-eight to thirty years old, who was of the country of Hainault and played better at hand-ball than any man had seen; and she played very strongly both forehand and backhand, very cunningly and very cleverly as any man could, and there were but few men whom she did not beat except the very best players. And it was the court in Paris where the best play was in the rue Grenier Saint-Lazare, which was called the Petit-Temple.'

It has been argued that if she played a backhand she must have had a racket, but this is not necessarily so. It is perfectly possible to play a backhand shot with the hand and may even be desirable in some circumstances – especially if one hand is stronger than the other.

Transition from hand to racket comes later – at the beginning of the next century. Pasquier (*Recherches sur la France* 1596) cites the evidence of an old man of over seventy-six who told him that in his youth he had been one of the leading players of Tennis in his day, but that the game had been quite different because they played with the hand only – and while some played with the naked hand, others, to make it less painful, wore double gloves. Still others, more confident, gave themselves some advantage over their companions by wearing cords and tendons, in order to hit the ball better and with less trouble, and this came to be general practice. Finally came the racket, at first a very primitive instrument but gradually developed into what we know today. Pasquier was born in 1528, which would suggest that the old man was talking about the latter part of the fifteenth century.

For a considerable time both hand and racket were used. When Henry VII entertained Philip, Archduke of Austria and King of Castile, at Windsor in 1506, he laid on some Tennis.

> *After the horse was Bayted Bothe Kyngs went to the Tennys playe … where played my Lord marques (of Dorset) the Lord Howard and two other knights togethare, and aftere the Kynge of Casteele had scene them play a whylle, he made partye with the Lord marques and then played the Kynge of Casteele with the Lord Marques of Dorset the Kynge Lookynge one them, but the King of Casteele played with the Rackete and gave the Lord Marques XV. and after that he had pled his pleasure and arrayed him selfe agene it was almost nighte, so both Kyngs Retorned agayne to their Lodginges.*

Clearly the racket gave the King of Castile an advantage over the Marquess of Dorset, for which compensation was made by a handicap of 15. Even so, the racket must have been a pretty primitive affair to have given a mere 15 to the opponent playing with his hand.

A few years later, in 1522, Erasmus in his *Colloquies* includes this dialogue:

NICHOLAS: *We'll sweat less if we play with a racket.*
JEROME: *No, let's leave the net to fishermen. Using your hand is finer.*

Jerome's answer is a pun in the original Latin – the word *reticulum* meaning both a racket and a net.

The derivation of the word *racket* has usually been attributed to the Arabic *rahat* meaning hands, but this is hardly tenable on linguistic grounds. Heiner Gillmeister, in an article published in *Journal für Geschichte* in March 1980, argues for a French origin of the word, which would be in keeping with the fact that most Tennis terms are French. As already mentioned, the earliest recorded name of the game was *cache*, the Picardian equivalent of the French *chasse*. The English words *catch* and *chase* mirror the different pronunciation in France of what was originally one word. In Picardy the verb *racacher* was used to denote the return of the ball, and a noun *racache* has survived in Picardian children's language meaning a sort of bat. It would seem probable, then, that some variant of these two words was the origin of 'racket', rather than a remote Arabic word, the use of which was confined to medical writings throughout the Middle Ages.

Even in 1555, when Scaino wrote his magnificent treatise, there were still courts built for play with the hand, and he includes plans for an open and a covered court; but clearly his own preference, and no doubt that of most of his contemporaries, was for the game with the racket.

In 1539, Vivès in his *Dialogues* describes a contemporary French racket strung with fairly thick gut, somewhat like the sixth or bass string of a lute.

By the end of the sixteenth century, the racket was the accepted thing and hands were only used to grip the racket. In his Italian/English phrasebook of 1591, John Florio makes no mistake in having one of his characters call out: 'What ho, boy, bring hither some balls and some rackets.'

Tennis rackets did not become the powerful instruments they are today until much later – probably the eighteenth century. The racket described and illustrated by François de Garsault in his *The Art of the Tennis-Racket-Marker and of Tennis* published in 1767 is the immediate ancestor of a modern racket with a much longer handle than had previously been used.

One noticeable difference is that in those days, the vertical strings were twice the thickness of the horizontal strings and that the latter were wound round each of the vertical strings instead of being threaded through them as they are now. This was the sort of racket used by Barcellon and Masson, and by Barre and Biboche.

Somewhere about 1856 the system of stringing changed; gut of equal thickness was used and the horizontal strings were threaded through the vertical. The French were the best makers of Tennis rackets and they included Borrelly, Lavergne, Tison and Leclercq. John Dynan and his son in the seventeenth century are the first known English makers and in about 1780 even the French acknowledged that an English professional Pilet (or Pillet) made a racket as good as theirs.

The great name in French racket-manufacture in the nineteenth century was Brouaye, an apprentice of Leclercq. His rackets, with their striking green centre-piece, are easily recognizable. They were as popular in

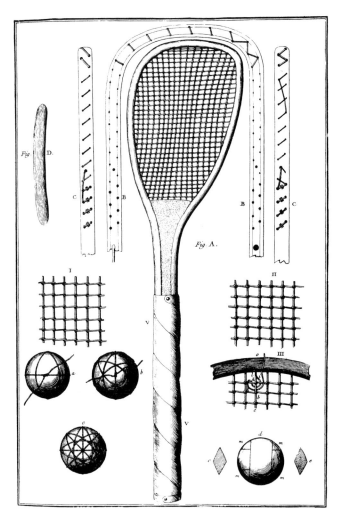

De Garsault's racket of 1767.

England as in France, although there were a number of English manufacturers such as Watkins, Pittman, Wilson, W. Birt, Cox, John Case and his son Henry Case.

The earliest known makers of Rackets rackets were Pittman and Wilson.

In about the 1880s, two London firms began to make first-class Tennis rackets: Prosser of Holloway Road, and Nusser of Dean Street, Soho. About 1913 Bennett, an apprentice of Nusser, started a new firm in Cambridge. In 1915 Nusser was interned as an enemy alien and his business was taken over by one of his principal assistants, G. Wilson. Other English makers of this period were Alfred White of Hampton Court and Arthur Twinn of Cambridge. In France two new firms started business, Gell and Cabart. The firm of H.J. Gray & Son was founded in Cambridge in 1855 by the Rackets champion of 1863–66 to make Rackets rackets.

In the twentieth century, Tennis and Rackets frames have evolved from a single ash hoop into a frame consisting of ash, hickory and, latterly, vulcanised fibre and willow laminations. Adhesive tape was used to bind the throat and shoulders of Rackets rackets. The introduction of modern adhesives has meant that the use of a wood screw to strengthen the throat is no longer necessary.

There have been a number of frame developments in reent years. Tennis frames have either the traditional square or rounded handles. One model, designed by former world champion Wayne Davies, features one less ash lamination to lighten the head. Another incorporates additional vulcanised fibre laminations inside and outside the head, which provide a stiffer, more durable frame. Paint finishes have improved and most clubs now have models specially made up in their

Early nineteenth-century rackets from Petworth House.

own club colours. An unsuccessful attempt to launch a graphite Tennis racket resulted in a change in the laws to stipulate that the racket must be made of wood or wood-related materials. Synthetic gut has replaced the natural variety and some professionals use alternative stringing patterns. Synthetic grips are now fitted to the handle.

In America, Bancroft of Rhode Island ceased production in the 1980s, having tried to manufacture Tennis frames in the Far East. Grays of Cambridge are thus the sole surviving manufacturers of Tennis and Rackets rackets. Grays were forced to close their factory in Benson Street in 1986 when graphite replaced wood in lawn-tennis and squash rackets, but production of Rackets and Tennis frames was transferred to their former sawmill in the nearby village of Coton, where production continues to this day. The firm continues to be wholly owned and controlled by the Gray family.

DEVELOPMENT OF THE BALL

BALLS FOR TENNIS have been made in much the same way since the game began. It was necessary to have a fairly hard, round ball that would bounce true on a stone surface and balls were made of leather or cloth stuffed with wool or hair. It wasn't until the use of rubber was understood that balls suitable for bouncing on grass were developed and lawn tennis began.

As one might expect, the first mention of ball-making comes from France, where it is recorded that in 1292 there were thirteen professionals (*paumiers*) making balls in Paris alone. French balls were exported to other Tennis-playing countries. When in 1386 French knights informed John I, King of Castile, that John of Gaunt and the English were preparing a military expedition against him, he replied:

> *When you left me last year I charged you to bring me some balls from Paris on your return to this country so that we might play a game of Tennis. But it would have been better had I charged you to bring me a helmet and good armour.*

In England there was strong opposition to foreign balls. In 1463/4 a petition was submitted to Edward IV to ban the import of a wide range of articles including 'Tenys Balles'.

> *'Pyteuously shewen and compleynen unto youre wisdomes, the Kynges true people, Artificers, Handcrafty men and women' of London and elsewhere in England and Wales have 'been gretely empoveryshed and greviously hurt and hyndred of their wordely encreace and daily livying' by goods imported 'by the handes of Straungers beyng the Kynges Ennemyes'.*

A century later a State paper of 1559 lists what were considered to be excessive imports, among them 'Balles, viz. Tennys balles, £1699'. And in 1591 Hugh Williams and Richard Kyd petitioned the Queen for a licence to make hand-balls and Tennis balls. They submitted that they could make better and cheaper balls than imported ones, which were sold at arbitrary and excessive prices, and that it would give employment to many poor working people. Evidently there was a duty on imported balls, for they offered to reimburse the Revenue by means of a tax.

But the main manufacturer of Tennis balls between about 1450 and 1550 was the Ironmongers' Company. Their records show receipts for balls supplied by them over nearly a hundred years, varying in price from one shilling to 1s 8d a gross.

Italy, too, was producing its own balls. In 1470 Galeazzo Maria Sforza ordered 100 balls from Florence, specifying that they should be a little larger than last time so that they would bounce more.

Evidently the standard of French balls had started to decline by 1480, when Louis XI, a keen Tennis player, issued a decree on 24 June that balls were to be stuffed with good hide and wool wadding and were not to contain sand, ground chalk, metal shavings, lime, bran, sawdust, ash, moss, powder or earth. The weight of these balls was about 1oz – very light compared with a modern ball of $2\frac{1}{2}$ to $2\frac{3}{4}$ozs, but of course they were for use by the hand or a fairly flimsy racket. The improvement in the quality of balls was further ensured in 1537 when François I granted letters patent to the professionals, authorising them alone to sell balls in the vicinity of Tennis courts. Finally, in 1581, Henri IV granted a charter to the master professionals of Paris which included standards for the manufacture of balls.

Esteufs, for use by the hand, had to weigh just under 1oz and be covered with sheepskin and tightly stuffed with wool; *balles*, for use with the racket, had to weigh about 1oz and be covered with new white cloth and stuffed with pieces of cloth tightly tied with good thread. In other words the ball, though lighter, was made in exactly the same way as it is today.

In 1539, Vivès in his *Dialogues* describes a contemporary French ball in contrast to that used in Spain. 'They hardly have any large balls as we do here [i.e. in Spain], but use smaller balls than yours, much harder and covered in white leather. The stuffing is not made of cloth as yours is but usually of dogs' hair and that is why they don't often play with the hand.'

The change from a leather cover to a cloth cover was noted by Sir Robert Dallington in 1598: 'You observe here [i.e. in France] that their Balles are of cloth, which fashion they have held this seven yeares: before which time they were of lether, like ours.'

In England balls were often stuffed with hair, normally dogs' hair, but if we are to believe Shakespeare, sometimes human hair:

DON PEDRO: *Has any man seen him at the barber's?*
CLAUDIO: *No; but the barber's man hath been seen with him; and the old ornament of his cheek hath already stuffed tennis balls.*
(*Much Ado about Nothing*)

A very interesting early ball found in the rafters of Westminster Hall is now in the Museum of London; it is made of leather stuffed with hair.

A press for making Tennis balls.

De Garsault gives a detailed account of the making of a ball together with illustrations, but a complete do-it-yourself guide was published just a few years ago (*How to Make the Real Tennis Ball from Core to Cover* by Richard Hamilton and Anthony Hobson).

In England between the wars, Tennis balls were made by Gradidge of Woolwich and A. Tompkins of Brighton. Balls from Prince's and Queen's were sent to A. Tompkins for re-covering, although at Queen's some were re-covered by E. Ratcliff and F. André. Alf White re-covered the balls at Hampton Court and for some of the private courts; at Manchester they were re-covered by J. Ronan and George Cooke under the direction of Charles Feldon.

In the Second World War both Gradidge and Tompkins ceased production of balls; for some time after the war there was a sufficient stock and little demand. The first stimulus to renewed production came from America. There a machine-made ball had been in use, extremely hard and very difficult to play with – especially for beginners. An approach was made to Dugald Macpherson for a supply of 3000 balls from Britain.

Macpherson sought the help of Henry Johns at Lord's, who had learnt the art of ball manufacture from Alf White. Johns made a dozen balls for approval and they were accepted. He tells the rest of the story himself:

As they were hand-made with strips of cloth torn from old coats and flannel trousers, I needed a great many pairs of trousers and lots of coats. Material was unobtainable as clothing was rationed and we were still using clothing coupons. All the old materials used had to be torn in $^3/_8$in. strips which took hours and hours before the actual making of the ball was started. I then asked the Americans which 'fall' was it they wanted them by, as the contract would take me at least six years (dollars bought most things those days except time). They settled for as many as could be made at any time, in fact the 3000 balls took five years to complete.

I was greatly assisted in this enormous exercise by George Beton and George Ferguson both at Lord's at this time. They made the kernel of the ball about an inch in diameter and I built them up to the required size and correct weight and tied them. My wife, Mona, and Mrs Beton had learnt to cover and re-cover them as required and this shortened the time-factor considerably.

Jimmy Dunn of Philadelphia was originally the only source of balls in the United States. He taught himself how to do it at the suggestion of Sammy Van Alen, and trained members of his staff in the art. Other professionals in the USA are skilled at re-covering both Tennis and Rackets balls.

The difficulty of ball production stimulated experiment and help was forthcoming from Guy Bassett-Smith of Dunlop although there was never any question of commercial gain. In 1960 he persuaded Sir Reay Geddes, then managing director of the company, to agree to the idea that the technical department of Dunlop Sports Co. at Speke be given the task of developing a machine-made ball with characteristics similar to the hand-made ball.

The department began by taking apart a typical ball from Manchester and found the best part of a Crimean War tunic in it.

The cover presented no difficulty; the normal lawn-tennis ball Melton cloth was suitable. The problem lay in finding a ball of normal weight with the same bounce characteristics. After patient experimentation, a ball was evolved by using a squash ball core and moulding pressureless lawn-tennis ball-compound around it. On first trial these balls were considered too lively and this was rectified by the addition of sawdust to the compound. Dunlop moulded the balls in manually operated presses and supplied them in quantities of about 200 dozen. Thanks to David Sealey, the sales and marketing manager of Dunlop, these were offered to clubs at manufacturing cost.

However, balls could not be relied upon to perform in the same way in every court and attempts to develop a manufactured ball continued, but without any further success. A return to traditional methods seemed the best solution and at present the balls are made by the professionals. Nevertheless, efforts have been made to standardize the balls and in the UK most are now constructed with a cork centre covered by several metres of half-inch cotton webbing. Every court in Britain except Lord's now uses fluorescent yellow cloth to cover the ball; Lord's continues to use white cloth.

THE MEDIEVAL GAME

IT WASN'T LONG BEFORE the attractions of Tennis spread from the street to the castle and it became the game of kings. Philippe IV of France, known as the Fair (1285–1314), had a court at the Hôtel de Nesle, which he bought in 1308, but there is no evidence that he played. The first French king who certainly played was his successor Louis X, the Quarrelsome (1314–16), and he owed his death to it. He played Tennis with great vigour in the forest of Vincennes, drank a beaker of cold water and went to rest in a nearby grotto. There he caught a chill, which turned to fever and he died.

It is likely that Louis X had been playing a game of *longue paume*. Side by side with the street game *courte paume* there developed an open-air game which needed no court. *Longue paume* never achieved the same degree of popularity as its sister game, but nevertheless it has survived into the twentieth century. In 1929 there were ninety-eight societies of *longue paume* in France, where it was played mostly in Picardy, and in Paris in the Luxembourg Gardens where it is still played.

Jean II, the Good (1350–64), also certainly played. His treasurer recorded a payment of 144 écus in 1355 for 'two sheets of Brussels cloth, bought to make four pairs of robes, lined with miniver, which the King gave to certain people to whom he had lost at Tennis.'

His son, Charles V (1364–80) was a keen player despite his poor health. He seems to have had a primitive court in the Louvre itself; he also played in a court on the rue Froidmantel, adjoining the Palace to the west, and in another, which he had built, in the rue Beautreillis.

Longue paume *in France.*

Charles VI (1380–1422) played and we know that in 1394 he lost 300 francs which he had to borrow from Jacques de Montmor, the Governor of Dauphiné. His brother, the Duke of Orléans, also incurred considerable debts at Tennis and must have been a keen player. Tennis being thus popular at the French court it was natural that in 1414 the Dauphin should send Henry V of England a present of Tennis balls, with the advice that he would be better employed playing games than making war.

Shakespeare records the English king's reply as follows:

When we have match'd our rackets to these balls,
We will, in France, by God's grace, play a set,
Shall strike his father's crown into the hazard.
Tell him he hath made a match with such a
wrangler,
That all the courts of France will be disturb'd
With chaces.

Shakespeare based his *Henry V* on *The famous victories of Henry V* of 1598, in which the Dauphin's presents are described as a 'guilded tunne of Tennis balles and a carpet'.

The incident is also described by several other writers. Thomas Otterbourne, living at the time, was the first to mention it. A fifteenth-century manuscript describing the Battle of Agincourt, Caxton in his continuation of Higden's *Polycronicon* printed in 1482, Hall in his *Chronicle* of 1548, and Holinshed in 1577, all give accounts of the same incident, although varying in detail.

In the reign of Charles VII (1422–61), France produced the first known lady player, Margot, who has already been mentioned (see page 25).

Louis XI (1461–83) took a keen interest in the game, as is shown by his decree on the manufacture of balls (see page 28).

From existing evidence, Tennis was played in Scotland, from the reign of Alexander III (1249–86), before it was played in England. Alexander's mother was a Frenchwoman, Marie de Couci, and the ties between the two countries were always strong. For King James I of Scotland it was fatal. He was at the Blackfriars Monastery in Perth when, on the night of 20 February 1437, a band of at least eight assassins led by Sir Robert Graham broke into the royal apartments. They slew a page on the staircase and rapidly approached the room where the King was alone with the Queen and some of her attendants. On hearing the noise of their approach, the Queen and her ladies sought to bar the door, but the traitorous Sir Robert

Stewart had removed the bolts. The story that Catherine Douglas thrust her arm through the bolt staples seems to be of later invention. Meantime, the King had tried the windows but found them strongly barred. Seizing an iron poker from the fireplace, he prized up a plank in the floor and lowered himself into the drain of the lavatory ('thordure of the privoy'). The only exit from this stone channel was a small square hole at the bottom intended for cleaning, but alas 'he maid to let stop hit well iij dayes afore hard with stone, bicause that whane he played there at the pawme the ballis he plaid withe oft ranne yn at that fowle hole, for ther was ordeyned without a faire playing place for the kyng.'

However, he remained hidden until he thought that all was quiet and then called up to the ladies to lower sheets down to him to pull him out. Unfortunately, one of the ladies, Elizabeth Douglas, fell in and the disturbance led to the discovery of the King's hiding place. He put up a stout fight but unarmed he was no match for his murderers and was killed.

James IV of Scotland also played Tennis as we know from the Lord High Treasurer's accounts.

At the end of the century another Tennis casualty occurred. Charles VIII of France, although mis-shapen and stunted in body, was an affable man who loved his wife, Anne of Brittany, and his château at Amboise. Here he built a Tennis court which was the scene of his death. (The remains of the court are still visible.) An eye-witness described the event.

The King left Queen Anne of Brittany's room and took her with him to watch the tennis players at the moat of the château where he had never taken her before; and they entered together a gallery called Haquelabac, the entrance of which was in disrepair, and the king struck his forehead against the lintel of the door, although he was quite small, and then watched the players for a long time and talked to everybody. Suddenly he fell backwards and lost the power of speech; it must have been two o'clock in the afternoon and he remained there until eleven o'clock the same night.

He was succeeded by his cousin, Louis XII (son of Charles, Duke of Orléans), a charming and well-liked young man who delighted in playing Tennis with his subjects, especially the citizens of his native Orléans.

But the popularity of Tennis had one drawback in the eyes of medieval kings and governors – it diverted the populace from more warlike sports, such as archery. So, while king and court continued to play

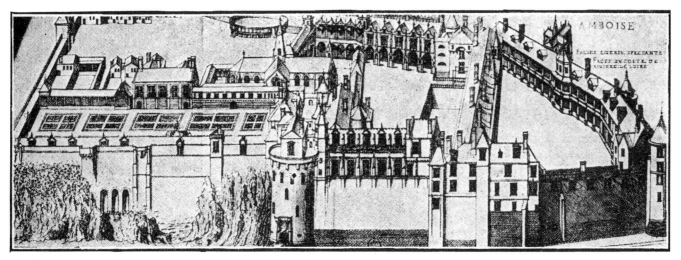

The Château d'Amboise.

with increasing keenness, it was forbidden to the humbler subject, though seemingly with little effect. Philippe IV of France was the first to prohibit it in 1292 and Charles V re-enacted the ban in 1365, the very same year that Edward III of England decreed:

June 12. To the sheriffs of London.
Order to cause proclamation to be made that every able bodied man of the said city on feast days when he has leisure shall in his sports use bows and arrows or pellets or bolts, and shall learn and practise the art of shooting, forbidding them under pain of imprisonment to meddle in hurling of stones, loggats and quoits, handball, football, club ball, cambuc, cock fighting or other vain games of no value; as the people of the realm, noble and simple, used heretofore to practise the said art in their sports, whence by God's help came forth honour to the kingdom and advantage to the king in his actions of war, and now the said art is almost wholly disused, and the people indulge in the games aforesaid and in other dishonest and unthrifty or idle games, whereby the realm is like to be without archers.

This was followed by a further prohibition in 1388 by Richard II, specifically including Tennis under the name *les jeues as pelotes* (*pelote* being the French for hand-ball). Servants and labourers were to have bows and arrows and to use them on Sundays and holidays, but, he adds, 'it is not the King's Mind that any prejudice be done to the Franchises of Lords, touching the Forfeitures due to them.'

Prohibition followed prohibition in France and England as each king came to the throne, although the Mayor of Paris slightly modified the complete ban in

1397 by permitting Tennis to be played on Sundays only. Henry IV confirmed it in 1410, imposing a penalty of six days' imprisonment on convicted offenders, a fine of twenty shillings on Mayors and Sheriffs, and six shillings and threepence on Constables who failed to put the Act into execution. Later Acts of 1476 and 1477 increased the penalty to forty shillings and six days' imprisonment and finally to twenty pounds and three years' imprisonment – a very stiff penalty indeed.

The first record of a prosecution under these Acts occurs in Canterbury about 1396. William Terrey was summoned before the Burgmote for permitting divers men to play 'le Closhe and le Tenesse' in his house.

In Lydd, Tennis was obviously so popular that public announcements were frequently necessary to forbid it, as these accounts show:

1429. *Itm paid to a man crying the Watch to be kept by the sea-side and that no man should play at the tenys.*
1462. *Itm paid for two Cries one for tenys-players and the other for the Watch.*
1476. *Itm paid for a proclamation made for tenys-players, dyse-players and boyle-players 1d.*

Further prosecutions are recorded in Oxford in 1450 when 'Thomas Blake, currier, William Whyte, Barber and John Karyn, glover, "husbandmen", appeared before us Master J. Beek, DD and Master Gilbert Kymer, Chancellor of this kindly University of Oxford and Comissary General (of the Bishop of Lincoln) with their hands on the Holy Gospels abjured the game of tennis within the City of Oxford and its precincts.'

At Exeter they even played illegally in the cloisters of the cathedral, as appears from this reply of the Bishop, Dean and Chapter to the Mayor's Articles in 1447:

Art. 5. Atte which tymes and in especiall in tyme of dyvyne service, ungoodly ruled peple most custumabely yong peple of the saide Comminalte within the saide cloistre have exercised unlawfull games as the toppe, penny prykke and most atte tenys, by the which the walles of the saide Cloistre have defowled and the glas wyndowes all to brost, as it openly sheweth, contrarie to all good and goostly godenesse...

In 1451 the canons of the Collegiate Church of Ottery St Mary and their lay friends defied their bishop's ban on 'tenys' and 'by vain, foul and prophane words, by senseless and swelling oaths, by torrents of unlawful perjuries, they shamelessly occasioned such brawling, contention and yelling in the sacred churchyard that the devotions of Christian people coming there to pray for souls departed were vilely and damnably disturbed.' (Letter from Professor G.R. Dunstan to *The Times*, 3 May 1977).

Detail from an early print showing the two original courts at Fontainebleau – marked 8.

SIXTEENTH-CENTURY TENNIS

WITH THE ACCESSION OF the kings of the House of Angoulême in France and the House of Tudor in England there began the golden age of Tennis which was to last throughout the sixteenth and seventeenth centuries.

In France, François I, Henri II, Charles IX and Henri IV were all keen players. It was the fashionable game at Court, and despite continued prohibition for the ordinary citizen it was much played throughout the country.

Herald of this golden age was the young François I, strong, healthy and handsome, a dashing cavalier who loved chivalry and splendour and violent exercise, a patron of the arts as well as sport. Here was a monarch very different from the ugly and depraved kings of the previous century. He played Tennis from his youth, and in order to be able to play whenever he wanted he built courts at all his principal residences. At the Louvre he built a new covered court by the rue d'Autriche in 1530. At Fontainebleau he built an open court near the fountain of Diana and two more covered courts at the Château of Saint-Germain.

The setting of one of these, in the forest above the Château de la Muette, has been described as 'paved with large paving stones, with pillars at intervals, on which were engraved in relief salamanders, the arms of France, and the letter "F" surmounted by a crown, which went right round this beautiful terrace on which one strolled, and from which sometimes one saw the hunt pass…and in particular there was a very lovely covered tennis court, which was on this terrace and from which there was a very lovely view.'

The King was evidently a useful player and always attracted a good audience, including the ladies of the Court with Catherine de Médicis at their head. It is said that 'a certain Monk, while playing with the King against two lords, made a brilliant stroke which decided the set in the King's favour, who then exclaimed "Ah, that is the stroke of a Monk". "Sire", replied the monk, "whenever it may please you, it shall be the stroke of an Abbot". An Abbey happened to be vacant at the moment and this the Monk received' – as he undoubtedly deserved.

It has been stated that the King played a match against the Emperor Charles V at Orléans, but there is no evidence of this. It has also been said that he played with Benvenuto Cellini. The King gave Cellini a triangular château up against the city wall, called Le Petit Nesle, which was unfortunately already let to the Mayor of Paris, although the latter made little use of it. However, he objected to Cellini moving in and it required violence to install the new tenant. Once in residence, Cellini writes: 'I had a tennis court in my castle from which I drew considerable profit.' He also tells of another pitched battle fought with stones, pikes and arquebuses without ball to expel a distiller who with the King's permission moved into the Tennis court and its lodgings. Cellini won this second battle and the King merely laughed at the incident. He does not mention playing Tennis with the King, which he surely would not have omitted were it in fact true.

François was envious of Henry VIII's navy and, determined not to be outdone, founded Le Havre and ordered a man-of-war even larger than Henry's famous *Great Harry*, which was over 180ft long with a burden of over 1000 tons. *La Grande Françoise*, built at Le Havre in 1532, was a third longer with a 2000 ton burden. She was four-masted with a mainmast of 25ft girth (nearly 8ft diameter) and 210ft high. She included a forge for mechanical repairs, a windmill to grind flour, a baker's oven and a private chapel. Between the castles, a Tennis court filled the waist of the ship with a huge awning stretched above it. The vessel attracted hundreds of sightseers and she was finally launched in September 1533. She did not go very far. Halfway across the harbour she disappeared into the estuary and grounded. She was freed and taken back to her berth, but on 14 November in a terrific storm she capsized at her moorings and sank. Eventually she was broken up and the St François district was built from her timbers.

The floating Tennis court experiment was repeated, however:

On the 3rd December 1539 the King embarked on the River Loire bound for Orléans; and the City Councillors sent ahead of the King to Gien ten or twelve boats, all covered in satin, on which were galleries, rooms, chimney-pieces and other furniture after the fashion of ships and there was one specially for the King, on which there were four rooms, galleries and a Tennis court.

Orléans was a thriving centre of Tennis which was particularly popular with the university students. There were forty courts in the city at the beginning of the sixteenth century, and some complaints that the sport was interfering with the young gentlemen's studies. Later, in 1556, the situation was sufficiently serious for a complaint to be made to the Duke of Orléans, who ordered eighteen courts to be closed. The students at Poitiers, too, were addicts of Tennis and had twenty-two courts on which to play.

Rabelais brought the young Pantagruel to Orléans, where he met the students and learned to play Tennis. He soon mastered it and when he graduated in law, one of his fellow students wrote of him:

Un esteuf en la braguette,
En la main une raquette,
Une loi en la cornette,
Une basse dance au talon
Vous voyez là passé Coquillon.

A ball in your pocket
A racket in your hand
A law in your hat
A low dance at your heel
You see you have passed the examiner.

The Dauphin François inherited a love of sports from his father, but unfortunately died at the age of eighteen in a somewhat similar way to Louis the Quarrelsome, having taken a cold drink while hot from playing Tennis – according to the doctors of the day. His brother Henri, who succeeded in 1547 as Henri II, had less charm than his father but had the same liking for vigorous exercise. He was certainly one of the foremost Tennis players of his day, if not indeed the best in the land. He built a second court at the Louvre, also on the rue d'Autriche side of the castle, at the other side of the main gates from his father's court. It

was also a larger court than usual, as Henri was very fond of playing doubles – or even trebles, with three players on either side of the net.

A contemporary described the King playing Tennis: 'At the large tennis court in the Louvre, dressed in white, wearing a doublet and a straw hat, he hits the ball enthusiastically; there is no formality except that the net is lifted when he wishes to go under it.' The white clothes lend a very modern touch to this picture, although designers today would hardly include a doublet and a straw hat. He must have been a delightful partner, for he shared his winnings with those on his side and paid all their losses himself. Henri's sporting activities led to his death. He took part in a tournament to celebrate the wedding of his daughter Elizabeth to Philip II of Spain and was mortally wounded in the eye by the lance of Montgomery, son of the Captain of the Guards.

His son François II was only fifteen and a sickly boy, who lived to reign for only one year. He was succeeded by his ten-year-old brother Charles IX, but effective power fell into the hands of Henri II's widow, Catherine de Medicis, who was faced with a critical situation in the rivalries of the Catholic and Protestant factions. She was naturally a leader in women's fashions and one of her hair styles was known as the racket style (*coiffure en raquette*), so called because the hair was criss-crossed in bands in the same way as the racket-makers crossed their strings. She evidently brought up Charles to play Tennis, for a drawing shows him at the age of two with a racket in hand.

Charles was weak, lazy and melancholic, but as the Venetian ambassador reported in 1561 'passionately fond of tennis and riding'. He fell under the influence of Admiral Coligny, much to the dislike of the Catholics, for Coligny was the political leader of the Huguenots. Catherine de Medicis was alarmed at the thought of this Protestant influence on the King and the result was an attempt to assassinate Coligny on 22 August 1572. Charles, as was his wont, was playing Tennis in the Louvre at the time, as described in the following account of the incident:

It was about 10.30 a.m. The Admiral left the Council... In front of the Louvre he met the King, who had just heard Mass celebrated at 10 o'clock in the Petit Bourbon chapel, and out of deference to the Sovereign he immediately retraced his steps and accompanied him to the tennis court, where the King and the Duke of Guise, having made a match with Téligny, the Admiral's son-in-law and another gentleman, played for a while. Leaving the tennis court the Admiral took the rue

Charles IX as a child.

d'Autriche… Then, being wounded by a shot from Maurevert's arquebus, he ordered Messrs de Piles and de Mouneins…to go without delay and inform the King of the attempt on his life. His orders were carried out at once. At that moment Charles IX was informed of the attempted assassination. Coligny's messengers had found him still in the tennis court and all witnesses agree on the spontaneous fury and bitterness with which he greeted the news. 'Will I never have any peace?' he exclaimed. 'Always new troubles.' Then throwing his racket on the ground he returned to the Louvre.

The attempted murder of Coligny brought things to a head. Catherine de Medicis and the Catholics realised that they could not let matters rest without imperilling their position. Charles gave in to his mother's advice and on 24 August, St Bartholomew's Day, at 1.30 in the morning, the alarm bells at St Germain-l'Auxerrois gave the signal for a massacre of the Huguenots. Coligny was killed. All the Protestant leaders were slaughtered except for the royal princes, Henri of Navarre and the Prince de Condé, who were imprisoned in the Louvre. In Paris alone three or four thousand Huguenots were killed.

One lucky man to escape was a certain Nompar de Caumont la Force, afterwards Marshal de la Force.

He was thirteen. The bodies of the three Caumonts lay at the end of the rue des Petits-Champs, near the city wall, where they had fallen. At about four o'clock in the afternoon, the doors of some houses opened, people appeared and approached the bloody scene. A professional from the Tennis court in the rue Verderet saw on the leg of one of the murdered Huguenots a cotton stocking which might suit him. He turned over the corpse, which was facing the ground. The youth of the face stirred him. Softly he said, 'Alas! He is only a poor child. Isn't it a shame. What wrong could he have done?' The child's head (it was that of Jacques Nompar) rose slowly, the mouth murmured, 'I am not dead, please save my life.' The man put his head down again. 'Don't move, for they are still here,' he said, and went away. Then came back. 'Get up,' he said, 'for they've gone.' Jacques Nompar put over his shoulders the dirty cloak that the man threw him. He walked in front of his saviour, who made pretence of beating him.

Later this Tennis professional received a pension from Marshal de la Force for his services and the Marshal became a keen player.

This kindly professional was no doubt one of those whose statutes had only recently been granted by the King. Originally the Tennis professionals had been members of a fraternity of makers of rackets and brushes. There were at least two branches of this fraternity in Paris in 1457, one of them meeting in the Chapel of St Barbe, their patron saint. Their arms show two types of brush and one racket.

Some time during the sixteenth century they broke away from the brush-makers and established their own corporation, calling themselves *maîtres-paumiers raquetiers* – master professionals and racket-makers. They adopted new arms and François I gave them letters patent. Charles IX granted them statutes in 1571.

The preamble to these was: 'Charles, by the grace of God, King of France, Tennis being one of the most honourable, worthy and healthy exercises which princes, peers, gentlemen and other distinguished persons can undertake, and which is today as much or more played and practised than any other by all the good towns of our kingdom, we have agreed the said

A member of the guild of rackets- and brush-makers.

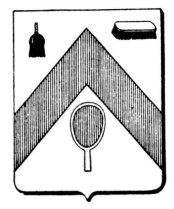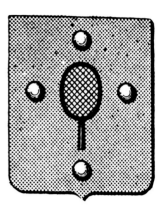

The arms of the rackets- and brush-makers and the later arms of the master-professionals and racket-makers.

requests and pleas of the Master Professionals…' The statutes go on to establish three grades of professional: the apprentice (minimum three years), the associate, and the master. The master could manage one court and employ one apprentice; he could also run a billiard saloon. A police licence stipulated the hours of opening and forbade play on feast days or during High Mass, the sermon and vespers, and banned the lending of money to players. The statutes also endowed the corporation with extensive rights over the manufacture of balls and rackets. These statutes were later confirmed by Henri IV and Louis XIII.

Besides the master professionals, associates and apprentices, there were many others employed at each court. There were markers, of whom two were required for each match, one to stand in each of the doorways leading into the court, marking the chases.

The score was kept by the marker on the service side by recording the games won in chalk on the stone floor. It was also the duty of a marker to massage players and to look after them when the game was over; this usually meant rubbing them down with a towel.

A similar guild of professionals is known to have existed in Florence in 1550.

The delicate King Charles did not long survive and died in 1574 at the age of twenty-four. His successor was Henri III, amusing and full of charm but effeminate in manner. He liked wearing costly clothes, necklaces and scent, and was even known to dress up as a woman for some Court festivities. He played Tennis but, as his demeanour suggests, does not seem to have been outstanding.

Henri of Navarre succeeded him in name, but he was not recognised by the still powerful Catholic League which was dominant in Paris. He had to fight for his throne against the League and its allies, the King of Spain and the Duke of Savoy. He was a brave man and a gallant soldier, popular with his Protestant subjects and merciful to his Catholic enemies. After four years of civil war, he sacrificed his religious principles to political practicalities and on 25 July 1593, at Saint-Denis, attired in white, he was accepted into the Catholic church and entered Paris as the acknowledged King of France.

He played Tennis wherever he found an opportunity and his early wanderings enabled him to visit courts in many parts of the country. Brought up in Béarn, he played frequently at Pau in the court in the rue du Château. In the disorders of 1569 this court was demolished to provide material for the fortification of the château, but it was soon reconstructed. The builders were ordered to be as economical as possible by Jeanne d'Albret, Queen of Navarre, Henri's mother, 'in order that our very well-beloved son may take some pleasure there.' He also played at Lectoure, Montauban and Nérac, where the Court established itself. In Paris he played in the court of the Sphère and in the two courts at the Louvre, and according to one version played Tennis in the Louvre when he was confined there on the morning of St Bartholomew.

After he became King of France, Henri IV played frequently and there are many accounts of his Tennis activities.

On 18 March 1590, the town of Nantes paid homage to the King who refreshed himself and passed the time by playing Tennis against the bakers of the town. They won his money and did not wish to give him his revenge, because they said that they had agreed to play a maximum of three sets. The King, to get the better of them, had it announced the next day that a small loaf would cost a penny-ha'penny, at which the bakers, very embarrassed, came to ask His Majesty to have mercy on them and to take whatever revenge he wished, except on their bread.

Three days after his conversion to Catholicism,

the King played tennis at Saint-Denis and, noticing that the court was full of ladies who wanted to watch him but could not because of his bodyguard, asked the latter to withdraw so that the ladies could watch him at their ease . . . and the same day the Duke of Elbeuf came to find the King in the tennis court at Saint-Denis. On seeing him the King left the court and said, 'I must meet this fat boy'.

Arriving in Paris on 15 September, after the surrender of Amiens, the King played Tennis the whole afternoon of the next day in the court of the Sphère. On 24 September, he was still there, his shirt torn at the back, his grey shoes tied in a 'dog-leg' knot; and not being able to get to the ball because he was tired, he said that he felt like a stumbling donkey.

The King mixed love and politics with his sport.

At the Sphère court, the Marchioness [of Verneuil, by whom he had three illegitimate children] and the Mesdames de Sourdize and de Sagone went every day to see him play; he allowed himself to borrow money from Madame de Monceaux, whom he caressed much and kissed in front of everybody; this did not prevent him from watching the Spaniards and he was ready when the moment came to abandon Tennis and love to throw himself upon Amiens with that flexibility of movement which tennis taught him.

And in 1598 after receiving the Spanish envoys,

the King went to play tennis in his court at the Louvre. Marshal de Biron had the court and the King partnered him against Prince de Joinville. There were foreigners there who watched him play; he was also watched by the ladies, amongst whom the Duchess of Beaufort was outstanding; the King made her unmask herself so that the Spaniards could see her more easily.

He went on playing until almost fifty and wrote to the Queen in 1601, 'You are awaited here with the greatest enthusiasm. Enough of writing – I am off to play tennis. I kiss you a thousand times.'

There are many entries in the royal accounts of the payment of the King's debts at Tennis, and it has been assumed that he cannot therefore have been a very good player. It should be remembered, however, that only his losses were recorded and his gains were received personally by him after each match. He was particularly careful not to let his winnings find their way into the treasury. On one occasion he put them in his hat, exclaiming 'by the belly of St Gris, I'll keep these to be certain no one will rob me, for they will not pass through the hands of my treasurer.' Naturally Henri IV built some new courts for himself. One was at Fontainebleau, where there already existed an open-air court. Henri built a covered court beside it, somewhat larger as, like Henri II, he preferred to play doubles. Another he built at Compiègne.

The vigour with which the game was played in France led to the occasional casualty. Poet Jean Passerat lost an eye through playing Tennis and Montaigne in his *Essays* wrote of a Tennis tragedy.

Captain Saint-Martin, twenty-three years old who had already given pretty good proof of his valour, while playing tennis was struck by a ball a little above the right ear, with no sign of contusion or wound. He did not sit down or rest, but five or six hours later he died of an apoplexy that this blow gave him.

An interesting court still exists at the Château of Suze-la-Rousse in the Drôme department of south-east France. It was built in 1566 (the story says in three days and nights) about fifty yards from the main entrance to the Château, when Charles IX paid a visit to Count François de la Baume Suze with the Queen Mother, Catherine de Medicis, and the future King Henri IV. It is an open court with a narrower and longer tambour than usual.

During this same period Tennis began to flourish in England under the Tudors. Henry VII played frequently, as his expenditure testifies, despite the fact that he re-enacted the restrictive legislation of previous reigns. His accounts tell us also some of the places where he played – Woodstock, Wycombe, Westminster, Sheen and Windsor. Westminster is an interesting location for there is no evidence of a court there; he may have played in one of the inner courtyards or perhaps even in Westminster Hall. The latter seems doubtful as it was then in use as law courts.

Nothing is known of a court at Wycombe, but a court at Woodstock is mentioned again in 1634 on the side of the house facing the town. Sheen Palace had a dramatic history. Built by Edward III, who died there, it was demolished by Richard II in 1394 out of grief at the death of his wife, Anne of Bohemia. Henry V rebuilt it, but in 1498, the very same year that Henry VII played Tennis there and while he was still in residence, it was totally destroyed by fire. It was again re-built by the King, re-named Richmond Palace and was to be the place where he, and later Queen Elizabeth I, died.

The site of the court at Windsor is shown in a view of the castle produced by John Norden in 1607 (page 41). It was in the old moat by the Round Tower, at the spot where now stands the equestrian statue of Charles II. It was an open court approached by a covered way from the keep. At Windsor Henry VII entertained Philip, Archduke of Austria and King of Castile in 1506. Philip was on his way from the Netherlands to take possession of his throne in Castile and had been driven to shelter at Weymouth by rough weather at sea. Henry entertained him with hunting, horse-baiting and Tennis, as described on page 25.

Henry VII also built a court at Kenilworth Castle in 1492/3.

Henry VIII was a great lover of sport and was especially keen on Tennis which he played frequently as a young man – and frequently lost, as the royal accounts bear witness. A contemporary author writes that 'the Kynge thys tyme (1510) was moche entysed to playe at tennes and at dice, which appetite, certayn craftie persones about hym perceyuynge, brought in Frenchmen and Lombardes, to make wagers with hym, and so he lost moch money.' A typical entry in Henry's accounts for 1519 reads:

to young Care for my lord's losses at tennis   8s.

As time went on he seems to have grown more reckless and Tennis debts are recorded in 1530 of forty-five shillings and in 1532 of forty-six pounds thirteen shillings and fourpence. The latter sum, lost by the King to the Cardinal of Lorraine and Monsieur le Guise, was a considerable one in those days compared to our present debased coinage. It is interesting to find that the very same day the King lost one hundred and sixteen pounds thirteen shillings and fourpence at dice to the same Cardinal, Lord Norfolk, Lord Suffolk and his Master of the Household. Many other interesting payments connected with Tennis are recorded in these accounts. It is clear that a certain Anthony Ansley was the King's professional, who supplied balls and rackets, and accompanied the King to play in various courts – even to France on one occasion in 1532, to play at Calais. Other courts mentioned in the accounts were at Richmond, Greenwich, Windsor and the Moore. The court at Richmond was the same as that at Sheen previously mentioned. The court at Greenwich formed part of the old Palace built by Humphrey, Duke of Gloucester, known as the Manor of Pleazaunce. The Moore court lay in the Manor of Rickmansworth and belonged to the Crown.

A good picture of the King at play in such courts as these was given by the Venetian Ambassador, Sebastian Giustiniani, writing in 1519.

His Majesty is twenty-nine years old and extremely handsome; nature could not have done more for him; he is much handsomer than any other sovereign in Christendom; a great deal handsomer than the King of France; very fair, and his whole frame admirably proportioned. On hearing that Francis I wore a beard he allowed his to grow, and as it is reddish, he has now got a beard which looks like gold. He is extremely fond of tennis, at which game it is the prettiest thing in the world to see him play, his fair skin glowing through a shirt of the finest texture.

Rawdon Brown in his *Four Years at the Court of Henry VIII*, adds in a note:

The shirts worn by persons of condition at this period were bordered with lace and curiously adorned with needlework. One which had belonged to Arthur, Prince of Wales, made of long lawn, and beautifully embroidered with blue silk round the collar and wrists, was in the possession of the late John Gage, Esquire, Director of the Society of Antiquaries.

On his way to and from the court, Henry evidently wore a black and blue velvet jacket, for in an inventory of his wardrobe in 1517 occur two entries listing: 'iij

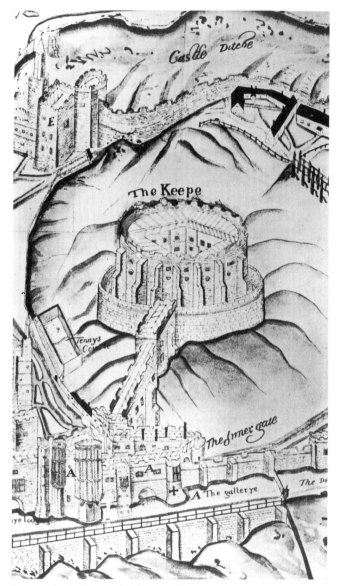

The court at Windsor Castle in 1607.

and in his suite in the Palace of Bridewell. Henry had built a long gallery, decked with tapestry, between the two, spanning the Fleet river and breaching the City wall. Here Hall records 'on Saterday the Kyng and the Emperor played at tennice at the Bayne against the princes of Orenge and the Marques of Brandenborow and on the Princes syde stopped the Erle of Deuonshyre and the lorde Edmond on the other syde, and they departed euen handes on both sydes after XI games fully played.'

How they managed to end up level after eleven games must remain another Tennis mystery! The Prince's partner was Albert, Marquis of Brandenburg, made a Cardinal in 1518. The two 'stoppers' were the Earl of Devonshire and probably Lord Edmund Howard, a member of the King's retinue at the Field of the Cloth of Gold. 'The Bayne' probably means the bath, and it seems likely that baths and Tennis court were combined in the same building – much in the same way as modern clubs combine games and swimming pools. It is not clear whether the court itself was at Blackfriars. Later evidence proves the existence of a court there in 1593 and certainly until 1918 a place named 'Tennis Court' existed off Church Entry, Carter Lane, Blackfriars. Expert research into the layout of the Dominican priory at Blackfriars, however, has not revealed the site of any Tennis court.

As might be expected of so keen a player as Henry VIII, he built several courts at his various palaces. One of them was at Hampton Court, where Tennis continues to be played to this day.

As a result of the research of Dr Howard Colvin, much more is now known about the early history of Tennis at Hampton Court Palace than hitherto. The first court, probably wooden, occupied the site of the present one and may have been built in Cardinal Wolsey's time. In 1532/3, Henry VIII built a new covered court at the northern end of the east front of the palace; its site is shown on the plan of the palace drawn up in George I's reign (marked AAAA, page 42). It measured 83ft x 27ft overall – much the same as the larger covered court at Whitehall. The two courts were connected by a gallery, the remains of which form the present garden wall. A description of this new court emerges from the accounts.

1. *Freemasons wourking upon all such dorys, wyndows and scouncyons for the new lodginges by the Tenys playe (April 1529).*
2. *8 standards and 2 staybarres for 2 wyndows servyng the new lodgings betwixt the galary and the Tenys playe. do.*

yerds qrto of blacke Velwete for a Tenes Cote for the Kings grace' and 'iij yerds qrto of blew Velwete for a Tenes Cote for the King'.

An item in the royal accounts gives an interesting sidelight on the King's Tennis shoes: 'It'm for sooling of syxe paire of shooys with feltys, to pleye in at tenneys, of oure great warderobe.'

In May 1527 the King injured his left foot playing Tennis and was forced to wear an easy slipper of black velvet for a time.

Great festivities took place in London in 1522, when the King received the Emperor Charles V. The two monarchs left the Palace at Greenwich on Friday, 6 June and came to Blackfriars. The Emperor was lodged in the guest-house of this Dominican priory

3. *Laying of gutters over the tennys play.*

4. *A vayn servyng for the stone typis at the gabull ende of the new Tennys play.*

5. *Payntyng and gyldyng of the vane uppon the type of the Tennys play, the Kynges armys wrought with fyne golde in oyle...4s.*

6. *To John Wylkynson for 200 redd ocker for pensellyng of the new tennys play at 20d. the 100.*

7. *For 12 wyndows of new glass, sett in the tennys play, every wyndow of 3 lightes, so the middle lights contain 39 footes, and every syde lyght conteyning 36? ft. In the lesser wyndowys 3 lyghts.*

8. *Carpenters workyng in makyng the hassardes in the close Tennys play agaynst the Kynges cummyng, every of them ratyd for every 9 howres 8d.*

9. *Master Wyre-drawers payd for the wyndows of the New Tennys Play some at 16d. the day, others at 8d.*

10. *Also payd to John Budd of Chiselhurst for*

4000 and a hundrithe pavyng tiles for the Close tennys play at Hampton Court of hym bought and delyverd at Hampton Court, at 16s. the thousand, by convencion 65s. 7d. (Nov. 1532).

It is clear from these accounts that the court was roofed and that the floor was constructed of paving stones. There were twelve windows, glazed and protected from stray balls by wire netting. There were lodgings at either end with windows allowing a view of the court.

York House was the property of the See of York and the London residence of the Archbishops of York when Thomas Wolsey succeeded to the Archbishopric in 1514 (becoming a Cardinal the following year). During his tenure he made many structural improvements to the building and entertained lavishly. Often he was host to the King there, and when in 1529

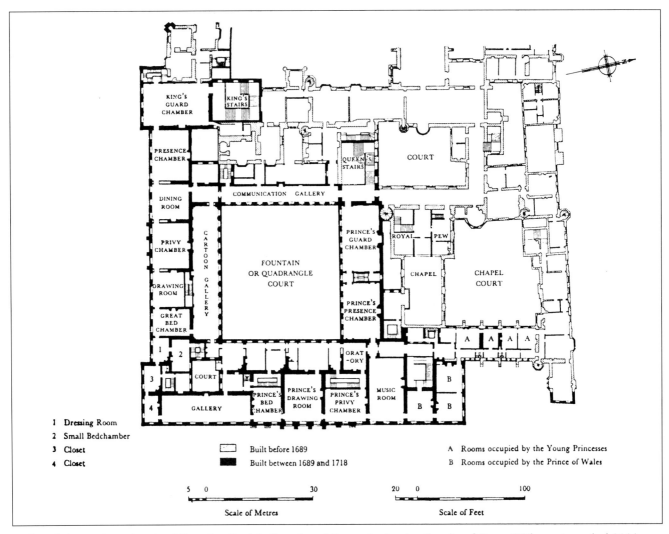

A plan of the royal apartments at Hampton Court in the reign of George 1, showing the site of Henry VIII's court, marked AAAA.

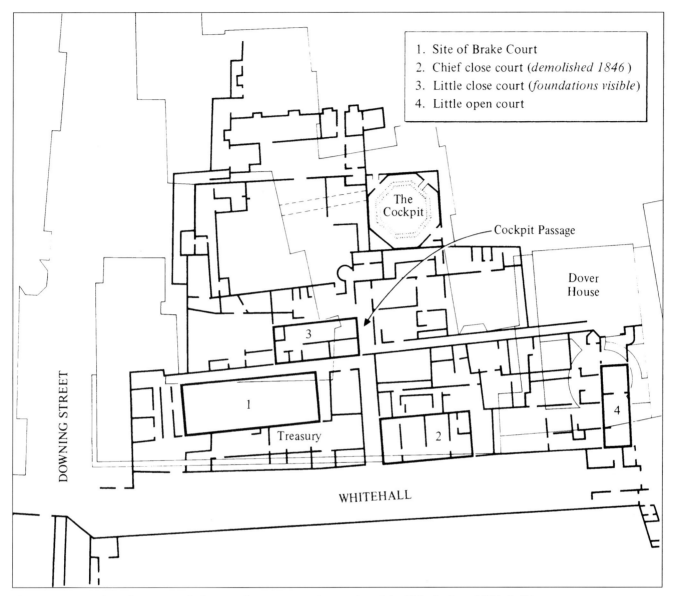

1. Site of Brake Court
2. Chief close court (*demolished 1846*)
3. Little close court (*foundations visible*)
4. Little open court

The Cockpit

Cockpit Passage

Dover House

DOWNING STREET

3

1

Treasury

2

4

WHITEHALL

The approximate sites of Henry VIII's four Tennis courts, superimposed on John Fisher's plan of Whitehall in 1670.

he fell from grace, Henry VIII was quick to seize the opportunity of acquiring the property, especially as his own Palace of Westminster, badly damaged by fire in 1512, was in a poor state of repair.

Once in possession, Henry wasted no time in embarking on an ambitious building programme and he renamed the palace Whitehall. As a keen sportsman and Tennis enthusiast, he made sure that Tennis courts were included in the building programme. There were four in all, two covered courts and two open. Their location is shown in the plan (above).

The most famous of these courts was the large open one south of the cockpit passage and known as the Brake – and it is another mystery of Tennis why it should have been so called. Rabelais, writing in 1532,

brought Gargantua to Paris to play Tennis with his friends at the 'Braque', and in his *Dialogues,* written in 1539, Vivès mentions the most famous court in Paris called the 'Braccha'. This was the court known as the *Jeu du Grand Braque Latin,* place de l'Estrapade, which bore the sign of *un chien braque* – a pointer. The King may have adopted the same name for his own great court because it was so well-known in Paris.

Great it certainly was. The paved area covered 5213sq.ft and it must have measured about 130 ft long x 40 ft wide. (Compare that with the present Lord's court, which measures 96 ft x 31 ft) It was even larger than the great court at the Louvre (illustrated by Scaino) which measured 114 ft x 37 ft 8 ins; but Henry VIII was always eager to surpass the French. No doubt in this huge court, as in the Louvre, it was usual to play three-a-side, if not four. It was also used to play *pallone* or balloon ball and was sometimes known as the balloon court.

The Brake remained a royal court in the early Stuart age. In 1604 it was repaired at a cost of £200, and later a dressing room was added for the use of Henry, Prince of Wales, when he played there. But it met its match in Oliver Cromwell, who turned it into a garden.

The main covered court lay just north of the Brake, fronting the street, and it was very much smaller than a modern court. The exact measurements are known to us from an interesting list of courts compiled in 1615 by the Clerk of Works at Petworth, who gives them as 78 ft x 22 ft. This may seem very small for an important court, but it has to be remembered that rackets were not the powerful instruments used today and that for the first half of the sixteenth century it was still quite usual to play with the hand, often protected by a thick glove.

This court, with its turrets and battlements, was a familiar landmark in Whitehall and although it, too, fell into disuse in Cromwell's time, its street façade survived until 1846 when it was demolished to make way for Sir Charles Barry's new Treasury offices.

There were two even smaller courts. One of them was open, and also appears on the Petworth list, with measurements of 72 ft x 18 ft. It adjoined the Tiltyard gallery and a building account of 1599/1600 suggests that it may have had wooden walls – 'lathing and laying of plaister with lyme and here (hair) on Tymber walles in the Tennys Court next the gallery to the tylte'. This court, too, disappeared under Cromwell.

The smaller covered court was sited west of the Brake at the end of Bowling Alley – its size is not known but from existing plans it would seem to have been about 60 ft x 18 ft. It was re-roofed in 1601, but in 1604/5 it was adapted for use by Princess Elizabeth as a kitchen and offices. Her lodgings were later used as a residence by Cromwell, until he moved to the main buildings of the palace in 1654. The foundations of this court can still be seen from Cockpit Passage, in the Cabinet Office.

The King built St James's Palace for himself and Anne Boleyn and naturally he included a Tennis court. It was situated in the angle between St James's Street and Pall Mall. In 1533 the keeper of St James's Park was put in charge of this 'Tenys playes'. Henry himself continued to play with great keenness, at least as late as 1538. In 1534 the Spanish ambassador wrote to the King's ex-partner, the Emperor Charles V, that 'there have been dances and games of tennis, and the King exercised himself in both.' A little later the same author

wrote that 'on St Andrew's Eve, instead of going to vespers, he [Henry] played Tennis with the [French] Admiral, and next day with another...' In 1538 some young Englishmen being educated in France told how they had seen the King play Tennis when he was supposed to be ill in bed.

The names of two holders of the office of Master of the King's Tennis Plays in Henry VIII's reign are known from an appointment of 9 December 1543:

Thos. Johns, a page of the Chamber. To be master of all the King's tennis plays within the palace of Westminster and elsewhere in England vice Oliver Kelly dec.

It is interesting to note that in the late twentieth century another Johns, Henry, became one of the most highly regarded professionals in the game.

Repressive legislation continued. Acts of 1535/6 and 1541/2 imposed such fines as 'fyve markes for evry moneth' and forty shillings for every day that a Tennis court was kept open. Anyone playing was liable to a fine of twenty shillings except at Christmas. Noblemen, however, and those with an income of over £100, were allowed to possess a court on their property. Others required a licence. In 1542 such a licence was granted to William Griffiths to keep a Tennis court in the Parish of Allhallows-the-Less, for the use of strangers born out of the King's dominions. In 1543 another licence was granted to Richard Kynwolmershe and his wife Elizabeth, to keep a Tennis court in the City for the recreation of 'young lords, knights, gentlemen and merchants'.

Bad sportsmanship seems to have been severely punished in Tudor days, at least within the precincts of a royal palace, for in 1541, 'Sir Edmund Knevet of Norfolk, Knight, was arraigned before the officers of the Green Cloth for striking one master Cleer of Norfolk within the Tennis Court of the King's House. Being found guilty he had judgement to lose his right hand and to forfeit all his lands and goods.' He besought the King that he might lose his left hand instead so that he might live to do the King good service with his right. Henry pardoned him.*

Although with the death of Henry VIII Tennis lost a great patron, it continued nevertheless to be very popular. Among the effects left by the young Duke of Suffolk on his death in 1551 were nine rackets. Etienne Perlin in his description of England and Scotland in

---

*Holinshed is the source of this story. According to Fuller's Worthies, it happened to Sir Edmund Wyndham not Sir Edmund Knevet.

1558 reported that 'you may commonly see artisans such as hatters and joiners playing at Tennis for a crown, which is not often seen elsewhere, particularly on a working day.' He didn't much like the English, writing: 'England is a good land with bad people, as the Spanish say,' and 'the people of this nation mortally hate the French…and we call them "or son" (whoreson).'

Queen Elizabeth I was a keen spectator of Tennis. John Nichols in *The Progresses of Queen Elizabeth* relates how ten Somersetshire men played Tennis in front of her window, 'to so great liking of her Highnes that she graciously deyned to behold their pastime more than an houre and a halfe.' If Nichols's timepiece was functioning correctly, we can conclude that the Queen would today be a regular visitor to the centre court at Wimbledon. On one occasion she was involved in an ugly scene, recounted in a letter from Thomas Randolphe to Sir Nicholas Throckmorton, dated 31 March 1565, at 'Edenbourge'.

Latlye the Dukes G. (of Norfolk) and my L. of L. (Leicester) were playinge at tennes the Q. beholdinge of them, and my L. Rob. being verie hotte and swetinge tooke the Q. napken owte of her hande and wyped his face, wch the Duke seinge saide that he was to sawcie and swhore y^t he wolde laye his racket vpon his face. Here vpon rose a great troble and the Q. offendid sore wth the Duke.

In 1577 it was reported that 'the Queene said she would have a gallerie from her Bed Chamber [in Windsor Castle] to go along over the Porter's lodge throughe the Cunstable's lodginge, and a Tennis Courte at thend.' The plans of the surveyor, Henry Hawthorne, for this gallery and Tennis court still exist. They show the projected court, measuring 76 ft x 28 ft westward of the Inner Gatehouse outside the wall of the Middle Ward. A window of several lights was to be made in the gatehouse turret from which the Queen might look out on the Tennis court below. The gallery was built in 1583, but not the Tennis court. Instead a new brick-built court was erected on the site of the old wooden one.

A new Master of the Queen's Tennis Plays, William Hope, was appointed on 22 April 1584; he held the office until his death eight years later. He was succeeded on 21 December 1592 by Edward Stone, 'footman'. The fee was 8d a day from Michaelmas 1591.

An interesting application for an exclusive licence was made in 1592 by one Thomas Bedingfield, 'for moving her Majesty to grant a licence for keeping certain houses in London and Westminster for playing at dice, cards, table-play, bowling and tennis, and to grant the forfeiture of others that keep such houses or places and use such plays contrary to statute.' For he says, 'She has power to grant such licences; the number of houses is at present very great, and many are kept by persons to whose houses the honester sort will not resort, whereby the worst sort have greater liberty to do evil; it is therefore meet to reduce the number, appoint good order and forbid from such places those who are not fit to play.' He goes on to propose that no one shall be allowed to play 'in the forenoon of any Sabbath day or during evening and morning prayers on holydays; that no swearing or blasphemy be suffered in any such places'. Lastly, 'none but noblemen, gentlemen and merchants, or such as shall be entered in the Book of Subsidies at 10*l.* in land or goods, shall be suffered to play within any such houses.' Five years later, in 1597, another grant reveals the existence of a Tennis court at Ludlow Castle. It was a 'grant to John Hartgell, on surrender of Rob. Bery of the portership of Ludlow Castle, and of the tennis play there; fee 4*l.* a year, to be taken out of the issues, fines, etc. assessed before Her Majesty's Council of the Marches of Wales.'

A picture of a game of Tennis in Elizabethan days is given in *The Parlement of Prattlers* by John Eliot, published in 1593.

THE TENISE-PLAY

JOHN: *Shall we play a set of tenise you and I?*
NICHOLAS: *Let's go to the great Bracke at White-hall.*
JOHN: *Where is the maister that keepes the tenise?*
MAN: *Here I am, sir, what is your pleasure?*
JOHN: *Giue us some soft and gentle shooes here. Rackets and bals bring here, ho.*
NICHOLAS: *Well play.*
JOHN: *I haue fifteene.*
NICHOLAS: *A losse, marke that chase there.*
JOHN: *Fifteene all.*
NICHOLAS: *This racket is not worth a rush.*
JOHN: *Some more rackets, ho.*
NICHOLAS: *Now giue me a faire ball. I cannot take a ball aboue hand, nor at rebound.*
JOHN: *The chase is mine.*
NICHOLAS: *I am thirtie.*
JOHN: *Thirtie all.*
NICHOLAS: *Aske standersby, I touched it not.*
JOHN: *Fortie fiue.*
NICHOLAS: *At dews then.*
JOHN: *A ball, I haue the advantage. The set is mine. I will bande a ball more than six-score paces mounting, with this racket which you refuse. Looke here.*
NICHOLAS: *O diuell! what a firking stroke is that! You haue an arme of yron.*

A sidelight on sixteenth-century behaviour after a game of Tennis is provided in George Chapman's *An Humourous Day's Mirth*, where the following dialogue occurs:

Enter Catalan, sweating.

CAT: *Boy, I prithee call for a coarse napkin. Good morrow, gentlemen! I would you had been at the tennis court, you should have seen me beat Monsieur Besan, and I gave him fifteen and all his faults.*

LEMOT: *Thou did more for him than ever God will do for thee.*

CAT: *Jaques, I prithee fetch me a cup of canary, three parts water.*

Evidently a coarse napkin took the place of the modern towel and a cup of canary with three parts water was the equivalent of the modern shandy. Sporting manners, however, have much improved and nowadays one would expect a sweating Catalan to offer his vanquished opponent a drink.

In Scotland, Tennis continued to be popular and James V built a court in 1539 at his palace of Falkland, Fife – where he later died of a broken heart, leaving the Scottish throne to his daughter, Mary, Queen of Scots. This court is still in use and a description of it can be found in Part III. It is the only remaining example of a *jeu quarré*.

Tennis was not exclusively royal. It seems to have flourished at Oxford despite official disapproval, and the annals of Merton College (today the landlords of the sole remaining court in Oxford) record in April 1492: 'Holt plays tennis and that in public. Comes late to Church.' This refers to Richard (or Robert) Holt, a Fellow of Merton from 1487 to 1493. Later, in 1508, Michael Clowe, William Philips, Richard Andrewes and Henry Busby were each fined sixpence for keeping 'tenys playes'. Seven years later two of them were convicted again of the same offence and fined a further sixpence each. Since the full penalty under the Act of 1495 was 'imprisonment by the space of a day in the stokkis openly', it doesn't appear that the law was very strictly enforced in Oxford.

In the year 1530 there were two Tennis courts in Oxford at Smith's Gate. The evidence of their existence is interesting. Under the Act making certain games illegal, the City Constables were to collect all tables, cards, dice and balls and to burn them in the market-place on market-days. A similar mandate was given to the Vice-Chancellor in respect of the University. The Mayor alleged that the Vice-Chancellor had failed to carry out his duty and had returned the equipment to the scholars. The Vice-Chancellor retorted that the City authorities 'allways do mayntene opynly unlawfull gamys of the tenys, as yn two houses of the rent [i.e. house property of the city] lying next to Smyth Gate, oon of the est side and a nother yn the west side, takyn more rent of the tenants of the said houses for the maynteyning of the said plays yerely.'

These two courts belonged to the City as opposed to the University; they were open courts and were on the present site of Hertford College. The one on the west side of Cat Street soon disappeared, but the other, which at its south end abutted on New College Lane, can be traced down to about 1690, when it was converted into two houses.

The first known University court was built by Christ Church shortly before 1546, in Blue Boar Lane, St Aldate's, on the same estate that included the Unicorn Inn. In 1587 the property was leased to John Lante MA, who later built the Merton Street court.

In about 1572 a new court was built in Oriel Street which remained in use until 1860, when it was converted into billiard rooms. In 1878 the site was acquired by Oriel College and the old Tennis court converted into lecture rooms. It now goes by the name of Old Lecture Rooms and is used for a variety of purposes such as bicycle storage and table tennis. But an imaginative plan for future development will allow the old Tennis court to remain, while new building will be carried out on a platform or podium above it. A curious feature of this old court was that a niche was cut in the centre of the main wall by the net hook to accommodate the marker. Presumably that was thought to be an improvement on the use of one or both of the doors, but it must have been a position of great danger.

Another court in Oxford is recorded in a lease of 1577, described as 'a certain sphaeristerium called le tenys court' on the east side of Vinehall Lane (now Alfred Street), somewhere at the back of the London and County Bank.

In 1595 Merton College granted a lease on Postmaster's Hall to John Lante MA which included 'a tennise court of late built and erected thereon by the said John Lante'. This was on the site of the present court, which was built about 1798. Tennis was popular in Oxford and J. Earle, a Fellow of Merton, wrote in 1628, describing an Oxford undergraduate: 'The two markes of his Senioritie, is the bare veluet of his gowne and his proficiencie at Tennis, where when hee can once play a Set, he is a Fresh-man no more.'

Oxford was very poorly provided with courts compared with Cambridge, where there were at least ten courts in the sixteenth and early seventeenth centuries:

Corpus Christi College in Penny-Farthing Lane. At some date between 1487 and 1515 the walls of a building intended for a bake-house and granary were carried up to sufficient height to play *pila palmaria*. In 1569 this court was converted to student rooms and a new roofed court built, shown in Hammond's map of Cambridge in 1592. It was pulled down in 1756.

Christ's College. Built 1564/5. Repaired 1597/8. Pulled down 1711.

Emmanuel College. Built 1584 or earlier. Originally roofed, but roof removed 1632. A College Order of 29 October 1651, reads:

The key of it shall be in the keeping of the Deane, who is to take care that the door is kept lockt, and none suffered to play during the howers hereafter mentioned, viz. from one of the clock till three in the afternoon and from eight of the clock at night till three the next morning; unless any of the fellows desire to play there in any of these howers, who may take any fellow commoner with them; yet soe as they cleare the court, shutt the doore, and return the key to the Deane at their comeing away.

This court was pulled down at some date before 1746.

Peterhouse. First mentioned 1572. Still in use 1677.

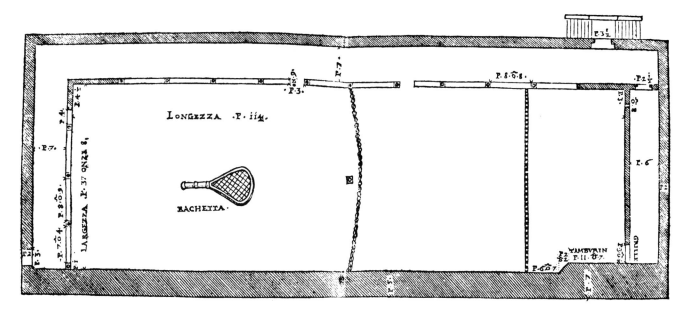

Scaino's plan of the court at the Louvre.

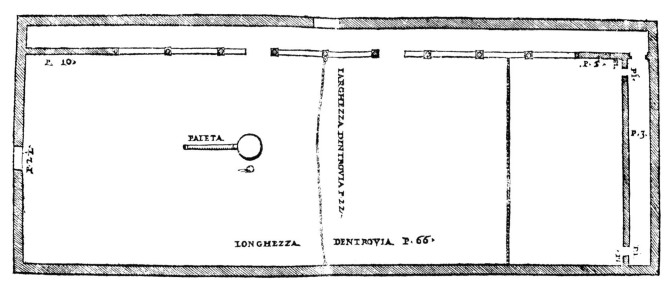

Scaino's plan of a jeu quarré.

St John's College. A wooden building in 1573/4 near the Master's garden. Pulled down 1598/9. Second court built on the other side of the river 1602/3.

Jesus College. First mentioned 1566/7. Rebuilt 1603/4.

King's College. A roofed court that certainly existed in 1569/70. Mention of 'chambers in the tenise courte', 1579.

Queen's College. Built before 1531. At east end of garden opposite the great gate. Accounts contain many entries recording repairs.

Trinity College. A court at the south-eastern corner of the college was repaired in 1585/6. Pulled down 1598. A new court was built in 1611 between the end of the north range of Nevile's court and the river, at a cost of £120. Two Tennis court keepers were appointed. Pulled down 1676 to make way for the Library.

Pembroke College. Abutting on Tennis Court Lane. Court built or re-paved in 1564. Rebuilt in 1734. Pulled down 1880.

Five of these courts – Corpus Christi, Christ's College, Emmanuel, Peterhouse and Pembroke – are all clearly marked and numbered on David Logan's plan of Cambridge in 1688. A sixth – St John's – is clearly shown but not numbered. The courts at Christ's College, Emmanuel and St John's also appear in the views of these individual colleges.

Another new court was built by Sir Henry Sidney, President of the Council, at Ludlow Castle.

The popularity of Tennis in the sixteenth century was by no means confined to England, France and Scotland. It was extensively played elsewhere in Europe; and it was in fact an Italian, Antonio Scaino da Salò, who wrote the first-ever treatise on the game in 1555.

Antonio Scaino came from Salò on Lake Garda. He worked at the University of Padua, where he lectured on Aristotle and St Augustine, and became a friend of the Duke, Alfonso II, who was a keen Tennis player. It was a disputed point in a game of Tennis that inspired Scaino to write his *Trattato del Giuoco della Palla.*

So enthusiastic was Scaino that he tells us that all the best people played Tennis – Julius Caesar and Alexander the Great included. And he tells us of the great players of his day – Gian Fernando the Spaniard and Gian Antonio the Neapolitan, who played with the hand, and Laches and Verdelot, Frenchmen, who played with a racket. Gian Fernando used to practise by using two cords stretched across the court less than a foot apart and playing the ball between them.

Scaino tells us of six different games:

1. *Pallone* is an open-air game usually played by four players on each side, using a large ball made of goatskin and filled with air. Each player wears an arm protector (*bracciale*) made of wood on his forearm, and with this he strikes the ball. Scaino includes a diagram showing the ball, the pump for inflating the ball and the *bracciale*. *Pallone* continued to be played in Italy up to the eighteenth century and an interesting picture in the MCC Museum at Lord's shows a game in progress.

2. A similar game uses a smaller air-filled ball struck with a kind of wooden bat (*scanno*), also illustrated by Scaino.

3 and 4. *Longue paume* is Tennis played out of doors, using either the bare hand or a racket. The balls for both *longue* and *courte paume* are the same, being stuffed with wool shearings, but the ball used for hand-play, larger and heavier than that for use with a racket, is more loosely stuffed to avoid injury to the hand.

5 and 6. *Courte paume* (called by Scaino the cord game) is Tennis as we now know it, but played either with the hand or with a racket.

Scaino includes two plans of Tennis courts. One is of the court at the Louvre in Paris, built by Henri II, and apart from its great size, this closely resembles a modern Tennis court. One slight difference is the entry to the court which is by a door on either side of the net (where the door gallery is today). In these doorways stood the two markers who kept the score and recorded the chases.

The cord (net) from which Tennis derived its Italian name, *giuoco della corda*, is clearly shown. It was a simple rope across the court with a fringe hanging from it to make it easier to determine whether the ball had gone over or under the cord. Scaino tells us it must be 3½ft above the floor at the centre.

The other plan is of a smaller court, known in France as a *jeu quarré*. The court at the Louvre, with dedans, grille and tambour, was called a *jeu à dedans*. The *jeu quarré*, of which the only remaining example is at Falkland Palace, had certain distinguishing features. It had no dedans and no tambour. Instead of the dedans it normally had various other winning openings which differed from court to court.

In Scaino's court there is one such winning opening on the service side, a square hole (*trou*) in the centre of the court 2½ft x 1½ft and 4½ft above the floor. On the hazard side the court illustrated is unusual in having no grille, but two small openings 1 ft from each corner, 10ins square and 5½ft above the floor.

In the normal *jeu quarré* there was another winning feature called *l'ais*. This was a board 6ft high by 1ft wide attached to the back wall on the service side in the corner by the gallery wall. The *trou* was usually found in the opposite corner of the service side, about 16ins square.

In some courts there was a further winning opening high up on the back wall of the service side. This was a round hole 8ins in diameter known as *la lune* – and a ball struck into it won a whole game outright. In the print of the court at Tübingen (on page 22) there appear to be two *lunes*, one at each end.

To complete his thorough survey Scaino includes two more diagrams of open and covered courts for Tennis played with the hand.

But of all the various ball games, Scaino considered the cord game to be the best:

> *Countless are those who place the cord game above all others, and among them I number myself. It is a game of great majesty and truly worthy of Gentlemen. Therefore we conclude by saying that, of all Ball-Games, the rarest and most honoured is the cord game.*
>
> *It is suitable for children, youths, men, almost for old men, too. It is dear to the jovial, pleasing to the melancholy, the serious and the severe, and suited to almost all humours and temperaments.*
>
> *What shall we say of the great gladness and contentment that the victor feels after a long and tiring battle? So great are they, indeed, that, unable to hide them, he jumps about, visibly and infinitely rejoicing in his victory.* [Compare the scorer of a goal in modern football.]

It is quite clear from all the evidence that courts differed very greatly in those early days and the rules had to take account of all sorts of natural hazards – especially in the case of *longue paume*. For example, Scaino discusses the way to treat a ball that lands on a passing cart and is then returned from the cart by an opponent. He advises that such a stroke is good if the ball was still moving on the cart, but if not, then a chase is made at the point where the cart was when the ball came to a stop; or, if a ball enters the window of a house and is returned to the court from another window, that is not good. He also records that there are often doorsteps of stone or wood or other such protuberances in Tennis courts which can lead to difficult decisions when struck by the ball.

He asserts that the ball is good if it hits one of the nails or hooks to which the net is attached and then passes over the net; a net cord is good in France but not in Italy.

Scaino also gives some tips to young players, emphasising in particular the need to watch the ball carefully, to keep to the centre of the court and to make good use of the back wall. Muddles between doubles partners were just as familiar then as now, and Scaino mentions that it is often effective to play the ball between two or more opponents, for each may well leave it to the other and neither return it. He particularly praises the cut stroke at which the French excel, and stresses the importance of constant practice.

All this advice reads very familiarly to modern ears and there is little difference between Scaino and a modern professional when it comes to coaching. But in the matter of what to wear for a game of Tennis, times have changed. Stockings, says Scaino, must be supple to allow the legs to bend; they may reach to the knee or, in 'modern' fashion, right up to the waist. The shirt must fit closely, provided the arms are free; and the shoes shall be light, soled for example with buffalo skin. Keep fit, says Scaino, and avoid a fat belly.

Curiously, he devotes one chapter to football, played twenty, thirty or forty to a side at Padua. He doesn't consider it so artistic a game as Tennis, but nevertheless it gives great pleasure to the spectators, especially when the players dash about in great disarray and fall upside-down almost as in a real battle.

Tennis seems to have been played in all the main Italian cities, as one might expect, but no traces of it remain today. We know it was played in Mantua in 1560, for the problem of 'whether or not it is allowed to play ball on Sabbaths and Holidays' by Jews was referred to the famous Rabbi, Moses Ben Abraham, later known as Moses Provençal. Mantua at the time was a haven for the persecuted Jews, thanks to the liberal policy of the Duke of Mantua, and there were probably some 2000 resident at the time. The Rabbi's ruling gives some glimpses of the game as it was played there.

Special buildings had been erected for it and some of them had open windows; occasionally the ball would go out through them, and 'the Sabbath is thus desecrated by the transfer of an object from private grounds to the field, which has the status of a quasi-public thoroughfare.' On the other hand, it was an advantage that the floor was of stone, thus obviating the need for minor repairs on the Sabbath. The ball was played, either with a kind of scoop, similar to the Basque *chistera* as used in *pelota*, or with 'small bows laced with guts, and netted with strings'.

Moses Provençal was particularly outspoken against the current habit of gambling on Tennis matches and condemned the practice of avoiding the prohibition of cash stakes on the Sabbath by betting in foodstuffs, such as flour and potatoes, later readily convertible into cash. 'Also,' he continues, 'it is not uncommon for the game to be conducted while the sermon is being preached in the Synagogue: this is by no means permissible.' He concludes that Tennis might only be played on the Sabbath with the hand; to use a racket was not allowed as 'the case was analagous to that of playing musical instruments on those days which were interdicted by the Rabbis, for fear that the player might attempt to mend the instrument that broke.'

We know that Tennis was introduced into Venice in 1595 and at least four courts seem to have existed there. In Rome in about 1600 a young painter, Caravaggio, quarrelled with a friend over a game and killed him. Permission was given to introduce Tennis to Milan in 1629 and another court existed at Turin.

In Spain, too, Tennis was well-known in royal circles, and like Louis X of France, two Spanish kings, Henry I in 1217 and Philip I in 1506, both of Castile, are said to have died as a result of drinking cold water after an energetic game.

The Hapsburg king, Philip III, was another royal patron of Tennis. 'He was at the age of twenty-four of small stature, but healthy and of a good complexion; very religious and an example of goodness and good manners. He ate well, but drank no wine; amused himself in hunting, which led him to be constantly in the country; he willingly undertook journeys; and passed the rest of his time in playing tennis and dancing.' The court in the Alcazar Palace in Madrid was repaired for him by the municipality and a corridor built from the Palace to the court for greater ease of access. Vivès, writing his Latin exercises in 1539, introduces a dialogue on the difference between the games in France and Spain. Scintilla has just returned from a visit to Paris:

BORGIA: *Do they play there in the same way as here?*
SCINTILLA: *Almost, except that the manager of the court provides shoes and caps for the players.*
BORGIA: *What are they like?*
SCINTILLA: *The shoes are made of felt.*
BORGIA: *Wouldn't these shoes suit us here?*
SCINTILLA: *Perhaps on a paved floor. In France and in Belgium they play on a flagstone floor, flat and level. The caps worn in summer are lighter, but in winter they are thick and fitted*

with straps under the chin, so that they do not come off.
BORGIA: *Here we only tie our caps under the chin when the wind is strong.*

Throughout central Europe the game flourished and at least one court existed in every main town and city. In the German states, forty-six towns possessed at least one court. The game was introduced to Vienna by the Emperor Ferdinand I, Charles V's younger brother, who had learnt it in his birthplace, Spain. In Sweden Eric IV built a court in Stockholm.

In Prague there were four courts, of which the most important was the royal court, known as Rudolf's *Ballhaus* in the castle gardens. This was built by an Italian architect for Ferdinand I about the year 1568 and was much patronised by the Emperor Rudolf II (1576–1612), who was a keen player. When his health deteriorated he remained a keen spectator and used to watch matches in progress, hidden from general view.

The French Marshal Bassompierre described in his memoirs how he played a game in Prague in January 1604 against Wallenstein with Rudolf II watching:

Playing tennis against the great Wallenstein, who was acting as the Emperor's great chamberlain since the death of Peter de Mollart a week previously, the Emperor came to see us play through a blind (jalousie) in a window that overlooked the court, and stayed there a long time.

In the early eighteenth century this royal court was used as a theatre, and in 1757 was heavily damaged during the siege of Prague. Later it became an arsenal and by 1945 was a total wreck. The magnificent exterior of the building has since been beautifully restored, but not, alas, the Tennis court itself.

There is a curious set of sixteenth-century pictures, each of which includes a view of a contemporary Tennis court. The series tells the story of David and Bathsheba. David is depicted twice – once gazing longingly from a balcony upon a nude Bathsheba beside a pool and once handing sealed instructions to her husband Uriah at the castle gate. The background to each picture contains a number of sports, Tennis most prominently, but also archery and a form of bowls. So far as the Tennis courts are concerned, some show a game of doubles, some singles. Most include markers sitting on a bench inside the court; three of them show markers actually marking a chase. In one there appears to be a sort of tambour, in another a winning-gallery. The pictures are individually owned in England, the United States and Italy. Their origin is another mystery of Tennis.

SEVENTEENTH-CENTURY TENNIS

THE ARRIVAL OF BOURBON KINGS on the French throne and Stuart kings in England did not signal an immediate decline in the popularity of Tennis, which continued to thrive for the first half of the seventeenth century.

Louis XIII was taught early to play Tennis. At eleven he was receiving lessons from a professional, Pierre Gentil, and at thirteen he played regularly three or four times a week, either in the court in the rue de Grenelle-Saint-Honoré, or at St Germain. Here is an extract from his doctor's diary:

> The 19th February, 1614. Goes by carriage to play tennis at Grenelle. The 28th, goes to the court at Grenelle; washed at M. Leclerc's; he eats there. 1st June, goes to the court at Grenelle, where he was struck in the teeth by a ball from the Chevalier de Soubré; he bleeds a little. 21st, plays tennis at St Germain-en-Laye.

Later in the year he went on a tour of western France and played Tennis whenever he had the chance. The same diary records games at Orléans, Châtellerault, Poitiers, Mirebeau, Angers, Nantes and Le Mans. He suffered another slight accident playing at Nantes, where he was struck by a ball in the right eye. He then fell ill and there are no further records of his play until 1617, when he returned to the Tennis courts.

Unfortunately, his doctor died that year and detailed records cease but he certainly retained his liking for the game and presumably continued to play. At any rate he played at La Rochelle in 1628, just after the capture of the town from the Huguenots, although he was seized by an attack of gout in the middle of the match.

One Tennis professional of the day was a certain La Lande; the King writes to Cardinal Richelieu that he had not been paid either his journey money or his fee.

The great popularity of Tennis necessitated the first common book of rules, and this was compiled by a master professional, Forbet. In 1592 he devised the earliest known rules, comprising twenty-four articles, which were published in 1599. They were re-edited and re-published in 1632 by Charles Hulpeau, under the title *Le Jeu Royal de la Paume*.

It is remarkable how closely these ancient rules resemble those in use today. Basically they differ on points of detail. The set consists of four or six games; in the case of a four-game set, if three games all is reached, a player has to attain a lead of two games to win it. The height of the net at the centre was to be such that a man standing at one end wall could just see the foot of the wall at the opposite end – with no mention of how tall the man should be! When there were two markers they stood in the two doors; when only one he stood in the door on the service side. If a marker's decision was disputed, a player could appeal to the spectators, whose majority decision was final.

Betting was normal on all matches and governed by rules. Very fairly, the winner was responsible for meeting such expenses as lost balls, bread, wine, firewood, shoes and markers' fees. The frontispiece of Hulpeau's book is an excellent reproduction of a seventeenth-century *jeu quarré*, although strangely enough it does not show the *ais*, mentioned in the text. In this particular court there seem to have been two *trous*, no *ais* and no *lune*.

An interesting description of a match in a *jeu quarré* is contained in Frissart's pamphlet of 1641, describing a game of Tennis between the French and Spanish kings, resulting in victory for the French. In this court there were a *trou*, an *ais* and a *lune*.

Naturally enough, Alexandre Dumas has his three musketeers play Tennis, but d'Artagnan calls the game off for fear of the power of Porthos's hitting.

A curious print by Jacques Callot records another casualty, but in this case resulting in a miraculous recovery. It shows a river scene near Mont St Michel, where the Prince's son has been killed by a blow from a Tennis ball. He is brought back to life by Jean Porcelet, Bishop of Toul.

A Tennis court in 1632, from Charles Hulpeau's book.

Paris. Those favoured in this way were two Jourdains, Le Pape, Clergé and Sercot.

A steady decline in the number of courts in Paris is recorded by the Dutch ambassador who wrote in 1657 that there were 114, although he was surprised there were not more. This compares with the 250 reported in 1596 (see page 17).

But there is no doubt that, in general, Tennis remained very popular in France. A Sicilian visitor wrote in 1692 that 'the young people amuse themselves with every sort of physical exercise, and especially Tennis.'

Some players, then as now, did not enjoy losing. One is reported to have had a habit of throwing balls, ball-baskets, rackets, clothes, and finally even himself into the grille. Another, more sporting, used to give a crown to his servant to go outside and utter a few strong oaths on his behalf.

An interesting account of the correct dress for Tennis occurs in the statutes of the master professionals of Bordeaux in 1684. 'No master professional may keep a court unless he has linen for the use of players: that is to say four dozen fine cloths to make caps, two dozen shirts, six dozen half-cloths for wiping, twelve pairs of trousers, the same number of vests, socks, shoes of leather and shoes of wool and eight pairs of sheets.' No doubt the woollen slippers and sheets were for use after the game, when waiting one's turn to be rubbed down by a marker.

As in France, so in England Tennis continued to be popular during the first half of the seventeenth century. James I was well aware of the merits of the game and recommended his eldest son, Prince Henry, to play. In his *Basilicon Doron*, written in 1598, when the Prince was aged four, he writes:

And amongst all vnnecessarie thinges that are lawfull and expedient, I thinke exercises of the bodie moste commendable to be vsed by a young Prince, in suche honest games or pastimes, as may further ability and maintaine health. For albeit I graunt it to be most requisite for a King to exercise his engine, whiche surelie with idlenesse will rouste and become blunt; yet certainly bodily exercises and games are verie commendable; as well for bannishing of idlenesse (the mother of all vice) as for making his bodie able and durable for trauell, whiche is necessaire for a King, but from this compte I debarre all rumling violent exercises as the fitball meither for laming nor making able the useris thairof, as lykeuayes sicc tumbling trikkis as onlie seruis for comœdians and gysairis to uinne

Louis XIII died in 1643 and was succeeded by his eldest son as Louis XIV, *Le Roi Soleil*. He was just four on his accession, but was soon on the Tennis court learning to play. Saint-Simon writes that, 'he excelled at dancing, pall-mall and tennis'.

In 1658, Louis paid a visit to Dijon, and 'passed part of his afternoons playing tennis in the Salamander court'. He also carried out some repairs to the court at the Louvre. But after Mazarin's death the burdens of state fell heavily upon him and he played less Tennis, preferring billiards, which he could play after the day's work was over.

However, he still enjoyed watching the best players, and was often to be seen at Fontainebleau on wet days until in 1702 a disastrous fire burnt out both courts there. He granted the best professionals the privilege of being allowed to advertise twice-weekly matches in *thaire breade with, but the exercises that I uolde haue you to use (althoch but moderatlie not making a crafte of thaime) are rinning, leaping, urestling, fensing, dansing & playing at the cache.*

The 'cache', usually spelt 'caitche', is the old Scots name for Tennis and the first public edition of 1603 reads 'playing at the caitche or tennise'.

No doubt for Henry's benefit, the King repaired the Brake Court at Whitehall. 'By Order, 2nd of September 1604. To Andrew Kerwyn, paymaster of His Highness's works, the sum of 200*l*., in prest, parcel of a more sum, limited by the said Privy Seal, towards the repair of the great Tennis-Courte, commonly called the Brake of Whitehall.' In 1612 he built a dressing room for the Prince, described as 'a small buildinge between twoe Brickwalls, adjoyneing to the Tennis-Courte or great Brake, beinge for the Prince to make himselfe ready in to play at Tennis there.'

Henry seems to have been hot-tempered on the Tennis court, and on two occasions was involved in a fierce quarrel. On the first he is said to have struck, or offered to strike, Robert Carr, Earl of Somerset, his father's favourite. On the second, Henry disputed a point of play with the young Earl of Essex. So violent was the argument that Henry called the Earl, 'son of a traitor', and Essex struck the Prince on the head with his racket, drawing blood. The affair was reported to the King who pardoned Essex when he heard a full account of the incident. He told Henry that the boy who had struck him would never be slow to smite his enemies for him. Another of the Prince's opponents was Sir John Harington. In a letter of 1609, Henry wrote to Sir John, 'When I see you (and let it be shortlie) you will find me your better at Tennis and Pike. Good Fellow, I write your friend, Henry.'

It was a great loss to the country when, in his eighteenth year, he fell ill and died. Thomas Birch, who wrote his biography in 1760, criticises his self-neglect. He would go swimming in the Thames after supper with a full stomach and this, according to Birch, stopped his nose bleeding but caused the fatal fever. On 24 October he played a great match at Tennis (probably at the Brake) clad only in his shirt despite the cold weather, and on going to bed complained of lassitude and headache. On 6 November he died.

His greatest diversion was at Tennis [Birch writes] *in which, it is acknowledged, he neither observed moderation, nor what suited his dignity and person, continuing often three or four hours at it.*

King James's second son, the Duke of York, later Charles I, was equally keen on Tennis. In the Exchequer records, under the date 6 December 1610, is entered, 'By order, to Jehu Webb, master of His Majesty's Tennis plays, the sum of 20*l*. for his attendance in teaching the Duke of York to play at Tennis, now one whole year ended at Michaelmas last, 1610, and for furnishing him with balls, rackets and other necessaries within the said year.' Another entry, on 8 November 1611, is authority to pay twenty pounds per annum and twenty pounds already due to John Webb, Master of the Tennis Plays, for instructing the Duke of York in that exercise, and providing rackets and balls for him. That the young Duke was no sluggard where Tennis was concerned is shown by a later entry which reads, 'Messenger to fetch Mr Clemman to come to his Highness next morning at St James by six in the Tennis Court, to play the match with Sir Thomas Howard.' He was also on occasion as impetuous as his elder brother and in 1618 quarrelled with the Duke of Buckingham in the court.

The Duke's Tennis teacher, John Webb, had been appointed 'master of the King's Tennis plays at Westminster, etc' on 7 February 1604. Three years later it is recorded that he was granted the moiety of £1600, old debts due to the Crown, to be recovered by him, and was confirmed in the office of 'Master of the King's tennis play throughout England'.

Two years later, in 1609, we find him suing Sir Thomas Knyvet, Knt, Lord Knyvet, John Freeburne and Roger Rolles in the Court of Common Pleas, alleging that they 'wrongfully, and without judgment, disseised him' of the office of Master of the Tennis-plays. He won his case, for the court held that the office of 'master of the King's Tennis-plays in West-minster, etc' included 'the tennis-plays for the King's household, and not only for the tennis-play when the King himself plays in his royal person; for the King is the head of his household, and therefore *a digniori parte*, the tennis-plays for his household may well be called the King's tennis-plays.' The record of the case mentions two courts at Whitehall, 'the close tennis court' and 'the Brake'.

John Webb's duties seem to have included the provision of balls, yet there existed another office – that of 'brinder or keeper of ballons and bracers for the tennis court', granted to Alex Narne, Gentleman waiter, for a fee of 2d a day with all profits, probably in 1604.

John Webb retired in January 1618 on a pension of £120 p.a. He was succeeded by Gideon Lozier and John Webb, who was probably his son. John Webb died in 1656.

The royal courts in London were the Brake at Whitehall and that at St James's, built by Henry VIII and repaired by James I. An interesting list of other courts existing in 1615 in the City is included in the Records of the Clerk of Works at Petworth, then the property of the Earl of Northumberland. The first two courts on the Petworth list are two other Whitehall courts; the larger covered court and the smaller open court. The other courts listed are 'Sommersett house, Essex house, Fetter lane, Fleetestreete, Blackfriers, Southampton, Charterhouse, Powles chaine, Abbchurch lane, St Laurence Pontne, Fanchurch streete, Cruchedfriers'.

The Charterhouse court was originally the court of Howard House, belonging to the Duke of Norfolk, on the site of the Carthusian monastery at Smithfield. In 1611 Charterhouse School was founded and soon afterwards the old Tennis court was converted to a boarding house for forty scholars, who at one time included John Wesley. It continued to be so used until 1872, when the school moved to its present site.

Many courts existed outside London. Henry VIII's court at Hampton Court flourished and James I included Tennis in the revels he organised there at Christmas 1604. The court at Windsor is shown in Norden's *Description of the Honor of Windsor*, in the year 1607. King James built a palace including a Tennis court at Newmarket, and in 1624 issued a warrant for the building of a court at Theobald's.

Courts also existed at this date in Ireland. In 1609 Lord Howth and Sir Roger Jones were involved in a brawl which led to bloodshed in a court in St Thomas's Street, Dublin.

By this time the old restrictive Acts were ignored, but it still required a licence to run a Tennis court. In 1620 James I granted to Clement Cotterell,

for the Term of his Life, sole Power and Authoritie to appoint, assigne, nominate and license such Persons as he shall think good, to have, maintain and keep, within the severall Places hereafter mentioned and not elsewhere, the severall nombers of Bowling Allies, Tennis Courts and suchlike Places of Honest Recreation, as are likewise in theis Presentes hereafter particularly mentioned, sett down and appoynted...videlicet...within the said Citties of London and Westminster, and in any place or places within two miles of the said citties, fowarteene Tennis Courtes.

This figure of fourteen courts is valuable confirmation of the accuracy of the Petworth list.

Charles continued to play Tennis enthusiastically on coming to the throne. On 6 November 1626 a warrant was issued to pay Thomas Hooker, keeper of the Tennis court at St James's, £798 3s 2d for balls and other accessories and for betting debts.

A later document of 1627 contains an instruction to Lord Treasurer Marlborough concerning 'his Majesty's pleasure that Hooker, the Tennis-court-keeper, be paid.'

The Treasury seems to have been very lax in settling the King's debts to Thomas Hooker, for after his death his wife, who succeeded him as keeper of the King's Tennis court at St James's, entered the following petition in 1637:

Before the death of her late husband, Thomas Hooker, there was due to him £3000 in 1630 whereof he abated £1000 for renewing the lease of the tennis court, and by his will left the other £2000 for the portions of his children. In May 1633 petitioner received £1000 and for the King's play since 1630 to 2nd May 1636 there is due £632. 7s. 0d. Prays a Privy Seal for £1632. 7s. 0d.

It seems likely that Charles I built the present court at Hampton Court Palace in about 1625, on the site of the old wooden court.

He also kept the Whitehall courts in good repair. A warrant of 21 October 1634 is addressed 'to the survayer, to cause the 3 Tennice courts at Whitehall to bee mended in places needfull'. In 1635/6 he re-paved the Brake court and money was paid 'to Nicholas Stone, Maurice and Richard Flewellein and other Masons...for taking up all the Purbecke paving in the Brake, and new squaring and layinge downe againe, V^mCCxiij foote of the said stone.'

About this time an investigation into the escape of a prisoner from the gatehouse mentions a certain Mr Gibbons, who keeps 'the Tennis-court in the Fields, unto whose house noblemen resort there and eat'. This reveals the existence of a new court in Lincoln's Inn Fields, built about 1633. It was situated in Bear Yard, Vere Street, Clare-market, and was usually known as Gibbons' Tennis court. Charles Gibbons lived close by the court until his death in 1668. This was one of two new courts near Lincoln's Inn Fields, built in this reign. The other was known as Lisle's Tennis court and was situated in Portugal Street on the site of the Royal College of Surgeons' Museum, blitzed in the Second World War.

In about 1634, the first of two courts was built in James Street (now Orange Street) off the Haymarket.

View of Hampton Court showing the present court as built by Charles I and the outer walls of Henry VIII's previous court.

It fell into disrepair and in 1680 Charles Hatton wrote to his brother:

> *Yesterday ye roof of ye Tennis cote in ye Haymarket fell down. Sir Charles Sidley being there had his skull broke, and it is thought it will be mortall.*

Even the outbreak of Civil War in England did not dampen the King's enthusiasm for Tennis, and he was playing the game with Prince Rupert in the Oriel Street court at Oxford on 28 December 1642 when a messenger arrived from Parliament with proposals for 'articles of accommodation'.

The match was 'at Mr Edwards his tennis court'. This was Richard Edwards, a surgeon, who was granted the lease of the property on 12 October 1636.

The King's absence from London was much lamented, and a pamphlet printed for NV and JB in 1642 is entitled: 'A Deep Sigh breathed through the lodgings at Whitehall, deploring the absence of the Court and the Miseries of the Pallace'.

It begins, 'A Pallace without a Presence! A White-Hall clad in sable vestments! A Court without a Court!', and later it reads:

> *There is no presse at the Wine-Sellor Dores and Windowes, no gaping noise amongst the angry Cookes in the Kitchings, no wayting for the opening of the Posterne-dore to take water at the Stayres, no racket nor balling in the Tenis Court...*

On one occasion the King found himself short of a Tennis suit and had to obtain Parliament's consent for the necessary material to be sent from London to Oxford. On 8 November 1643, it is recorded:

> *George Kirk, master of His Majesty's robes, applies for a pass for John Daintrey, one of the grooms in the office, to go to Oxford with his servant with 4 dozen of gloves, which are much wanted by His Majesty, and 4 yards of taby, 2 ells and $\frac{1}{4}$ of taffety to be a tennis-suit, and 2 pairs of garters and roses with silk buttons and other necessaries for making up of the said suit. Permission was granted by Parliament and it was ordered that John Daintrey shall have a pass to Oxon with a servant to carry down some things for the King's Majesty.*

At Oxford, Thomas Burnham keenly promoted Tennis. He had obtained a sub-lease of the Merton Street court in 1647 and issued a farthing token inscribed with a Tennis racket and ball and the words, 'Thomas Burnham at ye tennis Court in Oxford'. In 1667 he leased the Oriel Street court and in 1670 the Unicorn in Blue Boar Lane, 'where he built a fair and stately Racket court...covered overhead which it was not before.' He died in 1676, but his wife continued the business.

Tennis continued to be played in the Blue Boar Lane court until about 1835.

Oliver Cromwell did not approve of Tennis, and courts were put to military use.

John Hooker laid claim to the Tennis court at St James's. Probably he was a son of Thomas Hooker, whom Charles I had rewarded so generously for his services as Tennis court keeper at St James's. John Hooker received a peremptory order in July 1649 to hand over the key of the court of Colonel Thomas Pride, 'to enable him to quarter his soldiers there'.

A survey of the St James's Tennis court, made by order of Parliament in 1650, sheds some light on its construction.

One house called the Tennis Court built with bricks and covered with tiles and paved with tiles. The tiles well fitted and joined containing by admeasurement 100 ft. of assise in length and 35 ft. in breadth, also one leanto or walk lying on the east side of the said Tennis Court consisting of the length aforesaid, also one garden belonging to the same enclosed round with a strong brick wall of 20 ft. high, now in the occupation of John Hooker gentleman and is worth per annum £47.

We find that the late King by his letters patent bearing date the 12th day of August in the 7th year of his reign did grant to Thomas Hooker gentleman in consideration of his good service all that aforesaid Tennis Court and other the aforesaid premises for and during the full end and term of 80 years to commence at the end expiration or future or other determination of a former lease which did determine on the 25th day of March 1643 yielding and paying yearly during the aforesaid term of 80 years the sum of 12s. 4d....so that the aforesaid Thomas Hooker is the immediate tenant and hath yet to come 77 years and a half on the 29th day of September next ensuing...

The lessee covenants to repair uphold maintain and keep this Tennis Court and houses in good repair at his own cost and charges...

Examined for William Webb, Surveyor-General 1650

Ric Heinwood
Rowland Brasbridge
John Brudenell

Charles Gibbons' endeavours to build another court in 1654 found no favour in Puritan eyes.

October 17th. Petition of John Tilson, gentleman, and others, to the Protector and Council, to prohibit Charles Gibbons, a tennis-court-keeper near Lincoln's Inn Fields, from erecting another tennis court, to the disturbance of his neighbours and ill example of others in this time of reformation, he having one already which entertains company at unseasonable hours.

After the Restoration this court became a well-known theatre, but later it was used for sundry other purposes until finally burnt down in 1809.

Even under the Commonwealth, the office of Master of the Tennis Plays evidently continued, for on 8 March 1656 when John Webb died, Ralph Bird was appointed. He held office for a few years only, being replaced at the Restoration.

In exile, the Court continued to play Tennis in France. Charles I had brought up his sons, Charles and James, to play – a print of James at the age of eight in 1641 shows him racket in hand in an open court, probably the Brake in Whitehall, and accounts at Petworth record his playing there in 1647/48. When John Evelyn visited France in 1649 he wrote:

...on 13 September the King invited the Pr. of Condy [Prince de Condé] to supper at St Clo's [St Cloud]. There I kissed the Duke of Yorks hand in the Tennis Court, where I saw a famous match 'twixt Monsieur Saumeurs [perhaps Paul de Saumur] and Col Cooke, and so returned to Paris.

A letter from Sir Edward Hyde to Sir Edward Nicholas, dated 1657, reports that

The King spends his time not unpleasantly, nor uselessly, having entered into another kind of conversation with Don Juan, than is natural to an incognito condition. Yesterday they played at long poume, a Spanish play with balls filled with wire, and tomorrow they have a match at tennis.

Another story tells that Charles was playing a game of Tennis when news was brought to him of Oliver Cromwell's death in 1658.

The year 1660 marked not only the restoration of the monarchy, but the restoration of Tennis as the royal game. Charles II was the most enthusiastic monarch since Henry VIII to play it.

It was seldom that he passed a day without visiting the Tennis court as early as there was light enough to see clearly. In the summer he was there at five in the morning; on 5 October 1660, at eight, he told Clarendon at Council, 'I am now going to take my usual physicks at tennis.' It was in the Tennis courts that grave interviews were granted; when the Lords of the Hamilton party came in 1678 to press their cause against Lauderdale, they kissed hands in the lobby of the court; and it was in 1679 that he had his first serious illness from the chill which he caught, after a hard game, by sauntering along the waterside in St James's Park. He also played frequently at Hampton

Court and Stephen Charlton wrote to Sir R. Leveson in January 1661 that 'the King is in very good health and goes to Hampton Court often and back again the same day, but very private; most of his exercise is in the Tennis-court in the morning when he doth not ride abroad.' And in another letter he writes: 'His Majesty's only recreation as yet is at tennis [at Whitehall] by 5 o'clock in the morning for an hour or two.'

Charles was far from content with the courts that he found in England and immediately upon his restoration set to work to rebuild and restore them. He began in 1662 to build a new court at Whitehall, partly on the site of the Brake and partly on Lord Sandwich's garden, to replace the three courts of his father's reign. He issued a warrant in May of that year to 'pay Unto Thomas Cooke, his Ma^{ts} Servant, the Summe of 1500*l*. out of the Receipt of his Ma^{ts} Customes, to be by him employed in the building and erecting of a Tennis Court in the place of the Brake at his Ma^{ts} Pallace of Whitehall'. He sent Robert Long down to Hampton Court to take measurements and evidently entrusted to him much of the new construction. Long was paid for 'superviseinge & orderinge the workmen at the New Tennis Court nere the Cockpitt'. In fact, the court was commonly known as 'Long's'.

Samuel Pepys several times mentions the construction of this new court. On 26 July 1662, he notes: 'Here I find that my Lord (Sandwich) hath lost the garden to his lodgings, and that it is turning into a tennis-court.' Accounts of the Lord Chamberlain give details of some of the materials provided for the new court. A warrant of December 1662 was, 'to provide and deliver to Capt. Cook, Master of His Maties court at Whitehall…two chavres of two foot and an halfe wide in the seat one footstoole two velvett cushions, one velvett Carpett with gold fringe…Curtayne cloathes for the Tennis Court sixty yards of each side in length and six yards of each side deep in breadth, a corde, and Tarpaulin to goe round the court on the outside and black Bayes for the ends of the Court.' At the same time a bed and bedding were provided at the court for Robert Long, the marker, so that he might always be at hand.

There was a slight set-back some months later, and on 24 June 1663, Pepys writes, 'This day I observed the house, which I took to be the new Tennis-court, newly built next my Lord's lodgings, to be fallen down by the badness of the foundation or slight working, which my cozen Roger and his discontented party cry out upon, as an example how the King's worke is done.'

By the end of the year, however, the court was completed and Pepys watched the King play there on 28 December 1663. 'Walking through Whitehall I heard the King was gone to play at Tennis, so I down to the new Tennis-court, and saw him and Sir Arthur Slingsby play against my Lord of Suffolke and my Lord Chesterfield. The King beat three, and lost two sets, they all, and he particularly, playing well, I thought.' On 4 January 1664, he again visited the court and commented, 'but to see how the King's play was extolled, without any cause at all, was a loathsome sight, though sometimes, indeed, he did play very well, and deserved to be commended; but such open flattery is beastly.' He made another interesting visit to the court on 2 September 1667, and records it as follows:

> *I went to see a great match at tennis, between Prince Rupert and one Captain Cooke, against Bab May and the elder Chichly; where the King was, and Court; and it seems they are the best players at tennis in the nation. But this puts me in mind of what I observed in the morning, that the King, playing at tennis, had a steeleyard carried to him, and I was told it was to weigh him after he had done playing; and at noon Mr Ashburnham told me that it is only the King's curiosity, which he usually hath of weighing himself before and after his play, to see how much he loses in weight by playing; and this day he lost four and a half pounds.*

The site of this new Whitehall court is clearly shown on a Survey of the Royal Palace of Whitehall made in 1670 by John Fisher. It was surrounded by the apartments of Captain Cooke, Master of the Tennis Court. Charles himself kept a bed at the court. In 1673 he made over a 'Red Damask Tennis Court Bedd, with all things thereunto belonging' to the Duke of Monmouth. A few years later in 1677 an order was issued to the Master of the Robes to provide

> *a new bedd for his Ma^{ts} service in ye Tennis Court at Whitehall, (vizt.) a crymson damaske bedd with silke fringe of severall coloures, the bedd to be somewhat larger than ye other, the bedstead, quilts, bedding and blankets to be fitted up as for his Ma^{ts} other bedds, with one elbow chaire and 2 stooles with covers of crymson serge…2 window curtaines and a Portugall matt under the bedd.*

The new court appears to have been about the same width as a modern court, but somewhat longer. The overall dimensions given in a plan of 1793 are: width 39ft 1in (compare Hampton Court 39ft 7ins) and length 118ft 1½ ins (compare Hampton Court 110ft 11ins).

The other royal courts were certainly not neglected. The court at Hampton Court was repaired and in 1672 a warrant was sent 'to certify unto you his Maties pleasure that you provide and deliver...unto Thomas Cook Esqr Master of his Maties Tennis Courts such a proporcon of netts curtaynes and lynes for his Maties tennis Court at Hampton Court as Mr Cook shall inform yr L^dpp shall be necessary and convenient for his Maties service.'

In 1669 it was decided to convert the old Tudor court into lodgings for the Duchess of York (wife of the future James II). This conversion was completed in 1674 at a cost of £3000.

Another new court was built at Windsor. The old Tudor court still existed as late as 1672 when it was shown in a drawing by Wenceslas Hollar of the Upper Ward of Windsor Castle. Being an open court it was not in a very good state of repair. In 1676 it was decided to build a new covered court. The Treasury receipt of that year reads, 'Received of Mr Topham by order of King Charles the Second for a peice of ground sould to his Matie called Old Hawes to erect a Tennis Court – sixty pounds.' It was built south of the Lower Ward within the grounds of the Duke of St Albans' Lodge and is shown in Kip's views of 1709, which reveal a magnificent covered court measuring about the same as the new Whitehall court. Warrants of 1678 and 1679 show that it was furnished similarly to the courts at Hampton Court and Whitehall, with curtains, nets, lines, black hair-cloth and 'andyrons tongs'.

This court was still standing in 1742, but in 1782 the Queen's Lodge and later the Queen's Mews were built on the site.

King Charles also played in his court at Newmarket. Cosmo III, Grand Duke of Tuscany, described him playing there in 1669. 'After dinner the King, with the Duke [of York] and Prince Robert [Rupert], went on horseback to a place at a little distance from Newmarket and amused themselves with the game of tennis.' The King and the Duke of York also paid many visits to the James Street court.

Interesting figures for the number of courts in London in 1669 are provided by an Italian resident, who wrote,

before the Fire there were six different tennis courts, all built in the French fashion. Now there are only four, two having been burnt. The finest is that belonging to the King, just opposite the Palace, with which there is communication by a gallery over an arch. The King has a bedroom

there to change his clothes in, the window of which, guarded by an iron grating, looks upon the game. They generally play there three times a week, in the morning, in vests suited to the purpose.

Accounts show that the King continued to play later in his reign. Payments of the Wardrobe for 1679 show the following items bought for him:

Making a Paire of Tennis drawers	*xxx^d*
1 Ell of Taffata for Tennis drawers	*xxi^s vi^d*
1 Ell of Taffata for Tennis drawers	*xxi^s vi^d*
To John Pate for Shoos, Goloshoes, tennis shoes, Slippers & Bootes	*lxxxxiij l. x^s*

In 1682 the Tennis court bills submitted to the Master of the Great Wardrobe amounted to £111 12s 10d.

On Charles II's restoration there was considerable competition for court appointments. One of the first claimants for the post of Master of the Tennis Plays was Simon Smith, who had married John Webb's widow and claimed large sums of money owed to Webb on his death by the late King. His claim failed, however, and he had to be content with the post of Master of the Otter Hounds. Thomas Cooke was appointed Master of the King's Tennis Plays with Horatio Moore as his successor on his death.

Robert Long, who described himself as 'Clerk of the Chapel to the late King and keeper of balloons and paumes and of tennis shoes and ankle socks to his Majesty when Prince', petitioned in 1660 for the post of Groom of the Great Chamber. He was not successful but was compensated later the same year when appointed 'Marker in his Maties Tennis Courts, on the death of Mr Timothy Plesaunt'. A few months later, 'John Dynan ye younger, after the Decease of John Dynan, his ffather' was appointed 'Rackett Maker'.

Another claimant was John Hooker, who had laid claim to the court at St James's during the Commonwealth. He received £100 in 1662 in satisfaction of Tennis debts owed to him by Charles I.

Thomas Cooke remained Master of the King's Tennis Plays from the Restoration until 1689. However, in 1675 he transferred his rights in the Brake at Whitehall only, to Charles Cornwallis for the sum of £1500. The Crown granted Cornwallis a twenty-one-year lease on the Brake at a nominal rent with the stipulation that on the death of Cooke or on the expiry of the lease the property should pass to Horatio Moore.

When James II came to the throne in 1685, he confirmed Captain Cooke's position as the royal professional and by warrant of 17 June arranged for him to have the 'Bed, Bedding, etc. belonging to ye Bed which his late Matie used to lye in at ye Tennis Court at Whitehall'.

However, the King had many other preoccupations and little time for leisure pursuits.

On the accession of William and Mary, Horatio Moore lost no time in asserting his claim to be Master of the King's Tennis Plays elect. In April 1689 he issued a caveat that 'no grant pass relating to the place of Master of the Tennis Courts, till notice be first given to Horatio Moore, Esq., at Mr. Wait's house, a salesman, at the Golden Hart in the Strand, near the Savoy.'

The next month he made a petition for the grant of the office, alleging that he was entitled to it in reversion and claiming that it was vacant – presumably because Cooke was by this time an invalid. His claim was referred to the Attorney-General.

Another claimant was Henry Baker, a solicitor to the Treasury, who alleged that Cooke 'is above eighty and is bedrid' and sought to have Moore passed over in his favour.

The final decision was made by a grant dated 15 November 1689. The office of 'master of our Tennis Courts and Tennis Plays at Whitehall Hampton Court and elsewhere built and to be built for our Royall Disport and Recreation within this Our Kingdome of England' was granted to Henry Villiers. Excepted from the grant was

> all that Tennis Court with the appurtenances and other buildings there situate on a parcell of ground called the Brake adjoyning to the Cockpitt within Our Palace of Westminster built by Thomas Cooke Esquier and by his late Majesty King Charles the Second in the Twenty Seventh yeare of his Reigne granted to Charles Cornwallis Esquier for Twenty One yeares.

The grant was made to Henry Villiers 'for and during the naturall life of Thomas Cooke Gent'. He was to receive eightpence a day and £120 a year from the Exchequer.

Meanwhile Robert Long, the King's marker, secured the appointment of his son, also called Robert

The smaller seventeenth-century court in Stockholm.

Long, to succeed him in office. On 28 November 1669 'Robert Long ye younger, marker at Tennis and keeper of ye Long Paulins in order without ffee' was appointed 'to commence in ordinary with ffee upon the first avoydance or decease of his ffather'. His father died seven years later.

Under the Stuarts none of those repressive acts so common in Tudor times was passed. Tennis was in no way discouraged, and the only action taken was to regulate the amount of gambling on this and other sports by an 'Acte against deceitfull disorderly and excessive Gaming' in the year 1675. Import duties continued on foreign equipment; rackets were liable to duty at eightpence each and balls at £2 per thousand.

The granting of licences for public courts was part of the office of Groomporter. In 1678 John and Samuel Garrard were appointed to succeed Thomas and William Neale in that office with the oversight of 'all common billiard tables, bowling grounds, dicing houses, gaming houses and common tennis courts and the power of licensing the same'.

Tennis was popular throughout the seventeenth century in Europe. Two courts were built at Strasbourg in 1602; there were two at Leipzig, one in Berlin, several at Cologne, and the pattern repeated itself elsewhere on the continent. At Regensburg, a court was specially built for the meeting of the Diet of the Holy Roman Empire in 1652, and when the Diet met in Prague in 1663 the *Ballhaus* there was put at the disposal of visiting delegates.

In Switzerland there were courts in Basle, Berne, Geneva and Neuchâtel. In Sweden a magnificent royal court was built in Stockholm in 1627; it was 104ft long by 44ft wide and 28ft 4ins high. The original master professional was Mikael, but he was replaced in 1635 by a German called George Sippel.

Gustavus Adolphus II was a keen player and during the siege of Ingolstadt in 1631 expressed a desire for a game with his officers in the fortress court, but he did not succeed in capturing it.

The royal court being unable to meet the demand, another smaller court was built in the vicinity by Sippel between 1648 and 1653 on ground provided by the Empress Christina. This second court was eventually converted into a chapel in 1725.

In Vienna there were four courts. One of these, attached to the Imperial Palace, was burned in 1525 but reconstructed on a new site and eventually in 1741 converted into a theatre. Another remained in use until 1855 when it became first a museum and then the Chancellery (known as the *Ballplatz*).

In the seventeenth century, Tennis also spread to the New World. It is historically consistent that the first evidence should be in the form of a prohibition.

Peter Stuyvesant, Governor of New York, on 30 September 1659, proclaimed 15 October 'a day of Universal Fasting and Prayer. In order that it may be the better put into practice, we interdict and forbid during divine service on the day aforesaid, all exercise and games of tennis, ball-playing, hunting, fishing, ploughing and sowing...'

EIGHTEENTH-CENTURY TENNIS

THE DECLINE IN THE POPULARITY of Tennis which had begun by the end of the seventeenth century continued throughout the eighteenth century. Many old courts disappeared altogether and others were put to other uses, particularly as theatres.

Louis XV had been taught to play Tennis as a boy, but he was too lazy to play much. However, he built a new covered court at Fontainebleau to replace the two burnt down in 1702. This court was remarkable in having a niche in the main wall just under the net hook where the stakes were to be placed. Louis also reconstructed the Château at Compiègne, which involved the demolition and rebuilding of the Tennis court.

The Prince de Condé built a new court at Chantilly, but the game was generally in decline, except among students and soldiers. A decree of 30 May 1708 forbade Tennis court owners to allow students into the court during their working hours or to accept books or working equipment in settlement of debts. On 3 January 1731 they were forbidden to allow soldiers into the courts.

One keen player of this period was Philippe Egalité, father of Louis Philippe. He was playing in the Caille court at Orléans in 1787 when he received a letter from Louis XVI pointing out that he was to be exiled to Villiers-Cotteret instead of Orléans. He immediately dropped his racket and departed, comforted no doubt by the fact that there was also a Tennis court there where he could continue to play the game. To him is attributed the 'coup d'Orléans', a ball hit into the dedans after hitting the service wall.

Two books have provided us with a good knowledge of the game in France at this period, and of some of the great players. The authors were François de Garsault and de Manevieux.

François Alexandre Pierre de Garsault (1673–1778) was a member of the French Royal Academy of Sciences which published a comprehensive encyclopaedia of arts and crafts. His most interesting book *The Art of the Tennis-Racket-Marker and of Tennis* was part of that encyclopaedia and was first separately published in 1767. It is a goldmine of information on every aspect of Tennis in the eighteenth century.

Scaino was the first to give us details of the *jeu quarré* as distinct from the *jeu à dedans*. De Garsault gives us a complete description and plan. The winning openings are the grille (3 ft 4 ins high x 2 ft 9 ins wide) on the hazard side; the *trou* (16 ins square) on the service side, at floor level in the corner with the main wall; and the *ais*, a board (1 ft wide and 6 ft high) attached to the back wall in the corner with the gallery wall. There is no tambour.

The plan of the court still shows two doors, but only one marker is employed and he stands in the doorway on the service side, carrying a racket to protect himself. He also uses this racket to raise the centre of the net when players change ends to allow them to pass beneath. He keeps a record of sets and games won by each side with a piece of chalk on the flagstone at his feet. In a *jeu quarré*, there being no dedans, the balls were kept in the last gallery.

It is interesting that de Garsault was the first to mention the winning gallery. He describes it as the last gallery on the hazard side, but he makes it clear that a ball entering it wins a point outright. The chases are marked by lines and half-lines painted along the joints of the blocks of Caen stone, each 1 ft square, with which the floor is laid. There are fourteen chases on the service side but evidently none on the hazard side.

Clothing is supplied by the Master of the Court – caps, shorts, trousers, pullovers, stockings and shoes at an all-in charge of fifteen *sous* or at four *sous* each article except the cap which costs two *sous*.

The wearing of a cap might seem curious to us today, but perhaps with shaven heads on which to fit a full-bottomed wig, it was a necessity for keeping out the cold, especially in open courts. Certainly Vivès, writing in 1539, was familiar with the cap.

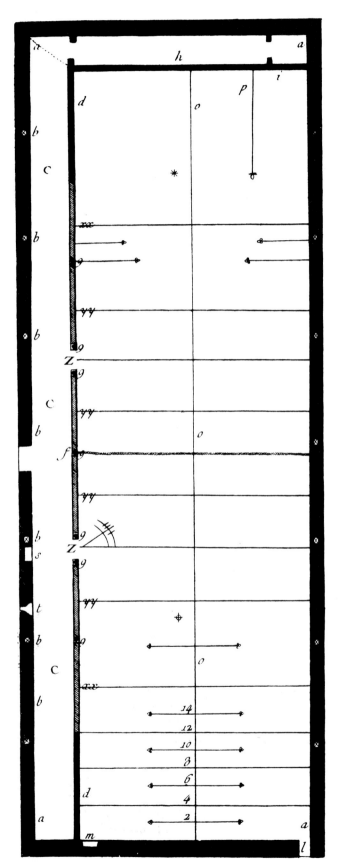

Plan of a jeu quarré *from de Garsault's book.*

Dressing-gowns were also supplied if required. The shoes were low-heeled or heel-less, made of undressed buffalo or calf hide, and tied with string. A buffet was provided including bread, wine and beer and in the corridor under the penthouse roof was a conduit for urine.

After the game, players were rubbed down in front of a good fire, but no beds were provided, since to sleep after a hard game and a good rub-down had resulted in fatal accidents.

De Garsault's book contains detailed instructions on the manufacture of both racket and ball, together with diagrams. He also gives us a recipe for blacking the inside of the court.

> *Take half a hogshead of ox blood, fourteen bushels of lamp-black, the gall of ten oxen to dissolve the lamp-black, and a bucket of urine to give sheen to the composition, mix it all cold.*

Imagine the smell of a newly painted court – and he recommends doing it twice a year!

Between 1751 and 1780 Messrs Diderot and d'Alembert were publishing the twenty-three volumes of *The Encyclopaedia or Reasoned Dictionary of Sciences, Arts and Crafts by a Society of Men of Letters.* Twelve volumes of plates accompanied the Encyclopaedia and in Volume IV, published in 1765, appear nine plates, very similar to those in de Garsault's book. Plans of a *jeu quarré* and a *jeu à dedans* are included and additional plans show a bird's eye view and a cross-section of these courts.

There is a slightly different illustration of a *jeu quarré* with a doubles match in progress, but all the features of the court are the same. However, there is no illustration of a *jeu à dedans*, but an additional plate shows a billiard room and the construction of a billiard table. There are also copious illustrations of implements used in the manufacture of rackets and balls closely resembling those in de Garsault's book.

De Manevieux's book, published in 1783, is less technical but full of interest. He describes the two sorts of court – *à dedans* and *quarré* – but differs in ruling that to win a point outright on the *ais* of a *jeu quarré* the ball must strike it full toss. He goes on to describe the ball and the racket, the rules and the method of scoring. In one *quarré* court in Paris, he tells us, as well as the *trou* and the *ais* there is another opening on the service side known as the *lune*. It is round, 8ins in diameter and 5ft off the floor. A player putting a ball into the *lune* wins a whole game outright.

However, he points out, most amateurs prefer the *jeu à dedans* and many master professionals had altered

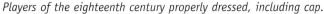

Players of the eighteenth century properly dressed, including cap.

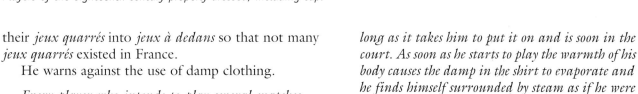

their *jeux quarrés* into *jeux à dedans* so that not many *jeux quarrés* existed in France.

He warns against the use of damp clothing.

Every player who intends to play several matches knows the need for a change of clothes, especially in the summer; but he must be sure that the shirts or vests that the master professional hires out to him are properly dry, since in a busy court, where the pro. is providing several shirts every day, the servant often only gives them a very hasty wash; each evening she takes all the shirts and clothes used during the day, shakes them in cold water while still impregnated with the player's sweat and hangs them out at once on a line. The mistress of the house thinks that it is useless to iron these clothes as they will be used the next day, so she folds them up half dry; a player impatient to play, only complains about the coldness of this shirt for as

long as it takes him to put it on and is soon in the court. As soon as he starts to play the warmth of his body causes the damp in the shirt to evaporate and he finds himself surrounded by steam as if he were in a steam-bath.

De Manevieux also tells us of the leading players of his time. Of the professionals of the 1740s and 1750s, he singles out Clergé, Farolais, La Fosse, Guillaume Barcellon and Barnéon. Barcellon was the King's professional (*paumier du roi*) in 1753 when his portrait was painted by E. Loys. His eldest son, Pierre, published a book entitled *Règles et Principes de la Paume* in 1800. Of his contemporaries, de Manevieux praises the pre-eminence of Raymond Masson, whom he considered better than all the previous five, and next to him, Charrier, the young Barcellon and Bergeron. This young Barcellon was probably Guillaume's nephew, Jean-Pierre, who married Pierrette Masson,

Raymond Masson.

Raymond Masson's sister. Of English professionals, he mentions two – Pilet and John Mucklow, Keeper of the Haymarket (James Street) court. In all he calculates there were about 160 professionals in circulation in France and abroad.

Masson is the first of the really great champions of Tennis whose achievements are on record. He was born in 1740 and by the age of twenty-five he was the outstanding player of his time. He could give 15 to his nearest rival, the elder Charrier. He won one remarkable match, watched by Louis XV and his court at Fontainebleau, against Clergé and Charrier, giving them half 15.

Against amateurs he had to submit to even greater handicaps such as on one occasion being seated in a barrel from which he had to emerge to play each stroke. All this was despite the fact recorded by de Manevieux that he wore spectacles.

Another rare distinction enjoyed by Masson was his

wife's prowess at Tennis. De Manevieux remarks that at the age of twenty-eight, Mme. Masson too was a skilful player.

As the century advanced, the number of Tennis courts in France declined. By 1767 there were only twelve master professionals in Paris, and in 1771 a decree forbade the recruitment of apprentices because of the small number of courts. When de Manevieux wrote his book in 1783, there were fifty-four courts in France, thirteen of them in Paris and three in Lyons. Not, perhaps, very many compared with the great days of the two previous centuries, but still a considerable number.

The French Revolution had a devastating effect on Tennis and the aristocracy, although curiously one of the first events took place in a Tennis court.

It is very odd that no Tennis court was incorporated in the design of the royal palace of Versailles; courts existed at all the King's other palaces – the Louvre, Vincennes, Fontainebleau, Compiègne, Saint-Germain. All that was available to the Court in 1684 was a game of *longue paume* in the avenues of the Trianon. For the story of the court at Versailles, I am indebted to M. Charles Vatel's book of 1883.

In charge of the royal Tennis courts (*maître paumier du roi*) at this time was Jean Bazin, proprietor of the court at Saint-Germain-en-Laye. He had a son, François, and a daughter, Jeanne, married to another Tennis professional, Nicholas Cretté. The three men determined to remedy the Versailles omission and to build a court on a site owned by them in the rue l'Hôtel-de-Lorge.

They planned the building with great care and the specification dated 1686 was minutely detailed. The floor was to be of Caen stone, white, without vein or marl, laid firm and level. The ceiling was to be painted blue, decorated with *fleurs-de-lis* in gold. Above the entrance was to be carved the royal emblem, a rising sun. Clearly it was expected that Louis XIV would play there.

It was also specified that the work should be completed in four months – and it was. But unfortunately, *le Roi Soleil* was unable to open it – he was ill throughout the year, underwent a major operation in November and was in bed until January the following year. So it was left to the Dauphin to confer royal approval on the court, which he did by playing there three days after it opened in December 1686.

However, it was not long after the King's recovery that he played Tennis on the new court, with all the pomp and ceremony that was then observed. It was the duty of one official (*le porte-manteau*) to hand the balls to His Majesty with one hand while with the other he held his sword. After he had played, the King was rubbed down in front of his officers and courtiers. He had to meet all the expenses, whether he won or lost, including a suitable meal for all his courtiers, laid on by the master professional.

Little is recorded of the court during the reigns of Louis XV and XVI. Neither King played there as far as is known, but certainly others did and it was well used. So it was readily available for the great event of 20 June 1789 which made history.

The King had summoned the full States-General, which comprised the Nobility, the Clergy and the Third Estate, to meet at Versailles in May 1789. But deadlock ensued on the seemingly important question of whether the three Estates should meet together or separately. Exasperated at the delay, the Third Estate met in the main hall on 17 June and voted to establish itself as the National Assembly, and this was followed on 19 June by a vote in the House of Clergy to meet with them. The King and his advisers were seriously alarmed at this prospect. They immediately announced a royal session of the States-General and troops occupied the main hall, where the Assembly had held its meetings, to prepare for it.

Bailly, President of the National Assembly, satisfied himself that the hall was occupied and a discussion ensued among the members on an alternative meeting-place. It is said that the suggestion of the Tennis court was made by Dr Joseph-Ignace Guillotin (a man of initiative, says M. Charles Vatel). Here the National Assembly met at 10.30 a.m. on 20 June 1789 and took the historic oath:

We swear never to dissolve and to meet whenever circumstances demand until the Constitution of the realm is firmly established on solid foundations.

This oath was unanimously approved and members were required to sign it individually. One demurred, but repercussions were averted by the President, who pointed out that one man's refusal to sign was witness to the liberty of their cause.

On the first anniversary of this historic oath, a bronze plaque was affixed to the wall of the court and ever since it has been regarded as a very special monument to the history of the French Revolution. In 1791 Jacques-Louis David was commissioned to paint a picture of the Tennis Court oath, 30 ft x 20 ft, for the sum of 36,000 *livres*.

In England, a parallel decline in the popularity of Tennis set in with the arrival of the Hanoverian monarchs. But in the first few years of the century further improvements were carried out to the court at Hampton Court Palace, which itself had been extensively rebuilt by Sir Christopher Wren. In 1700 Horatio Moore had submitted an estimate of £365, to include the laying of a stone floor 'without which no Ball can give a true bound'. But King George I preferred a brick floor, presumably for economy. In the event, however, the floor was laid with 1070 ft of Ketton stone.

Despite this, the King was not interested, and ordered the court to be fitted up as a 'Drawing Room' with an additional 'Side Kitchen' and a 'Necessary House for Persons of Quality'. He used to hold evening assemblies in the court.

The last flicker of royal interest was shown by Frederick, Prince of Wales, eldest son of George II, who played Tennis. Horace Walpole alleged that his death in 1751 was caused by a blow from a Tennis ball three years earlier.

The office of Master of Royal Tennis Courts continued. On 19 February 1708, Thomas Chaplin was appointed on the death of Horatio Moore. His appointment is described as:

A grant unto Thomas Chaplin of the office of Master or Keeper of the Tennis-court near the Cock-pit in Whitehall, and all other Tennis-courts which Horatio Moore, Esq., deceased lately enjoyed, with the buildings and appurtenances thereunto belonging, during her Majesty's pleasure (except the ground, building, and lodgings adjoining to the same Tennis-court near the Cock-pit, which are now enjoyed by the Duke of Montagu and Earl of Rochester, or either of them), with the fees of eightpence per diem, and 120l per annum, payable quarterly, out of the exchequer.

He was confirmed in office by King George I on his accession to the throne in 1714. He died in February 1728 and was succeeded by Charles Fitz-Roy.

The name of the marker in the James Street court at this time is also known, for a notice in the *Daily Courant* of 7 February 1732 reads: 'On Saturday last died Monsieur Latell, Marker of the King's Tennis Court in the Haymarket.'

In 1762, Richard Beresford succeeded Charles Fitz-Roy. He was replaced, from May 1764 to October 1765, by William Chetwynd Jr, but returned as Sir Richard Beresford and held the office until his death in 1791. In that year, Charles Meynell took over. Finally, in 1815, the Rt Hon. William Beresford was appointed. In his case, for the first time, there is no mention of the court at Whitehall, which had been demolished in 1809.

Some time before 1720 a new court was built in James Street, Haymarket, immediately adjoining the previous court and to the west of it. By this time, the old east court had been adapted for use as a theatre, but the new court came to be the centre of Tennis in England. A plan of the site indicates that the court measured overall 110 ft x 43 ft, identical to a modern court.

In 1757 it was taken over by Thomas Higginson, who seems to have specialised in the provision of facilities for Tennis and Rackets in the capital. An advertisement in the *Daily Advertiser* of 28 October 1742 reads:

To all Gentlemen that like the Exercise of Tennis, Fives or Billiards. There is a complete Tennis-Court, with a Tambour, and everything that makes it as good a Tennis-Court as any in England, at 1s. a set single, or 6d. a set double; with Fives-playing in the Tennis-Court, and Billiards at the same place. It's near the Bull and Gate Inn, Holborn, and near Lincoln's Inn Fields, by the Duke of Newcastle's, next door to Adlam's Coffee-House, opposite little Turnstile. It's kept by

THOMAS HIGGINSON

who keeps a Fives-Court at the bottom of St Martin's Street, on the left hand in Leicester-Fields. It's for Fives-playing only either with Racquets, Boards, or at Hand-Fives, at 2d., 3d., or 4d. a Game.

NOTE, *Any Gentleman may bespeak either Court for their own playing, and Care will be taken to keep it for them. Tennis-playing at 8d. a set with Tossing-Balls and Racquets, on agreeing before they begin to play, or else not less than 1s. a Set. Boards, Racquets, and all sorts of Ball, sold at the Tennis-Courts, Holborn.*

A subsequent advertisement states that the Holborn court adjoined the 'Six Cans' tavern.

Thomas Higginson opened a new court in Great Windmill Street in 1743 and advertised its facilities on 12 December:

TO ALL GENTLEMEN LOVERS OF EXERCISE

The New Tennis-Court in Great Windmill Street, facing St James's, Hay-Market, is completely finish'd and open'd, with complete Dressing-Rooms,

and everything fit for the Reception of Gentlemen, at 2s. for a six-game Set, with Advantage Game, or at 1s. or 8d. for four-game Sets. This Court is built after the Manner of that in James Street.

NOTE, *Another Tennis-Court in Holborn, or near to that Corner of Lincoln's Inn Fields turning up on the left Hand for the Duke of Newcastle's, with Tennis at 1s. or 8d. for four-game Sets, which is much cheaper than any other Courts in London, for they are 3s. 6d. a Set...*

By 1744 the court in St Martin's Street had been adapted for Tennis as well as for fives and Rackets, as an advertisement of 23 February makes clear. It was a *jeu quarré*, anglicised in the advertisement as a 'Carry-Tennis-Court':

There are now three new and complete Tennis-Courts built by Thomas Higginson.

These are the one in Windmill Street, price 2s. 6d. for a six-game set, or at 8d. or 12d. a four-game set 'when the Court's at Leisure'. The one at Holborn, where tennis is 8d. or 1s. in four-game sets.

And the other Tennis-Court is in St Martin's Street, next Door to the Stable-Yard, near Hedge Lane, Leicester Fields; it's built like the Tennis-Courts at Oxford or Cambridge; it's made out of the Fives-Court into a Carry-Tennis-Court; Tennis at 8d. or 12d. for a four-game Set.

NOTE, *Any Gentlemen may bespeak either Court for their own Play for any Day or Hour; or Fives-Playing; in either Court, with Tennis and other Balls, till they are wanted for Tennis, at 2d., 3d., or 4d. a Game.*

Thomas Higginson ran these three courts and the James Street court until his death in 1783, when John Mucklow took over at James Street.

Another fine court was built at Bath, the fashionable watering place, and thanks to the research of Mr R.R. Henshaw more is known about this court. He quotes the *New Bath Guide* for 1779:

Adjoining to the Riding School is erected an elegant and commodious Tennis Court by Richard Scrace, which was opened for play in 1777. The plan was presented to Mr Scrace by the Earl of Pembroke, and the dimensions of the Court were the same as that of the Duke of Orléans and Masson's in Paris – here are dressing rooms, dresses and everything necessary to render it as agreeable as possible. The terms of the play are the same as in London.

The court was built of Bath stone and the original flagged floor can still be seen. Adjacent are the changing rooms. The tambour still stands, and the markings of chases 1, 2 and 3 are visible. There also remain the nine large lights along each side of the court and an *oeuil de boeuf* in each gable end. It stands in Morford Street and is now an industrial museum. There is evidence of two additional courts in Bath.

Other new courts, outside London, were opened in Liverpool in 1750 and at Goodwood by the Duke of Richmond in 1760.

Another Tennis enthusiast was Francis, fifth Duke of Bedford. He built a court and riding school at Woburn Abbey in 1792 to a design by Henry Holland, which included a covered walk from the house and central dressing rooms serving both activities. A 'master of the court' and a 'tennis boy' were added to the household staff, the master being paid a salary of £84 per annum. Nets were supplied by Samuel Thatcher.

Unfortunately, this old court was gutted by fire in the early twentieth century, and in 1950 the discovery of dry rot necessitated the demolition of the whole building.

A primitive form of Tennis was also played in Wales. In keeping with history in other countries, the first known mention of the game is its prohibition in Cowbridge in 1610:

And also that there be noe tenyse playinge within the highe streate uppon payne of iij s iiij d. to be levied uppon every of them that playethe.

An early Welsh Tennis player was the martyr, Philip Evans, a Jesuit priest born in Monmouthshire in 1645. During the scare caused by the Titus Oates 'plot' he was arrested and imprisoned in Cardiff Castle. He was condemned to death, but the execution was deferred for eleven weeks during which time he was well treated and even allowed to play Tennis. He was on court when informed that he was to be hanged the next day, but he insisted on completing his game before returning to his cell.

About 1777 a court was built in Cardiff adjacent to the licensed premises attached to Nell's Brewery, once the Kemeys-Tynte Arms, later the Tennis Court Inn and then the Buccaneer. Before this court was built, a ball game was played against the north wall of St John's church tower and led to the usual prohibition as appears in the churchwardens' accounts of 1777:

To the Cryer for Proclaiming against Playing Ball against the Church 6d.

This court still existed in 1851, but can only have been of a very rudimentary sort, certainly an open court. There was another court in Chepstow.

Ball games of a sort were played in other parts of Wales. Three 'courts' existed at Llantrisant, and there was keen rivalry between Llantrisant and Cowbridge; a match between the two teams would draw a crowd of several hundred people.

John Richards, in *The Cowbridge Story*, gives an account of this game, which resembled fives or a primitive form of *jeu de paume*:

One of the most exciting games played at Cowbridge until the year 1880 was ball tennis. A very large high walled tennis court existed in East Village on the site now occupied by the Pavilion Cinema. The court was originally attached to the Tennis Court Inn which afterwards became the Wheelwright's Arms occupied by Mr Richard Aubrey, wheelwright. This game of tennis was played with the bare hand using a hard ball slightly larger than a golf ball and made of layers of rubber covered with white soft leather. The balls could not be purchased ready-made but were manufactured in the Borough by the local expert. The hop or tamp was extraordinary, and at the start of the season the players' hands would become red and swollen, later gradually hardening and becoming capable of the task. Competitions with players from other courts were a regular and popular feature arousing great enthusiasm in the Borough. Some of the last experts playing on the Cowbridge court were the brothers Traherne of Llantrisant, and the two Cowbridge stars Edmund John and John George, coal merchant. The pneumatic rubber ball was introduced about 1870 and replaced the hard leather ball.

At Nelson, games were played against the wall of the public house, now called the Nelson Inn, and much betting took place on the outcome. Sometime during the nineteenth century the present handball court at Nelson was built by some of the coal owners, and matches took place against teams from the Rhondda Valley. The large wall is reminiscent of a Basque *fronton*. The popularity of these games, even on Sunday, was noted by John Taylor, the poet, in his *Journey through Wales*, published in 1859:

There is no such zeale in many places and parishes in Wales; for they have neither service, prayer, sermon, minister, or preacher, nor any church door opened at all, so that people do exercise and edifie

T E N   [381]   T E N

Tennis. which means they can play as long as they please, without ever having occasion to stoop for a ball.

As to the odds at tennis, they are by no means fixed, but are generally laid as follow:

Upon the first stroke being won between even players, that is, fifteen love, the odds are of the single game

game	7	to 4
Thirty love	4	1
Forty love	8	1
Thirty fifteen	2	1
Forty fifteen	5	1
Forty thirty	3	1

The odds of a four game set when the

first game is won, are	7	4
When two games love	4	1
Three games love	8	to 1
When two games to one	2	1
Three games to one	5	1

The odds of a six game set when the

first game is won, are	3	2
When two games love	2	1
Three games love	4	1
Four games love	10	1
Five games love	21	1
When two games to one	8	5
Three games to one	5	2
Four games to one	5	1
Five games to one	15	1
When three games to two	7	4
Four games to two	4	1
Five games to two	10	1
When four games to three	2	1
Five games to three	5	1

The odds of an advantage set when

the first game is won, are	5	4
When two games love	7	4
Three games love	3	1
Four games love	5	1
Five games love	15	1
When two games to one	4	3
Three games to one	2	1
Four games to one	7	2
Five games to one	10	1
When three games to two	3	2
Four games to two	3	1
Five games to two	8	1
When four games to three	8	5
Five games to three	3	1
When five games to four	2	1
When six games to five	5	2

The foregoing odds, as beforesaid, are generally laid, but the chaces interfering makes the odds very precarious; for example, when there is a chace at half a yard, and a set is five games all, and in every other respect equal, the odds are a good five to four; and if it were six games to five, and forty thirty with the same chace, the odds then would be a guinea to a shilling; so that it is plain that the odds at this game differ from those of any other: for one stroke will reduce a set, supposing the players to be five games all, from an even wager to three to two, and so on in proportion to the stage of the set.

There are various methods of giving odds at tennis, in order to make a match equal; and that they may be understood, we shall give the following list of them, with their meanings, so that any person may form a judgment of the advantage received or given.

The lowest odds that can be given, excepting the choice of the sides, is what they call a *bisque*, that is, a stroke to be taken or scored whenever the player, who receives the advantage, thinks proper: for instance, suppose a critical game of the set to be forty thirty, by taking the *bisque*, he who is forty becomes game, and so in respect of two *bisques*, &c.

The next greater odds are *fifteen*, that is, a certain stroke given at the beginning of each game.

After these, *half thirty*, that is, fifteen one game, and thirty the next. Then follow the whole *thirty*, *forty*, &c.

There are also the following kind of odds which are given, viz.

Round services; those are services given round the penthouse, so as to render it easy for the *striker-out* (the player who is on the hazard side) to return the ball.

Half court, that is, being obliged or confined to play into the adversary's half-court; sometimes it is played straightwise, and at other times across; both which are great advantages given by him so confined, but the strait half-court is the greatest.

Touch-no-wall, that is, being obliged to play within the compass of the walls, or sides of the court. This is a considerable advantage to him who receives it; as all the balls must be played gently, and consequently they are much easier to take than those which are played hard, or according to the usual method of play.

Barring the hazards, that is, barring the dedans, tambour, grill, or the last gallery on the hazard-side, or any particular one or more of them.

These are the common kind of odds or advantages given; but there are many others, which are according to what is agreed by the players: such as playing with *board* against *racket*, *cricket-bat* against *racket*, &c.

The game of tennis is also played by four persons, two partners on each side. In this case, they are generally confined to their particular quarters, and one of each side appointed to serve and strike out; in every other respect, the game is played in the same manner as when two only play.

Any thing more to be said upon this subject would be needless, as nothing can be recommended, after reading this short account of tennis, but practice and attention, without which no one can become a proficient at the game.

TENOR, or TENOUR, the purport or content of a writing or instrument in law, &c.

TENOR, in music, the first mean, or middle part, or that which is the ordinary pitch of the voice, when neither raised to a treble nor lowered to a bass.

TENSE, in grammar, an inflection of verbs, whereby they are made to signify or distinguish the circumstance of time in what they affirm. See GRAMMAR.

TENT, in war, a pavilion or portable house. Tents are made of canvas, for officers and soldiers to lie under when in the field. The size of the officers tents is not fixed; some regiments have them of one size and some of another: a captain's tent and marquee is generally 10¼ feet broad, 14 deep, and 8 high: the subalterns are a foot less; the major's and lieutenant-colonel's a foot larger; and the colonel's two feet larger. The subalterns of foot lie two in a tent, and those of horse but one. The tents of private men are 6½ feet square, and 5 feet high, and hold five soldiers each. The tents for horse are 7 feet broad and 9 feet deep: they hold likewise five men and their horse accoutrements.—The word is formed from the Latin *tentorium*, of *tendo* "I stretch," because tents are usually made of canvas stretched out, and sustained by poles, with cords and pegs.

TENT, in surgery, a roll of lint made into the shape of a nail with a broad flat head, chiefly used in deep wounds and ulcers. They are of service, not only in conveying medicines to the most intimate recesses and sinuses of the wound, but to prevent the lips of the wound from uniting before it

Table of odds from the Encyclopaedia Britannica *of 1797.*

in the church yard, at the lawful and laudable games of trap, catt, stool-ball, racket, etc., on Sundayes.

The eighteenth century was an age of gambling, and betting on Tennis was as normal as it had been in Scaino's day. Joseph Fenn in 1772 wrote a forty-five-page booklet on the odds involved in a game. They were rather more simply listed in the *Encyclopaedia Britannica* of 1797. The *Annals of Gaming*, written in 1775 by 'a Connoisseur', warns against the risks run by the innocent Tennis punter:

So various are the deceptions of this game, that it is almost impossible for a stranger to go into a tennis-court, and bett without losing his money – so prostituted is this noble game to what it used to be, that instead of seeing only persons of the first rank in England, as formerly, we see the Dedans now thronged with some of the most notorious sharpers in London.

Another royal patron of the game in the eighteenth century was Philip V of Spain, a grandson of Louis XIV, whose hands are said to have been calloused from riding and playing Tennis. Louis I is reported by the French Ambassador, Maréchal de Tessé, to have played Tennis as soon as he had dined, and during the reign of Charles III the post of 'Judge of Ball and Racket Games' was created.

Certainly Tennis continued to be played in Italy, for Marchisio, the French professional of the early nineteenth century, was the son of the master of the Tennis court to the Court of Turin. An interesting picture by Bella shows a form of Tennis in Italy. It is very much closer to modern lawn tennis than to the traditional game with its four walls.

Tennis declined in popularity not only in France and England during the eighteenth century, but throughout the continent of Europe, and probably also in America, where it nevertheless continued to be played. An advertisement of 1763 in the *New York Gazette* offers for sale a tavern with 'a very fine Tennis-Court, or Five-Alley' and three years later a certain James Rivington was importing 'battledores and shuttlecocks, cricket-balls, pillets, best racquets for tennis and fives'.

About this time the first glimmerings of lawn tennis appear, in the form of Field Tennis, described by William Hickey in 1767.

In the summer we had another Club which met at the Red House in Battersea Fields, nearly opposite Ranelagh, a retired and pretty spot... This club

consisted of some very respectable persons, amongst them were Mr Powell of the pay office, Mr Jupp, the East India Company's architect, Mr Whitehead, a gentleman of independent fortune, King, the celebrated actor, Major Sturt of the Engineers and others. The game we played was an invention of our own and called Field Tennis, which afforded noble exercise... Our regular meetings were two days in each week, when we assembled at one o'clock, at two sat down to dinner, consisting of capital stewed grigs...a large joint of roast or boiled meat, with proper vegetables and a good sized pudding or pie; our drink consisting of malt liquors, cyder, port wine and punch. At four our sport commenced, continuing until dusk; during the exercise we refreshed ourselves with draughts of cool tankard, and other pleasant beverages. The field, which was of sixteen acres in extent, was kept in as high order and smooth as a bowling green... Besides our regular days some of the members met every evening during the summer months to have a little Field Tennis.*

The Graf von Wildenstein in a German court with curious chase markings.

Evidently the popularity of Field Tennis soon grew, perhaps owing to the liberal refreshment, which seems to have been an indispensable part of the game. At any rate, in 1793 the *Sporting Magazine* reported that,

> *Field Tennis threatens ere long to bowl out cricket. The former game is now patronized by Sir Peter Burrell; the latter has for some time back been given up by Sir Horace Mann.*

One player of the first rank still played Tennis in the James Street court in 1797 – Lord Lorne, later Duke of Argyll – and gave *The Times* an opportunity to record:

> *The once fashionable game of tennis is very much upon the decline. The court in the Haymarket seems to be now entirely forlorn.*

A game of Tennis in the eighteenth century.

NINETEENTH-CENTURY TENNIS

TENNIS IN ITS NATIVE LAND never recovered from the French Revolution. Napoleon played at Fontainebleau occasionally, as did Wellington, but neither had much talent. However, Napoleon kept this court and the one at Compiègne in good repair.

One court remained in Paris in the rue Mazarine until 1839, when it was replaced by another in the Passage Sandrié. This in turn was demolished in 1861 to make way for a new Opera House but, thanks to Napoleon III, Tennis continued in a new court in the Tuileries, opened in 1862 (with a match between Barre and Biboche) to which a second was added in 1882. Others were built in Deauville, Cannes and Pau, but most significant of all, the old court at Bordeaux was restored to use in 1878.

The court at Versailles had been neglected during the Empire and the Restoration, but took new life with the arrival of the 1848 Republic. The following year the meeting of the Congress of Peacelovers took place in Paris under the presidency of Victor Hugo. Afterwards the British delegation gave a banquet for the American delegation in the Tennis court at Versailles.

In 1855 it was actually re-opened for play with an exhibition match by the two leading players of the day, Barre and Biboche, but this revival didn't last long and on 20 June 1883, having been thoroughly restored at public expense, it was officially inaugurated as a museum of the Revolution.

In England, though, there was a distinct revival among the Victorian élite. Dukes, Marquesses and Earls, not to mention mere Barons, vied with each other to build courts on their country estates. The Duke of Wellington at Stratfield Saye; the Duke of Richmond at Goodwood; the Duke of Fife at East Sheen; the Marquess of Salisbury at Hatfield; the Earl of Craven at Coombe Abbey; the Earl of Plymouth at Hewell Grange; Lord Leconfield at Petworth; Lord Brougham and Vaux at Brougham Hall; Sir Edward Guinness at St Stephen's Green, Dublin; Sir George Prescott at Theobald's Park; Sir Thomas Fermor-Hesketh at Easton Neston; Sir Ivor Guest at Canford; Sir Andrew Noble at Jesmond Dene; Sir Charles Rose at Hardwick; Mr Albert Brassey at Heythrop House; Mr Edward Cazalet at Fairlawne; Mr J.P.F. Gundry at The Hyde; Mr Samuel Heilbut at Holyport Grange – all built courts at their stately homes during the course of the century.

All this was crowned by something of a revival of royal interest in the game.

In 1841, the year after their marriage, Queen Victoria and the Prince Consort visited Woburn Abbey as guests of Francis, seventh Duke of Bedford and his Duchess. On 28 July they inspected the Tennis court, where, according to Queen Victoria's diary, 'Albert tried to play at tennis.'

Evidently he enjoyed the experience for we find him playing again in the Duke of Wellington's court at Stratfield Saye in January 1845. Queen Victoria records in her diary:

Jan. 22. *A cold morning ... We sang Albert's Duet & then walked to the Tennis Court, where we watched the markers playing, & Albert tried it also a little. He afterwards, in spite of rain, went out shooting. – We lunched the same as yesterday, only that the Duke of Devonshire was also at our table. We then all went over to the Tennis Court & saw a fat man called Philips, the Duke's butler, who plays beautifully, – as well as the marker from Hampton Court & his son. When a great deal of the company had gone, Albert tried to play a little...*
Jan. 23. *I accompanied Albert down to the Tennis Court & watched him playing for a while. – At 11 we set off, just as we came, the good old Duke riding before us with Ld. Douro, etc, as before, on our arrival.*

The Prince Consort also announced his intention of playing at Hampton Court. A locker bearing his name is still in the dressing room there, but he played once

The court at the Tuileries in 1862.

only. The Prince of Wales (later Edward VII) played at Oxford and Cambridge and later at Hampton Court and Prince's Club.

For those not possessing their own court, several club courts were available. First in importance, until its closure in 1866, was the James Street court, off the Haymarket.

About 1820, Mr Robert Lukin became secretary of a club based on the court at James Street. A Silver Racquet was competed for annually, and, to all intents and purposes, this was the British amateur championship. The first University match was played here in 1859.

In 1822 Mr Lukin published a *Treatise on Tennis*, dedicated to George William, Duke of Argyll, 'an ardent admirer and patron of the game of tennis'. This contains the rules of Tennis at the time and hints on playing, and it is interesting to see that these rules differ very little from those of the modern game. There are one or two oddities, of course. The 'match of three' for instance, in which one player opposed two, was not unusual and he devotes a couple of pages to it. Certainly the great Barre often played against two

others because he was so much better than anyone else. He played Peter Tompkins and W.J. Cox at Brighton in 1843; and Peter Tompkins and his son, Edmund, at Brighton in 1849.

Not only were the French still the best players but they also made the best rackets. 'The French Racket is far superior to any other, the preparation or seasoning of the wood being well understood in that country; those that have hitherto been made in England are but little admired,' says Lukin.

Clearly, betting in the course of the game was still commonplace, as he includes a table of 'Odds, as usually betted'.

In 1818, the Prince Regent gave orders that the court at Hampton Court should be put in order, and play continued there throughout the rest of the century. Near the court were rooms allotted to the Master of the Tennis Court and these were occupied by the last holder of that title, the Rt Hon. Major William Beresford, whose tenure of office was from 1815 until his death in 1883.

New courts were built at Brighton (1836) and Leamington (1846). In 1893, Prince's formed a link

The James Street court.

with the Brighton court which became known as Prince's Club, Brighton. For the next twenty years or so, it was the main court for world championships.

On 15 October 1838, Mr Aislabie, then secretary of the MCC, laid the foundation stone of a Tennis court at Lord's, situated on the east side of the ground. It cost Mr J.H. Dark, the lessee of the ground, over £4000, but it resulted in a very considerable increase in membership.

'Patrons can be furnished with as many as 100 warm and 100 cold baths per diem, with dressing rooms; couches have also been provided for their temporary use after a heavy practice, and there are two of the best billiard-tables that can be manufactured.' The interior dimensions of the court were 96 ft ½ in x 31 ft 8 ins. A Rackets court was added in 1844.

When the James Street court closed in 1866, the MCC decided to make the court at Lord's the best in London. They re-paved the floor, but a plan for lighting the court from the roof was abandoned as too expensive. They also decided that it was necessary to glaze one side of the roof only. New blinds had been

installed in 1865, which shows that the top of the side walls had been open – as was the case with most courts – and covered with blinds. At the same time, £250 was spent on the Rackets court. The roof and front wall were badly in need of repair.

It soon became apparent that Biggs, the head professional, was not up to the job. Several players could give him odds and there were complaints of his untidy habits. He was dismissed and replaced by George Lambert, from Hampton Court, assisted by his brother William.

The court was re-opened on 12 March 1867 and became the home of the MCC prizes competition, which superseded the James Street Silver Racquet. The MCC Gold Racquet was won by J.M. Heathcote every year from 1867 to 1881 and again in 1883 and 1886. For fifteen years, Heathcote never lost a set to an amateur on level terms. His main rival in later years was the Hon. Alfred Lyttelton, who defeated him in 1882, 1884, 1885, 1887 and then retained the Gold Racquet every year until 1895.

The University match was transferred from James Street to Lord's in 1867.

J.M. Heathcote.

Some indication of the staff and wages at this time is given by the 1883 staff list:

George Lambert (head pro)	£2 a week
William Lambert	£1 10s a week
James Fennell	£1 5s a week
John Fennell (a boy presumably)	15d a week
B. Peggs (Rackets marker)	£1 5s a week
R. Gaby (lawn tennis)	£1 1s a week

Charges were 5d for 2 hours' singles (4d for 1½ hours), 6d for 2 hours' doubles (5d for 1½ hours), 2d extra for non-members.

Gaby was the father of Richard Gaby, the Club Superintendent. The MCC presented a silver salver to father and son to mark the centenary of their fifty years of service to the Club.

Lambert's career at Lord's came to a sad end in 1889, when he retired, suffering from gout and bankruptcy, owing money to Alfred Tompkins for balls and to Biboche for rackets. Fortunately, he found another post at the East Road court at Cambridge and was succeeded at Lord's by James Fennell.

The MCC published their *Rules of Tennis* in 1872 and they differ little from modern rules. In the old court at Lord's there were 'fly nets' at the top four corners of the court and a ball that rebounded off them was in play. A pass neutralised a previous fault, but the rule that striker-out could take a pass was expunged in 1875.

In 1854 Prince's Club was opened on a site where Hans Place now stands. In addition to spacious club rooms, it contained two Tennis courts, seven Rackets courts, a cricket ground and, later, a skating rink, when roller-skating became fashionable.

An account of the club in 1872 is given in *Clubs and Club Life in London* by John Timbs.

> *The Club, established in 1854, is built upon the Pavilion estate, in the rear of the north side of Sloane-street, the principal entrance being from Hans-place. The grounds are of considerable extent, and were originally laid out by Capability Brown. They were almost environed with lofty timber-trees; and the genius of landscape gardening fostered by wealth, rendered this glade in the Brompton groves of old a sort of rural elysium.*
>
> *The Pavilion estate was once the property of Holland, the well-known architect, who planned Sloane-street and Hans Place, as a building speculation; and, in the grounds nearly between them, built himself what was then considered a handsome villa, the front of which was originally designed by Holland as a model for the Prince of Wales estate. In the grounds, among the remains of Brown's ornamental work, was an icehouse, amidst the imitative ruins of a priory. Here, also, were the Ionic Columns (isolated) which were formerly in the screen of Carlton House.*
>
> *The Club buildings comprise seven closed courts; a tennis court; gallery and refreshment rooms; baths, and a Turkish bath.*
>
> *Prince's Club is a subscription establishment; and its government is vested in a committee. Gentlemen desirous of becoming members of the Club must be proposed and seconded by two of its members. Two of the rules enact – that members have the privilege of introducing two friends, but that such visitors, if they play, be charged double the rate charged to members; and that no hazard, dice, or game of chance be allowed in the Club. Their Royal Highnesses the Prince of Wales and the Duke of Cambridge are members.*

It was a most popular club until property development caused it to close down in 1886. Immediately plans for

The Rackets court at the original Prince's Club.

a new Prince's were put in hand and the new club opened in 1888, just off Knightsbridge on a site once occupied by the Japanese village of the Great Exhibition of 1851.

The new club comprised two Tennis and two Rackets courts, two bowling alleys, a Turkish bath and various club rooms, including a pleasant sitting room, the Oak Room. It flourished for the next twenty years. The Prince of Wales (later Edward VII) was present at the opening of the first Tennis court when the Hon. Alfred Lyttelton played a match against Charles Saunders; the next Prince of Wales (later George V) was often in the club, sometimes accompanied by one or more of his sons. Two of them, Edward (later the Duke of Windsor) and George (later George VI), played many games of squash there.

Many officers of the Household Brigade found it convenient to be members, especially those quartered at Knightsbridge Barracks just across the road. In fact, the Orderly Officer at Knightsbridge was specifically allowed out of barracks to visit the club.

Rackets had been played in Manchester since 1876, but the Racquet Club's premises, including the two Rackets courts, were compulsorily acquired by the London and North-Western Railway Company little more than a year later. A new site was found in Blackfriars Road, Salford, and there the club reopened in December 1880, under the title of the Manchester Tennis & Racquet Club with one Tennis and one Rackets court. It remains the foremost club in the North of England.

In January 1888 two new courts were opened in London at the Queen's Club, West Kensington, where two Rackets courts had been opened the previous year. The Queen's Club Open tournament, instituted in 1888, became the British Amateur championship the following year and has continued to be held on the east court ever since, apart from occasional visits to other courts.

Tennis continued to be played at Oxford and Cambridge. When Peter Tompkins left Merton Street for the Brighton court in 1836, Thomas Sabin took over the management and ran the court with great success for thirty years. He instituted the Oxford Prize Racquet in 1850 and was responsible for training several first-class apprentices: E. (Ted) Hunt, who later went to Boston and taught Tom Pettitt, Thomas Lambert, and his younger brother George.

In 1866 the court reverted to Tompkins's management when the James Street court was closed, and Edmund Tompkins went to Merton Street. There he remained until 1887 when he was succeeded by his son-in-law J.H. Dickinson.

At the other Oxford court in Oriel Street, James Russell was in charge, with an assistant called Foulkes, until the court was converted into billiard rooms in 1860. Russell had club feet and was nicknamed 'Duck-legged Jim'. He would sometimes play with a ginger-beer bottle with a wooden peg stuck in the mouth for a handle. He was greatly respected as a teacher.

The Prince of Wales (later Edward VII) used to play in both Oxford courts and when Oriel Street was closed in 1860, he attended a benefit match for Duck-legged Jim in the Merton Street court.

At Cambridge, the Pembroke court had been rebuilt in 1734 and continued to be much used. J.M. Heathcote, the dominant amateur from 1867 to 1888, learnt to play there. As with so many courts at that time, the side windows were not glazed and he recalled how snow (and presumably rain) would come gusting in. There was no net in the dedans, to the great peril of any spectators. Nevertheless, Heathcote described it as 'a charming court, rather small and rather fast'. The Prince of Wales used to play in this court, too, which was then managed by Charles Phillips, with Henry Harradine as marker. When it was demolished in about 1880 the flagstones were used for the new court at Hewell Grange.

Meantime, two new courts had been built. When Phillips, the professional at Stratfield Saye and father of Charles and James Phillips, retired, the Duke of Wellington built a court for him at Parker's Piece, East Road, with a Rackets court as well. It was opened in 1853/54. The floor was of slate and rather slow according to J.M. Heathcote. On Phillips's death the court was managed by a Mr Chawner, a don at Emmanuel College, with Henry Harradine and John Bracher as markers. Bracher took over as manager in 1887, and George Lambert leased the court from 1889 to 1891 when it was closed.

Another court was built in 1866 at the top of Burrell's Walk, known as the Clare & Trinity court. The first manager was James Phillips, brother of Charles, who had two assistants, sons of Henry Harradine of the Pembroke court. The elder left after two or three years to become a non-conformist writer, but the younger, James, carried on and eventually took over from James Phillips in 1882. He remained in charge until 1910, when he handed over to his nephew, Arthur Twinn.

J.J. Russell.

A second court was built on the same site in 1890 and opened with a prestigious match between Peter Latham and Charles Saunders. About 1900 a curious match was played in one of these courts between Edgar Baerlein and Lord Howick – both mounted on bicycles.

This surge of court-building in England spread to the United States and Australia.

In 1876 Hollis Hunnewell and Nathaniel Thayer built a private court in Buckingham Street, Boston. They brought Ted Hunt over from Oxford to run it, and to assist him they engaged a twelve-year-old English boy, Tom Pettitt, who was later to achieve great things.

In 1879 another court was built at the Newport Casino on Rhode Island. The story of its origin is remarkable.

James Gordon Bennett, the publisher of the *New York Herald* and a world-wide traveller and explorer, thought it would be a great joke to have one of his polo ponies ridden into the club, the Newport Reading Room, by one of his young English friends, Captain Candy.

NINETEENTH-CENTURY TENNIS

Alfred Tompkins.

The result was not received with any enthusiasm – in fact there was quite a row. It seems that the horse was not on its best behaviour. Bennett resigned from the Reading Room and left the club.

On thinking it over he decided that he had been rash and went back early next morning to retrieve his letter of resignation. To his dismay, he found that the committee had already met and that his resignation had been accepted.

To retrieve the situation he engaged the firm of McKim, Mead and White to build, opposite his own house on Bellevue Avenue, the Casino Club, with twenty-two lawn-tennis courts, a Tennis court, a theatre, a squash tennis court, and club rooms above.

This complex was completed in time for the national lawn-tennis tournament to be held there in 1880. As head professional, Tom Pettitt was engaged from Boston's Buckingham Street court. He forged a link with the Boston Tennis & Racquet Club in 1904, which he maintained until his retirement in 1927. At the Casino he was a legendary figure, continuing to serve it every summer until his death in 1946 at the age of eighty-seven.

The Tennis court was never much used owing to the humidity in the summer, and in 1945 the roof was destroyed by fire. In 1979 it was restored at a cost of over $250,000.

Another court was opened in Boston in December 1888 by the Boston Athletic Association, and Tennis grew steadily in popularity.

New York followed suit in 1891. The Racquet Court Club, opened in 1876 at 55 West 26th Street, moved to 27 West 43rd Street and built a Tennis court as well as two Rackets courts. The club wrote to Frederick Tompkins, then professional at the Duke of Wellington's court at Stratfield Saye, to offer him the post of Tennis professional. Tompkins went to see his eldest brother, Alfred, then running a hotel in Notting Hill, to borrow money for his passage to the United States, but Alfred decided to go himself and it was he, not Frederick, who took over the Tennis court. Before his arrival Robert Moore ran both the Tennis and Rackets courts, assisted by Stanley Lambert. In 1892, when Moore returned to England, George Standing took over the Rackets courts.

In 1893 the Chicago Athletic Association built a Tennis court, two Rackets courts and a squash tennis court. Harry Boakes from Quebec was put in charge with Eddie Rodgers, William Joyce and Jim Fellman to assist him, but the venture was not a success and the Tennis court was converted into bowling alleys in 1901.

The first court in Australia was built by Samuel Smith Travers in 1875 in Hobart, Tasmania, modelled on the famous James Street court. Smith Travers took with him as professional to the new court Thomas Stone, who had learnt his trade at Hampton Court, James Street and Oxford.

But in 1882 Stone was lured away to take over a new court in Melbourne, at a salary of £250 p.a. plus 10 per cent of the gross receipts from play. He gave wonderful service to this club for over forty years. At a crisis in the club's finances in 1916 he even offered to forego his salary until things improved, and was grateful when it was decided merely to reduce his salary to £150 p.a. He remained secretary of the Melbourne club until the year of his death at the age of eighty-five in 1924.

Elsewhere, in Europe, as in France, the game was on the decline. There was spasmodic play in Vienna and a court at St Petersburg remained open until 1866. Otherwise there is little evidence of activity.

Yet despite the swing in popularity from France to the English-speaking world, the first half of the century continued to be dominated by great French players.

The court at St Petersburg.

Joseph Barcellon, son of Guillaume, was a frequent visitor to England. He played a match on 1 May 1802 against Philip Cox (later known as 'Old' Cox, but at that time aged twenty-three).

Philip Cox was born in Oxford in 1779. He trained as a marker in the Oxford court and came to the James Street court in 1798 as assistant to John Mucklow. A contemporary report records:

On Saturday, May 1st, at one o'clock at the Royal Tennis Court, St James's Street, was played a very famous match between the two best players in Europe, Monsieur Barcellon, a Parisian, and Mr Cox, junior, of London, a youth of about twenty years of age. The superior skill and knowledge of the former, obliged him to give fifteen for two bisques. The party was made for One Hundred Guineas, the best in five sets... The match was won by Monsieur Barcellon.

It seems likely that Barcellon was the best player of his day.

In 1813, Old Cox took a lease on the James Street court from John Mucklow and his mortgagees, paying £250 a year. The lease expired in 1832 when it was extended for a further forty years.

In 1816, Cox played a match for the world championship against Marchisio of Paris, son of the professional in charge of the Turin court and presumably by then the champion of France. The match was for 100 guineas and played over three days; Marchisio won. Three years later Amédée Charrier was champion of France and Cox had another chance at the world title. This time he won the match, played over two days, and was recognised as world champion for the next ten years.

It was remarkable that all these matches were played at James Street, Cox's home court, which must have given him a considerable advantage. Charrier's supporters offered to back him for £300 against Cox in Paris, but there is no record of that match being played.

But these ten years of an Englishman's superiority

Edmond Barre.

Charles Delahaye, nicknamed 'Biboche'.

were only a brief interlude, for there then arrived on the scene one of the great players of all time, J. Edmond Barre, who played and defeated Cox for the world title at James Street in 1829, and dominated the game for the next thirty years.

Barre was born in Grenoble in 1802. His father was a *paumier* of the second rank who moved to Paris and ran a court in the rue Mazarine. Here Barre learnt to play and soon made such an impression that in 1827 he played a match against Marchisio and Amédée Charrier at Fontainebleau in the presence of the King and his son, the Duc de Berry. His performance was so outstanding that he was appointed *paumier du roi*.

At the height of his powers in 1839 he could give Peter Tompkins, the best English player, half 30 and a bisque. In 1845 he played against Peter Tompkins and W.J. Cox (son of Philip Cox) and gave them half 15 and a bisque (reported in *Bell's Life* as 'seven and a half and a bisque').

Familiarly known in England as 'Papa' Barre, he was as much respected for his warm and friendly personality as for his outstanding prowess. He enjoyed playing for eccentric bets and there are many stories of these. On one occasion he played a match against the Comte de Reignac at Fontainebleau giving him 'all the walls' and having walked to the court from Paris. He left at dawn and arrived about 3 p.m., having covered the forty-three miles in ten hours. After an hour's rest he played and won the match. The next morning he walked back to Paris, accompanied by his colleague Louis Labbé who greatly enlivened the return journey by his antics. The latter on one occasion also played a freak match, carrying a marker on his back.

Barre was also known to play the ball between his legs (a dangerous shot for the novice) or with the handle of the racket.

In 1855, he was appointed *paumier de l'Empereur* and he held the world title undefeated until 1862.

Such was Barre's pre-eminence that another great French player never even contested the world championship: Charles Delahaye, known as 'Biboche'. Born in 1825 of an old family of Tennis professionals, he was attached to the court in the Passage Sandrié in 1840. There he had the opportunity of playing with Barre and with an outstanding amateur, M. Mosneron, and soon he was second in prowess only to Barre himself. He defeated Peter Tompkins at Hampton Court in 1848, and in 1851 defeated his son, Edmund, at Oxford and at James Street. In 1860, he added another victory in Paris by 5 sets to 2 in a three-day match. He played a famous match against Barre to mark the re-opening of the Versailles court in 1856.

Biboche eventually became manager of the Passage Sandrié court until its demolition in 1861 when he took over the new court at the Tuileries. Again, Biboche played a match against Barre to mark the court's opening.

Biboche, too, was fond of bizarre handicaps and once played a match wearing the full dress uniform of the National Guard, even carrying a musket with fixed bayonet in his left hand.

Biographies and pictures of some of these great players are included in a book by Eugène Chapus published in 1862 under the title *Le Jeu de Paume – son Histoire et sa Déscription*. Biboche and his father, Henri Delahaye, Barre, Peter Tompkins and Masson are included. This was the year of the opening of the new court at the Tuileries, and the book has a chapter on it, together with an illustration.

The book also contains an extract from the club rules. Evidently, three professionals were always on duty and, if the court was empty, a member had the right to ask the professionals to play a match for which he would pay them.

As well as much other information on the history and playing of Tennis, there are also details of *longue paume* as played in the Luxembourg Gardens in Paris.

Barre finally yielded the championship to Edmund Tompkins in a great match at the James Street court in 1862. Barre was sixty, Tompkins thirty-six and at his peak; yet it was a tremendous struggle and officially declared a draw. The match was to be the best of fifteen sets. The rules required advantage sets to be played (i.e., after 5-all one player had to achieve a lead of two games to win the set) so only two or three sets could be played each day. It seems that if the set continued too long it could be treated as a draw – no tie-breaks then to suit television schedules.

On the first day, 16 May, the first set was drawn, the second won by Barre. On 20 May, Barre won two sets, Tompkins one. On 25 May, Tompkins won two sets, Barre one. On 28 May, the first set was drawn and the next two won by Tompkins. On 10 June, the first and third sets were drawn and the second won by

Edmund Tompkins.

Tompkins. By then of fourteen sets played, four had been drawn, six won by Tompkins, four by Barre. It was a tremendous performance by Barre, but he could do no more and although the match was declared a draw, Edmund Tompkins was regarded as champion of the world from then on, and the era of great French players came to an end.

The Tompkins were one of the great families of English Tennis. Originally from Waterperry in Ireland, Peter Tompkins's grandfather took over the lease of the Merton Street court, Oxford in 1758, but his father moved to London to manage the court at Windmill Street. Peter himself (1802–63) – his real name was Edmund – started at Windmill Street, then returned to Oxford to the Merton Street court and finally, in 1836, took over the newly opened court in Brighton, where he remained until his death in 1863.

Peter had three sons. Edmund (1826–1905), world champion 1862–71, started at Leamington in 1846, took charge at the James Street court in 1849 and, when that court closed in 1866, returned to the family

George Lambert.

Tom Pettitt.

home in Oxford as lessee of the Merton Street court. Alfred (1832–1913) was assistant to his brother at James Street from 1849 to 1864, then moved to Brighton, where he ran a Rackets court in Middle Street. He became the principal maker of balls at Upper Lewes Road, Brighton, until his death. John (1836–1903) spent his whole career at Brighton, first as assistant to his father until his death, and then as manager until 1893.

In the next generation, Edmund's daughter married J.H. Dickinson, and he took on the Merton Street lease from his father-in-law. Their son, R.C.E. Dickinson, became head professional at Prince's Club from 1910 to 1923, when he returned to the Merton Street court as lessee on his father's death.

John Tompkins had seventeen children, of whom two sons followed the family tradition. J. Alfred became senior professional at Manchester from 1880 to 1887 and later went to New York. Frederick had experience at Prince's, Stratfield Saye and Malta (Rackets) before becoming Rackets professional to the

Walnut Street Racquet Club, Philadelphia, in 1904. When, in 1907, the Walnut Street Club moved to new premises on 16th Street with the addition of a Tennis court, Frederick became manager of Tennis and Rackets.

But the supremacy of the Tompkins family came to be challenged by another great family of Tennis players, the Lamberts. Joseph Lambert (1814–1905), head professional at Hatfield from 1849 to 1905, played until he was over eighty years of age. His son George (1842–1915) trained with Thomas Sabin at the Merton Street court, Oxford (1859–66), managed Hampton Court (1866–69), Lord's (1869–89) and East Road, Cambridge (1889–1891).

In 1871, aged twenty-nine, George Lambert challenged Edmund Tompkins for the world title and Tompkins yielded it without a match. Such was Lambert's dominance of the Tennis scene for the next fourteen years that no one challenged him for the title and, when a challenger finally appeared in 1885, he was from the United States: Thomas Pettitt.

81

Pettitt had visited England in 1883, returning the following year, and had made a great impression with his aggressive play. One writer described his style as 'strange, wild, barbaric, untutored and apparently developed out of an inner consciousness'. He shocked the critics, used to a more delicate style of play, but he also shocked the leading players. Neville Lytton wrote: 'Then Pettitt appeared on the scene. He had quite different principles. He was revolutionary, almost a Bolshevist. He used to say: "When I get a fair sight of the ball I hit it, and I hit it d—d hard."'

Eustace Miles gave him high praise:

Tom Pettitt is famous for his strength and agility. It is said that he can take up a man and throw him as he would throw a ball. The best of his strokes have never been equalled, and can only be realised by those who stand up against him on a dark day. His resource is incalculable. No ball is ever dead while Pettitt is in the Court. Last, but not least, he conceals the direction of his strokes in a way which I can never imagine to be rivalled. He has done more than any one else to change ancient into modern Tennis; having once shown that the modern game was more paying than the ancient game, he was bound to have his followers. He forced hard where others would have played with a heavy cut for the corners. But the great point of his game is not his sheer Force. I have always considered one of his finest strokes to be his stroke for the length of the Court: he hits the ball into the Nick time after time. This stroke is among his most effective, and I have never met a critic who recognised the skill which it implies.

The championship match was played in 1885 at Hampton Court and was to be the best of thirteen sets, with no advantage sets. On the first day, 11 May, Lambert won three sets, Pettitt one. On 13 May, each player won two sets. On 15 May, Pettitt won all four sets and the match, although the final set was a tremendous struggle before Lambert lost it 5–6. In the end Lambert's age told against him in this gruelling encounter; he was forty-five to Pettitt's twenty-five.

But although the reign of the Lamberts was at an end, the family continued to give service to the game. George's elder brother, Thomas, served with Thomas Sabin at Oxford; his younger brother, William, at Hampton Court, Lord's and Hewell Grange; his next brother, Alfred, at Prince's Club; and his youngest brother, Charles, at Hatfield. George's son, Henry Charles, served at Lord's and Petworth; William's son, Stanley, at Hampton Court and Oxford; and Charles's

Charles Saunders.

son, Edgar, at Hatfield, Queen's and Jesmond Dene, which he managed from 1894.

The next world championship match took place in 1890. Charles Saunders, a great stylist from Prince's Club, had established himself as the top British player by defeating George Lambert in a home-and-home match at Prince's and Lord's in 1886. He then challenged Pettitt and, in a bid for complete fairness, a most extraordinary match was arranged. It was to be played on Sir Edward Guinness's court – which had marble walls – at St Stephen's Green, Dublin. French balls were to be used and no practice was allowed on the court beforehand.

In these curious conditions, Saunders gained an early lead. On the first day, 26 May, Saunders led by 3 sets to 1. On 28 May, Pettitt squared the match at 4 sets all. On 30 May, Pettitt won by 3 sets to 1, thus retaining his title. But in September of the same year Pettitt decided he had had enough of competitive play and resigned, leaving Saunders as champion in name.

By now a new star had started to rise, one of the all-time greats of Tennis – and equally great at Rackets – Peter Latham. His early career and his great

NINETEENTH-CENTURY TENNIS

Peter Latham.

achievements in the Rackets court are described on pages 140–141.

In 1888 he became head professional at the newly opened Queen's Club, where he remained for the next ten years. In 1895, already Rackets world champion, he played Charles Saunders at Brighton for the Tennis world championship. On the first day he dominated the match, winning all four sets and losing only seven games. On the second day the sets were shared, two each, and on the third Latham won the first set to gain the title and become the only man to hold the world championships of Tennis and Rackets simultaneously.

In 1898 he defended his title against the former champion from America, Tom Pettitt, but the match, played at Brighton for £500 a side, was very one-sided, with Latham winning by 7 sets to 0, despite Pettitt's newly invented railroad service.

At the turn of the century, Latham was dominant in Tennis and Rackets as no man has been before or since.

In America, the growth of amateur interest in the game was marked by holding national competitions.

The Tennis singles championship of America was first played in 1892 and won by R.D. Sears of Boston.

Apart from two victories in 1894 and 1895 by B.S. de Garmendia of New York, it was won by players from Boston until the year 1900, when E.H. Miles became the first Englishman to win it.

Our knowledge of the game in this century is extensive thanks largely to *The Annals of Tennis* by Julian Marshall, published in 1878. It is a scholarly book on every aspect of the game – its history, its equipment, its laws, its method of play. The research involved in its production must have been prodigious. Certainly every subsequent author on this subject, including this one, is indebted to Julian Marshall for his comprehensive and authoritative work.

Also of interest are the chapters on Tennis in the Badminton Library, written by J.M. Heathcote and published in 1890. They add nothing historically to Julian Marshall's book but provide a background to the contemporary game and its leading players.

STICKÉ

In the last quarter of the nineteenth century a curious hybrid game developed called stické – an abbreviation of sphairistike, the name given by Major Wingfield to his game of lawn tennis. It was a form of lawn tennis, played in a type of Tennis court, using lawn-tennis rackets and a lawn-tennis net.

Julian Marshall.

The court was somewhat smaller than a normal Tennis court and constructed entirely of wood. Within the court there was no standard lay-out; some had a penthouse, some not; some had a grille, some a dedans, some a tambour; but none had chases. Rallies tended to go on for a long time, unless a player trained at Tennis knew how to cut the ball and bring it down sharply off the back wall.

The Tennis and Rackets Association minutes reveal that the Royal Artillery built a court at Shoeburyness in 1874 and that officers there and RE officers at Chatham drew up a code of rules for the game. They mention other courts at Gosport, Lydd, Esher (R. Howell, Esq), Jubbulpore, Rawalpindi, Halifax (Nova Scotia), Pretoria and Malta. Clearly, soldiers had carried the game overseas with them. In its early days, stické was played with a soft, uncovered india-rubber ball, $2\frac{1}{2}$ in in diameter and weighing $1\frac{1}{2}$ oz, supplied by F.H. Ayres.

There was at one time a court at Buckingham Palace, later converted into a swimming pool. Other courts existed at Easton Neston (the Tennis court converted), Taplow (later used for other purposes), Wildcroft (demolished), Mongewell, Cliveden, Greenlands, Kirtlington, Esher, Clandeboye, Avon Tyrrell, Longford, Digswell and Queen's Club.

Overseas there were courts in Ottawa and Cooch Behar and at Vice-Regal Lodge, Simla.

The court at Avon Tyrrell was built by the third Baron Manners, who built the house in about 1892. It was converted into a squash court in about 1930. When the fourth Baron gave the house to the National Association of Youth Clubs, it was adapted for use as a sports hall.

The court at Longford Castle, belonging to the Earl of Radnor, was burnt down in the 1960s. The one at Greenlands, in use until 1945, was subsequently converted by the Staff College into squash courts.

Colonel A.W. Acland remembers the court at Digswell, built by his father. It had one side penthouse only and was lit by electric light supplied from a private generator.

The Heathcote-Amory family own an excellent court at Knightshayes, near Tiverton in Devon, built in 1903 and still in almost daily use. It has a penthouse round three walls, and the game is played with lawn-tennis balls dyed bright red.

Dugald Macpherson used to play in Sir Samuel Scott's court at Westbury in the 1920s. His opponent was Gerald Robarts, the well-known squash player who won the American and Canadian championships in 1924.

Stické court at Corsham, Wiltshire.

Another excellent example of a stické court still stands at Hartham Park, Corsham, in Wiltshire. It is built entirely of wood with a penthouse along one side only and is equipped with a changing room and upper gallery. It was built by Sir John Dickson-Poynder, MP for Chippenham from 1892 until 1910 when, as Lord Islington, he was appointed Governor of New Zealand. Later he was Under-Secretary of State for the Colonies (1914–15) and for India (1915–19). It is a much larger court than usual, suitable only for doubles, and is regularly used by the family and friends of Earl Cairns, especially at weekends.

In Wales, Sir Stafford Howard built a court at his house Cilymaenllwyd in Llanelli, which he bought in 1910 from the Rees family. Mrs Garnons Williams remembered the game being played with lawn-tennis balls coloured red.

Another interesting version of a stické court is to be seen at Ryston Hall in Norfolk. De Luze mistakenly described it as 'an old dedans court, built about 1670 by Sir Roger Pratt, a courtier of Charles II, and still owned by the same family.' It is to this day owned by that family, but the building is in fact an old tithe barn, converted for stické by the addition of a grille and a very small dedans.

On 19 May 1891, a poem entitled 'Parker's Piece' by J.K. Stephen was published in the *Cambridge Review*.

Stephen died nine months later at the early age of thirty-three, but the poem is of interest in mentioning some of the great players of the age – three world champions (Lambert, Saunders and Pettitt), two leading amateurs (Alfred Lyttelton and J.M. Heathcote) and the leading professional at Cambridge (James Harradine).

To see good Tennis! What diviner joy
Can fill our leisure, or our minds employ?
Not Sylvia's self is more supremely fair
Than balls that hurtle through the conscious air.
Not Stella's form instinct with truer grace
Than Lambert's racket poised to win the Chase.
Not Chloe's harp more native to the ear
Than the tense strings which smite the flying sphere.
    When Lambert boasts the super-human Force,
Or splits the echoing Grille *without remorse:*
When Harradine, as graceful as of yore,
Wins 'Better-than-a-yard,' *upon the floor;*
When Alfred's ringing cheer proclaims success,
Or Saunders' volleys in resistlessness;
When Heathcote's Service *makes the Dedans ring*
With just applause, and own its honoured king;
When Pettitt's prowess all our zeal awoke
Till high Olympus shuddered at the stroke;
Or when receiving 'Thirty and the floor'
The novice serves a dozen Faults *or more;*
Or some plump don, perspiring and profane,
Assails the roof and breaks the exalted pane;
When 'Vantage, five games all, the Door' *is called,*
And Europe pauses, breathless and appalled,
Till lo! the ball by cunning hands caressed
Finds in the Winning Gallery *a nest;*
These are the moments, this the bliss supreme,
Which make the artist's joy, the poet's dream.
    Let Cricketers await the tardy sun,
Break one another's shins and call it fun;
Let Scotia's Golfers through the affrighted land
With crooked knee and glaring eyeball stand;
Let Football rowdies show their straining thews,
And tell their triumphs to a mud-stained Muse;
Let india-rubber pellets dance on grass,
Where female arts the ruder sex surpass;
Let other people play at other things;
The King of Games is still the Game of Kings.

The curious hybrid game of stické.

TWENTIETH-CENTURY TENNIS

1900–80

NEW COURTS

IN PARIS THE TWO COURTS at the Tuileries did not survive long into the twentieth century. In 1907, they were converted into picture galleries, now well-known for their collection of Impressionist paintings. But thanks to the efforts of J. Jameson, W. Bazin and their supporters, two new courts were built on the second floor of 74ter, rue Lauriston, and opened in 1909. The master professional was Charles Lesueur, assisted by Ferdinand Garcin and Georges Cott, a grandson of Barre.

In 1899 the Raquette d'Or had been instituted in the Tuileries courts. This was confined to French residents and was, in effect, the French amateur championship. The competition was transferred to the rue Lauriston in 1910 and, at the same time, a new competition was introduced, the Coupe de Paris, open to all amateurs.

The only other French courts to survive were those at Bordeaux and Pau.

In Britain the boom continued until the outbreak of war in 1914. At Lord's the old court was demolished in 1898 to provide better seating accommodation and a new one built in 1900 in its present position behind the Pavilion. The paving stones of the old court were transferred to the new.

Sir Charles Rose, in addition to his court at Hardwick, built another at Suffolk House, Newmarket. It was opened in 1901 with a match between Peter Latham and Cecil 'Punch' Fairs. Finding his original court at Hardwick slightly further from his house than he wished, he built a second there in 1907, allegedly on his wife's rose garden while she was abroad on holiday!

In 1905 J.O.M. Clark built a new court at Troon in Ayrshire, the first in Scotland since Falkland Palace. In 1906 C.T. Garland opened his magnificent court at Moreton Morrell, Warwickshire, still one of the best in England. In 1907 Lady Wentworth opened her court at Crabbet Park, Sussex, with G.F. Covey as head professional. Lady Wentworth was undoubtedly one of the best lady players ever to have played the game. She described herself in *Who's Who* as World's Lady Tennis Champion – a title she assumed without challenge. In 1899 she had married the Hon. N.S. Lytton, a distinguished amateur player, who twice defeated Edgar Baerlein, in 1911 and 1913, to win the amateur championship.

In 1909 Alderson Horne opened a curious miniature court at Ditton Place, Balcombe, Sussex – later the headquarters of the Penthouse Club; the floor measured 78 ft x 28½ ft. Another miniature court came into play in the 1970s when Ted Allerman converted the chapel of his house at Tuxedo into a half-size Tennis court.

In 1912 J.F. Marshall opened his court at Seacourt, Hayling Island, with another Latham v. Fairs exhibition match. This latter court had a dramatic history according to Marshall's daughter, Mrs Joan Grant, in her book *Time out of Mind*.

At the end of what was going to be the garden Father had built a real tennis court and a billiard room. One morning I was in the tennis court with Father watching the walls being covered with a special kind of cement. Thirty men were working up ladders and the man who had invented the cement, who was called Mr Bickley, was there too. Suddenly Mother rushed in and shouted, 'Out, all of you! The roof is going to fall in!'

Everyone stared at her and then looked up at the roof – a glass roof with iron girders that had been put in by a firm which roofed railway stations. It looked perfectly solid, but Mother became so angry at not being obeyed that Father ordered the men to stop work; so they climbed down the ladders and filed out of the building. For about five minutes they stood about, trying not to show that they thought Mother was being ridiculous. Mr

The opening of the Tennis court at Suffolk House, Newmarket in 1901. Front row (left to right): *J. Bickley, E. Dealtry, E. Nusser, F. Covey, A. Dooley, E. Gray, P. Latham, C. Fairs, J. Fennell, W. Stevens, J. Harradine, G. Lambert, F. Tompkins, W. Payne, W. Webb.*
Second row (left to right): *E.F. Newton, A. White, G.W. Smale, G.E.A. Ross, C. Saunders, T. White, P. Ashworth, J.F. Marshall.*
Back row (left to right): *W.H. Cohen, S. Heilbut, C.D. Rose, Baron E. d'Erlanger, Maj. E.W. Baird, E. Crawley.*

Bickley was saying to Father that if the walls cracked because the work had been interrupted he could not be held responsible. Mother was holding me by the arm in case I tried to run back into the court, which I had no intention of doing. Suddenly there was a grinding noise and an enormous crash. Clouds of dust belched out of the openings where the side-gallery windows were going to be. 'My God, it has fallen!' said Father. Mr Bickley looked as though he was going to be sick. Some of the workmen swore under their breath, and I saw three of them take off their caps and cross themselves. The only person quite unmoved was Mother, who said calmly, 'What did I tell you, Jack? You must admit there are advantages in being married to a witch.'

Joseph Bickley was a famous figure in the Tennis world as a builder of courts, and his patent methods had a great influence on the development of the modern game. He built the two courts opened at Queen's Club in 1888 and the Tuxedo Club court in New York opened in 1900. From then on, most courts in England and America were built by him or in his manner, and some existing courts treated by his process, here described by Allison Danzig:

The walls and floor are made of a concrete material that has a base of atlas cement mixed with sand that is screened through a sieve that has 2000 squares to the square inch. This base is soaked every twelve hours for a period of thirty days. When work is started on the finishing coat, which

looks like lamp black, and whose composition remains a secret, it must be continued day and night to obtain the uniformly smooth, even surface. Both the material and the laborers are sent out by the company from London to America, France, Australia or wherever the court is to be built.

This Bickley process enabled the floor to be laid in six large slabs rather than with paving stones, thus obviating false bounces at the joints, but it would be alarmingly expensive in overtime today. Joseph Bickley died in 1923 at the age of eighty-eight.

Mrs Grant, in *Time Out of Mind*, also writes of the professional at Seacourt.

Duncan Duncan Wilson, our tennis professional, came into my life when I was four. He had been christened Duncan Duncan because he had a paternal and a maternal uncle with the same name, and his parents wanted to make sure that neither of them was offended. Long before he started teaching me to play the game, which was not until I was seven, I used to watch him stringing rackets or re-covering tennis balls, nine dozen to each basket of them, in his room at the end of the court while he talked about tennis. He told me there were grossly ignorant people who confused it with lawn tennis, a very inferior game played outdoors which should be referred to by the well instructed as pat-ball or lawners. It was, of course, our tennis that was the Game of Kings. Henry V might not have beaten the French so thoroughly at Agincourt, after the Dauphin had started the war by sending him a basket of tennis balls as an insult, unless he had been determined to prove that he could win as easily on the battlefield as he could in the court. Anne Boleyn might have kept her head if she had taken the trouble to appreciate the game. 'She probably annoyed the king by clapping when he lost a chase, or by forgetting to clap when he put a nice shot into the winning gallery,' said Wilson.

At about the same time several old courts were renovated, including Petworth, Canford, Hatfield, Hewell Grange and Fairlawne. But the outbreak of war in 1914 cast a deep shadow over the game of Tennis.

After the war, only two new courts were built. One, constructed in 1922, was an open court with a penthouse along both sides on Lambay Island, Co. Dublin. It belonged to the Hon. Cecil Baring, later Lord Revelstoke. The other, opened in 1924, was converted by W.N. McClean from an 1886 long fives court at Rusthall House, Tunbridge Wells.

In the United States a very fine court, built with the aid of Bickley, was opened at the Tuxedo Club, Tuxedo Park in 1900. Robert Moore returned from England to take over as head professional and was later joined by Arthur Forester as Tennis professional. Forester took charge when Moore left in 1920. The Gold Racquet competition was first played in 1903.

In the same year, George Gould opened a private court at Georgian Court, Lakewood, New Jersey, together with a Rackets court, which became the 'nursery' of his son Jay Gould. To coach his two sons, Gould engaged Frank Forester, trained at Prince's, who had been in New York since 1898. When Forester left in 1914, Alfred White took over for a couple of years and after that there was no further play. The court was resurfaced by Bickley in 1906. It became a girls' seminary, but in 1966 was re-opened for an exhibition match between Jimmy Dunn and Tommy Greevy.

In 1902, the Myopia Hunt Club opened a court at Hamilton, Massachusetts with Alfred Kirton as professional, and in the same year William C. Whitney sponsored a new court at Aiken, South Carolina. This was especially popular during the winter polo season when an outside professional was engaged. At one time this was Jack White from New York, later David Kenney from Newport and then Pierre Etchebaster.

In 1904 a second court was added at the New York Racquet and Tennis Club, and the Boston Tennis and Racquet Club opened a magnificent new building at the corner of Boylston and Hereford Streets with a Tennis court, a Rackets court, and squash courts. Tom Pettitt came to take charge and remained with the club until his retirement in 1927.

Philadelphia followed in 1907 when a Tennis court was built in the new Racquet Club building on 16th Street. This time Frederick Tompkins, supplanted in an earlier appointment by his brother, successfully arrived to take charge of both games. He brought over Jock Soutar to assist him. The national doubles championship was first played here in 1909.

In 1908, the first American University court was opened at Harvard, principally thanks to the efforts of H.J. Coolidge, together with a Rackets court and two squash courts, known as the Randolph Tennis and Racquet Courts. The first professional, a man by the name of Clark, was later succeeded by Alfred Kirton. In 1916 these courts were converted into squash courts.

The following year, Clarence Mackay opened a magnificent new private court at Roslyn, Long Island and put Robert Moore Jr in charge. He was succeeded in 1915 by the former world champion Punch Fairs.

An equally luxurious private court was built in 1915 by Payne Whitney at Greentree, Manhasset, Long Island, with Frank Forester from Lakewood as the resident professional. On Forester's retirement, William 'Blondy' Standing, nephew of George Standing, took over.

In 1918, the New York Racquet and Tennis Club moved to its present site at 370 Park Avenue with two Tennis courts and a Rackets court.

The last court to be built in America was in Chicago by the Chicago Racquet Club in 1923. Charles Williams took charge and Rackets still flourishes there. The Tennis court has unfortunately been adapted for use as an indoor lawn-tennis court.

In Melbourne in 1971, an event took place that turned out to be of enormous significance to Tennis generally. At the eighty-ninth Annual General Meeting of the club in June of that year, the President, Richard Allen, won approval for the sale of the property in Exhibition Street for a sum of A$675,000 on the understanding that a new club would be built within a few miles on less expensive land. A new site was bought in Sherwood Street, Richmond for A$131,000 and the design of the new buildings entrusted to architect Daryl Jackson. After careful research in Britain, he built two magnificent new courts, remarkable not only for the excellence of their playing properties but also for the wonderful natural lighting.

The floor is red-coloured granolithic paving laid over concrete. The walls are of reinforced concrete, coloured

Payne Whitney.

olive green. The penthouse roof is of hardwood boards (Eucalyptus Regnans), sanded and left as natural wood. Sections of the roof arc covered with perspex acrylic sheeting to admit diffused light. Behind a small dedans runs a glass partition through which spectators may watch play without distracting the players. There is also a large spectator gallery running the whole length of the north court high above the penthouse and this is able to accommodate at least 100 people.

In addition to the two Tennis courts, there were two squash courts, changing rooms, a children's pool and a flat for a resident professional.

The first to occupy the flat were Chris Ronaldson and his wife, Lesley, who arrived from Oxford early in December 1973. Ronaldson played many fine matches against his rival professional from Hobart, Barry Toates, and was responsible for a considerable raising of the standard of play in Melbourne. His wife gained

a worthy reputation as a modern successor to Margot, the renowned early fifteen-century player.

The new courts were ready in 1974 and the official opening by the author, as President of the British Tennis and Rackets Association, took place on 23 March 1975. It was attended by numerous distinguished visitors from overseas, including two former world champions, Pierre Etchebaster, then retired and living in St Jean-de-Luz, and Northrup Knox. Unfortunately, an injury prevented Knox from playing. The full Bathurst Cup was played for the first time in Australia and was won by Britain (Alan Lovell and Andrew Windham), who beat both Australia and the USA by 5 matches to 0. Other visitors were invited to participate in various competitions as well as to partake in the lavish hospitality.

All those who had played in Melbourne moved on south to celebrate the centenary of the old court in Hobart. To mark the occasion a magnificent new trophy, the Governor's Cup, had been presented by the Governor of Tasmania, Sir Stanley Burbury, for an open competition to be held regularly from then on. It was won on this first occasion by Frank Willis from Manchester, who beat Barry Toates in the final by 3 sets to 2.

Where Australia had shown the way, France soon followed and in 1978 a magnificent new court was opened in the Avenue de Verdun, Mérignac, Bordeaux. The initiative for selling the old court in the rue Rolland and re-building in the Avenue de Verdun came from a senior civil servant, Claude Quancard. His enthusiasm, charm and ability overcame all difficulties. Unfortunately, soon after the court was completed he died suddenly. The club bears his name in honour of his great achievement.

The old premises were sold for 2,100,000 francs and for almost exactly the same sum the new buildings were erected – the Tennis court, four squash courts and excellent club accommodation. In addition, there were site costs of 345,000 francs and other expenses, but with the aid of a bank loan on favourable terms and a Government grant towards the squash courts (the first ever to be built in Bordeaux) the project was made possible.

The architect was Francisque Perrier, assisted by Lechêne. The first professional, Henri St Germain, had been coaching lawn tennis since his defeat by Jim Dear at Holyport in 1954.

The Tennis court is named after the greatest French player of the twentieth century, Pierre Etchebaster. An international competition was held there in April 1979 to mark the opening, and Etchebaster was presented with the medal of *L'Ordre du Mérite National* by M. Chaban-Delmas, President of the National Assembly, Mayor of Bordeaux and a talented player of many games, including Tennis.

The four squash courts are named after de Suduiraut, de Luze, Biboche and Talbot.

Manchester, which had established particularly close links with Bordeaux, gave the club a stained glass window with a Tennis design, and Hayling Island provided the grille. The Tennis and Rackets Association presented them with a cabinet, and Petworth gave them two ancient rackets. The Knox brothers (Norty and Seymour) donated a challenge cup to be named after Etchebaster. Other clubs from Australia and Britain presented various books and prints in honour of the occasion.

CHAMPIONS OF THE EARLY TWENTIETH CENTURY

In 1901, Latham left Queen's Club to work for Sir Charles Rose, one of his greatest patrons. He went first to Sir Charles's court at Newmarket (1901–7), then to his second court at Hardwick (1907–13).

In 1904, he was challenged by Punch Fairs for the world title. The match was played at Brighton on 16, 18 and 20 May. It was clear from the start that Latham was not quite as formidable as he had been in the last championship match against Pettitt, and that Fairs was a greatly improved player.

The first day's play was even and hard fought; Latham emerged the winner 6–5, 6–3, 6–4, 3–6 – 21 games to 18. Fairs got off to a flying start to lead by 5 games to 1 in the first set, but then Latham established

Jock Soutar and Cecil 'Punch' Fairs.

his mastery to win that set and the next two. He played very severely and accurately, and volleyed most effectively, but Fairs had the better service.

On the second day, Latham was at his best. After two close sets shared 6–3, 4–6, he dominated the match and won the remaining two sets 6–1, 6–1. His return was outstanding, his accuracy in finding the winning openings was remarkable and again he volleyed powerfully. Fairs' service was still the better and won him the second set of the day.

That left Latham with one set to win on the final day to retain the championship, but Fairs did not give up without a fight. He had little to lose and, although Latham was not at his best and less accurate than previously, Fairs played outstandingly well. It was he who dominated the play in the first two sets, winning them 6–3, 6–3. The third set was a great struggle. In one game, Fairs hit the grille three times in succession before finally winning 6–5. He was now just one set behind in the match.

All seemed over when Latham led by 5 games to 1 in the fourth set, but again Fairs hit back and levelled the score at 5 all. Latham won the final game, however, to achieve the set he needed for victory.

Clearly Fairs had every right to challenge again and this he did the following year. A rather curious match was arranged on a home-and-home basis at Queen's and Prince's, four sets at each and, in the event of an equality, a final five sets at Brighton to settle the match.

The first leg was played on 7 October 1905 at Queen's, Latham's home court, and he made a disastrous start, losing the first three sets 0–6, 3–6, 4–6. Fairs was certainly playing well, but Latham had an off day. He made a lot of mistakes and missed too many easy shots, although every so often producing one of his great forces or making a superb retrieval. He managed to salvage the last set, winning it 6–1.

He faced a hard task, therefore, in the second leg on Fairs' home court at Prince's, and it proved too much for him. He was playing much better, but Fairs, too, was on top form. There was some excellent classical play on the floor. However, Fairs won the first set 6–2 and the second 6–5 (after Latham had led 4–2) to win the championship.

Next came a challenge from the leading French player, Ferdinand Garcin, who played Fairs at Brighton in 1906. On the first day, 21 April, he gave the champion a shock by winning 3 sets to 1. But Fairs reversed the score on 24 April to square the match at 4 sets all. On the third day, 28 April, Fairs crushed his opponent, winning the three sets required to retain the title by 7 sets to 4.

But his dominance didn't last for long. Latham had been licking his wounds and was ready to make a come-back. He challenged Fairs and a match was arranged at Brighton.

On the first day, 6 May 1907, it became obvious that the old champion was back to form. He set a very fast pace all through the match, boasting and forcing marvellously and showing all his old powers of return. The first two sets were a magnificent display of Tennis, with many long and brilliant rests. At critical points Latham brought out his best and he won both sets, 6–5, 6–5.

He dominated Fairs in the third set, winning it 6–3, but, tiring, he lost the fourth 3–6, so ending the day leading by 3 sets to 1. He started the second day, 8 May, as if he intended to sweep Fairs off the court, leading 4–0 and 5–1, but Fairs fought back to 5 all before finally losing the set 5–6. Latham continued to dominate the play, taking the next set 6–3 and going on to lead 5–3 in the third. Unfortunately, at this point the light deteriorated to such an extent that play almost had to be abandoned. After a great struggle, Fairs won the set 6–5 and, with Latham tiring and suffering from cramp, took the next set 6–1, leaving the overall score 5–3 in Latham's favour.

On the final day, 11 May, Latham made certain of regaining his title by winning both sets played, the first easily 6–2, the second after a tremendous struggle 6–5. The strain had told on both players and the quality on this final day was less good, but nevertheless it was a magnificent achievement by Latham – one day after his forty-second birthday.

Immediately afterwards he resigned the title, which was re-assumed by Fairs. Latham continued to play in exhibition matches and handicap events for many years, however, and was especially highly regarded as a teacher. He returned to Queen's Club in 1916 and was there able to play a part in the post-war revival of Tennis. In 1919 he played two fine matches against the redoubtable Edgar Baerlein, the amateur champion, giving him odds of half 15.

When Latham died at the age of eighty-eight, Edgar Baerlein wrote of him:

One Tennis and two Rackets players are mentioned as possibly his equals. I cannot believe it. His ability was of a character that was not fully evident to a spectator. If an opponent had any effective attack, Peter would seem to say to himself 'we're not having that to-day' – and we didn't. He found a way of stopping it.

He was said not to have a very good service. It did not look remarkable but if you had a favourite return he saw to it that you had few opportunities of using it. His service at either game might win few aces but it gave him the attack and put hand-out on the defensive.

He was very quick to start and to move, so was able to wait, balanced, near the centre line until his opponent could no longer alter the direction in which his shot would go. The result was that it looked as if the ball was always being hit to him.

In fact, magnificent though he appeared to be as a player, he was an outstanding example of one who was 'better than he looked'.

Further, he was an artist, ever seeking perfection. For him it was not enough that a stroke should be a winner. It had to be that and more, the more being that even he could not improve it.

Finally he was a delightful opponent. Everything he did in the court made it a pleasure to play against him, and out of court his experience, intelligence, and natural courtesy, made him a popular figure wherever tennis and rackets were played.

Fairs was soon challenged again by Edward (Ted) Johnson, then the professional at Moreton Morrell, but he retained the title fairly easily at Brighton in June/July 1908 by 7 sets to 2. Two years later, he was called upon to defend the championship against Fred Covey, Lady Wentworth's professional at Crabbet Park.

The match again took place at Brighton and was extremely close. On 4 May the sets were shared two each. On 6 May Fairs, making good use of his high drop service, secured a lead of 5 sets to 3. On the final day, 9 May, Covey won the first set, Fairs the second to make it 6 sets to 4. Fairs made a tremendous effort to clinch the match in the next set, but lost it 5–6. The older man, he had taken a lot out of himself in the attempt and lost the next set 1–6, making the score 6 sets all. But in the end Fairs was the fitter of the two and, playing beautifully, he won the final set 6–1 to retain his title.

A return match was played in 1912 at Prince's Club, where the court had been recently renovated. It began on 29 April and seemed likely to be another very close contest, the day ending at 2 sets all. But when they met again on 1 May, Fairs was suffering from rheumatism, and Covey ran away with all four sets to lead 6 sets to 2. On 4 May, Fairs won the first set, but Covey easily won the next to win the match and become the new world champion.

This same year a somewhat curious situation arose over a challenge to Covey by Ted Johnson of Moreton Morrell. The Tennis, Racket (sic) and Fives Association (TRFA) issued a notice that unless Covey played him within twenty-one days of the 4 May 1913, they would recognise Johnson as champion.

This unwise decision elicited a stinging letter to *The Field* from the Hon. Neville Lytton. He pointed out that the world title was not in the gift of the TRFA, that the committee mainly consisted of Rackets players, that Covey's doctor forbade him to play a match before October and that Johnson had never beaten Covey or Fairs on level terms. Lytton also announced his resignation from the TRFA. Evidently this letter had the desired effect, for no more was heard of Johnson's challenge.

By now a new star had risen in the Tennis firmament and, for the first time, this was an amateur player, Jay Gould from Georgian Court, Lakewood, New Jersey. Jay Gould, born in 1888, had started playing Tennis at a very young age. He was introduced to the game at his father's new court at Lakewood when he was twelve. Frank Forester from Prince's Club had been engaged by his father to teach Jay and his brother Kingdon to play Rackets and Tennis. On his arrival in March 1900, he began teaching the two boys Rackets; in the spring of 1901 he gave them their first Tennis lesson.

Jay soon gave up Rackets and began to play Tennis regularly. Many of the leading players would visit Lakewood and he had plenty of opportunity to learn from them. In 1903 one of these visitors was E.A. Thomson from New York, and from him Jay learnt the railroad service that was destined to be such a distinctive characteristic of his game.

In 1905, at the age of seventeen, he played in the Tuxedo Gold Racquet tournament, reached the final, but was beaten by Charles E. Sands. The same year he gave a good game to Peter Latham at Lakewood, receiving 15. By the following year he had developed

Left to right: *Jay Gould, George Standing, Frank Forester.*

into the best amateur in the USA. He won the Tuxedo Gold Racquet in March 1906 and went on to win the national championship.

Full of confidence and anxious to widen his experience, he cabled his entry for the British amateur championship and sailed for England three days after winning the American national. At that time, the two finalists of the previous year stood out of the competition, and the winner of the contest had the right to challenge the previous year's second prize-winner – the winner of that match having the right to challenge the holder.

Jay Gould won the competition with ease. He went on to defeat the second prize-winner, V.H. Pennell, by 3 sets to 1 and to challenge the holder, Eustace Miles. He won the first set, but lost the next three and the match.

Eustace Miles was the author of *Racquets, Tennis and Squash,* published in 1902, in which he put forward his somewhat eccentric views on training, including breathing, diet and exercise. These are followed by some miscellaneous notes on fatness ('Fatness, beyond a certain degree, is a positive disadvantage'), staleness ('A usual remedy for staleness is champagne and a large dinner') and constipation ('It has been said that nine-tenths of the English people are constipated').

The main section is devoted to a detailed analysis of the techniques of the three games, with much advice on methods of play. The book ends with a historical and personal section, including some accounts of the principal players of his day and the winners of various competitions.

The next year, Gould returned to England, met Eustace Miles again in the challenge round, and defeated him to become the first American to win the British amateur championship. In 1908 he again defeated Miles, not only in the amateur championship but also to win the Gold Medal in the Olympic Games in London, which included Tennis for the only time in history.

In his own country, he dominated the amateur game from 1906 until he retired in 1926. Not only did he win the national championship every year, but no one could even take a set off him. From 1907 until his retirement he lost just one match – that was to Edgar Baerlein in the Bathurst Cup in Paris in 1923. Baerlein won 4–8, 8–5, 8–4, but Gould had not been in the best of health and was probably affected by the death of his father shortly before. At any rate he beat Baerlein 3–0 the following year in the same competition in London.

In 1913 he challenged Covey for the world championship, and a match was arranged for the following year in Philadelphia and London.

The match was played in Philadelphia on 16 and 18 March 1914, and was decisively won by Jay Gould, by 7 sets to 1. On the first day Covey could capture only eight games in four sets. On the second day he managed to take the third set at 6–5, but won only five games in the other three sets.

This overwhelming victory stirred up considerable controversy about whether the world championship was at stake, or whether this was the first leg of a home-and-home match. Robert W. Henderson carried out considerable research into the matter, and his conclusions are based on very firm evidence.

Despite the disadvantage of playing on an American court with American balls, Covey's backers accepted Gould's challenge and there can be no doubt that Gould won it in March 1914. However, Gould made a gentleman's agreement that, should he win in Philadelphia, he would play Covey at Prince's Club, London by June of that year. The articles governing the match gave him a year's grace and provided for a return match in or before March 1915.

June 1914 was still two months before the outbreak of war and even after that Covey, having been rejected for military service, offered to play Gould and give his share of the gate money to hospitals for the wounded. Gould wrote to Covey on 22 November 1916, relinquishing the world title, but from the available evidence it seems right to conclude that he forfeited the title according to the articles in March 1915.

The next championship match featured another American challenger, Walter Kinsella.

Kinsella was a native American, unlike many of the other leading American professionals who were of British birth. William C. Whitney introduced him to squash, at which game he was to hold the American championship from 1914 to 1926. With Whitney he went to Aiken and learnt to play Tennis. After Whitney's death, he was employed at the New York Racquet and Tennis Club as a Tennis professional under George Standing.

In 1915 he won the American professional championship in a match against Jack White and he successfully defended that title against Punch Fairs the following year.

In December 1919 he was beaten by Jay Gould at Philadelphia for the American Open championship in a best-of-thirteen sets match. On the first day Gould swept to a 4–0 lead (6–3, 6–4, 6–3, 6–5) and went on to win the first set on the second day 6–0. Kinsella rallied to win the next three sets (6–3, 6–5, 6–1), but Gould clinched victory on the third day (6–3, 3–6, 6–2). Nevertheless, it was Kinsella who played Covey for the world title.

The match was played in 1922 at Prince's Club. On 15 May, Covey led 3–1; on 17 May, 6–2, and by winning the second set on 20 May he secured the championship by an overall margin of 7 sets to 3.

Lord Revelstoke recalls asking both players for their autographs.

Kinsella wrote: 'I am now returning to the States to learn how to "cut" the ball.' He did just that, and in a return match the following year he made an early breakthrough, winning the first three sets, but Covey struck back to take the next seven sets and the match, again by 7 sets to 3.

There now appeared on the scene another of the all-time greats of Tennis – not for the first time, a Frenchman. Pierre Etchebaster, born on 8 December 1893, was brought up in the Basque traditional games of *pelota*. He excelled at them, but his sporting career seemed thwarted when he was apprenticed to an uncle in Chile in 1909 and then called up for military service in 1914. However, demobilised in 1919, he resumed the Basque games and was soon champion of them all.

His recruitment to Tennis was due to Jacques Worth, couturier, brother-in-law of Cartier, winner of the Raquette d'Or in 1921 and 1922, and President of the club at rue Lauriston. He was on the look-out for a replacement for Ferdinand Garcin, who wished to retire, and he engaged Etchebaster in 1922. Although Pierre had never played the game before, he was soon the best in Paris. After two years he visited England and won the professional handicap competition at Manchester. In 1927 he challenged Covey for the world title.

The match was played at Prince's in May, and Etchebaster made a brilliant start by winning the first set 6–0, playing the traditional French game on the floor. Covey was too experienced to panic, and he fought back to win the second set 6–4. He went on to take the next set 6–4, to lead by 2 sets to 1. Now it was Etchebaster's turn to react, and he swept ahead to lead by 4 games to 0 and 40-love. It looked as if he was likely to win the first and final sets of the day's play to love.

But it is a great tribute to the champion's determination and skill that he fought back in masterly fashion to square the score at 4 all in about five minutes, and to win the next two games and the set at 6–4. Thus he led, somewhat unexpectedly, by 3 sets to 1 at the end of the first day's play.

The Times correspondent was so impressed with Etchebaster's talent in this match that he accurately predicted that he would 'one day be so good a player that later followers of Tennis will know him as "Pierre" only.' The correspondent paid tribute to both players, stating that the packed dedans considered the match to be the best exhibition of pure Tennis since the time of Peter Latham.

There was bound to be a reaction to the brilliance of the first day's play and although the game was closely contested on the second day, its quality was lower. Covey again emerged the winner by 3 sets to 1 (6–3, 5–6, 6–3, 6–5). Experience had given him a lead of 6 sets to 2 and he required one more set on the final day to retain his championship. It looked as if the match was over.

But not in Etchebaster's view. He started brilliantly on the third day, winning the first two sets 6–3, 6–4, and leading 3–1 in the third. Covey caught up to make it 4 all, then 5 all. Etchebaster led 40–15 in the final game but failed to hold his advantage and Covey won the set to retain his title by 7 sets to 4.

Etchebaster had proved that he was a worthy contender, but another rival had emerged in America, Jock Soutar, professional at Philadelphia. It was agreed that Etchebaster and Soutar should play a match to decide who should challenge Covey, and Etchebaster paid his first visit to the USA. The match was played in Philadelphia in February 1928 and easily won by Etchebaster, by 7 sets to 1. He had established his right to have another go at Covey.

The match took place at Prince's Club on 7, 9 and 12 May 1928. This time Etchebaster had improved considerably in all departments – he served more accurately, volleyed better and played a more severe stroke. Covey was now forty-seven, and his game had lost some of its edge.

Etchebaster swept to a 3–1 lead on the first day, winning both the first and last sets to love, 6–0, 2–6, 6–1, 6–0. Play on the second day started with a set of the highest quality, in which Covey showed his old skill against a younger opponent who was cutting the ball down and rarely making a chase worse than 2. At 5 all there was a tremendous battle for the final game. Covey led 15–0 and served a double fault; he led 30–15 and 40–30; he had advantage four times to Etchebaster's twice, before finally securing the two consecutive points and the set.

But the effort tired him. Etchebaster went on to seize the next three sets 6–3, 6–0, 6–1 to lead by 6 sets to 2, leaving him one set to win on the third day for the title. He started nervously and it was Covey who

Pierre Etchebaster.

took the first set, but Etchebaster made sure of the next, 6–2. He had begun his unbroken reign of twenty-six years. Soon after his victory, he joined the New York Racquet Club as senior Tennis professional.

His first challenger was Walter Kinsella, in 1930, and the match was again played at Prince's Club, on 26 and 28 May. Kinsella played a hard-hitting game of boast and force, but Etchebaster showed his supreme skill in controlling the ball and dominated the first day's play, winning all four sets 6–3, 6–1, 6–3, 6–2. On the second day he went on to take the fifth set 6–3, but in the sixth Kinsella, now desperate, started a wholesale bombardment of dedans and grille, which for a time was effective and took him to a lead of 5–2. Etchebaster regained control and caught him at 5–5,

but Kinsella won the set. It was his only set, for Etchebaster went on to win the next two 6–2, 6–4 and the match by 7 sets to 1.

In 1937 Etchebaster faced a challenge from the outstanding American amateur Ogden Phipps, who won the amateur championship every year from 1934 to 1939 – except 1938, when he lost to his principal rival, Jimmy Van Alen, in the semi-final. Phipps had established his right to challenge Etchebaster in 1936, with an easy victory over Kinsella at Greentree in a challenge match for the American Open championship. Phipps won by 3 sets to 0. He was twenty-eight at the time, Kinsella fifty-one.

The match took place at Tuxedo in December 1937. Etchebaster soon established his superiority with beautiful strokes on the floor and deadly marksmanship for the winning openings, although Phipps had the more heavily cut stroke. Etchebaster served better and was effective in volleying Phipps's railroad service. He won the first two sets 6–3, 6–2. Phipps took the third 6–4, but Etchebaster won the fourth 6–1. Unfortunately, in the penultimate game of the last set Phipps, chasing a ball that had hit the wall above the dedans, slipped and fell into the gully under the net, twisting his ankle. This injury forced him to retire from the match, and not long afterwards the war intervened.

The competition for the British Open championship (Prince's Club Shield) was first played in 1931. In a remarkable first-round match lasting three hours and twenty-four minutes, Lord Aberdare beat Ted Johnson 5–6, 5–6, 6–5, 6–5, 6–5. The match took a lot out of both players and Aberdare fell an easy victim to Jack Groom in the semi-final. In the other semi-final, Edgar Baerlein beat E. Ratcliff. The final was another remarkable match. Groom was leading by 2 sets to 1 and 5–1. Twice he had a match point at 40–30 and advantage. But in the end, Baerlein took the set 6–5 and went on to win the final set and the championship 6–1 – a very fine achievement at the age of fifty-one.

LITERATURE BETWEEN THE WARS

The years between the two world wars were rich in books on Tennis, regrettably less so on Rackets. First came the two volumes of *A History of Tennis* by E.B. Noel and J.O.M. Clark, published in 1924. Julian Marshall had done so thorough a job of research into Tennis history that there was not much to add, but in every other way these two volumes are a treasure trove of information about the game and its personalities.

In the first volume, the game's history is carried on from where Julian Marshall left off in 1878. The great championship matches are described, as are the characters of the champions, not only professional but also amateur, and not only in Britain, but in France, the USA and Australia. The final five chapters detail the history of the University matches.

The second volume contains chapters on the literature of Tennis, the laws of Tennis, rackets, balls and courts, hints on play and handicapping. At the end are a number of appendices containing invaluable information on courts and their dimensions, winners of events, professional and amateur players.

In the pages of these two books is everything anyone could wish to know about Tennis in the post-Marshall period up to 1924. It is a remarkable record on which this present work has drawn heavily and gratefully.

Not content with his book on Tennis, E.B. Noel collaborated with C.N. Bruce (later Lord Aberdare) to publish *First Steps to Rackets* in 1926. This is a very slim volume by contrast, and is mainly devoted to practical instruction as its title implies, but it has a useful chapter on the history of Rackets, as well as details of the more important championships as an appendix.

The Thirties were even more prolific, with two especially valuable books, *La Magnifique Histoire du Jeu de Paume* by Albert de Luze, published in 1933, and *The Racquet Game* by Allison Danzig, published in 1930. The former is one of those great works of scholarship in the Marshall tradition, but this time treating of Tennis in the land of its origin.

What Marshall did by patient research for the history of the game in England, de Luze did for it in France. After describing its history century by century, he writes of courts in the different *départements* of France – a tremendous task – as well as of courts abroad. In the second part, he gives details of courts, balls, rackets, professionals, championships and even of *parties excentriques* and *coups extraordinaires*. An excellent English translation by Sir Richard Hamilton, Bt. was published in 1979.

Once again the author of this present book unashamedly acknowledges his indebtedness to de Luze on all matters concerning the game in France. Equally, for its history in the United States there is no more authoritative account than that contained in Allison Danzig's book. It is all the more valuable in that it covers Rackets as well – not to mention squash rackets and squash tennis.

Another intriguing title appeared in 1932: *Tennis Origins and Mysteries* by Malcolm D. Whitman. This is a fascinating series of essays on all the unsolved problems, philological and historical, of Tennis, and some useful accounts of the origins of both Tennis and lawn tennis in the USA. It also contains (as an appendix) an invaluable bibliography of Tennis, compiled by Robert W. Henderson. As well as his own book, *Ball, Bat and Bishop*, Henderson wrote many articles on Tennis and Rackets.

Also in the Thirties, a volume on Rackets, squash, Tennis, fives and badminton was published in the Lonsdale Library series. It includes a most interesting section on the history of ball games by John Armitage, and some chapters on the playing of Tennis and Rackets by Edgar Baerlein.

POST-WAR CHAMPIONS

In 1948 Ogden Phipps once again won the US amateur singles, having been absent on active service in the Navy since 1939. In the final he overwhelmed Alastair B. Martin, who had a blistered hand, 6–0, 6–0, 6–2, and challenged Etchebaster, then aged fifty-four, for his world title. The match was played in New York in April.

On the first day Etchebaster was in command. Phipps played his usual strong floor game, cutting the ball heavily, but Etchebaster had an answer to his every stroke and kept returning the ball remorselessly to a perfect length. He served better, too, varying from sidewall to underhand twist, whereas Phipps exclusively served the railroad which Etchebaster took well. The result was a 3–1 lead for the champion, 6–3, 5–6, 6–0, 6–2.

Phipps played much better on the second day and only Etchebaster's skill at critical moments secured him the first three sets. After winning the first set 6–4, he was 0–4 and 2–5 down in the second before capturing it 6–5. He snatched the third, too, 6–5, and Phipps must have been very disheartened. He was also suffering from cramp, but went gamely on until Etchebaster showed signs of fatigue. Phipps deservedly took the fourth set 6–5. This left Etchebaster with one more set to win, and he accomplished this on the third day by 6–2 to retain his title.

Later the same year, Etchebaster faced another challenge, this time from the other side of the Atlantic, from Jim Dear.

Dear was a pupil of Peter Latham's and an outstanding player of both Tennis and Rackets, and also of squash. For three years in succession (1935–37), he had been narrowly defeated for the

British Open squash championship by the outstanding Amr Bey; in 1938 he was a worthy winner. At Rackets, he was British Open champion from 1946 to 1954 and again in 1960; he was world champion from 1947 to 1954. At Tennis, he was British Open champion from 1938 to 1950 and again from 1951 to 1962. He fully deserved the award of the MBE bestowed on him in 1960 for his unique services to Rackets, Tennis and squash.

His Tennis was marked by the same all-round ability as his Rackets. His eye and swiftness of foot gave him great power of return in defence, and in attack he was very accurate on the winning openings, particularly the dedans, often off the main wall. He played a very effective volley, an attacking rather than a purely defensive stroke. Not a railroad server, he had a wide range of different services for different occasions, including the high drop and the underhand twist.

Dear found conditions in New York very different from London. The balls were lighter and very difficult to cut; Etchebaster had perfected the type of game best suited to the conditions, using his outstanding ability to control the ball superbly and stroke it into the corners. Dear could only seek to mirror this game and to retrieve all he could with an occasional blast for one of the winning openings.

Etchebaster got off to a good start by winning three of the four sets on the first day, although Dear was unlucky not to win the second. The score was 6–1, 6–5, 6–3, 3–6. On the second day the sets were shared 2 all, 6–2, 1–6, 3–6, 6–3, and despite being almost seventeen years younger, it was Dear who appeared tired at the end. On the third day, Etchebaster started nervously to lose the first set 4–6, but at that point, in Dear's own words, 'my legs just died on me' and Etchebaster ran away to victory 6–0, 6–1. Dear believes that his leg failure may have been caused by electrical treatment which he received for a muscle strain.

As holder of the championship, Etchebaster had to be beaten on his own court. Had Dear been able to play him home-and-home, as he did Johnson in 1955, there might have been a different result.

In December 1949, Ogden Phipps had another go at the then fifty-six-year-old master. Phipps was at the height of his powers, having won the US Amateur singles for the seventh time and the British Amateur championship. Etchebaster had conceded four sets to Dear and might be thought to have passed his peak; but he proved it to be quite otherwise. Playing with flawless accuracy, he completely dominated the first day's play and allowed Phipps just four games in all.

Pierre Etchebaster serving his familiar railroad.

Sadly for Phipps, he found the champion on one of his greatest days, when all the magic of his Basque origin came to his aid and he was invincible. He won 6–0, 6–2, 6–0, 6–2.

It was an overwhelming lead for Phipps to face on the second day's play, but he was a fighter and surely Etchebaster could not again find such a sure touch. So it seemed when Phipps won the first set 6–4 and led 4–1 in the second. Then the master re-asserted his authority. He won the next five games to take the second set 6–4, and went on to win the next two sets 6–2, 6–3, retaining his world title by a superb exhibition of mastery and skill.

More evidence of his outstanding brilliance was yet to come. The following year an even younger opponent challenged him. Alastair Martin was the new US Amateur champion, and like his predecessor, he had added the British Amateur championship to his laurels. He was twenty years younger than Etchebaster, but he could do little better than Phipps against the superb authority of the champion. Etchebaster won the first set 6–2 and led 5–3 in the second. Then Martin made a great effort, drew level at 5–5, saving several set points in the process, and had a set point for 6–5. But Etchebaster won the set and effectively the match. He went on to win the next two sets 6–1, 6–0.

On the second day Martin fought back courageously, but however hard he tried he could not shake the uncanny control of the champion, who took the first two sets 6–4, 6–1 and went on to lead 4–2 in the third. Martin again made a tremendous effort to come back and squared the set at 5 all, but the pressure was too great and Etchebaster won the final game and the set to retain his title by 7 sets to 0.

Alastair Martin had a second challenge match against the champion, now aged fifty-eight, in November 1952. He fared little better. Etchebaster won on the first day by 3 sets to 1 (6–1, 5–6, 6–1, 6–0) and by the same margin on the second day (6–3, 6–3, 6–3, 5–6). He had to win just one set on the third, and despite a brave effort by Martin, he won the first set 6–5 to retain the championship.

Early in 1955, aged over sixty-one, Pierre Etchebaster resigned and a great reign came to an end. If he had started playing Tennis as young as some of his great predecessors, that reign might have been ten years longer, but his early preoccupation with Basque games and the intervention of the First World War prevented that. It is impossible to compare champions of one age with those of another, if only because playing conditions differ, but it is certain that Etchebaster has to be reckoned one of the great Tennis players of all time.

Not only was his greatness registered in his unbeaten record of victories up to the age of sixty, but he was also a great master of the science of ball games. He didn't play the game just by instinct; he thought deeply about technique and he was for that reason an outstanding teacher. Always make use of the spin already on the ball, he would explain; never try to impart the opposite spin. Always make use of the lower part of the net in the centre – don't try to be too clever and hit your ball over the high part. He would spend hours in the court, practising one particular stroke

The Van Alen Trophy match of 1956 at Lord's. Standing (left to right): *S.A.M. Collins (Oxford), G. Reindel (Princeton), M.R.M. Love (Cambridge), E. Harding (Harvard), H. Johns (MCC Head Professional), G. Unhoch (Yale), O.J. Colman (Cambridge), R. Hackett (Harvard), N.F. Robinson (Cambridge).* Sitting (left to right): *R.B. Bloomfield (Oxford), J. Van Alen II (Yale), M.H. Searby (Cambridge), James Van Alen, R. Aird (Secretary MCC), N. Ludington (Harvard), M. Coulman (Oxford), W. Van Alen Jr (Pennsylvania).*

Jim Dear and Albert (Jack) Johnson.

until it was to his satisfaction. Sufficient to quote the words of Allison Danzig:

> *No athlete I saw in nearly half a century of reporting Tennis, football, the Olympic Games, rowing, golf, baseball made winning seem so easy, perfection so commonplace, as did Pierre in Court Tennis.*

And Jim Dear:

> *His game is his own. There can only be one Pierre. No-one will ever study the game as he did in order to be such an artist at it.*

Etchebaster's retirement left the world championship vacant and it was necessary to arrange a home-and-home contest between the two best players on either side of the Atlantic. In Europe, Jim Dear first played a match at Holyport against the leading French professional, Henri St Germain from Bordeaux, and won comfortably. He then played Ronald Hughes for the Open championship.

Surprisingly, he had much greater difficulty in winning on his home court, Queen's, where the first leg was played. Having won the first two sets narrowly 6–5, 6–5, he went on to lead 4–2 in the third. Hughes fought back to win that set 6–4 and the fourth set 6–4 to square the match.

This encounter provided some of the best Tennis seen in Britain since the war. The pace and elegance of Hughes's ground strokes were met by Dear's brilliance and variation of attack.

Five days later at Manchester, Dear ran out an easy winner 6–4, 6–2, 6–1, Hughes making too many mistakes.

In America, Albert (Jack) Johnson, son of Ted Johnson of Moreton Morrell, who had joined the professional staff of the New York Racquet Club, first beat Jimmy Dunn of Philadelphia for the Professional championship (in Philadelphia 6–2, 6–2, 7–5; in New York 6–3, 7–5, 6–3) and then beat Alastair Martin for the Open championship in New York (6–5, 5–6, 6–1, 6–4, 6–4, 6–3, 6–2, 6–3).

The Dear v. Johnson match was played in New York and London in 1955. This time Dear was the older and Johnson had shown considerable improvement since his arrival in New York. On 25 February, they finished 2 sets all. On 28 February, Johnson dominated the play and looked like winning all four sets, but Dear made a tremendous effort and won the last set to make the score 5 sets to 3 in Johnson's favour. On 2 March, Dear won the first set, but Johnson narrowly won the next two 6–5, 6–5 to give him an overall lead of 7 sets to 4.

On 25 April the match was continued at Queen's Club. It began with Johnson looking a likely winner. He took the first set 6–3 and a terrific struggle ensued for the second set, clinched by Dear 6–5. By now Johnson was tiring and Dear was on top – he won the next two sets 6–3, 6–2 to lead by 3 sets to 1. On 27 April the situation was reversed. Dear started at a great pace to take the first set 6–0, but Johnson rallied and, after Dear had won the second set 6–5, went on to take the remaining two sets 6–5, 6–5 to leave the match 5 sets to 3 in Dear's favour.

On the final day, 30 April, it was necessary for Dear to win the first two sets to give himself a margin of 7 sets to 3 over Johnson's 7 sets to 4 in New York.

A pulled leg muscle made it look an impossible task. He consulted Dr Stephen Ward, who asked him how long he needed to play and Dear told him about an hour. It was enough – he won the two sets necessary in convincing fashion, 6–3, 6–1, to add the Tennis world championship to that of Rackets and, to all intents and purposes, of squash. He had very narrowly failed to equal Peter Latham's record of holding both Tennis and Rackets world championships at the same time, for he had lost the Rackets title to Geoffrey Atkins the previous year.

Johnson had his revenge two years later. A return match was played at Queen's on 25 and 29 May and 1 June 1957. On the first day Johnson won the first set 6–3, but Dear then struck his best form. In a brilliant burst he won the second set 6–1 and went to 3–1 in the third. But Johnson was very fit and full of return, while Dear was now forty-eight and as Rackets professional at Wellington had not had a great deal of match practice. Johnson took the next two sets to lead on the day by 3 sets to 1.

On the second day it was essential for Dear to get a good start and he led all the way through the first set to 5–4, but Johnson's return was sure and he never let go. It was he who eventually won the set 6–5. Dear managed to capture the next 6–4, but Johnson took the last two 6–4, 6–3 to gain a formidable lead of 6 sets to 2.

Northrup Knox and Alastair Martin.

On the third day, therefore, Johnson needed one set for victory and it seemed to be all over when he raced to a 4–1 lead in the first set. But Dear struck what *The Times* correspondent called 'a patch of pure purple' and, playing magnificent attacking Tennis, won the next five games for the set. He couldn't keep it up. Johnson re-established his smooth, fast game to win the second set 6–2 and the match. There had been much fine retrieving by both players during the match; Dear was the more adventurous in attack, but Johnson played a sound, steady game which in the end prevailed and the title went back to America.

In 1959 an amateur won the world championship for the second time – Northrup R. Knox, winner of the US Amateur singles in 1957 and 1958. He challenged Johnson for the world title and the match was played in New York in February 1959. Knox led after the first day's play by 3 sets to 1, but it could have been very different. Johnson started well, winning the first set 6–3 and leading 4–1 in the second. Knox hit back to win the second set 6–5 and the third 6–0. In the fourth, Johnson led 4–2 and 5–3, but it was Knox who eventually won it 6–5.

The pattern was reversed at the start of the second day's play. Knox began better, took the first set 6–3 and led 3–1 in the second. Johnson rallied to win the second set 6–4 and to lead 3–2 in the third. The pendulum swung again and Knox won the third 6–4. The all-important fourth set was a bitter struggle with Johnson playing well on the floor, but Knox the more accurate on the winning openings. At 5 all Knox led 40–15 with two set points, but Johnson put two successive balls into the grille and a third on to the tambour to stand at set point. Two good services by Knox gave him set point again and this time he took it to lead by 6 sets to 2.

He now needed one more set for the championship, and he won this 6–2 on the third day.

His first challenger in 1966 was a new British Open champion, Ronald Hughes. Hughes played hard and well, but in unfamiliar conditions Knox was too good for him and won overwhelmingly by 7 sets to 0.

Then two remarkable brothers, talented at all ball games, came on the American scene – G.H. (Pete) and J.F.C. (Jimmy) Bostwick of New York. Jimmy, the younger, was in fact the first to win the Amateur singles in 1959 at the age of twenty-two, defeating Knox by 3 sets to 1 in the final (6–3, 5–6, 6–3, 6–3) and even leading 5–2 in the second set. He played with great brilliance, but it must be remembered that Knox had only just emerged from an exhausting world title match with Johnson.

Knox re-established his superiority by winning the Amateur singles from 1960 to 1963. Meantime, Jimmy Bostwick won the Open championship, first in 1960, again in 1961, and then in 1962 with a convincing victory by 3 sets to 0 over his elder brother, Pete. In 1964, Knox did not defend his Amateur title and in a very close match Jimmy repeated his victory over Pete by 3 sets to 2 (25 games to 23).

In 1965 it was Pete's turn. He won the Amateur championship, which he held until 1969 and won again in 1971. In 1966 he added the American Open championship at Tuxedo, but lost it again the following year to brother Jimmy. In partnership, they won the Amateur doubles in 1969 and 1973.

In 1967, Pete challenged Knox for his world title and the match took place in New York in February 1968. Knox won by 7 sets to 3, but the match was a great deal closer than the score in sets suggests.

On the first day, Knox was dominant, serving better than Bostwick and finding more winning openings. He won by 3 sets to 1 (6–5, 2–6, 6–3, 6–3). He won again on the second day by the same margin, playing with beautiful control and great accuracy. The last two sets were of high quality, but in the end Knox took both (2–6, 6–3, 6–4, 6–4). On the third day, Bostwick at his most brilliant outplayed Knox in the first set, which he won 6–2, and went on to lead 4–2. Knox fought back to level the score at 5 all and won it 6–5 after Bostwick had had a point for the set. He retained his title, therefore, by 7 sets to 3, but in games the margin was narrow – 48 to 45.

On 10 February, Knox retired and again the championship was vacant. A match was arranged home-and-home between the US and British Open champions of the day, Pete Bostwick and Frank Willis, a professional from Manchester. The first leg was played at the New York Racquet Club on 28 and 30 April and 2 May 1969.

On the first day Willis made a good start, leading 3–0 and almost 4–0 in the first set, but Bostwick started to play well and Willis found the strange conditions difficult. The result was a 4–0 lead for Bostwick (6–4, 6–3, 6–2, 6–2). The second day's play was much closer and Willis did well to halve the four sets played after Bostwick had won the first two (6–3, 6–3, 4–6, 4–6). On the third day, Willis won the first set 6–5, but lost the next 2–6 to give Bostwick an overall lead in New York of 7 sets to 3.

Willis, therefore, seemed to have an evens chance at least, playing on his home court at Manchester and, indeed, he started well by winning the first set 6–3. But then Bostwick began to play superb Tennis and swept to victory in the next three sets 6–4, 6–3, 6–3, for an overall lead of 10 sets to 4. His supporters' hopes, dashed by the first day's play, rose rapidly when on the second day Willis won all four sets 6–3, 6–5, 6–1, 6–3. But on the final day he lost the first set 3–6 and Bostwick took the title by an overall 11 sets to 8.

Bostwick's first challenger was none other than his younger brother Jimmy. The match was played at the New York Racquet Club on 16 and 19 October 1970. Jimmy began in brilliant style to win the first set 6–4, but Pete, after a slow start, began to show his true form and won the next three sets 6–4, 6–5, 6–2. On the second day he continued where he had left off and won all four sets 6–5, 6–5, 6–2, 6–0 to retain his title.

As the score in the first two sets of the second day indicates, however, his victory was by no means easy. The match was spectacular, with long rallies. Both players covered the court magnificently and returned balls that seemed irretrievable. But Pete was slightly the more severe in stroke and deserved to win.

In 1972, again in New York, Jimmy turned the tables and won the title by 7 sets to 2. The full score was 6–3, 2–6, 6–5, 6–4, 6–2, 5–6, 6–5, 6–4, 6–2.

Above *Jimmy Bostwick in 1975.*

Below *Jimmy Bostwick and Howard Angus.*

At this point another remarkable all-round games player appeared: Howard Angus. Angus won the Amateur Rackets title from 1972 to 1975 and was Open champion from 1971 to 1973 and 1975–6. He won the Amateur Tennis singles and the MCC Gold Racquet from 1966 to 1980, the Cutty Sark championship in 1974, 1976 and 1977, and was Open Tennis champion from 1970 to 1979, despite four challenges by Frank Willis.

In 1973, Angus crowned his Rackets career with a decisive victory over Willie Surtees to become Rackets world champion. He sought to add the Tennis world championship and thus equal Peter Latham's record. It was agreed that before he should have the right to challenge Jimmy Bostwick for the title, there should be an eliminator between him and the US Open champion, Eugene Scott. This took place at Queen's Club on 29 and 31 March, and in New York on 8 and 10 April 1974.

Angus started badly, losing by 1 set to 3 at Queen's on the first day, and losing the first set on the second day to go 1–4 down. However, he fought back remorselessly, slowing down the pace intelligently, and won the next four sets. He thus finished the London leg leading by 5 sets to 4, not a very satisfactory lead on his home court. But by now Angus had sized up his

Hampton Court, June 1977 – Howard Angus (centre) successfully defends his world title against Gene Scott (third from right). Also in the group are (left to right) Alastair Martin, David Warburg, Pat Barker, Jimmy Van Alen and Alan Lovell.

opponent and he played with great skill in New York to win by 5 sets to 1 and prove his right to challenge for the world title.

The world championship match that followed was one of the most curious in the history of this event and Angus was desperately unlucky. It is typical of his good sportsmanship that he has never grumbled about events that might have sent others to seek the help of the Samaritans.

The match was scheduled for 16, 18 and 20 April in New York and, although feeling unwell, Angus won all four sets on the first day. He was examined by a doctor that evening, who recorded a temperature of 102 and diagnosed a respiratory infection. Angus asked for a postponement of the second day's play.

The USCTA, who had overall control of the challenge, did not come back to Angus with a decision on whether the postponement was granted or not, but he read in the *New York Times* that the first day's play had been declared null and void. A completely new match was proposed. Angus felt passionately that he should have been given the option, if no postponement was offered, of forfeiting the second day's play and playing from 4 sets all on the third day. The doctor had stipulated that Angus should not consider playing until his temperature had been normal for thirty-six hours. Angus turned up on 20 April and played one set against his trainer, Norwood Cripps, just to show he could have played on the third day, but it was a futile gesture.

In the intense negotiations to get the match re-scheduled, Angus was adamant that he wanted to play straightaway and not have to come back to New York at some future date. Luckily, David Norman happened to fly into New York at that moment and took up the negotiations on behalf of Angus and the Tennis and Rackets Association. Eventually, he reached agreement with the USCTA and Jimmy Bostwick to re-start the match on 1 May, with Angus undertaking to switch to Bancroft rackets since his 'frying-pan' church-type Grays racket, although three-quarters of an inch inside the USCTA's 1973 ruling on racket size, had attracted some criticism for being 'too wide'.

On the first day the sets were shared two all, Angus winning 20 games to Bostwick's 19. On the second day, however, Bostwick produced some of his most brilliant Tennis and won all four sets to attain a commanding lead of 6 sets to 2. Angus needed to win 5 sets on the last day to beat the champion. He nearly accomplished this seemingly impossible task. He won the first three sets 6–4, 6–3, 6–2, to make the score 5 sets to 6. The next set was a real cliff-hanger. Angus had a set point at 5 games to 4, but Bostwick made it 5 all. Angus had three more set points to square the match, but finally Bostwick won this all-important set to retain his title by a total of 7 sets to 5.

The next year Jimmy Bostwick retired and the world championship was once again vacant. The two obvious contenders were Howard Angus and Eugene Scott. A match was arranged in New York on 29 and 31 March and 1 April, and in London on 11 and 13 April 1976. Scott made a good start on the first day in New York, winning the first three sets and ending the day 3 sets to 1 up. On the second day, Angus repeated his achievement in the eliminator match two years previously and won four sets in succession to lead by 5 sets to 3. On the third day, there was only one man in it and Angus easily took the first two sets and the New York leg by 7 sets to 3. Having lost the first three sets, this was a remarkable achievement and made Scott's task on a foreign court look very daunting.

Indeed it was. On the first day at Queen's, Angus established a 3–1 lead. On the second he won the first set to make sure of the title. Although he had narrowly missed Peter Latham's record of holding both Rackets and Tennis world titles simultaneously, he had equalled Jim Dear's record of holding the titles individually and he was the first amateur ever to do so, and the first left-hander.

The next year a return contest took place on 8, 10 and 12 June – this time on the royal court at Hampton Court Palace, the first time that a world championship match had been played on this historic court since 1885. In that year, in another Anglo-American encounter, Tom Pettitt had beaten George Lambert. On this occasion the tables were turned and the British holder emerged the victor.

On the first day honours were even at 2 sets all. On the second there was a hard battle for the first two sets, which Angus eventually won 6–5, 6–4. Scott, showing signs of weariness in the face of Angus's determined retrieving of the most difficult shots, lost the next two sets outright, giving Angus a commanding 6 sets to 2 lead overall. On the third day, Angus won the first set to clinch his victory and retain his title.

Up to this date there had been no trophy for the Tennis world championship, but the omission was made good on this occasion with the presentation by the Tennis and Rackets Association of a silver salver engraved with the names of all previous holders, and with the outline of the four Tennis-playing countries and the names of their courts.

Howard Angus agreed to defend his title again in 1979, and challenges were received from leading players in Britain and the United States. To establish a British challenger, a match was played between Chris Ronaldson (Troon) and Norwood Cripps (Queen's), won by Ronaldson 5 sets to 1. In the United States, Jimmy Burke (Philadelphia) beat Eugene Scott (New York) by 5 sets to 3.

In the final eliminator, Chris Ronaldson beat Jimmy Burke by 7 sets to 1 at Hampton Court in April 1979. Burke began nervously, having not had more than a few days to get used to the strange conditions, and lost the first two sets 3–6, 3–6. He fought hard to win the third set 6–4, but lost the next 4–6 to leave Ronaldson with a lead of 3 sets to 1.

The second day's play produced some marvellous Tennis and Burke was unlucky not to win either of the first two sets. In the first he led at 5–4, 40-love, but Ronaldson was never better than when he had his back to the wall and he rallied to win it 6–5. He went on to take the next two sets 6–5, 6–0. In the fourth set he was 4–5 down again, but once more came from behind to win it and the match 6–5.

Both players had produced some lovely shots and Burke's return of Ronaldson's heavily cut stroke in the forehand corner was remarkable. Ronaldson was much the stronger at service and on the volley.

The challenge match for the world and British Open championship took place at Hampton Court in April 1979. Ronaldson had the advantage of youth, of having had to play several top-class matches to reach the challenge stage, and of having defeated Angus in the final of the 1978 Cutty Sark competition. Angus had had trouble with his back. Few people would have guessed that the champion would retain his title by 7 sets to 0, perhaps least of all Howard Angus himself.

The first day's play on 17 April produced an excellent match. There were many fine rallies and some quite extraordinary returns. Angus set a very fierce pace and his service was always aggressive. Despite this, Ronaldson certainly deserved to win one set – particularly the fourth in which he led at one point by 5 games to 4. Nevertheless, the final score to Angus was 6–4, 6–4, 6–5, 6–5.

That was a formidable lead for Ronaldson to face on the second day and it proved too great for him. He failed to produce the form he had shown previously, made too many mistakes and allowed Angus to win 6–3, 6–2, 6–3 and easily and worthily retain his world championship title.

Angus's record compares with the greatest players of all time. Apart from his domestic achievements (noted on page 102), he was Tennis world champion from 1976 to 1979. Few indeed are those players who can claim to have recorded a victory over him in a major championship. His Rackets achievements are recorded elsewhere (pages 155–157) and as a player of both games his record is quite outstanding.

PROMINENT PLAYERS

Apart from those few distinguished players involved at world championship level, there were many fine players of the game. Outstanding among English amateurs in the early years of the century was E.H. Miles, winner of the Amateur championship from 1899 to 1903, 1905–6 and 1909–10; winner of the Gold Prize 1897–99, 1901–06 and 1908–13.

An even more dominating figure came to prominence in 1912 – Edgar Baerlein, already established as a leading Rackets player and then aged thirty-nine. He first won the Amateur championship in that year, lost narrowly to the Hon. N.S. Lytton in 1913, and won again in 1914. After the war he won it every year from 1919 to 1927 and again in 1929 and 1930. He won the MCC Gold Prize every year from 1921 to 1929 and again in 1931.

As at Rackets, one of his chief rivals was the Hon. C.N. Bruce (later Lord Aberdare) but only once did Bruce beat him in a major championship. That was for the MCC Gold Prize in 1930.

Baerlein became the first winner of the Prince's Club Shield for the Open championship, when he beat

Edgar Baerlein.

105

W.A. (Jack) Groom 3–2 in 1931 at the age of fifty-one. His other great achievement was to defeat Jay Gould in Paris in 1923 in the course of the Bathurst Cup.

The mantle of Baerlein fell upon the shoulders of Lowther Lees, a fellow Mancunian of powerful physique. Lees won the Amateur singles in 1928, 1931 (when he beat Baerlein 3–0 at Manchester), 1933 to 1937 and 1946, when it was played at Lord's because of war damage to the roof of the Queen's court. He also won the Open championship by beating Jack Groom 7–1 in 1934 and 7–2 in 1935. He lost it in 1938 to Jim Dear, who won 5–1.

Among the professionals, Jack Groom of Lord's, Willy Ratcliff of Queen's and E.J.G. Johnson, son of Ted Johnson, were pre-eminent.

Ratcliff defeated Johnson 3–1 for the British Open in 1931 and Groom defeated Ratcliff 7–1 in 1932. Just before the Second World War, Dear started to make his presence felt, winning the Professional championship in 1937 and the Open in 1938. Had the war not intervened, Dear's record might have been even more astonishing than it was, but in 1939 he joined the RAF and Tennis and Rackets were out for the duration. All he managed was an occasional game of squash when the opportunity arose.

After the war, Dear did not defend his Open championship, being too busy with Rackets, and a match took place in 1950 in which Ronald Hughes, the Rackets professional at Malvern, beat Henry Johns of Lord's 5–3. Dear, however, returned to the fray in 1951 to regain his title by beating Hughes.

When Dear resigned as Open champion in 1962, Hughes regained the title by beating David Warburg 5–1. He in turn lost to Frank Willis of Manchester in 1967. Willis was potentially one of the great players of the day, but he was of too easygoing a nature to win as often as he might. He managed to stave off a challenge from Howard Angus in 1968, but he lost to Angus in 1970 and the latter held the title for the following four years.

In 1965, *The Field* gave a magnificent trophy for an annual open competition. Mostly this was won by Hughes, Willis and Angus, but three other names appear among the list of victors – Norwood Cripps, then at Queen's and now Rackets professional at Eton, had two fine victories over Willis in 1971 and 1973, and played in the final on six other occasions; Chris Ennis, who defeated Cripps in 1975; and Chris Ronaldson, who beat Angus in 1978.

Among post-war amateurs none was dominant before Angus in 1966, but competition was keen.

Dugald Macpherson, who had won both the Amateur championship and the MCC Gold Prize in 1939, won the Gold Prize from 1947 to 1949 and in 1951 and 1952. The author won the Amateur championship in 1953 and 1954, and 1956 and 1957, and the Gold Prize from 1954 to 1958.

Beating Macpherson for the Gold Prize in 1950, and then defeating Bruce in the semi-final and Peter Kershaw in the final of the Amateur in 1955, Robert Riseley showed what a fine player he was. Unfortunately, ill-health never allowed him to attain the heights of success that he deserved. Lord Cullen, who had previously won the Amateur in 1947 when he defeated Kershaw on his home court at Manchester, played brilliantly to beat Riseley in the final of 1952 by 3 sets to 2.

David Warburg had a successful record over a considerable period. He first won the Amateur championship in 1959 and repeated this success in 1961 and 1965. He was even more successful in the MCC prizes, winning the Gold Prize in 1953 and 1960–65.

Another outstanding player of beautiful style was Rackets champion Geoffrey Atkins. He won the Amateur in 1960 and 1962–63. In 1960 and 1963 he had the distinction of winning the Amateur singles title at both Tennis and Rackets. Anthony Tufton was a worthy winner in 1964 and Alan Lovell featured in five finals against Angus, taking him to five sets in 1977.

A great contributor to both Tennis and Rackets in the post-war years was Michael Pugh. Although never in the top flight as a player, he devoted his energies to spreading enthusiasm for both games and encouraging young players. His greatest playing achievement was to win the Bailey Cup (now the Tennis Amateur doubles, then an inter-club competition) for Manchester in 1951 in partnership with Peter Kershaw. He also played third string in the victorious Old Rugbeian Henry Leaf Cup teams in 1949, 1959, 1953–57 and 1959–60.

AMERICAN CHAMPIONS

In America in the early years of the century, Boston players enjoyed continuing success in the singles championship, in particular J. Crane Jr who won it from 1901 to 1904. There then arose that new champion of world class, Jay Gould, who won without defeat from 1906 to 1925 – except for 1918 and 1919 when no championship took place.

With the retirement of Jay Gould the competition became more open and a number of other players won

Jay Gould.

it: C. Suydam Cutting, Hewitt Morgan, William C. Wright and two British visitors, George Huband and Lord Aberdare.

In 1934 another player of world class took the title for the first time – Ogden Phipps, who won it five times in six years and again (twice) after an interruption caused by the Second World War. His principal rival in the early days was Jimmy Van Alen and they had some terrific struggles. In 1933 the singles were played for the first time in Philadelphia and Van Alen beat Phipps 3–0 in the semi-final, going on to beat W.C. Wright in the final and win the championship.

The following year Phipps turned the tables to take the title for the first time, but Van Alen still managed to beat him in the Tuxedo Gold Racquet in a closely contested five-set match. In 1936 Van Alen came very near to victory again in the Amateur singles, but eventually Phipps won by 6–0, 5–6, 5–6, 6–4, 8–6, after Van Alen had led 6–5 and advantage in the final set. He went on to win the Open championship in a challenge match against Walter Kinsella at Greentree. Kinsella was aged fifty-one to Phipps's twenty-eight and Phipps won easily 6–2, 6–1, 7–5.

Thereafter, Phipps dominated the Tennis scene, although Van Alen twice won the singles again in 1938 and 1940, when Phipps did not compete. Phipps's matches with Pierre Etchebaster have been mentioned earlier.

After Phipps came Alastair Martin, winner in 1941 and every year from 1950 to 1956. He, too, twice challenged Etchebaster for the world title without success. In 1954, playing brilliantly, he defeated a much younger opponent, Northrup R. Knox, in the final conceding just three games, but Knox, a favourite pupil of Etchebaster, could not be held down for long. The following year he took a set off Martin; in 1956 a knee injured playing polo prevented him from playing; in 1957 Knox won, and held the title for six out of seven years.

Knox successfully challenged Jack Johnson for the world title in 1959 and no doubt in reaction to that splendid effort lost his Amateur title to another rising star, twenty-two-year-old Jimmy Bostwick. The younger man played brilliantly to win 6–3, 5–6, 6–3, 6–3 – having also led 5–2 in the second set.

Knox did not defend his world title in 1964 and from then until 1972 it was shared by the two Bostwick brothers, Pete and Jimmy, both of them in turn world champions. In 1973 Howard Angus visited the United States and won the title. Until 1980 it was won consistently by Gene Scott except for 1979 when he was beaten by R.E. Howe.

A doubles championship was started in 1909 and many of the same players came to dominate it with various partners. Jay Gould won it in all nineteen times with three different partners.

A notable victory was that of the Van Alen brothers, J.H. (Jimmy) and W.L. (Sammy) in 1940. Even more remarkable, two more Van Alen brothers, J.L. and W.L. Jr (sons of Sammy), won the championship in 1967. The Van Alen family have been great supporters of Tennis in the United States. Jimmy originated the biennial match between undergraduates from Britain and America for the trophy which bears his name. Sammy was the first President of the US Court Tennis Association from 1955 to 1970, and is highly respected on both sides of the Atlantic.

Three sets of victorious brothers: (left to right) W.L. Van Alen, J.H. Van Alen, N.R. Knox, S.H. Knox III, G.H. Bostwick Jr, J.F.C. Bostwick.

It is remarkable that the doubles championship has been won by seven sets of brothers. Apart from the Van Alens, there were the Cuttings (1925), the Martin twins (1951), the Knox brothers (1958–59 and 1961), the Bostwicks (1969 and 1973) and the Howes (1974).

In 1956 the US Open championship was revived. The first player to have been recognised as Open champion was Jay Gould in 1921 when he beat Jock Soutar, but on his retirement the title was dropped. In fact, if not in title, his successors were Kinsella, Soutar and Etchebaster.

Etchebaster's retirement in 1954, and the founding of the US Court Tennis Association in 1955, were the main reasons for the institution of an Open championship. At first the professionals continued to prevail; for the first four years Albert (Jack) Johnson, then at New York, defeated Jimmy Dunn of Philadelphia in the final. But from 1960 to 1972 the championship was dominated by the Bostwick brothers; in those thirteen years Jimmy Bostwick won the title seven times and Pete Bostwick three times. Only Johnson, who won again in 1963 and 1965, and Ronald Hughes from England, who won in 1964, interrupted their monopoly.

From 1972 to 1977 the championship was dominated by another amateur, Gene Scott, but from 1978 professionals won again: J.J. Burke Jr of Philadelphia in 1978, Barry Toates of Boston in 1979 and Chris Ronaldson of Hampton Court in 1980.

In 1960 an Open doubles championship was first played. In its early years Jimmy Dunn was the most successful player, winning in 1960 and 1962 with W.I. Forbes Jr and from 1964 to 1967 with W.T. Vogt. The brothers Bostwick won in 1961 (when Dunn and Forbes had to scratch in the final owing to an injury to Dunn's leg), and from 1968 to 1970. The only non-American winners of the championship up until 1980 were Norwood Cripps, then at Queen's Club, and Chris Ronaldson, then at Melbourne, in 1977.

1980–2000

The explosion of interest in Tennis that occurred in the last decade of the twentieth century was built on a slow revival in the 1980s. In May 1981, the Jesmond Dene Tennis Court in Newcastle was re-opened, followed in 1986 by the restoration of the court at Holyport. No new Tennis court had been built in Britain since 1912 until the Oratory School did so in 1990, largely due to the initiative of its headmaster, Adrian Snow. Then in 1993, the Harbour Club court opened in London, its location in the basement involving a lower ceiling than normal. The Newmarket court was restored in 1995 thanks to the efforts of John Shneerson and Anthony Coles. A new court was built in 1997 for the Bristol and Bath club in the grounds of Clifton College with the aid of a lottery grant, and the previous court at the Hyde, Bridport was restored, also with a grant from the National Lottery. Both these last two courts were officially opened in 1998 by HRH the Earl of Wessex, who had performed the same service for the Harbour Club five years earlier.

The latest additions include two new courts, one of which has a glass grille wall, at the Prested Hall Racket Club near Chelmsford in Essex, built as part of a sports centre planned by Mike Carter. The second court at Cambridge has been restored and a magnificent new court at Middlesex University built with the aid of a very generous grant from Mr and Mrs Peter Luck-Hille. The latter was also opened by the Earl of Wessex, on 16 January 2000.

Although the court at Troon was closed in 1990, this is a net increase of ten courts making a total of twenty-six in Great Britain.

Unfortunately, the only remaining court in Ireland, built in black marble in the centre of Dublin by the Guinness family and currently owned by Dublin University College, is under threat. It is required for use as a concert hall.

In the United States, a new court – Prince's Court – has been opened in McLean, Virginia, a suburb of Washington D.C., and courts have been reopened at Lakewood, New Jersey (the Georgian Court) and Newport, Rhode Island (the National Tennis Club).

In Australia, new courts have been built at Ballarat in 1984 with invaluable support from John Gilbert; in Sydney in 1997 at Macquarie University, thanks to the determination of the University's Executive Officer Robert Lawton and the generous financial support of Wayne Davies; and at Romsey in 1999 where Gordon Cope-Williams was the driving force. In harmony with this new-found interest in Royal Tennis, Australia has produced some of the world's top players. Australia won the Bathurst Cup in 1982, for the first time ever, and the following year the Australian Royal Tennis Association was formed under the chairmanship of Bill Hepworth, largely made possible by generous sponsorship.

The men's world championship remains the pinnacle of international competition. It is still contested on a challenge basis over two legs. Each playing nation – Britain, Australia, America and France – has its own open championship and a challenger to the world champion is found from among the winners of these.

A new world champion emerged in 1981when Chris Ronaldson, the senior professional at Hampton Court, defeated the holder, Howard Angus. In the British eliminator, Ronaldson had beaten Frank Willis by 7 sets to 0 and in the final eliminator beat Barry Toates 7 sets to 4. In the championship match, Ronaldson won all four sets in the first leg 6–5, 6–5, 6–5, 6–2. In the second leg, Angus won the first set 6–2 and Ronaldson the second 6–2. Ronaldson was

Chris Ronaldson: among the cream of the world's professionals.

Chris Ronaldson (second left) retained his world Tennis title at Hampton Court in 1983, beating Wayne Davies 7–4. Others pictured: Lord Aberdare (left), Sir Clifford Chetwood and David Norman.

leading 5–4 in the third when Angus tore a calf muscle and had to retire, conceding the match to a very worthy new champion.

Chris Ronaldson's interest in Tennis began in 1971 when he joined the Oxford court as assistant to Peter Dawes and later became senior professional. On the opening of the two new courts in Melbourne in 1974, he was appointed senior professional and made a major contribution to their success. In 1978, he moved to Troon in Scotland and in 1979 to Hampton Court where he remains the senior professional.

He has written several books on the game including *Tennis: A Cut above the Rest*, which has an accompanying video, and has made a considerable contribution in the realms of administration and coaching. He has been called in to help with development plans at Bordeaux, Fairlawne and Holyport.

Chris Ronaldson first defended his title in 1983. Wayne Davies, a young Australian professional working at the New York Racquet and Tennis Club, had defeated a fellow Australian, Colin Lumley, in the eliminator. Ronaldson defeated Davies at Hampton Court by 7 sets to 4 to retain his title.

In 1984, Ronaldson became the first player to take the grand slam in one calendar year, winning all four open championships – British, French, US and Australian. In 1985, he rebuffed Davies in a second challenge by 7 sets to 1 at the Queen's Club to establish his complete supremacy at the time.

In 1987, he faced a third challenge. In the eliminators Lachlan Deuchar beat Graham Hyland and Wayne Davies beat Deuchar to emerge once again as the challenger to Ronaldson. In the challenge match at the Queen's Club, Davies beat Ronaldson by 7 sets to 4 and became the new world champion. He faced a challenge from Lachlan Deuchar in 1988, but won without difficulty by 7 sets to 1 on his home court in New York.

Lachlan Deuchar challenged again in 1991, having defeated Graham Hyland by 7 sets to love to qualify. Deuchar had a remarkable record. He had not lost a single match for almost two years and had won all four Open championships in the 1990–91 season. Davies, on the other hand, had had recurring injury problems including operations on both knees. The challenge match was played at the New York Racquet Club over three days in 1991 and after some closely fought sets Davies retained his title by 7 sets to 4.

Deuchar launched yet another challenge to Davies in 1993, having first defeated the leading amateur player, Julian Snow, in an eliminator in Melbourne.

Wayne Davies: first Australian to become world champion.

The challenge match was dramatic and the score towards the end of the final day was six sets all. Deuchar's giraffe service had proved very effective. However, Davies rallied and finally won the deciding set by 6 games to 1 to retain his title. This was a sad result for Deuchar whose record includes winning the British Open championship for six consecutive years, equalling the achievement of Chris Ronaldson.

Davies faced another challenge in 1994, on a home-and-away basis, this time from Robert Fahey, an Australian based at Hobart who had won the US, Australian and French Open championships in 1993. He was injured when leading by 1 set to 0 in the final of the British against Julian Snow but went on to eliminate Snow as a world championship challenger by 12 sets to 7, in a home-and-away match.

The first leg of the championship match was played at Hobart where, on his home court, Fahey won by 7 sets to 1. The second leg took place in New York. Davies made a huge effort to offset Fahey's lead, winning the first three sets, but Fahey won the fourth. Fahey needed just one more set to win the match on the second day. Davies won the first set, but Fahey took the second and with it the match and the world title.

Fahey's first challenger emerged in 1995 after three elimination matches. In the first, Chris Bray, the professional at Petworth, beat Julian Snow at Hampton Court. In the second, Bray played Deuchar at Hobart and was leading by 6 sets to 1 when Deuchar had to retire with an ankle injury. Bray then played Davies in the third eliminator and lost to him by 7 sets to 1, leaving a repeat match, Davies v. Fahey, for the championship.

Once again a splendid match was spoilt by injury. Fahey was leading by 6 sets to 2 after the second day's play when Davies retired with a back injury and Fahey remained champion.

The following year, 1996, brought forth a number of potential challengers. Davies was the US Open champion, Frank Filippelli the Australian and Mike Gooding the French. Fahey had beaten Deuchar in the final of the British. In the eliminator matches, Gooding beat Filippelli and Davies beat Gooding. The final challenge match was played in Melbourne when Fahey soundly defeated Davies by 7 sets to 1.

Julian Snow has dominated the the British Amateur championship, winning for thirteen years out of fourteen. He won the British Open in 1992, 1993, 1994 and 1998, when he beat Steve Virgona, an up-and-coming young Australian player, in the final. In 1998 he also won the Open doubles with James Male. By winning the 1997 US Open he qualified to challenge for the world championship in 1998. He defeated Chris Bray at Lord's by 5 sets to 2, Mike Gooding in Melbourne by 7 sets to 2 and challenged Fahey for the crown. He made a very gallant attempt

Robert Fahey, perhaps the finest player of our time, took the world championship in 1994 at the age of 23.

Julian Snow: dominated amateur Tennis from 1987 into the twenty-first century.

to dethrone the champion – the match stood at 3 sets all and 5 games all at one point – but eventually lost by 4 sets to 7.

The candidates for the 2000 challenge were Chris Bray, who won the British Open in 1997, the US Open in 1998 and the Australian Open in August 1999, beating Fahey in 4 sets in the final; and Wayne Davies, winner of the US Open of 1999 at the age of 43. A preliminary eliminator took place at Hobart in February 2000. Bray led by 3 sets to 1 on the first day and, after the second day, by 5 sets to 3. On the final day some magnificent tennis was played as Davies fought back to level the score at 5 sets all and to win the last two sets and the match by 7 sets to 5. It was a famous victory, entitling Davies to challenge Fahey for the championship, his tenth appearance in the final of this great event.

The championship match was played at Hobart later in February and was dominated by Fahey who won by 7 sets to love. Davies never gave up and was unlucky not to win the sixth set after being 5 games all, but he found the champion in overpowering form.

On 20 November 2000, Fahey defeated Chris Bray in the final of the British Open championship at the Queen's Club to achieve the Grand Slam of winning all four national championships in the same calendar year. The only previous occasion when this was achieved was in 1984 by Chris Ronaldson.

Apart from the world championship and the national Open championships, singles and doubles, many other competitions are held regularly. The UK annual fixture list includes championships for amateur and professional players of all ages and standards, both men and ladies. In addition to the well-established championships for the leading players, i.e. the Professional and Amateur singles and doubles, there are championships for every age group from the under 12s to the over 70s and for every handicap group. The inter-club championships are run in two divisions for the Field Trophy and the Brodie Cup; and the national league, which is run by the Real Tennis Professionals Association (RTPA), involves approximately 200 players in seven divisions. The Bathurst Cup attracts entrants from the four main Tennis-playing countries and rotates every two years between them. Apart from the major competitions run by the Tennis and Rackets Association, there are innumerable club competitions played in every court worldwide.

Lord Aberdare, President of the T&RA, with one of the game's major sponsors, John Ritblat of British Land.

LADIES' TENNIS

IN May 1981, at Moreton Morrell Tennis Club, a men's world tournament was taking place. Chris Ronaldson, who two weeks earlier had wrested the world championship from Howard Angus at Queen's Club, was playing. Outside the rain-sodden marquee, Alan Lovell, then Chairman of the Tennis Committee of the Tennis and Rackets Association, turned to Chris's wife Lesley and said, 'Have you thought of starting a Ladies' Association? You would have the blessing of the Tennis and Rackets Association.' Lesley,

British Ladies' champion in 1979, 1980, 1981 and 1987, needed no further encouragement.

With Chris's help, a draft constitution was prepared for discussion at a meeting arranged for 31 October 1981 at Moreton Morrell during the British Ladies' singles handicap tournament. The constitution was approved unanimously and the Ladies' Real Tennis Association was on its way. Nominations for a Chairman, Hon. Secretary and Hon. Treasurer were requested to arrive before the next meeting, to be held

Penny Lumley, world champion.

Lesley Ronaldson, British champion in the eighties.

on 16 January at Hampton Court during the first British Ladies' Open doubles championship. Lesley Ronaldson was elected Chairman, Vivian Dawes Hon. Secretary and Alex Warren-Piper Hon. Treasurer. A lady member was invited to sit on the Tennis Committee, and Sheila Mackintosh was duly nominated and elected.

At the tournament, Sheila Mackintosh and Jill Cottrell became the Ladies' doubles champions, beating Evelyn David (US) and Lesley Ronaldson.

Lesley led the Association, diligently and with great enthusiasm, for its first ten years. Sheila Mackintosh, a former Captain of the Great Britain ladies' squash team, took over the chairmanship of the Ladies' Association in 1991, quietly asserting her authority as the Association expanded. In 1998, she handed over to Sarah McGivern, ably qualified professionally to steer the Association in an increasingly technological world.

In 1998 the Council decided to invite the LRTA Chairman to be a member of the Council by right.

Supported by the hard-working committee, they were responsible for the organisation and running of the British Open singles and doubles tournaments, the ladies' handicap (division 1 and 2) tournaments, the Ladies' Masters, the LRTA International, and the Billy Ross-Skinner Invitation Mixed Doubles. A tournament for beginners and under twenty-fives was introduced, as was a handicap mixed doubles; an unofficial tournament took place annually in Paris; and a golf and Tennis day became an established and popular annual event, as did a mothers and daughters tournament.

The continued work and loyalty given by Treasurer Alex Garside (née Warren-Piper) and Secretary Vivian Dawes ensured that Association enjoyed invaluable stability over many years. In 1978, Vivian Dawes's husband Peter, along with Paul Danby, suggested the first British Ladies' Open be held at Seacourt.

Front row (left to right): *Maggie Wright, Jane Lippincott (US), Charlotte Cornwallis, Clare Southwell, Sally Jones, Susie Falkner, Jill Newby.* Back row (left to right): *Sheilagh Owens, Brenda Sabbag (US), Anne Balcerkiewicz, Gitte Dunkley, Catherine Walker, Christine Anies (France), Alex Garside, Evelyn David (US), Melvyn Pignon, Sarah McGivern, Ros Lake, Caroline Harding, Jane Vaughan, Sheila Macintosh, Viv Dawes, Lesley Ronaldson, Carolyn Armstrong-Smith, Kate Leeming (Aus), Sue Haswell, Fiona Deuchar (Aus).*

Sally Jones, a fine all-round sportswoman.

As the number of players and thus international liaison increased, the first world championship – played as a tournament and not a challenge – took place in 1985 in Melbourne. Talented Australian Judy Clarke beat Lesley Ronaldson in the closest of finals 6–3, 5–6, 6–5. Judy also won the second world championship, in 1987 – it was held every two years – beating Katrina Allen (Queen's Club) 6–5, 6–4 at Seacourt.

Katrina Allen had already made her name as British champion from 1983–86. A player of great natural talent, her flamboyance at times gave the impression that even she did not know what stroke she would play next. During her career she was world doubles champion with Lesley Ronaldson (1987), French champion (singles and doubles), US champion (singles and doubles) and Australian champion (singles and doubles).

Then came the phenomenal career of Penny Lumley (previously Fellows, née Bland). Penny won the world championship in 1989 in Philadelphia, beating Sally Jones 6–4, 5–6, 6–3; in 1991 in Hobart, again beating Sally Jones 6–4, 5–6, 6–4; in 1995 in Newport, Rhode Island, beating Sue Haswell 5–6,

6–4, 6–0; in 1997 in Ballarat, again with victory over Sue Haswell 6-3, 6-1; and for a fifth time in 1999 at the Royal Court, Hampton Court, beating Sue Haswell 6–4, 4–6, 6–4.

Penny Lumley was undoubtedly one of the outstanding sportswomen of the 1990s. In a span of ten years she won five world championship titles, four world doubles titles, was British Open champion eight times and the British Open doubles champion four times. In 1996–97 she achieved the ultimate when she won the Grand Slam, taking the British, French, American and Australian Opens and the world singles and doubles titles. In 1996 she was awarded the Greenwood Trophy for the most improved player of the year, and also the Baerlein Cup. In 1998 and 1999 she was again awarded the Baerlein Cup by the Tennis and Rackets Association in recognition of the best amateur performance (male or female). With a marvellous temperament, Penny was a wonderful ambassadress for the game.

By the end of the century, a small but established nucleus of world-class players had formed. Headed by Penny, they included Sue Haswell (RTC), Katrina Allen (Queen's Club), Sally Jones (Moreton Morrell), Alex Garside (Seacourt), Fiona Deuchar (Australia and RTC), Charlotte Cornwallis (Bristol and Bath) and Kate Leeming (Australia and the Oratory), the last two having turned professional.

Of these, the career of Sally Jones merits attention. She has twice been runner-up to Penny Lumley in the world championship (1989 and 1991), each time taking the match to three sets; she was world champion in 1993 beating Charlotte Cornwallis in Bordeaux; and she and her regular partner Alex Garside have taken the world doubles title twice. She has been the British champion twice, and the British doubles champion seven times, six of those with Alex Garside. Strong and athletic, Sally is a talented all-round sportswoman. She was a British schoolgirl lawn-tennis champion, played lawn tennis for Warwickshire, squash for South Wales, and managed five blues at Oxford. As a sports journalist, she continues to make a valuable contribution to the growth of the ladies' game.

Ladies' tennis has come a long way since those early days in the 1960s when just a handful of women knew the game and most of those would be playing at Queen's, Seacourt or Hampton Court. That first British Open in 1978 was won by Anna Moore, a lawn-tennis player who had been playing real tennis with men at Seacourt since the club was formed in 1965. Entrants for the Open numbered ten – six from Seacourt and four others.

Four outstanding players: (left to right) world champion Penny Lumley, Charlotte Cornwallis, Alex Garside and Sally Jones.

In the UK, lady players are now eligible for selection for their club teams and to compete in the National League, the Field Trophy and the Brodie Cup, the Bridgeman Cup, the Seacourt Silver Racquet and the Henry Leaf Cup. Annual category tournaments are open to men and women, and matches with mixed teams are common, giving those lady players with equal handicaps the chance to play against men of similar standards in everything but strength.

PART II

RACKETS

The King's Bench prison in 1822 showing the Rackets courts in the background.

HOW RACKETS BEGAN

TRACING THE HISTORY OF TENNIS from its early beginnings in about the twelfth century, it clearly emerges that a number of different games were played under the general umbrella of what Scaino called *giuoco della palla*. There was *pallone* (balloon ball), *jeu quarré*, *jeu à dedans*, *longue paume* and other variations played with various implements, or none at all. But the theme running through them all is that of two sides engaged in combat across a dividing line. Scaino calls it a battle.

Rackets is quite different from this family of ball games in being played against a wall and not across a net. The only game that resembles it is pelota in its various forms. Pelota is of Basque origin and *frontons* are to be found in many a Basque village and town, but they never spread to Northern Europe. Joseph Strutt, in his *Sports and Pastimes of the People of England*, makes no mention of a game of Rackets. The truth is that Rackets started in the debtors' prisons, the Fleet and the King's Bench, in the mid-eighteenth century.

Many a gentleman confined for debt was able to lead a reasonable life if he had friends to support him and many of them, familiar with the game of Tennis, brought their rackets into the prison to while away the tedious hours. They found the high prison walls ideal for this purpose.

Rackets was certainly played at the Fleet in 1749. A humorous poem of that date, written by 'a Gentleman of the College' contains these lines:

Within whose ample Oval is a Court,
Where the more active and robust resort,
And glowing, exercise a manly Sport
(Strong exercise with mod'rate Food is good,
It drives in sprightful streams the circling Blood;)
While those with Rackets struck the flying Ball,
Some play at Nine Pins, Wrestlers take a Fall;

Beneath a Tent some drink, and some above
Are slily in their Chambers making Love;
Venus and Bacchus each keeps here a Shrine,
And many Vot'ries have to Love and Wine.

An illustration accompanying this poem shows a new arrival being introduced to the cook by the chamberlain; he has evidently already met the tapster and the gaoler. In the background a game of Rackets is in progress, from which it is quite clear that Tennis rackets were being used at this early period in the game's history.

In 1780 John Howard published a report on *The State of the Prisons in England and Wales*. He had visited the Fleet in 1776, and writes at one point in his report: 'I mentioned the billiard table. They also play in the yard at skittles, missisippi*, fives, tennis, etc.'

The situation was similar at another debtors' prison, the King's Bench in Southwark. John Howard wrote of the King's Bench: 'One can scarcely even enter the walls without seeing parties of skittles, missisippi, portobello, tennis, fives, etc.'; and later James Neild recorded: 'Part of the ground next the wall is appropriated for playing at rackets and fives.'

In 1780 the old Fleet Prison was destroyed during the Gordon Riots, but it was soon rebuilt, and reopened in 1782. Rackets continued to be popular there and a good view of 'the Bare' or Rackets ground in 1808 is contained in Pugin and Rowlandson's *Microcosm of London*. Rackets at the King's Bench is also illustrated in the *Microcosm of London* and in a print drawn by Theo. Lane, engraved by Geo. Hunt and published by Charles Hunt of Covent Garden.

---

*A form of bagatelle, normally played on a board, but in this case no doubt on the ground.

James Neild wrote on the general state of prisons in England, Scotland and Wales in 1812. He notes that at the Fleet there was:

Surgeon, none. No medical assistance in case of sickness [but] a spacious yard behind the Prison, in which the Prisoners play at skittles, fives, and tennis, etc.

Fives was sometimes confused with Rackets, as appears in a print of 1788 in the Crace collection entitled 'Fives, Played at the Tennis Court, Leicester Fields'. Here again the game involved is clearly Rackets and the print provides the first evidence of the game being played outside prison walls.

A game of Rackets at the Fleet is described in *Finish to Life in London*, by Pierce Egan in 1829.

The fat Knight, it appears, had flattered himself that having received lessons from the late celebrated players at racket, Messrs Davies and Powel, and also some instructions as to the game of fives, under that phenomenon, the late Pat Cavanagh, he laughed outright at the efforts of the 'Young One' and the Corinthian, as mere commoners; and, over his wine, offered to make a match with our heroes, for a 'rump and a dozen!' The proposition was immediately accepted by Tom and Jerry; and Logic was quite pleased that it would afford him a fine opportunity of visiting his

A new arrival at the Fleet Prison.

old acquaintances and friends on board the 'Fleet'! But the 'uncommonly big gentleman' soon found out his mistake, to his cost and ridicule; also, that talking and doing were widely different; and the loud laugh was now turned against the fat Knight, on his being floored by a false step, in his eagerness to strike the ball. 'Well, my friend,' said Old Mordecai, who was 'blowing his cloud', and watching the movements of the game, with a grin upon his countenance, 'Vere's your rump now? Vat, you have dropped down upon your knees! I vill bet de synagogue to a vatch-box, that Young Lambert does not get upon his legs again, vidout some help. Vy, you have made de valls of de Fleet shake again!' The whole of the spectators joined in the laugh at the ridiculous situation of Sir John Blubber; and several of them offered to run for a doctor, 'as they were sure his latter end must have been very much injured by so severe a fall'. Logic and Jerry immediately offered the 'fat Knight' their assistance, who, upon obtaining the use of his legs, was quite out of temper at the satirical remarks and jests levelled against his bulky frame, but more especially with Old Mordecai, and immediately Sir John gave up the match in favour of his opponents.

In 1832 Pierce Egan published his *Book of Sports and Mirror of Life* in periodic issues at threepence each. Number XV was entitled 'The Game of Rackets'.

It includes William Hazlitt's magnificent obituary of John Cavanagh, the fives player, from his essay, 'The Indian Jugglers'. No greater tribute has ever been paid to any sportsman than this eloquent piece of prose.

The full text of Pierce Egan's article is as follows:

THE GAME OF RACKETS is a truly pleasing Sport; not only for the spirit and amusement which it affords to the mind, but the good results which the constitution derives from such active exercise; there is no game, perhaps, not even cricket itself, which combines so well skill with so much bustle, that even an indolent man must be alive to all the movements of the game, while the bat is in his hand. The racket player is always on the move; standing still is entirely out of the question; and two or three games at rackets are calculated to do more good towards the restoration of health, and keep the frame clear from the effects of gout and rheumatism, than the whole contents of Apothecary's Hall. In an enclosed court it may be played all the year round; while in an open court it can only be played in the summer.

It is now eight or ten years since old one-eyed Powell's establishment (so designated from having lost one of his eyes by a ball, while playing a game at rackets) was broken up by his Court being broken down. All who have any acquaintance with rackets recollect him, in his day, a first-rate player, and, after his day, competent to cool the consequence of many who fancied themselves good performers.

The game of rackets is not like tennis, which is played by dropping a ball over a central net, on each side of which the players stand; but, at rackets, the ball is struck against what is called a head-wall, and returned at the bound to the same wall, each player endeavouring so to strike it against the wall that his adversary may not be able to return it; he who does not return it, either loses a point (or, as it is technically termed, 'an ace') or has his 'hand out' that is to say, forfeits the situation in which he would be able to add to his score of the game. People, in general, are not aware of the skill required to play the game well, and the fact is, the better it is played the more easy it appears.

There are several open Racket Courts, independent of the King's Bench and the Fleet Prisons, where gentlemen seldom go voluntarily for the sake of playing, although they take it now and then 'upon compulsion'. There is a good open Court at the Belvidere, Pentonville; another at the Eagle Tavern, in the City Road; and the proprietor of White Conduit House a third; but the fault of these places is that the company is not sufficiently select, and that a gentleman who is fond of the game (and all are fond of it who can play at all) are there compelled to join a miscellany of very respectable persons no doubt, but not of the highest grade in society. As it is, the ardour of some individuals of rank and education in pursuit of the game induces them to overlook the inconvenience to which we have alluded, and we must do the proprietors of the Courts we have named the justice to say that they contrive to keep persons of really questionable character and appearance at a distance.

Independent of 'the old school', there are many first-rate players at present in the height of their performances. There can be no objection to naming and describing the qualifications of a few of the professors, who, generally speaking, have other and very reputable employment besides being racket players. There is no question that Pittman is the best player in England – we do not mean Thomas Pittman, who some years ago held this envied station, but his younger brother John, who is most accomplished at all points – the volley, that is, returning a ball before it touches the ground; the cut, a sharp hit which strikes the ball so low against the wall, and so swiftly, that on its return, there is little or no hop to enable the adversary to strike it; and the twisting drop, given gently and quietly from the racket, in consequence of which, the ball, after it reaches the head-wall, falls dead at once, and a return is almost impossible. In these respects, and more, John Pittman is perhaps the most perfect player that ever existed, and probably better than his brother Tom, in his best day.

We know that Tom has some old friends who will deny this position, but our opinion is formed after seeing both perform, the one ten years, and the other a short time since. Tom Pittman is still capital, and superior to John in cramp matches, where he plays under certain disadvantages, in order to make the contest with an inferior player more equal. With his back-hand he can beat nearly all the amateurs, and there are few that can compete with him when his hands are tied together at the wrist, and he is consequently obliged to hold the racket with both; he has beaten tolerable players in this way, and with the addition of a couple of flat irons fastened to his ankles on the inside. If we mistake not, it was he who, some years ago, played with a rolling pin instead of a racket, and won his match. Matthew Pittman may also be reckoned a good player, but he is not to be named in the same century with his two brothers. John Pittman's principal rival is a person called 'Tawney Sam', a small but active little man, who hits with the greatest nicety and precision, and who last year carried away the prize-racket from some excellent competitors, among them a person named Morris, who in some points of the game is superior to Sam, but who is by no means so certain.

Morris has a fine free hit, perhaps the severest in England, and is a fine partner in a four match. His play and that of 'Tawney Sam' are in some respects contrasted, for Sam is all delicacy and finesse, and Morris all force and vigour. Morris has a one-eyed friend, whose name we do not know, who is celebrated for playing under his leg, and who in this manner will contend against any man in England, although, in other points, he is inferior to several. Sowden has been a player quite from his childhood, and, on the whole, is perhaps only inferior to one or two, while, in some particulars, he exceeds them; he would unquestionably be first-rate, and on a level with John Pittman, if he had a good back-hand; but there he fails, and is often put to a difficulty in order to get at a ball with his front-hand, that ought to be returned with his back-hand. He is a capital player to give odds, for then he is

perfectly confident; but he seems a little nervous when opposed to a man of equal or greater skill.

These are the prime players of London, and so good that any of them could give what is called 'the odd hand' to country performers: giving the odd hand is about equal to giving one-third of the game. Besides these, there are Lamb and Chapman, and half a score more second raters, besides the players who are in the habit of exhibiting in the King's Bench and Fleet, of whose merits we are not competent to speak. Many distinguished members of the Prize Ring have been good players at fives and rackets, and it may be remembered that the celebrated Jem Belcher lost his eye at the game.

The game of rackets in the Fleet and King's Bench Prisons, has often turned out a source of livelihood to a number of the prisoners who have been attached to the sport. The following anecdote of a man of the name of Hoskins, who was at one period of his confinement the *racket-master*, a capital player, and who altered the game from 11 to 15, may not altogether prove uninteresting to the reader: Hoskins made the Fives Court, which is so much played in during the summer time by the prisoners, and also visitors to the King's Bench Prison; he was an industrious and sober man, and also from his knowledge of the game continually in practice; and waiting upon gentlemen with the bats and balls, and frequently taking a hand in a match, he was enabled to support his family of seven children with credit to himself, and with variable success, until at length a disease settled in his legs, and totally incapacitated him for nearly the last twenty years of his life from following any employment.

Poor Hoskins might have exclaimed with Sterne's Starling – 'I can't get out!' In the year 1798, a material part of the King's Bench was consumed by fire, whether by accident or design was never ascertained; the arched chambers will show where the fire raged, they are the rebuilt part, and said to be fire-proof, so that a fire taking place in any one of these chambers cannot extend beyond it. Hoskins' life was one of continued vicissitudes, which even imprisonment could not abate; he was once the Post-master of the prison. Hoskins was a Cornish man, and of a very good family; his father was a respectable surgeon, and Hoskins was brought up a gentleman; he was here THIRTY-EIGHT years, at the suit of a single creditor, one whom he once called friend and benefactor, and for a disputed debt which he vowed he would never pay. He was a good-tempered, convivial, amiable and benevolent man.

A word of advice from an old professional in a debtors' prison.

Hoskins was one of the burnt out: he had been at the time so many years a prisoner that no connection remained to draw him back to the world he had quitted; the BENCH was *his* world! and he surveyed its ruins with a pensive and powerful feeling; as though the work of desolation had done its worst, and robbed him of his home. In this state of mind he reared himself a shed from the scattered fragments of the former pile, and lived amidst the ruins, seemingly content, sharing his meal with a poor mouse, who every morning visited him at the breakfast hour, and was fed. Hoskins and the mouse found a home amidst desolation, and they sojourned together in unabated friendship, until the builder's hand disturbed their good harmony and good fellowship.

It is, however, due to Mr Jones, the Marshall, to confess his kindness to this forlorn individual; he supported him for the last two years of his life, and buried him on his decease, in the month of December 1823, after an *uninterrupted imprisonment of* THIRTY-EIGHT *years!!!*

During the *Swellish* times, as they have been since termed by those persons who were in the habit of 'making money' by the rich debtors, when those high-bred ones the late Honorable *Tom* Coventry, and the late Captain *Tom* Best (whose memorable but unfortunate duel with Lord Camelford, gave him great notoriety in the fashionable and sporting world), *sojourned* within the walls of BANCO REGIS, or were otherwise lodged within its *Rules* prescribed for the health of the patients of the Marshall – the GAME OF RACKETS was in high estimation, and very large sums of money were lost and won upon it.

The King's Bench Prison at that period was one continued scene of *gaiety* and *dash* – indeed, it was like any thing else but a place of confinement. The promenade, almost every evening, until the cry of 'all out' occurred, was a complete picture of *le beau monde*. It exhibited some of the most elegant dressed females in the kingdom; the finest, nay, fashionable women who felt not the slightest reproach by visiting their unfortunate friends in 'durance vile'.

In truth, in this 'place of retirement' from the eye of the public, a number of men of fortune, who had 'outrun the constable', had taken up their abode in order to avoid the bore, threatenings, and a thousand other 'little disagreeables' from those persons who 'only ask for their own', to enjoy a bit of *quiet* life, and join in the well-known *chant* –

Welcome, welcome, brother debtor,
To this poor, but merry place;
Where no Bailiff, Dun, or Setter,
Dares to shew his measly face!

The game of rackets was carried on with great spirit under the patronage of the above fashionable leaders; and the ground was frequently covered with visitors of the most elegant description to witness the trials of skill, and great matches between those celebrated players of the game, Messrs Lewis, Mackey, and Smith.

Since the above period, indeed, almost to a very recent date, the brave Major Campbell has been the principal hero in the field respecting his superiority at the game of rackets. It is too true that the Major had rather a 'long innings', nearly fourteen years in the situation of a lodger to Mr Jones. The high spirit of the Major – his fine stamina – his great activity – and his attachment to rackets – united with considerable experience, and his 'long practice' in the Racket Court, rendered him a first-rate player in every point of view. As a 'gentleman' he had scarcely any thing like a competitor; and with the very best professed players of the day, the Major always proved himself a most powerful opponent. But he is now restored to the society of his friends and enjoying the 'Sweets of Liberty'; and should his king and his country demand his services he is quite ready to make use of *balls* of another description.

Ireland has also given birth to some celebrated racket players – Mr Carney, a gentleman well known in the sporting circles at the West end of the Town, distinguished himself in a number of great matches, not only as a first-rate player, but with eminent success, under the patronage of the late Duke of Richmond: indeed, Mr Carney was viewed by his countrymen as the *crack* player in Ireland. He is also a capital wrestler. Mr Carney won a double match in March 1825, for 300*l* made on the spur of the moment between him and the celebrated Mr Hayne, by defeating the '*great gun*' of Windsor, Tom Cannon, in a trial of skill at wrestling, at Ireland's garden, Brighton. Mr Carney likewise won the billiard match with Jonathan Kempfield, on his own table, and also acknowledged the first player in the world; but it is only justice to state that Jonathan gave *seventy* points out of one hundred to Mr Carney. The latter person is also distinguished for throwing a heavy weight to a much greater distance than any other man in the kingdom.

We flatter ourselves that the following sketch of the late *Pat Cavanagh*, so truly celebrated as a Fives player, and also a 'good one' at rackets, will prove highly interesting to the readers of the BOOK OF SPORTS:–

'When a person dies,* who does any thing better than any one else in the world, which so many others are trying to do well, it leaves a gap in society. It is not likely that any one will now see the game of Fives played in its perfection for many years to come – for Cavanagh is dead, and has not left his peer behind him. It may be said there are things of more importance than striking a ball against a wall – there are things, indeed, that make more noise and do as little good, such as making war and peace, making speeches and answering them, making verses and blotting them, making money and throwing it away. But the Game of Fives is what no one despises who has ever played at it. It is the finest exercise for the body, and the best relaxation for the mind. The Roman poet said that "Care mounted behind the horseman and stuck to his

skirts." But this remark would not have applied to the Fives player. He who takes to playing at Fives is twice young. He feels neither the past nor the future "in the instant". Debts, taxes, "domestic treason, foreign levy, nothing can touch him further". He has no other wish, no other thought, from the moment the game begins, but that of striking the ball, of placing it, of *making* it. This Cavanagh was sure to do. Whenever he touched the ball there was an end of the chase. His eye was certain, his hand fatal, his presence of mind complete. He could do what he pleased, and he always knew exactly what to do. He saw the whole game, and played it; took instant advantage of his adversary's weakness, and recovered balls, as if by a miracle and sudden thought, that every one gave for lost. He had equal power and skill, quickness and judgment. He could either outwit his antagonist by finesse, or beat him by main strength. Sometimes, when he seemed preparing to send the ball with the full swing of his arm, he would by a slight turn of his wrist drop it within an inch of the line. In general, the ball came from his hand, as if from a racket, in a straight horizontal line; so that it was in vain to attempt to overtake or stop it. As it was said of a great orator, that he never was at a loss for a word, and for the properest word, so Cavanagh always could tell the degree of force necessary to be given to a ball, and the precise direction in which it should be sent. He did his work with the greatest ease; never took more pains than was necessary, and while others were fagging themselves to death, was as cool and collected as if he had just entered the court. His style of play was as remarkable as his power of execution; he had no affectation, no trifling.

He did not throw away the game to show off an attitude or try an experiment. He was a fine, sensible, manly player, who did what he could, but that was more than any one could even affect to do. His blows were not undecided and ineffectual – lumbering like Mr Wordsworth's epic poetry, nor wavering like Mr Coleridge's lyric prose, nor short of the mark like Mr Brougham's speeches, nor wide of it like Mr Canning's wit, nor foul like the *Quarterly*, nor *let* balls like the *Edinburgh Review*. Cobbett and Junius together would have made a Cavanagh. He was the best *up-hill* player in the world; even when his adversary was fourteen, he would play on the same or better, and as he never flung away the game through carelessness and conceit, he never gave it up through laziness or want of heart. The only peculiarity of his play was that he never *volleyed*, but let the balls hop; but if they rose an inch from the ground he never missed having them. There was not only nobody equal, but nobody second

---

*John Cavanagh died in January 1810, in Burbage Street, St Giles's.

to him. It is supposed that he could give any other player half the game, or beat them with his left hand. His service was tremendous. He once played Woodward and Meredith together (two of the best players in England) in the Fives Court, St Martin's Street, and made seven and twenty aces following, by services alone – a thing unheard of. He another time played Peru, who was considered a first-rate Fives player, a match of the best out of five games, and in the three first games, which of course decided the match, Peru got only one ace. Cavanagh was an Irishman by birth, and a house-painter by profession. He had once laid aside his working-dress, and walked up, in his smartest clothes, to the Rosemary Branch, to have an afternoon's pleasure. A person accosted him, and asked him if he would have a game. So they agreed to play for half-a-crown a game, and a bottle of cider. The first game began – it was seven, eight, ten, thirteen, fourteen, all. Cavanagh won it. The next was the same. They played on, and each game was hardly contested. 'There,' said the unconscious Fives player, 'there was a stroke that Cavanagh could not take: I never played better in my life, and yet I can't win a game. I don't know how it is.' However, they played on, Cavanagh winning every game, and the by-standers drinking the cider, and laughing all the time. In the twelfth game, when Cavanagh was only four, and the stranger thirteen, a person came in and said, 'What! are you here, Cavanagh?' The words were no sooner pronounced than the astonished player let the ball drop from his hand, and saying, "What! have I been breaking my heart all this time to beat Cavanagh?" refused to make another effort. "And yet, I give you my word," said Cavanagh, telling the story with some triumph, "I played all the while with my clenched fist." He used frequently to play matches at Copenhagen-house for wagers and dinners. The wall against which they play is the same that supports the kitchen-chimney, and when the wall resounded louder than usual, the cooks exclaimed, "Those are the Irishman's balls," and the joints trembled on the spit!

Goldsmith consoled himself that there were places where he too was admired; and Cavanagh was the admiration of all the Fives Courts where he ever played. Mr Powell, when he played matches in the Court in St Martin's Street, used to fill his gallery at half-a-crown a head, with amateurs and admirers of talent in whatever department it is shown. He could not have shown himself in any ground in England, but he would have been immediately surrounded with inquisitive gazers, trying to find out in what part of his frame his unrivalled skill lay, as politicians wonder to see the balance of Europe suspended in Lord Castlereagh's face, and admire the trophies of the British Navy lurking under Mr Croker's hanging brow. Now Cavanagh was as good looking a man as the Noble Lord, and much better looking than the Right Honorable Secretary. He had a clear, open countenance, and did not look sideways, or down, like Mr Murray the book-seller. He was a young fellow of sense, humour, and courage. He once had a quarrel with a waterman at Hungerford-stairs, and, they say, served him out in great style. In a word, there are hundreds at this day who cannot mention his name without admiration, as the best fives-player that perhaps ever lived (the greatest excellence of which they have any notion), and the noisy shout of the ring happily stood him instead of the unheard voice of posterity! The only person who seems to have excelled as much in another way as Cavanagh did in his, was the late John Davies, the racket-player. It was remarked of him that he did not seem to follow the ball, but the ball seemed to follow him. Give him a foot of wall, and he was sure to make the ball. The four best racket-players of that day, were Jack Spines, Jem Harding, Armitage and Church. Davies could give any one of these two hands a time, that is, half the game, and each of these, at their best, could give the best player now in London, the same odds.

Such are the gradations in all exertions of human skill and art. He once played four capital players together and beat them. He was also a first-rate tennis player, and an excellent fives player. In the Fleet or King's Bench he would have stood against Powell, who was reckoned the best open-ground player of his time. This last-mentioned player, till lately, was keeper of the Fives Court, and might have used for a motto over his door – '*Who enters here forgets himself, his country, and his friends.*' And the best of it is that by the calculation of the odds, none of the three are worth remembering! Cavanagh died from the bursting of a blood-vessel, which prevented him from playing for the last two or three years. This, he was often heard to say, he thought hard upon him. He was fast recovering, however, when he was suddenly carried off, to the regret of all who knew him. As Mr Peel made it a qualification of the present Speaker, Mr Manners Sutton, that he was an excellent moral character, so Jack Cavanagh was a zealous Catholic, and could not be persuaded to eat meat on a Friday, the day on which he died. We have paid this willing tribute to his memory:

Let no rude hand deface it,
And his forlorn – Hic jacet.'

Cavanagh must have been a wonderful player to evoke such a paean of praise from Hazlitt.

Charles Dickens was familiar with Rackets at the Fleet and mentions it on several occasions when Mr Pickwick was unfortunate enough to find himself in that prison. For example:

> *The area formed by the wall in that part of Fleet in which Mr Pickwick stood was just wide enough to make a good racket court, one side being formed, of course, by the wall itself, and the other by that portion of the prison which looked (or rather would have looked, but for the wall) towards St Paul's Cathedral. Sauntering or sitting about, in every possible attitude of listless idleness, were a great number of debtors... Some were shabby, some were smart, many dirty, a few clean... Lolling from the windows which commanded a view of the promenade were a number of persons, some in noisy conversation with their acquaintance below, others playing at ball with some adventurous throwers outside; and others looking on at the racket players, or watching the boys as they cried the game.*

The popularity of Rackets at the debtors' prisons made the post of Racket master one that was highly prized. In 1814 there were six Racket masters at the King's Bench prison, administering four courts. They would provide rackets, balls and a ball-boy for a fee. A new racket cost a guinea and the court fee was sixpence. Out of this the Racket master paid fourpence for two new balls and a halfpenny to the ball-boy, retaining three-halfpence for himself. Extra balls were charged for, and some strong players, we are told, used four balls in a game.

At the King's Bench the appointment of Racket master was made by the authorities, but at the Fleet he was elected twice a year by the prisoners themselves.

The situation drew comment from the Committee of the House of Commons on the King's Bench, Fleet and Marshalsea prisons in respect of the King's Bench:

> *There is however a practice, which, though it would be injudicious altogether to prevent, might still be put under regulation. The practice alluded to arises out of the racket-grounds. For a long period, a portion of the court has been divided into four racket-grounds, which are held by six masters; the successor to each ground pays something to the first occupant, on his quitting the prison, partly for the purchase of rackets, and partly for the goodwill. One of the present racket-masters paid as*

large a sum as six guineas. A small fee is paid by the players: and though it be said that any one may play there who chuses, whether he pays or not, yet it is also said that this circumstance hardly ever happens, there being a point of honor felt by the prisoners upon this subject. The objection seems to be, the permission given to strangers to play there; it is an open place, where any one may play, and as such it may become the resort of the idle and the dissolute. As an exercise and amusement to the prisoners it is unobjectionable; as a place of resort, from the opportunity it may furnish to gambling, it is fitting that some regulation should be adopted to limit the practice as at present existing.

And of the Fleet the Committee concluded:

> *The system of letting the Racket-grounds within the prison exists here as in the King's bench; but from the situation of the Fleet, they are more frequented by strangers. Mr Nixon says that the profit to the holder of each racket-ground may amount to one guinea per week. Your Committee are of the opinion, that this practice requires the same regulations as that which they have pointed out, when reporting on a similar usage existing in the King's Bench prison.*

The following is an example of a Racket master's election address of 1841 – interestingly, seeking support from ladies as well as gentlemen:

> *Ladies and Gentlemen,*
> *The time having now arrived when, in conformity with the established rules of the place of which we are at present inmates, it is customary for such persons as are desirous of becoming elected as Masters of the Racquet Grounds, to canvass your votes, I do myself the honour of addressing you, to request a continuance of the support that on a former occasion procured me that appointment.*
>
> *I hope I may say my past conduct has been such as to render any protestations for the future, save that it shall be the same, unnecessary.*
>
> *I feel the situation is one that requires attention and unceasing exertion – not so much from the individual position, as from the circumstance that the amusement and (what is still more vitally important), the health of my fellow inmates is in some measure placed in the hands of the person appointed; and I beg to assure such as may kindly favour me with their votes, and the members of our community in general, that no attention on my part shall be wanted to render the*

Racquet Court as eligible as possible, and the necessary 'materiel' such as to ensure the approbation of the players.

I believe my application is somewhat late, but I feel confident, by your kind support, of finding myself appointed to the office I now respectfully solicit. I shall do myself the pleasure of waiting on you, for an answer; and have the honor to be,

Ladies and Gentlemen,
Yours obediently,
JOHN ALDRIDGE

2 Coffee Gallery
Fleet Prison
Dec. 11th 1841

Until 1 August 1850 the Racket master was one of the prisoners, and it was not unknown for him to make enough money to pay off his debts and regain his freedom. From that date, however, visitors were barred from the prison courts and the master had to be appointed from outside.

We are given some idea of the amount of play at these courts – and possibly the lack of skill of at least some of the players – by the fact that at the annual restoration of the four courts at the King's Bench, some 250 dozen balls were recovered from neighbouring roofs and gutters.

From the prisons Rackets spread to the taverns, where it was first played in an open court, consisting of little more than a front wall.

A description and rules of the open game are given in Donald Walker's *Games and Sports*, published in 1837.

The Racket-ground presents, in the first place, a very high wall of about forty or more feet in width; and at the top of the wall is a net-work of about five feet in height to prevent those balls going over that happen to be struck above the coping of the wall... The player who commences, or the server, stands in the centre of the ground, in a space marked out for the purpose... If he fail to serve it above the red line, it is called a 'cut' ball; and if it falls inside the line, it is called a short ball, and his opponent may accept it or not, as he chooses... The in-player or server is out if he serves three cut balls, if he strikes the wood which runs along the wall at about eighteen inches from the bottom, if he misses the ball twice with his racket in attempting to serve it, if the ball fall out of bounds, or if he wilfully obstruct his opponent's stroke... If a ball falls on the line, it is called a line ball, and is played again... A marker is always required at

this game. His duty is to keep the balls well covered with chalk, so that they may leave a mark upon the wall, to watch carefully whether the ball falls in or out of bounds, to call the game as each stroke is made, and to be ready to be referred to, if necessary, by the players.

From this account it appears that the server had three chances to produce a good service so far as the service line on the front wall was concerned, but seemingly he could serve any number of short services; hand-out could take a short service, but not a 'cut'.

We learn more about the early game of Rackets from J.R. Atkins, a civil servant, whose *Book of Racquets* was published in 1872. It is of very great interest not only in its description of how the game was played, but especially for its illustrations of various types of court and some basic shots.

He, too, in his historical introduction, refers to the game in the singular as 'the game of Racquet'. He ascribes the growth in its popularity to the general spread of 'muscular Christianity' in Britain, and blames the French defeat by the Germans in 1870 'in some measure to the neglect and decay of active recreations in the school life of the French youth of our time'.

Atkins gives a full and illustrated account of all the various types of court that existed in this transitional period – and some that didn't exist which he thought should.

The open court is the same as that previously described by Walker but with the added information that the front wall is about 45ft high. One refinement is that the wood or tiles on the floor marking the boundaries of the court are now coloured with ochre, so that a ball that bounces on them will show a red mark. By this time, too, the server was allowed two attempts at a good service, not three as previously. Game was 11 points in the open court game, 15 in the covered court. Two of the markers' cries unfamiliar to modern ears were 'Over' (beyond the back line) and 'Gone away' (out of court).

In doubles it was necessary to serve alternately into either side of the court. Having done so, the server was responsible for taking balls at the back of the court, while his partner looked after the short balls. Walker notes the vulnerability of an open court to weather, but stresses its great advantage in allowing ample space for spectators.

He describes the covered court, which is identical to those in use today, and the semi-open court, which was popular in Ireland. This was the same as the open court except that it had two side walls sloping

Diagram of the open court.

gradually downwards from the top of the front wall to a height of about 10 to 15ft at the back. He also describes a small wooden court suitable for a garden and allegedly used in the United States.

He puts forward his own ideas for new types of court. The Great Match Gallery Court is covered, with no back wall, so that large numbers of spectators can be accommodated in galleries at the back of the court. The Tent Court and the Covered Open Court are essentially open with either a temporary or a permanent roof. The Gaslight Close Court is a covered court artificially lit, possibly, he suggests, using white walls and a somewhat larger-than-usual black ball. 'The fact that racquet could be played by gaslight would mark a decided era in the history of the game.'

Atkins offers his readers some advice on playing the game. 'A graceful attitude and mode of delivery and return should also be studied from the outset. A loose and awkward manner of hitting a ball on the part of the player detracts greatly from the pleasure of the spectator.' As for clothes:

...a racquet suit can scarcely be too thin. A pair of trousers of white flannel, with a fancy flannel shirt and belt is the costume most in vogue, at least in close courts; but in open and close courts alike a Jersey or vest of some light material – silk, cotton,

A well-dressed player, illustrated by J.R. Atkins.

128

Diagram of the covered court.

Atkins' idea for a Great Match gallery court.

or merino – is frequently adopted, instead of the shirt, open at the throat. In all cases India-rubber-soled canvas shoes should be worn, to insure firmness of tread and immunity from slipping on the court. Some players (especially in open courts, where there is a danger of a draught) always wear a thin white kerchief round the neck, to avoid cold, and also a light cricket cap. But those appendages are seldom adopted by close-court players.

He has some sound advice for the young on drinking.

Some young players are apt to indulge too freely in copious draughts of bitter beer and other drinks in the course of a morning rubber. This is unwise, for the result is profuse and excessive perspiration, which is weakening. No doubt a novice, at the outset of his career, is apt to feel rather dry in the mouth, with a parching sensation about the tongue and lips, and he is sorely tempted to 'moisten his clay' as often as he can. Well, this he may do, if 'moistening' is to be taken in the literal sense of the term. The best plan is to wash the mouth out occasionally with a little mild brandy and water, or water pure and simple – retaining it in the mouth for a few seconds before ejecting it… After the play is over, however, we recommend a little brandy and water, or sherry and water, to keep the body from cooling too rapidly. Pale ale or claret at this time, however tempting, is apt with some persons to produce a chilling sensation inwardly – but if the constitution be robust, and the circulation powerful, these drinks may be taken with impunity.

At the end of the book there is an account of the cost of the game: full-sized rackets were from 7s 6d each, boys' rackets from 6s and balls 14s a gross.

The names of some of the taverns where Rackets was popular are known. The most famous, where open court championships were frequently played, was the Belvedere (sometimes spelt Belvidere), Pentonville.

Other courts were to be found in London at the Eagle, City Road; the Yorkshire Stingo, Marylebone Road; the Oxford & Cambridge, Chalk Farm Road; White Conduit House; the White Bear, Kennington; the Rosemary Branch, Peckham; and the Boileau Arms, Castelnau, Hammersmith. Outside London there were courts at the Eglinton Arms, Bristol; the Griffin and Porter Butt, Bath; and the Three Blackbirds, Bristol, as well as at taverns in Cork, Belfast and Birmingham. The Earl of Eglinton and Winton had a court at Eglinton Castle in Scotland.

A contributor to *Baily's Magazine of Sports and Pastimes* wrote that 'it was very much a public house game, and savoured of drinking boxes, long pipes, and beer; but in itself it really was a fine manly game.'

When Disraeli, then aged twenty-six, visited Malta in 1830 as part of a Grand Tour of the Mediterranean and Near East, he wrote of the occasion:

The Belvedere Rackets court.

Affection tells here even better than art. Yesterday at the racket court sitting in the gallery among strangers, the ball entered, and lightly struck me, and fell at my feet. I picked it up, and observing a young rifleman excessively stiff, I humbly requested him to forward its passage into the court, as I had really never thrown a ball in my life. This incident has been the general subject of conversation at all the messes today!

The earliest known racket-maker was Pittman in 1834 – no doubt one of the early champions, Thomas or John, or at least a member of that family. He was succeeded by Jefferies of Woolwich, P. Wilson, E. Bluck, T.H. Prosser of Pentonville Road, F.H. Ayres, Buchanan and Malings, the successor to Jefferies in Woolwich. Today the only firm making rackets is Grays of Cambridge. Pittman also made balls, and after his death the father of John Mitchell, champion in 1846, took over. Later they too were made by Malings.

Rackets at the White Bear, Kennington, in 1846.

NINETEENTH-CENTURY RACKETS

THE POPULAR SPECTATOR SPORT of the taverns was destined for a different future in the exclusive circles of public schools and private clubs.

Harrow can claim to have been the first public school to play Rackets, developed in the school yard when that was enlarged in 1821. The sixth and fifth forms used the west wall of the Old Schools, with the east wall of the Milling Ground as a back wall; the rest of the school used the high south boundary wall, which was pulled down in 1889. These 'courts' were full of natural hazards such as chimneys, wire-covered windows, drain-pipes and other architectural features, necessitating an elaborate code of rules.

The game was played with leather-covered balls called 'best fives' and old Tennis rackets, cut down and lightened. Balls and rackets were originally sold by an old lady called Arnold, commonly known as 'Old Polly'; later by Sam Hoare, the Custos (head porter).

Two new courts were built at Harrow in 1850 just west of the Milling Ground, known as the Shell and Fifth Form courts. Both were open and the Fifth Form court had only one side wall.

The earliest covered court was built by the Royal Artillery at their Woolwich Depot. The MCC built a court at Lord's next to the old Tennis court in 1844, and Prince's Club opened its doors in Hans Place in 1853 with several Rackets courts, two Tennis courts and later a cricket ground.

The main Rackets court measured 60ft x 30ft and set the standard measurements for the future. Before that it had been the practice in open courts to play doubles in a larger version (80ft x 40ft) in which two players would cover the front of the court and two the back. The popularity of the game grew rapidly and at one time there were seven courts at Prince's, but one sad result of the vogue for the covered court was the gradual disappearance of public courts attached to taverns. Rackets lost its popular appeal and became a game for the well-to-do.

A court was built in 1857 by Colonel Lord West at Buckhurst Park, in Sussex, to commemorate the capture of Sebastopol, where he had commanded the 21st Royal North British Fusiliers. About the turn of the century Joseph Bickley re-faced the walls. During the Second World War the court was requisitioned by the Army, but little harm was done.

Thanks to the support of Earl de la Warr it remains the only private court in the country.

Both Oxford and Cambridge had courts and this led to the first University match in 1855. This was limited to doubles, but in 1858 a singles match was also played between the first strings. This remained the pattern until 1921 when two singles matches were played, although the second did not count towards the result until 1937. The first match in 1855 was played at Oxford, but subsequent matches took place at Prince's until that club was demolished in 1886. The match was played at Manchester in 1887 and thereafter at Queen's.

The Victoria Club, Torquay was built at 23 Victoria Parade by Henry Day, in 1859. It included a Rackets court as well as billiard and reading rooms. Rackets was popular at first, but interest waned in the Eighties and by the end of the century the court was being used for badminton. It also served as an overflow dormitory for the adjacent Sailors' Rest when the Fleet was in Torbay. It was reported that 'its sepulchral qualities were occasionally used to good effect in reducing bibulous sailors to awe-struck silence.'

The first covered court at Harrow was opened in 1865 immediately adjoining the Fifth Form court to the west. It is slightly larger than standard and remains in use today.

The Public Schools Rackets championship began in 1868 at Prince's, was played at Lord's in 1887 and thereafter at Queen's, except for 1941 when the final was played at Wellington.

An interesting former Rackets court still stands in Eastbourne at the Winter Gardens, although it has been partly walled up for other purposes and is now mainly used for storage. The walls are intact, however, the glass roof only partly replaced with corrugated iron and above the entrance are still the words 'Racquet Court'.

It was built about 1870 as part of the recreational area known as Devonshire Park, which also comprised two swimming pools (male and female), lawn-tennis courts, Turkish baths, athletic facilities and later, squash courts. Teas and concerts were organised at the Winter Garden. The game also spread rapidly to Army posts in India, Canada, Malta, Gibraltar and Hong Kong.

The growing popularity of Rackets led to the building of several club courts: in 1876 two courts at Manchester and in 1888 two others at the new Prince's Club, Knightsbridge, and two at the Queen's Club, West Kensington.

In 1877 the Liverpool Racquet Club was opened, with two Rackets courts and a bowling alley, at a cost of £7000. In 1894 the bowling alley was converted into two courts, for Eton fives and Rugby fives, although not long afterwards the latter came to be used for squash. In 1912 one of the Rackets courts became a small squash court with adjoining squash tennis court, and in 1928 the second was converted into a standard squash court.

In 1919 Archie Hathrill joined the club as Rackets professional. He had been trained at Marlborough and was badly wounded on the Somme during the First World War. When the last Rackets court disappeared he took up the coaching of squash, lawn tennis and fives, and after the club courts were destroyed by enemy action in the Second World War he became Steward. In 1969 he completed fifty years' service with the club.

In Oxford there were two covered courts near St John's College and two more were built about mid century in St Aldate's, close to Christ Church.

Sir William Hart-Dyke, who was at Oxford from 1856 to 1861, recalls that at that time the service line was higher and a high drop service falling awkwardly into the corner was demanded. This was usually returned on the volley. Great use was made of drop shots and it was common in doubles for two players to guard the front of the court in order to get back drop shots, and two the back. There were often long rallies. The game in general was much slower than the modern game.

In Cambridge, Rackets began, as elsewhere, in open courts attached to public houses. One of these, at the University Arms, was kept by H.J. Gray for eleven years before he went to the East Road or Wellington court at the invitation of its owner, Phillips.

In 1858 St John's College opened two new courts (one open and one closed) built at a cost of £1689 5s 9½d and owned by shareholders. H.J. Gray was approached to run both. At first he demurred, having been not long with Phillips at the Wellington court, and suggested his younger brother, William. But William was only twelve at the time and considered too young, so in the end Harry Gray accepted.

The rules of these courts allowed shareholders to book them after 9.00 a.m. and members of the College after 10.00 a.m. The subscription was half-a-guinea a quarter and court charges were:

	Subscribers	Non-Subscribers
Single-wall game	2s	3s
Four-wall game	3s	4s
Each ball	2d	3d

No play was allowed except in slippers. *

In 1864 new shares were issued to cover the cost of roofing over the open court for about £330. In 1883 the shareholders were repaid at par and a fourteen-year lease was granted to Harry Gray at a rent of £100 p.a. Gray surrendered the lease in 1895 and soon afterwards the courts were demolished.

Meanwhile, in 1892, St John's leased a plot of land in Portugal Street to the Rev. R. St John Parry and others, for ninety-nine years from 29 September 1887 at a rent of £18 6s 8d p.a., on which were built two Rackets courts and fives courts. Latterly, the Rackets courts were used for badminton, one even had a wooden floor, and there were also two Eton and two Rugby fives courts and three squash courts; but the whole complex has now been demolished.

The St John's College Archives contain various accounts relating to the Rackets courts, which are interesting in throwing light on the suppliers of balls. The earliest were supplied from 1858 to 1860 by George Erwood, once master of the Royal Artillery court at Woolwich. He charged sixteen shillings a gross for new balls and ten shillings a gross for re-covered balls; and he charged £10 in December 1858 for supervising the protection of the roof windows of the closed court with wire-netting and the staining of the floor.

From 1859 to 1870 balls were supplied by the firm of Jefferies and Malings of Woolwich, who also charged sixteen shillings a gross and allowed a rebate of six shillings a gross returned.

*St John's College Archives.

In 1862, T.H. Prosser, later well-known as makers of Tennis rackets, entered the scene. Evidently, Prosser had trained at Jefferies and Malings, as he proudly claimed on his invoice, together with the fact that he was 'patronized by the Princes' Club'. By 1866 he had moved to Pentonville Road, and in 1882 claimed the patronage not only of Prince's Club, but also of Oxford and Cambridge Universities, Harrow, Eton, Rugby, Cheltenham, Marlborough, Winchester and 'Hailesbury' Schools. He, too, originally charged sixteen shillings a gross for new balls, but by 1882 this had risen to one guinea. For re-covering old balls he charged fifteen shillings a gross, and gave a rebate of six shillings a gross for balls returned.

H. Day of Lisson Grove near Lord's supplied one batch of ten gross of balls at eighteen shillings a gross in 1866, and it seems balls must have been in short supply, for the next year a batch was ordered from T. Watters of Dublin and he continued to supply them for several years. His charge was one pound a gross for new balls, allowing a rebate of four shillings and sixpence for balls returned.

In 1873, Henry Malings of Woolwich appears, describing himself as 'late of the Firm of Jefferies & Malings' and 'By Special Appointment to the Marylebone Club (Lord's)'. He charged eighteen shillings a gross and gave a rebate of five shillings.

H.J. Gray first sent in an account in 1878, describing himself as 'Racquet Manufacturer'. By 1882 he had become H.J. Gray & Sons, 'Racquet & Lawn Tennis Manufacturers'. He charged eighteen shillings and sixpence a gross for Rackets balls and forty-eight shillings a gross for fives balls.

In 1860, members of University Hall, London raised money to build a Rackets court on their premises. This project failed after three years of negotiation with the freeholders, but in 1864 an agreement was reached with the council of University College, London, that they would provide a site, on condition that it was primarily for the use of students of the College and the Hall.

Construction began in August 1864 and the court was completed in November 1865. The architect was Horace Field and the main subscriber, anonymous at the time, Henry Crabb-Robinson. In 1868, Edward Enfield gave a silver cup for the best student of the session, first won by E.B. Hume. A Racquet Club was formed in 1892, controlled by a committee, and an annual dinner inaugurated. In 1895, extensive repairs were carried out to the floor and to front and back walls. A single door was installed to replace the previous double doors in the back wall.

The first home match took place in November 1896 against two Oxford University players, B.N. Bosworth-Smith and H.D.G. Leveson-Gower, University College being represented by C.E. Marriott and G.J.E. Pittman. The same year the court acquired its first professional, N. Naylor, who had recently retired from Clifton College. He was allowed to use the court for practice and to give lessons at one shilling an hour.

In 1898, a silver cup was purchased for the singles championship, and in 1907 it was agreed to present the winner with an inscribed medal. The court was closed during the 1914–18 war but returned to use afterwards. It was still in play in 1930, but shortly thereafter was converted to provide two squash courts and accommodation for the dramatic society and the presidents of the two union societies.

In 1888 Antony Gibbs, grandfather of Lord Wraxall, moved into Tyntesfield near Bristol. He had been a keen Rackets player at Exeter College, Oxford, and decided to build himself a court.

Not far from Tyntesfield he owned another house, Belmont, built in 1780 by William Turner in the shape of a centre block and two wings. The centre block was gutted to provide a Rackets court and the library converted into a boiler house and changing rooms. A complete glass roof was built over the court to give maximum light.

In 1920, Belmont House was required as accommodation for the estate's agent and considerable rebuilding took place. A squash court was built across the middle of the Rackets court, rooms were rebuilt on the ground and first floors and a garage was constructed.

Another court was built in the nineteenth century at Elvaston Castle near Derby, once the home of the Earls of Harrington.

A most noteworthy event was the building of a court in Melbourne in 1876 by the Melbourne Club. The idea was first mooted in 1868, but other improvements in club facilities, such as a new billiard room, took priority over the Racket court. However, a meeting of forty-five members on 11 February 1876 unanimously passed a resolution proposed by Molesworth Greene and seconded by Captain Standish to erect a court on the Little Collins Street frontage.

The contract went to G.W.T. Freeman and by the end of August the building was virtually complete at a total cost of some £1600. In September a marker was engaged at £1 per week, including clothes and board. Balls cost twenty-four shillings a gross, shoes eighteen shillings a pair and rackets £1 each.

But its success was short-lived and by 1890 it was being used as a servants' dormitory. In 1891, new quarters were built for the servants and the court restored to use at a cost of £30. There were bursts of activity in the court in 1901 and 1911 but in 1912 the committee accepted a proposal in the suggestion book that the court should be converted to two squash courts. By May 1913, the work had been carried out at a total cost of £120, including a bath and hot shower. Later the site became used as a store-room and then a garage.

NINETEENTH-CENTURY CHAMPIONS

All the early champions up to 1862 were trained at the Fleet or King's Bench prisons in the open courts that existed there. The first names known to us are those mentioned by Pierce Egan, and it is difficult to distinguish a true champion with any certainty until Thomas Pittman in 1825. Before him, William Hazlitt refers to John Davies as the outstanding player of his day and to Powell, 'who was reckoned the best open-ground player of his time'. The same two names are mentioned by Pierce Egan, who tells us that the 'fat knight' prided himself on having had lessons from them.

However, Robert Mackay (or Mackey) is usually recognised as the first champion, as he was the first to claim the title in 1820, having defeated James Lewis at the King's Bench. His claim cannot be considered very good, as Pierce Egan makes no mention of it and merely refers to 'those celebrated players of the game [at the King's Bench] Messrs Lewis, Mackey, and Smith'. It seems likely that there was little competition between players in the two prisons, and that Mackay should more realistically be considered champion of the King's Bench.

Another outstanding player of those early days was Matthew Pittman, father of Thomas, John and Matthew junior. It was to Thomas Pittman that Robert Mackay resigned his championship claim when ill-health forced him to relinquish it. Thomas Pittman issued a challenge to all-comers to play him on 26 June 1825 at the Belvedere Gardens, Pentonville, for any sum between £5 and £500. Bad weather prevented play and the match was postponed, but even so no challenger came forward. From that date, therefore, Thomas Pittman can clearly be considered the champion, as Pierce Egan acknowledges.

His first challenger was Thomas Butler of Birmingham. Rackets had been introduced there by a Mr Atkins at the Islington near Pie Bridge, where Butler had learnt to play.

The match took place in the Birmingham court on 21 July 1828, and Pittman won the best of nine games to retain his title.

In November 1834, Thomas Pittman resigned in favour of his younger brother John, who was renowned not only as a great player of volley, drop and cut, but also introduced a new shot, the twist. In 1837, John Pittman played an informal match with John Lamb at what was now the Queen's Bench prison. Lamb won the match, which was thus described in the *New Sporting Magazine*:

> *...a hasty, unprepared, crude match, knocked up and knocked off – brilliant, but unsatisfactory – smartness, judgment and energy mixed up with those sad antidotes to such qualities – viz. fatness, and previous long and pampered inactivity on one side, and bodily malady and uncultured strength on the other.*

This led to a formal challenge, and a match was arranged to take place on 11 June 1838 at the Belvedere court for £100-a-side, the best of fifteen games, each game then being of 11 points. The players were to be allowed a half-minute rest between rallies and two minutes between games. A special box was built for the referee and umpires. Pittman trained for the match under J. Sowden, one of the players mentioned by Pierce Egan and later the Racket master at the Boileau Arms court. Unfortunately, a thunderstorm prevented play and the match had to be postponed.

It took place on 19 June, and was described by the *New Sporting Magazine* of October 1838:

> *The great struggle for superiority in the art of racquet-playing, was brought to a focus by a match being at length made upon the fairest possible terms, for Lamb to play John Pitman the best of fifteen games, for 100l. a-side, at the Belvedere Court, near Islington, and we attended, with a sincere anxiety for a true game, truly played, and success to the best. The ground was in perfect order, having been attended to with unceasing care by Thomas Pitman, the owner of it, and the well-known brother of the player in the match. The chalking the lines of the court, and other preliminaries were carefully completed. The first of the players we saw, was John Pitman. He was wrapped in a large beaver great-coat; but the neat and powerful shoes carefully put on, clean white cottoned ankles just seen expanding into muscle, under the skirts of the coat, met at the other extremity by the light and quiet eye, clear*

complexion, firm neck, and pale forehead; no man could look better to enter a ring for any athletic sport:— He reminded us strongly of poor honest Tom Shelton, in his palmy days! We shortly afterwards saw Lamb, as quiet and unassuming as his namesake. He looked slim and pale, but there was a good-heartedness about his confidence, and an unaffectedness attending his attire, that could not but pleasantly strike the looker-on.

John Pitman is by very far a more athletic man than Lamb; he has, perhaps, a harder face; a more resolute carriage; but no one could act, on this occasion, with a more controlled temper, or submit with finer moderation to adverse decisions (during the match) than this admirable player. The hour of play, however, arrived; and the coats were thrown aside – the umpires taking their places on an elevated platform in front of the stage. It was an anxious moment!

Pitman first appeared in the court, and showed through his flannel shirt and tight lower white clothing, great muscular symmetry and power. He flashed, or idled, a ball against the court-wall as a race-horse canters before the stand, to give a glimpse of his condition, his action, and his confidence. Lamb was slower to appear; and when he did, there was a lathiness *about his figure which bore not a favourable contrast with the iron frame of his competitor. He was dressed in trousers (always "a questionable shape" with those who come forth as the* Athletae*), and there looked a painful inwardness of the points of the shoulders which promised unfavourably for* lasting.

The Two shook hands. The racquet was tossed up, and Pitman won the hand. *And from this moment nothing could be more cool, precise, or energetic than the exertions of each. Pitman played with the greater strength; Lamb with the finer niceties of the science.*

There can be no doubt in an unprejudiced mind, that the result of this match exhibited the best player. Pitman played with infinite resolution up to the last game, but one; *and there the jading of an up-hill journey told upon his harassed spirits, and baffled skill. His temper, however, was maintained with admirable evenness to the last. His early strength, however, was lavished and wasted upon the calm science of Lamb; and (to descend for an instant to* minutiae*), we thought he too regularly* served *Lamb in his favourite corner.*

The match lasted for two hours and twenty minutes, and was won by John Lamb by 8 games to 4. The full score

was 11–7, 7–11, 11–6, 7–11, 11–8, 11–7, 11–9, 11–7, 10–11, 9–11, 11–6, 11–5. While his delighted backers collected their debts, Lamb was rewarded with £10. T.J. Gem described Lamb as a 'fair-haired, muscular, little man, very quick upon his legs, with an imperturbable temper, and a head that never lost a chance'.

In September the same year, Lamb was so confident of his prowess that he offered to play anyone, giving them two points in a 15-point game for £100-a-side, but no challenger came forward. Two years later he died of consumption. The championship was now vacant and three claimants appeared. All of them issued challenges to meet anyone on their own court, but none was accepted and during that six-year stalemate the championship must be considered to have been in abeyance. The three contenders were George Erwood, a left-hander trained in the Fleet and then master of the Royal Artillery court at Woolwich; John Pittman, the former champion from the Belvedere court; and Samuel Young from Birmingham.

Eventually, in 1846, John Charles Mitchell, trained

John Mitchell.

at the Queen's Bench and later Lord Eglinton's marker in Scotland, took up Young's challenge. At the time, Mitchell was landlord of the Sea-Horse, Maudlin Street, Bristol (re-named the Eglinton Arms in 1853) where there was a court; he also played at the Three Blackbirds, Ellbroad Street, Bristol, and at the Griffin and the Porter Butt in Bath. Mitchell was another who enjoyed playing at unusual odds. He would often take on a lesser opponent using a kitchen brush, the handle of a racket or a soda-water bottle. On one occasion, he won a match against a certain member of the peerage, giving him 99 points in 100.

The match, the best of nine games, took place at a recently built close court in Bath Street, Birmingham, and Mitchell won by five games to love. This was the first championship played in a close court and for some time afterwards there were separate championships for close and open courts. However, the main interest gradually shifted to the close-court game of which Mitchell remained champion for the next fourteen years.

T.J. Gem, one of the founders of lawn tennis at Leamington, was among those who regretted the change. He wrote in 1873:

It was the old open-court rackets, the London game, as played in the Queen's Bench and the Fleet, and at the Belvidere ground, Pentonville, that taught men to hit. The play-ground being indicated by white lines, and there being no back or side walls, a man must use his head, as well as his hand, and hit to points, or be out of bounds. There was no hitting with outstretched arm, and trusting to the chapter of accidents there. Those who remember the 'drops' of old John Lamb and George Erwood will know the accuracy that was attained, or have seen the Pitmans, John and Tom, and John Mitchell, with the arm close to the side, swing the racket down below the calf of the leg and give a 'crusher' that took all 'rise' out of the ball, can testify the hits that could be made. It is not contended that nobody can do this now; but certainly the pleasant mode of playing this excellent game does not make it a necessity.

Mitchell's successor at Eglinton Castle was Patrick Devitt. Lord Eglinton had great faith in his prowess, especially as he had defeated Francis Erwood by

Exterior of the court at Eglinton in 1980.

3 games to love in January 1847 and Billy Magrath, from the Kildare court in Dublin, by the same score in January 1848. After this match, a letter appeared in *Bell's Life*, alleging that Devitt was invincible in his own court. This led to an immediate response from Mitchell and Young.

Matches were soon arranged for £100-a-side to be played at Eglinton and Birmingham. On 22 March at Eglinton, Young beat Devitt by 4 games to 2, and on 24 March Mitchell did likewise by 4 games to 3 after a match lasting two hours and twenty-four minutes. At Birmingham in April, Devitt again lost both matches: to Young 0–4 and to Mitchell 2–4.

These details come from the match book of the Racket Court at Eglinton Castle covering the period December 1846 to January 1849 (kindly lent by the Earl of Eglinton). It records matches played between members of the leading families of Ayrshire, Lord Eglinton himself playing in many of them.

The court at Eglinton still stands, although most of the plaster has come off the walls and the gallery has been removed. It is used for storage.

In 1859, Francis Erwood – originally trained at Lord's and then at Woolwich with his brother George – challenged Mitchell for the championship. The match was to be home-and-home, the best of seven games at each court, for £200 each match. The first match was played at Woolwich on 6 March 1860, the referee being Mr George Prince, founder of Prince's Club, and was won by Erwood, 15–11, 15–2, 15–8, 15–6.

This was a daunting lead for Erwood before the next match at the Eglinton Arms, Bristol, but the courts varied considerably and Mitchell's backers were still confident that he would turn the tables. A packed gallery cheered both players on to the court on 27 March. Erwood won the first two games 15–6, 15–6; Mitchell the third 15–11. The fourth game was vital to any hope that Mitchell had of winning this leg and saving his backers a further £200. It lasted more than half-an-hour and was of very high quality. At 14–14 Erwood was serving at game ball – evidently there was no rule about 'setting' at the time. He won the rally despite a protest that the ball was 'foul' (presumably 'not up') and went on to win the next game 15–9. So the match was his, and the championship. Mitchell was the last great exponent of both the close and open-court game.

Francis Erwood was now champion of the close court and his brother George of the open court game. The latter had issued several challenges to all-comers, but no one had come forward. A Mr Ede had on occasion taken up the challenge but on the day no one appeared and he lost his deposit. It was suggested by some that these were ploys to allow Erwood to retain his championship without having to defend it, so when Mr Ede once again took up the challenge for a match on 27 June 1863 no one paid much attention, least of all Erwood who had put on weight and was in poor training.

However, on this occasion Mr Ede's dark horse appeared at the last moment in the shape of Edmund Bailey. Erwood took the lead (11–10, 11–7) with the odds 5–2 in his favour. But his lack of training became apparent and he lost the next two games (7–11, 6–11) to square the match at 2 games all. The final game took place amid tremendous excitement and uproarious cheering; Bailey finally emerged the victor by 11–10.

About this period, the influence of public school and university Rackets began to be felt – particularly in the person of Sir William Hart-Dyke, who learnt the game at Harrow School.

Sir William won the first Oxford v. Cambridge singles for Oxford in 1858 and repeated his victory in

Sir William Hart-Dyke.

1859 and 1860. In those three years he also won the University doubles match in partnership with J.P.F. Gundry.

In 1862, he challenged Francis Erwood for the championship and the match was played at Woolwich and Prince's for £50-a-side. He won at Woolwich 5–15, 15–7, 15–11, 15–5, 17–18, 15–2, and at Prince's, 14–17, 15–6, 15–3, 15–12, 15–14, to become the first amateur to win the championship – and the first player not to have had his initial training in a debtors' prison! Unluckily, not long afterwards Erwood was struck in the face by a ball while playing against an officer at Woolwich. The injury affected his left eye and he was obliged thereafter to give up match play, so that when Sir William resigned the title the following year he was unable to contest it. Sir William's resignation was to allow him to pursue his political career. He was an MP for forty-one years and among other offices was Chief Whip in Disraeli's government of 1874. He died in 1931 at the age of ninety-three.

Although Sir William himself triumphed in the covered court, he retained a considerable respect for the earlier open-air game that he had known in his youth. 'The close-court game has no doubt wrought changes for the worse so far as the best features of Rackets are concerned,' he wrote. 'The game as played in open courts against a single wall was a severe test of skill and judgment in placing the ball, and accuracy as regards strength and measuring distance.'

The resignation of Sir William heralded the reign of the eldest of the famous five Gray brothers of Cambridge, who laid the foundations of the firm of Gray's of Cambridge, which has served court games so well by the provision of first-class rackets and equipment for so long.

The eldest was Henry John Gray, born in 1837 and introduced to Rackets at the age of ten at the open court of the University Arms. In 1855, he founded the firm, making rackets at the St John's College courts, where he was then the professional. He remained there for many years and taught the game to his four brothers. He challenged Erwood, whose injury prevented him from playing, and H.J. Gray assumed the title in 1863.

In 1866 he resigned in favour of the second brother, William, born in 1846. At the age of sixteen, William had become champion of Ireland by beating Dalton, the marker at the Vice-Regal Lodge court in Dublin. He was soon called on to defend the title when a challenge came from Joseph Foy of Aldershot.

The match took place for £200-a-side in 1866. William won the first leg 4–0 on 26 February at the University Club court in Dublin and the second 4–2 on 19 March at Aldershot.

William is generally regarded as one of the outstanding players of all time for skill and grace. Alfred Lyttelton wrote of him:

> *When the greatest masters of various games are passed in review, none seem to have quite equalled Gray in the combination of absolute success with absolute gracefulness... But if perfection in a game be attained by combining success in results with beauty of style...no one to my mind, has brought any game to such perfection as that to which William Gray raised the game of Rackets.*

Present at this match was Auguste La Montagne, a Canadian, who with the support of friends had built a court on 13th Street, New York, near Sixth Avenue, called the Gymnasium Club.

La Montagne offered to match the American champion Fred Foulkes against Gray in a home-and-home match. Gray at once accepted this challenge for £1000-a-side, but La Montagne considered this too high and the match was eventually made at £500-a-side.

Gray, accompanied by his sixteen-year-old brother Joseph and his trainer, Walters, arrived in New York aboard the steamer *City of Washington* on Monday, 25 March 1867 and took up residence at the Buck's Head Hotel, 15/17, Crosby Street. He immediately started to practise at 53/55, West 13th Street, finding the court strange as it was 10 ft longer than an English court, with a wooden floor.

The *New York Clipper* described him as 'a handsome, intelligent, young fellow, twenty-one years of age, about 5 ft 8 ins in height and of a slender, well-knit frame, combining strength and activity in admirable proportions'.

Frederick Foulkes was an Englishman by birth, from Leamington. He had trained in Rackets at Oxford before emigrating to Canada in 1858. From there he won the American championship in a match against Billy Devoe. In 1865 he again defeated Devoe and was engaged by the New York Gymnasium Club. The *New York Clipper* described him as 'about thirty-four years of age, stands 5 ft 6 ins and is light and active in build'.

The first leg of the contest began on Monday, 22 April and the gallery was crowded to capacity, not only by members but also by 'the élite of the sporting and turf men of the city'. Betting was fierce and, having started at 100–80 on, Foulkes, by the start of the match, was at evens.

Gray started brilliantly, won the first game 15–5 and the betting on him went to 100–60. But Foulkes evened the match by winning the next game 15–5. Gray won the third game 15–6 and a very close fourth game followed which after 13 all and set 5 Foulkes won 18–15 to even the score again. Gray came back strongly in the fifth game and led by 14–8, looking a certain winner, when he broke his racket. Foulkes scored six points in succession to make it 14 all and went on to win the next three points and the game 17–14. By now the betting was 500–400 on Foulkes, but with the score 6–5 in Gray's favour, a storm broke and the light deteriorated to such an extent that further play had to be postponed until the following day.

On resumption, Gray was in top form. He won the unfinished game 15–8 and the final game 15–0. 'This decided the American half of the game and amid loud cheers Gray tossed up his Racquet.'

The second leg was played at the Ulster Club in Belfast on 6 July 1867. There the match was reported by the *Belfast News*, which described Gray as 'exceedingly graceful, presenting an open, expressive and intelligent countenance. Like his opponent Foulkes, he is very quiet and gentlemanly in his manner, and possesses a frame combining strength, activity and symmetry in an unusual degree.' Gray's practice was somewhat hindered by an injury to his thumb, sustained on the passage from America in the *City of New York*.

This second match began as closely as the first. Foulkes won a hard-fought first game 15–8. Gray made sure of the second 15–3. Another close game was won by Foulkes 15–10, followed by another game to Gray 15–12. Then Gray broke away to win the next two games and the championship 15–5, 15–9.

The *Belfast News* concluded its account: 'The game was carefully marked and most audibly too by Richard Armstrong.' How rarely do we give praise to all those markers who give such wonderful service to the game of Rackets.

Gray was now undisputed world champion, but alas, in 1875, at the early age of twenty-nine, he died at Eton College, where he was in charge of Rackets.

A match was arranged for the vacant title between Joseph Gray, another brother, then the Rackets professional at Rugby School, and H.B. Fairs. Fairs and Stevens were Rackets professionals at Prince's Club, known to the members as 'Punch' and 'Judy'. The nickname 'Punch' passed from father to son and 'Punch' Fairs Junior was later to become Tennis world champion. 'Judy' Stevens was for many years the Rackets professional at Harrow.

The match was played in January 1876 at Prince's and Rugby; each player was allowed four days' practice in his opponent's court. The stake was £250-a-side and, as in prize-fighting, the players were weighed in. Fairs, almost twenty-seven, scaled 8 st 10 lbs in playing costume, and Gray, aged twenty-five, 9 st 12 lbs.

After a nervous start by both players, Fairs won the first leg at Prince's 15–7, 15–1, 15–9, 6–15, 15–12. Gray put up greater resistance at Rugby, where the court was 5ft longer and 2ft wider than that at Prince's with a paved floor and poor light. Nevertheless, Fairs was victorious again 15–3, 18–14, 8–15, 15–11, 3–15, 17–14, and became the new champion. E.O. Pleydell-Bouverie wrote of this match in the Badminton Library:

The 1876 match presented great differences of style, Gray's self-contained neatness being in marked contrast to 'Punch's' slashing sweep. 'Punch' was a little man, standing somewhere about 5ft. 4ins., but the manner in which he reached the ball would lead one to suppose that he had the length of arm of a six-foot man. That arm too was extraordinarily loose. To see him hit gave rather the impression of a racket being slung at the end of a rope, so flexible were his joints. As he played it seemed as though H. Fairs was an arm and a racket, the rest of him being a mere appendage.

Once again tragedy intervened and Fairs died two years later. Joseph Gray became the third brother to hold the championship and he did so unchallenged for nine years.

Joseph Gray went to New York in 1881 to play a match for $1000 against the American champion, Harry Boakes, professional in charge of the Quebec court. Joseph was accompanied by his brother Walter, and Boakes practised with the New York professional, Robert Moore. In a preliminary to the challenge match, Walter Gray easily defeated Robert Moore. In the words of the *New York Herald* reporter: 'he played with Moore as a cat would do with a mouse…Moore was simply a novice in the hands of Gray.'

Reporting on the challenge match itself, he writes:

The grandest exhibition of scientific manipulation of the racket ball that has ever been witnessed in this city was the great championship match yesterday afternoon at the New York Racket Club.

Joseph Gray started a clear favourite, but Boakes played brilliantly to win the first game 15–12. The second game was fiercely fought, Boakes making much

Harry Boakes and Joseph Gray.

When that club was compulsorily acquired by the London and North Western Railway Company for their Exchange Station, he moved with the club to their new premises in Blackfriars Road, Salford.

There he prospered and gave notice to the champion of his ability when in 1886 he defeated Walter Gray by 4 games to 2.

The challenge match was played on 20 April 1887 in the new court at Rugby and on 27 April at Manchester. Immediately under the announcement of the match in *The Field* appears an interesting advertisement for 'Naylor's Racquet Court Wall Black'.

Gray was considerably the elder of the two players – he was thirty-seven, Latham twenty-two. He put up a tremendous struggle in his home court and after a very close match with many long rallies emerged the victor by 4 games to 3, (15–7, 10–15, 9–15, 15–10, 15–9, 8–15, 15–8; 87 points to 79).

But at Manchester, Latham had it all his own way, largely thanks to his service, and won 4–0 (15–2, 15–4, 15–11, 15–9). The account of the match in *The Field* is of interest in mentioning that balls of excellent quality were supplied by Gradedge (*sic.*) of Woolwich, H. Gray of Cambridge, and Prosser of London.

This was too much for the Grays to tolerate, and the following year Latham was challenged by brother Walter, the Rackets professional at Harrow from 1873 to 1878 and after that at Charterhouse. Again, largely thanks to his dominating service, Latham swept ahead in the first leg played on 25 April 1888 in the recently opened court at Queen's Club, where he was in charge of Rackets. He won 2–15, 15–12, 15–7, 16–14, 15–6. In the second leg, played on 2 May at Charterhouse, he faced a partisan gallery, who cheered Gray's every stroke and largely ignored Latham's. The match was close but he won the two games necessary for overall victory out of four games played, the score being 8–15, 15–4, 12–15, 15–9.

This was the last time that one of the Gray brothers competed in a world title match. Four out of five brothers had contested the title over twenty-five years and three of them had held it for twenty-one – an astonishing performance. The fifth brother, George, born in 1852, was also an accomplished player and was in charge of Rackets at Haileybury.

Another American challenge was received in 1891 for a stake of $5000 from George Standing, originally trained at Prince's Club but then Rackets professional at the New York Racquet Club and the outstanding player in the USA. The match was played on 25 April at Prince's Club and on 2 May at Queen's Club, Latham winning with great ease by 5 games to 0. At

use of the drop shot, while Gray played a more orthodox straight up-and-down game. Eventually Boakes won it 18–15 and went on to take the third game easily 15–7. Gray appeared exhausted by his efforts in the second game and Boakes relaxed. It was a costly mistake. Gray won the fourth game 15–4, the fifth game 15–5, and the sixth game 15–5, to square the match at 3 games all.

Boakes seemed thoroughly rattled and Gray was completely on top. The last game was a cliff-hanger, as Boakes pulled himself together and made a final effort. The score reached 7 all, 12 all, 13 all, set 5. Amid intense excitement Gray just won it at 18–15.

'Never has such a thrillingly exciting contest been played in racket circles in this city,' proclaimed the *New York Herald*. 'The play was of the sharpest nature, and of a rarer description than the lovers of the game here have been accustomed to seeing.'

The first challenge to Gray's title came from Peter Latham of Manchester.

Latham was born in Manchester on 10 May 1865. He started his career as a boy, aged eleven, at the opening of the Manchester Racquet Club in 1876.

Prince's the score was 15–6, 15–12, 15–9, 15–5. Latham required one more game at Queen's to assure himself of overall victory and this he won 15–6.

Latham's predominance at Rackets enabled him to turn his attention to Tennis with an ambition to win the world championship of that game too – a feat he accomplished in 1895.

He was challenged again for his Rackets title by George Standing in 1897 and this time the match was to be played in England and America, for a stake of £2000. Standing practised with Walter Gray at Charterhouse; Latham retired to the salubrious air of Blackpool and practised at Manchester and Liverpool.

The first leg was played at Queen's on 16 October 1897. The marker was André of Winchester. Latham had played very little Rackets since his victory over Standing in 1891, as he had been preoccupied with winning the Tennis world championship. He started the match in fine form, however, serving well, showing his old power of return and mercilessly killing the easy ball. He won the first game 15–11, the second 15–13 after being 0–9 down, the third 15–10 and went on to lead 9–3 in the fourth. Standing rallied at this point, caught up at 13 all and won the game 18–15, but Latham took the next 15–4 to lead by 4 games to 1.

The second leg was played in New York on 27 November. 'Reporters were not admitted,' wrote *The Times* correspondent, so that the exact score of the match is not easily determined, although Latham certainly won it by 4 games to 3. He started well to take the first game 15–2. The second was a particularly brilliant game, just clinched by Standing 18–16. Standing went on to win the third game 15–3, but the tremendous pace had told on him and he could not prevent Latham from seizing the fourth game and so retaining his title. The match was played out, the score of the last three games from Latham's viewpoint being 9–15, 16–15 (or 17–16), 15–1.

Latham's last defence of his title was in April 1902, against Gilbert Browne of Prince's Club. This match evoked very little interest and the gallery was at half capacity to see the champion retain his title with the greatest of ease, by 4 games to love at the Queen's Club – 16–13, 15–10, 15–0, 15–2 – and 1 game to love at Prince's, 15–11.

After this match Latham resigned the title, undefeated. He was undoubtedly one of the outstanding Rackets players of all time. He dominated the world scene for fifteen years and was Tennis world champion for ten. When he died in November 1953, at the age of eighty-eight, *The Times* obituary was headed 'A Peerless Player of Rackets and Tennis', and of his Rackets play recorded that his 'wonderful wrist, balance, and footwork gave him a grace and perfection of style and movement, and there was no weak point in his armour.'

George Standing v.
Peter Latham in New York 1899.

TWENTIETH-CENTURY RACKETS

1900–80

IN AN ARTICLE in the *National Review*, E.B. Noel gives some interesting facts about Rackets courts at the beginning of the century. Those that had gone out of play between 1900 and 1919 were at Eastbourne, Oxford, Torquay, Newcastle, Liverpool, Leamington and some private courts. Existing in 1914, in addition to those at public schools, were courts at Queen's (two), Prince's, Lord's, University College London, Manchester, Cardiff, Cambridge, RA Woolwich, RMA Woolwich, RE Chatham, RMC Sandhurst, Aldershot, Colchester and Shorncliffe.

Abroad there were courts in Malta, Gibraltar, Hong Kong, and at the Hurlingham Club, Buenos Aires, where the Argentinian championship was played.

Thanks to the South Glamorgan Library, the story of the Rackets court in Cardiff is known. It was built in 1878 for £2300 by the 'Cardiff Racquet and Fives Court' Company in Westgate Street, adjoining Cardiff Arms Park. At that time it was the only building on the west side of Westgate Street. In 1880 lawn tennis courts were added.

The premises, known as Jackson's Hall, were later used as offices.

The Rackets court in Cardiff.

WORLD CHAMPIONS UP TO 1939

When Peter Latham resigned as world champion, a match was arranged to decide his successor between Gilbert Browne, Latham's last unsuccessful challenger in 1902, and J. Jamsetji, a professional from Bombay and the best player in India. Despite the very different playing conditions in England, where the game was somewhat faster, Jamsetji was victorious by 6 games to 2 in a match played at Queen's Club and Prince's Club in May 1903. This was a dull and disappointing match and a considerable anti-climax after the great days of Latham. At Queen's Club, Jamsetji won 15–11, 18–16, 13–16, 15–8, 15–4, and he won the necessary two games at Prince's, 15–5, 11–15, 15–5, to become the first overseas player to hold the championship – and as yet the only player not to come from Britain or America. Perhaps sadly for Rackets, his very talented countrymen from the Indian continent have taken to squash rackets.

A unique event took place in 1908 when Rackets for the first and last time was included in the Olympic Games, held that year in London. The competition was played at Queen's and comprised both singles and doubles. It was hardly an Olympic event – indeed it was a bit of a farce.

Only English players entered and the Amateur champion and likely winner, E.M. Baerlein, retired before playing a match. In the second round, just one match was played as three players retired. Worse still, in the final, H.M. Leaf scratched as a result of an injured hand and the Gold Medal was won by E.B. Noel. Noel had won the Amateur championship in 1907 and was runner-up to Edgar Baerlein in 1908, but his Gold Medal should more deservedly have been awarded to him for his service to Tennis and Rackets as historian and Queen's Club secretary.

The doubles, a similar fiasco, was won by V.H. Pennell and J.J. Astor.

Jamsetji was challenged in 1911 by Charles Williams, a brilliant young professional who at the time had just gone to Harrow. Williams, when at Prince's, had defeated T. Jennings of Aldershot in a home-and-home match in April 1909. He had then challenged Walter Hawes of Wellington for the Professional championship and beaten him too, in a match played at Queen's and Princes's in June 1909.

A match for the British Open championship was arranged between Williams and Edgar Baerlein, but had to be postponed (owing to an accident involving Baerlein). It took place eventually in January 1911 and provided a marvellous match for spectators. Williams was one of the hardest hitters of the ball, with a wonderful backhand; Baerlein was full of skill and determination. In the first leg at Queen's, Williams easily won the first game 15–2, but Baerlein took the next two 18–15, 15–6. Unfortunately, he was hit on the elbow at the end of the third game, and this caused him difficulty in throwing up the ball for service. He fought hard but just lost the fourth game 10–15. Thereafter Williams, hitting harder than ever, swept away to win the last two games 15–3, 15–3.

The second leg at Manchester also provided a magnificent match, but Williams was at his best, making few mistakes, and Baerlein was mainly on the defensive. Williams again won 4–2 (15–8, 7–15, 15–2, 18–16, 8–15, 15–2).

It was hardly surprising, therefore, that when he played Jamsetji for the world title he overwhelmed him. On 25 April at Queen's he won 4–0 (18–15, 15–2, 15–9, 15–8) and on 13 May at Prince's he won the necessary game for the match (15–7). Jamsetji at the time was thirty-nine, Williams twenty-two.

Charles Williams was a remarkable player and a terrific hitter of the ball. Practising for a championship match, he would play single-handed against a formidable amateur pair, Cyril Simpson and Roddy Williams, and beat them. As a young man he had the alternative of becoming a Rackets professional or a welterweight boxer. He used to say that he regretted his choice as he'd have 'murdered' his pugilistic opponents as he did his Rackets ones.

Charles Williams and Jock Soutar.

The next twenty-five years were dominated by two great rivals, Charles Williams and Jock Soutar, who had trained together as junior professionals at Prince's Club. Soutar was a Scotsman, brought over to Philadelphia in 1907 by Frederick Tompkins to assist him at Rackets. He was also no mean Tennis player, and held the US Professional Tennis championship from 1925 to 1928 until the arrival of Pierre Etchebaster. He also dominated the American squash rackets scene from 1916 to 1925.

However, in 1912 George Standing was still American Open champion and it was he who challenged Williams for the world title. Williams was on his way to America to play this match on the maiden voyage of the *Titanic* when she struck an iceberg and sank on 14/15 April 1912, with the loss of 1513 lives. He spent nine hours adrift in a small boat before being rescued, and naturally the match was called off. By 1913, Standing had retired and Williams agreed to meet Soutar in a home-and-away match.

The first leg, played at Queen's Club, was distinguished by hard and accurate hitting and by Soutar's heavily cut service, which never rose from the

World Rackets championship, 1914. Standing (left to right): *G. Standing, F.C. Tompkins, Jay Gould, Tom Pettitt, W. Wilson Potter, Edgar Scott, Milton Berger.* Seated (left to right): *Peter Latham, Foxhall Keene, James Potter, Charles Williams, W.H.T. Huhn, Jock Soutar, Percy Houghton, George H. Brooke.*

back wall. Williams took this formidable service on the volley and his brilliant backhand and speed about the court brought him victory by 4 games to 2 (6–15, 15–12, 15–11, 15–10, 9–15, 15–6).

Soutar won the second leg in Philadelphia with great ease by 4 games to 0 (15–2, 15–8, 15–4, 15–3). The day was extremely hot and Williams never showed his true form in the conditions. His hard hitting broke all his best rackets, but he refused to accept the offer of one of Soutar's – indeed every encounter of these two friends was marked by good sportsmanship. Soutar thus became the first American world champion.

The war years prevented any further matches between them until 1922, when a return match was played in Philadelphia and New York. Williams gained a modest lead in Philadelphia by 4 games to 3, but in New York, Soutar again won four games in succession to retain his title by 7 games to 4.

Soutar's next challenger in 1927 was a fellow-American, William 'Blondy' Standing, nephew of George Standing. But Standing was unable to cope with Soutar's mighty service and lost by 8 games to 1 in a match played in New York and Philadelphia.

In 1923, Charles Williams went to America to join the Chicago Racquet Club as senior professional. In 1929 he made a third effort to defeat Jock Soutar, this

time successfully. Once again he started well, winning the first leg in Philadelphia by 4 games to 2, but this time he made no mistake in the second leg in Chicago, winning by 3 games to 1 – an overall victory of 7 games to 3. He was champion again, eighteen years after he first won the title and sixteen years after losing it to Soutar. He was now undisputed master of the game.

Charles Williams's death in 1935 left the world title vacant, and an Anglo-American home-and-home match was arranged to fill it. From Britain came David Milford.

Milford was a remarkable master of the game; not a hard hitter but with perfect control which enabled him to place the ball with consummate skill and bring off an unexpected winner from a difficult position. He had an astonishing record, which would have been even better but for the intervention of Hitler.

He first distinguished himself at Rugby, winning the Public Schools championship in 1923 and 1924. At Oxford he represented the University for four consecutive years (1925 to 1928), winning all four doubles matches against Cambridge and two out of the three singles played. His only defeat was in 1927 at the hands of Peter Kemp-Welch.

He first won the Amateur singles in 1930. That same year he won his first hockey cap and gave up Rackets to concentrate on hockey. He did not enter for the Amateur Rackets again until 1935, when he won it, beating Ian Akers-Douglas in the final. The following year he won the final by 3 games to 1 against John Pawle. The match was very close at 1 game all and 9 all in the third when Milford was hit on the back of the head by a ball off the back wall. After a short break the match was resumed and Milford never lost another point.

The same year he challenged Albert Cooper for the British Open championship and beat him by 8 games to 3. Milford rates the first leg of this match as the best Rackets he ever played. After losing the first game 17–18, he went on to win by 4 games to 2. This victory gave him his chance to win the world championship in 1937. Quite unexpectedly, Norbert Setzler had beaten Bobby Grant for the North American Open, so it was Setzler not Grant who opposed him. Had it been Grant, Milford modestly doubts the outcome, for in three matches he played against him (admittedly two of them 'friendly'), he never won a game.

The first leg was played at the New York Racquet Club on 16 January 1937 and provided a thrilling match. The first four games were exactly divided, the score being, from Setzler's viewpoint, 9–15, 15–9, 10–15, 15–10. Setzler won the fifth game 15–8, but lost the sixth 12–15 to make the score 3 games all. In the final game, Milford led most of the way up to 11–9, but Setzler made a great effort, overtook him and went on to win the game 15–12 and the match by 4 games to 3.

Setzler played some magnificent, hard-hitting Rackets, but Milford showed how good he was at varying the pace and length of his shots. He did well to hold Setzler to so close a score on the New York court.

The second leg was played at Queen's Club on 10 April 1937 immediately following Milford's fourth (and third consecutive) win in the Amateur singles. This time the match was one-sided and Milford ran out an easy winner by 4 games to 0 (15–4, 15–4, 15–9, 15–12). He was amazingly quick about the court, with a wonderful eye and wrist, and at times played strokes of sheer genius when caught on the wrong foot. He also served much better than Setzler.

Milford was a very worthy world champion and the first amateur to hold the title since Sir William Hart-Dyke in 1862. He retained his Amateur title in 1937 and 1938, beating Robert Riseley and Ian Akers-Douglas in the finals, but did not enter in 1939. The doubles took place in term-time and Milford was a master at Marlborough, so he entered just once, in 1938, partnered by Peter Whitehouse – and won.

OTHER CHAMPIONS UP TO 1939

Between the wars many fine matches were played for the British Open championship. Until he left for Chicago in 1925, Charles Williams was the dominant player and was recognised as such without challenge. Cosmo Crawley recalls asking Walter Hawes why no Professional championship was held between 1918 and 1925 and receiving the reply: 'What's the good of having a Professional championship with Charlie here? He could give any of us at least 10.'

On his departure, however, a Professional championship was held at Queen's in January 1925 and won by Charles Read without conceding a game. This made him Professional champion of Rackets and squash; he had previously been Professional champion of lawn tennis too.

In April 1929, the first match was played at Queen's for the Open championship between Read and J.C.F. (Cyril) Simpson, the brilliant left-hander who had won the Amateur championship in 1926, 1927 and 1928. Simpson set a fast pace and won the first leg by 4 games to 1. On the second day he won the first two games to secure the championship.

A return match was played in April/May of the following year, again at Queen's. Simpson was recovering from a bad cold and knew he could not last a long match. He threw everything into one great effort to win by 4 games to 0, but the last game was very close with Read starting to play well.

In the second leg, Simpson needed one game for the match and this he won 15–10. Read was no mean opponent, as the score might suggest. The match was played out on the second day and he won all four of the next games.

Cyril Simpson was an attractive personality and player. He was none too good in the morning, and he was apt to do most of his training at the Café de Paris. On one occasion, however, he recalls arriving at Queen's in this pyjamas for a 10 a.m. match and winning. It was a great loss to the game when he broke both wrists in an accident and was unable to play again.

He had a wonderful doubles partner in R.C.O. (Roddy) Williams, and together they toured Canada and the USA in 1925. They met the redoubtable C.C. Pell and S.G. Mortimer in the Canadian final and scored a remarkable victory after trailing by 1 game to 3 and 7–14. However, the tables were turned in New York when Pell and Mortimer won by 4 games to 2.

Simpson recalls that in those days in the United States, instead of the receiver asking for a let if he was in danger of hitting the server, he would shout out 'turning' and strike the ball as he pleased. This was a terrifying situation for the server, and Jay Gould recalled two occasions when a player lost an eye as a result of turning.

Simpson also noticed that American players laid their spare rackets in the court under the board. He was told by Peter Latham that there was a good reason for this. When he played George Standing for the world championship in 1897, he broke a string and went out for a new racket to find that the strings of all his rackets had been 'nicked'!

In 1931 Lord Aberdare had won the Amateur championship and beaten Simpson in the process. He challenged him for the Open, and the match was played at Queen's in January 1932. Aberdare was forty-six, and there was some doubt about whether he could last a long match against a younger opponent. But in the event he won by 6 games to 2, mainly thanks to his murderous service – 'probably the best in the world', wrote *The Times* reporter. However, even his service could not prevent him losing the title the following year to Ian Akers-Douglas, Amateur champion from 1932 to 1934. Akers-Douglas easily won the first leg in March 1933 (4–0) and Aberdare retired.

In 1934 Akers-Douglas was challenged by Albert Cooper, then Professional champion. It is remarkable that in 1932 Charles Read, then aged forty-two, had been able to beat Cooper in the final of the Professional championship (3–2), but in a challenge match the following year Cooper had his revenge, winning (6–3).

The match took place at Queen's in February 1934. Cooper won the first leg 4–2 (15–4, 15–12, 15–9, 8–15, 9–15, 18–13). His victory was due almost entirely to service and he made fifty-two service aces in the course of this leg of the match. This enabled him to sweep ahead and lead by 3 games to 0. He appeared to tire, however, and Akers-Douglas played brilliantly to win the fourth game, his last stroke being a wonderful 'get' off the back wall, played between his legs. He continued to dominate in the next game and when he went to 9–1 in the sixth it looked as if he might well square the match. Cooper fought back hard, caught him at 13 all and went on to clinch the match by winning the set to 5.

On the second day, Cooper needed three games to win the title, but the match was far from over when Akers-Douglas, very fast about the court and serving well, won the first two games 17–15, 15–13 and went on to lead 8–0 and 12–4 in the third. This was the vital game. Cooper, making a great effort, levelled the score

at 13 all and won it 18–14. In the fourth game, Akers-Douglas began to slow up as the terrific pace of the match began to tell, and Cooper won it 15–10 to make the score 2 games all.

The final game was all Cooper's. He raced ahead to 12–0, then served his hand out. Akers-Douglas managed to take 2 points, but Cooper got back in and went to 14–2. At match point, there was an accident. Akers-Douglas, in his anxiety to win the point, ran right across in front of Cooper as the latter was about to make a forehand kill. Cooper checked his stroke but the ball hit Akers-Douglas on the back of the head. He reeled and collapsed in the corner. After a five-minute interval, although still dizzy from the blow, he gallantly insisted on resuming the match. One service from Cooper won him the game 15–2 and the Open championship.

In 1936 Cooper lost the Open title to David Milford. The first leg was played at Queen's in April and produced a gem of a match. The first game, won by Cooper 18–17, was a wonderful exhibition of Rackets. Cooper's glorious hitting was matched by Milford's speed of foot and wonderful ball control. Milford emerged the winner by 4 games to 2. The second leg was inevitably disappointing by comparison. Milford's persistence of return wore the edge off Cooper's powerful hitting and he won by 4 games to 1.

The first international Rackets match between Great Britain and the United States took place in America in 1928, when a cup was presented recording an American victory by 3 matches to 2. The United States team comprised Clarence C. Pell, Stanley G. Mortimer, Hewitt Morgan and Charles J. Coulter; the British team was Cyril Simpson, the Hon. Clarence Bruce, Peter Kemp-Welch and George Huband. During the visit Bruce won the Canadian singles and Bruce and Simpson won the US doubles.

A second match, in 1930, resulted in another American victory by 5 matches to 1. The American team was largely the same: Pell, Mortimer, Morgan and Coulter, with the addition of E.M. Edwards; for Britain, Bruce (then Lord Aberdare) and Kemp-Welch returned and were accompanied by Dr H.W. Leatham and L.D. Cambridge.

THE PRINCE'S CLUB

Many players had happy memories of the Prince's Club in Knightsbridge, and its atmosphere of sportsmanship and good company. It enjoyed royal patronage – Edward VII, then Prince of Wales, was present at a match to open the first Tennis court between the Hon.

Alfred Lyttelton and Charles Saunders; George V was often in the club and his sons, later George VI and Duke of Windsor, played many games of squash there. It was particularly convenient for officers stationed at Knightsbridge Barracks and, in fact, by special dispensation the orderly officer was allowed out of barracks to use its facilities.

Originally it contained two Tennis courts, two Rackets courts, two bowling alleys, a billiards and card room, a Turkish bath and club rooms, including a luncheon room and the famous Oak Room. It was very much a male preserve except for Miss Shepherd, who sat in a box by the main door and presented members with their bills for games, meals, baths, and suchlike before they left the building. But in its last few years, ladies were admitted to play squash and to dine.

Soon after the First World War, one of the Rackets courts was converted into three squash courts, none of them standard size, all with a stone floor and all with one wooden side wall formed by the partition – except for the centre court which had two wooden side walls.

Two games were played in the bowling alleys: American nine-pin bowls with 14lb balls (with no finger holes) and 'cocked hat', played with three pins and a small ball. The boys would get sixpence an hour for replacing the pins, apparently an enjoyable task except when the Earl of Stair was playing. He was 6ft 8ins tall, immensely strong, and would pick up the largest ball as if it were a mere golf ball and hurl it furiously down the hog-backed alley, to the terror of everyone in the vicinity, while at the same time instructing the pins in stentorian tones what to do. They usually did.

Many of these boys were later to become great names in Tennis or Rackets or both. Henry Johns had been a ball-boy at Queen's before going to Prince's in 1925; Jim Dear followed him there in 1927, when E.J.G. Johnson, Ted's eldest son, went to Brighton. At that time R.C. Dickinson was the head professional, with William Webb and Alfred Dooley to assist him. Other boys were Bill Tutt and Geoffrey Dawson.

The courts were the scene of many famous matches – seven Tennis world matches and four Rackets world matches. Here, too, the Army and Navy Rackets championships were regularly played and the inter-regimental doubles. Despite its popularity, the club was often facing financial crises.

One such, in the early Thirties, led to the appointment of a new board of directors of Prince's Club Limited, with Max Heilbut as chairman. This did not affect the club committee, which continued under the chairmanship of Douglas Barry. A deputation from the board, led by Max Heilbut, visited the landlords – the Prudential Assurance Company Limited – who always treated the club most generously. As a result of this meeting the rent was reduced, and four standard squash courts were built in one of the Tennis courts. A small end of the Tennis court was left over, and much thought and ingenuity went into ideas for a new game – without success. Other improvements were made. The club was now to remain open for dinner, having previously closed at 6 p.m., and periodically club dinners were held, followed by exhibitions of Tennis and Rackets by leading players. Some remarkable – and uninhibited – matches were played.

A proposal to redevelop the site and reconstruct the club on the top floor was abandoned because of the weight factor. During the Second World War, the premises were taken over by the Army Post Office and afterwards were demolished to make way for flats. All that can now be seen of this famous old club is the tambour of one of the Tennis courts.

POST-WAR REVIVAL

The end of the war led to a burst of Rackets activity everywhere and the start of two new competitions. The Army Open Rackets (Victory) competition was first played in 1946 when the old-timers, Cosmo Crawley and Peter Cazalet, won a remarkable victory over the much younger Geoffrey Atkins and Ronnie Taylor. The following year, Crawley won again, in partnership with Kenneth Wagg, and in 1948, the last year it was played, the winners were R.A.A. 'Bimby' Holt and Kenneth Wagg.

More enduring were the Combined Services (past and present) competitions, first played in 1949, when Geoffrey Atkins won the singles, and the doubles in partnership with Ronnie Taylor. The singles were last played in 1967, but the doubles have continued and have been won by many different pairs. The brothers Pugh (Tim and Tom) have won it on three occasions.

To mark the end of the Second World War and the revival of Rackets, Cosmo Crawley and Clarry Pell planned a British Rackets team tour of North America to take place in January/February 1947. The British team consisted of Cosmo Crawley (captain), Ian Akers-Douglas, Bimby Holt, John Pawle, Ronnie Taylor and Kenneth Wagg. They were accompanied by Jim Dear, who was on his way to play for the world championship and able to give them invaluable practice, beginning with some keep-fit squash on the *Mauritania* at sea.

The hospitality extended to the team wherever they went was beyond praise – in fact, it was remarkable that

A toast to conclude the 1947 tour of America – standing (left to right, those in full view): Jim Dear, Eddie Rogers (drinking), Clarry Pell, Bobby Grant, Malcolm Kirkbride, Cosmo Crawley, Ronnie Taylor. Seated: Bimby Holt, Ian Akers-Douglas, John Pawle.

they managed to achieve such excellent results in the circumstances! Their position was made the more embarrassing by the strict financial controls of the immediate post-war years, but American generosity and some assistance from Lord Astor of Hever overcame all difficulties. In the Rackets world at least, the tour was a practical expression of Anglo-American solidarity in defence of freedom, individual achievement and good sportsmanship.

The tour began in Chicago with the Western Amateur championships. This was a tuning-up affair in the absence of the best American players and resulted in all-British finals. Bimby Holt won the singles, defeating his doubles partner, Ronnie Taylor, in the final by 3 games to 2, and Cosmo Crawley and John Pawle won the doubles, beating Holt and Taylor 4–2 in the final.

Next port of call was Montreal, for the Canadian Amateur championships. This visit produced the best singles match of the whole tour when, in the final, Bobby Grant beat John Pawle by 3 games to 2 (13–18,

12–15, 15–9, 15–8, 15–10). It was an outstanding match between two brilliant players, both of whom believed in classical Rackets, hitting the ball hard and low, going out for the kill at every stroke. The score indicates how close the match was, but not the tension of the final game when Pawle led 9–3. This magnificent match was witnessed by the Governor-General of Canada, Earl Alexander of Tunis, who presented the trophy.

In the doubles, Crawley and Pawle were again victorious, this time beating the best American pair, Grant and Pell, by 3 games to 1.

Next stop on the tour was Tuxedo, for the Gold Racquet, where the team failed to distinguish itself and left Grant to win it in a final against fellow American F.F. de Rham.

They moved on to New York, for the US singles championship. In the semi-finals, Holt had an unexpectedly easy victory over Grant by 3 games to 0 (16–14, 15–8, 15–8) and Dick Leonard beat Pell by 3 games to 2. In the final, Holt easily won the first two

Anthony Ward and Richard Greenwood, the Eton pair in 1944.

THE WORLD CHAMPIONSHIP AFTER 1946

In 1946, Milford resigned his world and Open titles, but continued to play in the Amateur, appearing in eight finals between 1947 and 1955, of which he won two, in 1950 and 1951. He was narrowly defeated by John Pawle (3–2) in the finals of 1947, 1948 and 1949. In the 1948 final, he actually had two match points in the fourth game and in the fifth led 10–0. Pawle, with a badly blistered hand, was forced to change his grip and served a stream of aces to win the match.

In the doubles he found a magnificent partner in his Marlborough colleague, John Thompson. They won ten times – 1948, 1950–52 and 1954–59.

Milford's resignation meant a vacancy for world champion; moreover, Cooper decided not to defend his Professional championship, and there was no North American champion. To fill these gaps, a considerable programme of matches was organised in 1946.

First, the Amateur championship was revived, and in the event was won by John Pawle. Then a match was arranged at Rugby and Queen's Club between Peter Gray and Jim Dear for the Professional championship – won by Dear 8–0. Then Dear, rather unfairly it seems in retrospect, was to play first John Pawle, then Peter Kershaw, Amateur champion in 1939, for the Open championship.

Dear won both these matches. On the first day at Queen's against Pawle, he won 4–2. This was a very closely fought match for the first four games, but then Pawle faded and lost the last two games, 0–15, 1–15. Dear took the second leg at Queen's 4–1. He went on to play Kershaw at Manchester where he won 4–0, although Kershaw put up stiff resistance in the last game, leading by 14–8 and eventually losing it 15–17. In the second leg at Queen's, Dear won 4–1, but only after Kershaw had put up a fierce fight for the first three games.

Bobby Grant, the brilliant American amateur from New York, was expected to beat Kenneth Chantler, the Montreal professional, for the North American Open, so Dear went off to start practising in New York. Unexpectedly, Chantler beat Grant in a very close match 15–6, 16–18, 13–16, 15–9, 15–1, 11–15, 18–15 after Grant had led 10–4 in the final game.

Dear had to play in Montreal with only a few days' practice. However, he won a convincing victory (15–9, 16–17, 15–10, 15–11, 15–11). Chantler put up a good fight. There were many long rallies and plenty of hard hitting, but it was Dear who, every so often, played a very effective drop shot to win a valuable point.

In his own court Dear swept to victory by 4 games to 0, having in reality won the championship when he

games (15–8, 15–2) but Leonard took the next three (15–11, 15–12, 15–7) to win the championship. Holt, however, had his revenge in the Pell Cup, beating Leonard by 4 games to 0 (15–2, 15–5, 15–7, 15–6).

The US doubles championship was played in Philadelphia and won by Holt and Taylor, who beat Leonard and M. Kirkbride 3–0 in the final.

The highlight of the tour was the international match played at the New York Racquet Club on 31 January and 1 February and won by Great Britain by 5 matches to 2. Three doubles matches were played on the first day: Crawley and Pawle beat Grant and Pell by 3 games to 1; Holt and Taylor beat Leonard and M. Kirkbride by 3 games to 1; Akers-Douglas and Wagg lost to R.L. Gerry and F.F. de Rham by 3 games to 1. Great Britain thus had a 2–1 lead.

In the singles Pawle lost to Grant by 0 games to 3; Holt beat Leonard by 3 games to 0; Taylor beat de Rham by 3 very close games to 0 (16–15, 17–15, 15–12); Crawley beat Pell after a real cliff-hanger match by 3 games to 2 (15–12, 5–15, 8–15, 15–6, 18–17).

Jim Dear and Jack Johnson.

won the second game. But great praise is due to Chantler. He was the first Canadian to dispute the world championship and he did not have the advantage of close competition in Montreal. The game of Rackets, particularly in Canada, is greatly indebted to him. His enthusiasm and encouragement have introduced many a young player to the game and his friends are to be found wherever there is a Rackets court.

Jim Dear was born in Fulham in 1910, two years after his brother William. Both started work as ball-boys at Queen's, aged fourteen. William was very good at lawn tennis; Jim hated games and was nearly sacked when he was seventeen for showing no promise. In 1927, he was offered an apprentice post at Prince's, when E.J.G. Johnson left for Brighton; he accepted it reluctantly and joined Bill Tutt, Bill Webb, Alfred Dooley and Henry Johns.

At Prince's he was the only Rackets and squash professional, playing squash on the sub-standard courts converted from the second Rackets court. On one of these courts he beat Amr Bey, who was practising for a Bath Club Cup match against Sir John Child, and from that day on Amr Bey would take him to other courts in London to practise with him. Dear won the Professional Squash championship in 1935, beating Donald Butcher at the Conservative Club and Prince's, but he lost the Open to Amr Bey in 1935, 1936 and 1937. Finally he won the Open championship he so richly deserved in 1938, defeating A.E. Biddle.

He gained some Tennis experience by playing Tutt from time to time for a glass of beer.

During the Second World War, Dear was in the RAF, grounded by a perforated ear-drum, and able to play just the occasional game of squash. Prince's closed during the war and he returned to Queen's in 1946.

As a player, Dear was outstanding for his all-round ability on the court and his wonderful ball control. Not an especially hard hitter, he was a master of the angles and of change of pace. He could produce a beautifully timed drop shot even from a volley, which earned him many an important point. He was vulnerable, perhaps, against a really hard hitter such as Bobby Grant, but in general his accurate eye and swift footwork made him difficult to beat.

After Chantler, Dear faced a sterner task. John Pawle had emerged as the outstanding amateur of the post-war years. He won the Amateur championship in 1946, defeating Ian Akers-Douglas in the final, and in 1947, defeating David Milford, albeit narrowly, in the final. Now he challenged Dear for his world title.

The match took place at Queen's Club on 21 and 28 January 1948. The first day's play was of the highest quality and must be considered one of the greatest matches ever played at this level. Dear won the first game 15–5, and no one can have given Pawle much hope at this stage. But in the second game, he started to serve well and play brilliantly in the rallies. Full of confidence, he surged ahead to take the next three games, 15–6, 15–12, 15–9. Unfortunately in so doing he injured his back, and Dear, playing consistently well, fought back to win the next two games, 15–9, 15–5, and square the match at 3 games all. The final game was a tremendous struggle with Dear always slightly ahead. He reached 13–9; Pawle crept up to make it 12–13, but after several changes in hand Dear finished it off at 15–12 to lead by 4 games to 3 on the first leg.

After the brilliance of this first leg, the second was almost inevitably an anti-climax. It started well, Pawle winning a very close first game 18–15 and Dear the second 15–10. But in the third game Pawle's back again handicapped him greatly. Dear won that game 15–1 and the next 15–7. Pawle put up a courageous fight for the fifth game, but Dear emerged the winner 16–13 to retain his title.

John Pawle had another go at Dear in 1951, the match taking place at Queen's on the 24 February and 3 March. Dear won the first game 15–6. Pawle fought back to win the next two games 15–7, 15–12, and lead by 2 games to 1. But from then on Dear was in control, covering the court with amazing speed and winning the next three games 15–2, 15–7, 15–6. In the second match, Dear was even more dominant and won the three games necessary for overall victory 15–9, 15–9, 15–6, as well as the fourth game 15–8.

His next challenger was Geoffrey Atkins, who had learnt to play Rackets at Rugby and was to be the

Geoffrey Atkins.

outstanding player of the next fifteen years. He had won the British Amateur singles in 1952 and 1953 and also held the American and Canadian Amateur singles titles when he challenged Dear for the world and British Open championships.

The match was played at Queen's Club on the 15 and 22 April 1954. In the first leg, Atkins took an early lead and Dear, who was somewhat out of match practice, was having great difficulty taking his underhand twist service. Atkins won the first three games 15–9, 15–1, 15–8, playing brilliantly and seemingly invincible. But Dear's experience as a match player and his fighting qualities came to his rescue. From 2–5 down in the fourth game he won 13 consecutive points to take the game 15–5 and went on to lead 14–10 in the next. But Atkins caught up at 14 all and Dear set 3. This was the crucial moment of the whole match and the pendulum swung this way and that in an agony of suspense for the players and spectators.

Atkins went to 1–0. Dear put him out and went to 2–1. The game seesawed and Dear had three game points. Finally, luck took a turn, and Atkins put him out with a winner off the wood. He went on to win the next two points and the game to lead 4–1.

Dear, however, was not down-hearted and started the second leg of the match in overwhelming fashion. He won the first game 15–10 and, after a fierce struggle, the second 18–17. He took the third game 15–6 to lead by 3 games to 0.

Atkins rallied splendidly in the fourth game and won it 15–10. Now came the vital game. If Dear could seize it, he would win the second leg 4 games to 1 and the match would have to be decided on points. Such was the points situation that he had to prevent Atkins from getting more than 7 points. In the event, Atkins was now in full flood and forged ahead to 7–3. One magnificent service and he had won the championship. In fact, he went on to win the game 15–10 and lose the final game 16–18.

Another great champion had arrived. He had shown his mettle in this splendid match, and a sporting temperament that refused to be panicked. Whenever and wherever he played, Geoffrey Atkins was always a shining example to all of perfect court manners.

His style of play was not unlike that of Dear, relying more on accuracy and consistency than big hitting. He seldom put the ball on the back wall and at his best seemed never to make a mistake. His footwork was phenomenal and he covered the court seemingly without effort. His forehand was particularly good and his service very effective. These qualities enabled him to take Willie Surtees to five games in the US Open in New York and the US Amateur in Chicago in 1971 at the age of forty-four.

With this match, Dear lost the British Open championship as well, but it was typical of his fighting spirit that in 1960, at the age of fifty, he regained it, defeating John Thompson by 7 games to 4.

The same year, Atkins went to work in Chicago and his name was engraved often on the board of winners of the American and Canadian national championships. He won the US singles in 1954, 1955 and 1956, when he also won the British singles, and in 1959 and 1960. In that year he returned to Britain and again won the singles.

His first challenger for the world title was J.W. (James) Leonard, who had won the Amateur championship in 1961 and repeated his success in 1962, narrowly defeating Atkins in the final by 3 games to 2. This established his right to challenge, and the match took place at Queen's Club on 19 and 26 January 1963. Atkins won the first two closely contested games (17–15, 15–12), lost the third (8–15) but won the next two (15–11, 15–6) to lead by 4 games to 1 at the end of the first day's play. On the second day, he won the first two games (15–8, 15–6) and thus retained his title by 6 games to 1.

Leonard was an intellectual player, concentrating on length and placing the ball. His very heavily cut service was awkward to take and he made few errors in the rallies. He was calm and intelligent, never easy to beat.

The next challenger was Charles Swallow, who had narrowly beaten Atkins by 3 games to 2 in the final of the 1964 Amateur championship. The match was played at Queen's on 31 March and 4 April 1964. Swallow started well and was leading by 2 games to 1 when he had to stop for a while, suffering from cramp in his right hand. On play being resumed, Atkins narrowly won the next game (18–14) but took the last two games with ease (15–6, 15–2) to end the day 4 games to 2 up.

On the second day, Swallow again started in great form. He won the first two games (15–9, 15–11) and led 13–12 in the third. This was a vital turning point; Swallow could have won the championship had he won this game. But Atkins, always at his best in a crisis and showing no emotion, went coolly on his way to win that game (18–14) and the next (15–12), squaring the match at 2 games all. Swallow was still in with a chance when he took the fifth game (15–12), but Atkins made sure of overall victory by winning the sixth game (15–8). The second day's play provided a crowded

James Leonard.

Chicago, 30 March 1967. Geoffrey Atkins (seated second from the right) still unruffled after his 4–2 win in the first leg of his world title defence against James Leonard (racket in hand).

gallery with a magnificent spectacle. Swallow at his peak was one of the finest strikers of the ball in the classical tradition and seemed at times invincible. Only Atkins's calm temperament, speed of foot and power of return enabled him to weather the storm and emerge victorious.

Swallow came very near to being the greatest player of his day and his matches with Atkins were great demonstrations of Rackets at its best.

From 1964 to 1966 Atkins was working in Japan and played no Rackets. When he returned to Chicago, he decided to resign the British Open championship. A match was arranged for the vacant title between the two best players of the day, Leonard and Swallow, and was won by the former, by 7 games to 4. Leonard then challenged Atkins again for the world title. The first leg of the match took place at the Chicago Racquet Club on 30 March 1967, the second at Queen's Club a week later.

In Chicago, Atkins established a lead of 4 games to 2. In London, he dominated play, winning the first three games and conceding just 18 points.

Three years later, it was Swallow's turn again to have a go at the champion, having clearly proved his right to do so by winning the Amateur championship in 1968 and 1969 and the British Open championship in January 1970, defeating Leonard by 7 games to 4.

The match was played in Chicago and London in April 1970. In Chicago, Swallow had shown excellent form in practice with Mark Faber and looked a likely winner; but pre-match nerves and a sleepless night when opposed to the almost casual confidence of Atkins got him off to a bad start. He rallied towards the end and the last two games were hard-fought, but Atkins emerged the winner by 4 games to 1.

This was a heavy handicap with which to start the London leg, played as usual at Queen's Club.

Nevertheless, Swallow made a tremendous effort.

H.R.H. the Duke of Edinburgh and the author at the 1968 T&RA dinner.

The first game produced Rackets of the highest quality and was just won by Swallow 18–16. He swept on to take the second game 15–4, but he could do no more. Inexorably, Atkins fought back to win the next two games 15–7, 15–5 and retain his title.

The following year Geoffrey Atkins, now aged forty-four, resigned the world championship after a record reign of seventeen years, a tremendous achievement amid fierce competition from many younger players.

It was agreed to arrange an Anglo-American match to decide the next holder of the title. The North American Racquets Association nominated Willie Surtees, an Englishman resident in the United States. Surtees had learnt his Rackets at Rugby, too, and was first string in the pair that won the Public Schools Rackets championship in 1965.

It was not easy for the British Tennis and Rackets Association to nominate anyone. The year before, Swallow had decided to resign as British Open champion

and the title had become vacant. It was agreed that a preliminary competition should be held between Charles Hue Williams, Tom Pugh, Richard Gracey and James Leonard to decide who should have the right to play the Amateur champion, Martin Smith, for the vacant title.

In the event, Pugh won the eliminator, but unfortunately contracted a virus infection that prevented him from playing Smith, who was recognized as British Open champion. When the world title fell vacant in 1971, Howard Angus had not yet won the Amateur championship. He was narrowly defeated by Smith in the final, but reversed this in 1972. Nevertheless, it was agreed that Angus would meet Pugh in a play-off to find the world championship challenger – the winner of that match would play Smith for the British Open title and the right to play Surtees for the world title.

Angus never dominated the Rackets scene as he did Tennis, but his great speed and wonderful footwork made him a formidable player. He had a good, accurate service, but it was his power of retrieval, backed with his physical fitness, that won him many matches. He had shown Rackets talent since his time at Winchester, where he was in the pairs reaching the final of the Public Schools championship in 1962 and 1963. In 1965 and 1966, he played Rackets for Cambridge and thereafter he embarked upon his outstandingly successful Tennis career with victory in the Amateur championship and the MCC Gold Prize in 1966.

In the play-off, Angus beat Pugh 4–0 and Smith 6–2. He played Surtees for the world title in two legs, at Queen's Club on 7 January and in Chicago on 15 January 1972. Angus romped home at Queen's Club, winning by 4 games to 1. Surtees was unlucky not to win the last game, having led by 13–6 and 14–10, but eventually lost it 14–17.

Surtees started with that considerable disadvantage in the second leg in Chicago. However, Angus too

Willie Surtees in play against Howard Angus.

suffered from disadvantages. He was not familiar with the court and, because of central heating, necessary when the outside temperature was 50 degrees below freezing, the gut strings of his rackets had to be replaced with nylon. This had a considerable effect on his service, not helped by the one-service rule. In the first game, Surtees raced ahead to 13–7, serving well; Angus caught him at 14 all, but lost the game 16–17. Surtees won the second game 15–10 and swept on to an easy win in the third. The tension during the fourth game was even greater than in the first, with the championship at stake.

Angus fought gamely to lead 6–1, 12–8 and 13–11, but Surtees levelled the game at 13 all and went on to win the next five points and the world championship.

The following year, 1973, Angus turned the tables in no uncertain fashion. He had already retained his Amateur singles title when he went to the USA with a Jesters team. In the course of this visit, he began with Tennis, winning the Tuxedo Gold Racquet, beating Eugene Scott in the Bathurst Cup and winning the US Amateur Tennis title with victories over both brothers Bostwick. He then turned to Rackets and was due to play Surtees in the final of the US Amateur Rackets championship in Boston. Unfortunately, following an accident, Surtees had to have six stitches in his right eyelid, and the match was postponed. Nevertheless, the world title match went ahead as planned. It was played at the Chicago Racquet Club on 17 March during the Club's fiftieth anniversary celebrations.

Surtees started the first game in fine form and led 14–9, but Angus fought back to equalise at 14 all and won the game 17–15.

Angus went from strength to strength and, although Surtees had a chance in the third game, Angus won the next three games to lead 4–0 in the first leg. This match was also counted as the postponed final of the US Amateur championship, and as a consequence Angus achieved the feat of being Amateur champion of Rackets and Tennis on both sides of the Atlantic. The next day they played again for the North American Open Rackets title and this time Surtees had his revenge after a fine match, by 3 games to 2.

The second leg took place on 24 March, as usual at Queen's Club. After losing the first game 8–15, Angus won the second 15–3 to become the first left-handed world champion. He went on to crown this fantastic year of success by winning the British Amateur Tennis championship and the MCC Gold Racquet – both for the eighth year running. His ambition was now set on the Tennis world championship, so as to hold both

Rackets and Tennis titles simultaneously and equal the achievement of Peter Latham.

However, Angus retained his Rackets amateur title in 1974 and 1975 and played another match with Surtees for the world title in March 1975. This time the position was reversed. Surtees won the first leg in Chicago by a 4 games to 0 and came to Queen's Club requiring one game to give him back the title. The first game was very hard fought and Angus emerged the victor at 15–12. He now seemed to be in with a chance, reaching 11–1 in the second game. At this point, Surtees struck his best form, but Angus struggled on to reach 13–8. Surtees took the next three points to trail 11–13, but then Angus served an ace to reach game-ball at 14–11. He failed to clinch the game and, although he had another point for the game, Surtees finally won it 17–14, to reclaim his title.

The following year, Angus triumphed over Eugene Scott to win the Tennis world championship and needed to win back the Rackets title if he was to hold both at the same time. He challenged Surtees once again and a fourth match was arranged between the two rivals.

The first leg was played at Chicago on 5 March 1977 and resulted in an overwhelming victory for Surtees by 4 games to 0. Angus fought hard in the final game and lost it by the barest margin 16–17, but in the other three games he could manage no more than 18 points against a champion in top form.

When the second leg was played at Queen's on 12 March, Surtees required one game to retain the championship; he won the first game 15–11 in less than a quarter of an hour.

Surtees's style of play was good to watch. He had few weaknesses, an outstanding backhand, and he hit the ball hard and low. He was very fit and had plenty of stamina for a long match. He had many of those match-winning qualities that distinguished Geoffrey Atkins in his day as world champion.

OTHER PROMINENT PLAYERS, 1900–1980

One outstanding amateur player of Rackets and Tennis was Edgar Baerlein, beaten by Charles Williams in an eliminating contest for the World Rackets championship. He was also a brilliant all-round games player. He considered himself the best at the Eton field game and certainly expected to get a Blue for either rugger or soccer at Cambridge until he broke a knee playing Rackets in his first term. He played golf, lawn tennis and ice-hockey for Lancashire.

At Rackets, he first came to prominence in the Oxford and Cambridge match, winning all four of his

Edgar Baerlein.

singles matches from 1899 to 1902 and the doubles in 1899, 1901 and 1902 with E.B. Noel and F.B. Wilson as his partners. In his first year after leaving university, he won the Amateur singles, lost in the final of 1904 to the great H.K. Foster, but won again in 1905, 1908 to 1911, 1920–21 and 1923. He won the doubles while still at university in 1902, from 1904 to 1905 with E.H. Miles, in 1909 with Percy Ashworth, and in 1914 and 1920 with G.G. Kershaw.

But even he would admit that when he was Amateur champion Peter Latham could give him 7.

Ronny Aird recalls playing as Baerlein's partner in the Amateur Rackets doubles in the 1920s. During a long rally he took a ball just inside Baerlein's half of the court. The next shot went straight to Baerlein, who left it and lost the point. To an astonished Aird he explained, 'After you took the last one, I thought there was no need for the further play on my part.' Aird also recalls Baerlein's wise advice when hand-in to try to hit the ball between one and two feet above the board, but when hand-out between one and two inches.

His achievements at Tennis are listed elsewhere and, although he never played much lawn tennis, it was the general opinion that he would have been among the top flight of players.

James Agate, the well-known critic, was an admirer of Baerlein's ball-playing skill and makes mention of him in his writing. Of his character he writes that his passion was an ice-cold demonstration of superiority and the quickest, most exact brain he had ever known. He reports that Baerlein told him he would have been Rackets world champion but for his extraordinarily long wrist, which got him out of difficulties into which, without it, he wouldn't have dared to get; and also that he had calculated the odds against an after-life at a shade worse than 5–2.

One of his great rivals at both Rackets and Tennis was the Hon. C.N. Bruce, later Lord Aberdare, a brilliant player of all ball games and an especially attractive batsman for Middlesex.

Bruce had won the Public Schools Rackets championship for Winchester in 1904, the University singles for Oxford in 1908 and the University doubles the same year with H. Brougham. Four years in succession (1920–23) he played Baerlein in the final of

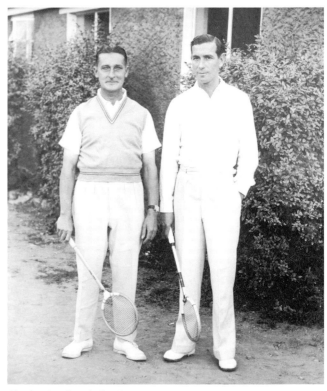

Charles Read and Jim Dear.

The Hon. C.N. Bruce (later Lord Aberdare) and Dr H.W. Leatham.

the Amateur singles, but on only one occasion did he win, in 1922. He reached the final again in 1927 and 1928, when Cyril Simpson was at the top of his form, and Simpson won on both occasions.

Bruce was a very fit man, however, and seemingly ageless. In 1931, at the age of forty-five, he defeated a much younger Ian Akers-Douglas to win the Amateur singles, and the following year defeated Cyril Simpson by 9 games to 2 for the Open championship.

Undoubtedly his greatest achievements were as a doubles player. He won the Amateur doubles ten times between 1910 and 1934 with four different partners, mostly H.W. Leatham, the Charterhouse doctor. They won on six occasions. Bruce also won the US doubles with Cyril Simpson in 1928, and the US and the Canadian doubles with Leatham in 1930.

In 1939, at the age of fifty-three, he entered the Amateur doubles with yet another partner, his eldest son, the author, then aged nineteen. This ill-sorted pair managed to reach the final, where they were beaten by Cosmo Crawley and John Pawle by 4 games to 3. The Second World War put an end to any second attempt.

Cyril Simpson was a brilliant left-hander, whose half-volley left his opponent standing and the spectators gasping. He won the Amateur singles from 1926 to 28, and was the first holder of the Sheppard Cup for the Open championship, beating Charles Read in 1929 and 1930. He lost this in 1932 to Lord Aberdare, who in turn lost to Ian Akers-Douglas in 1933. Akers-Douglas was Amateur champion from 1932 to 1934 and with Kenneth Wagg made up a formidable doubles pair, winning in 1932–33 and 1935.

Another outstanding doubles player of this period was Cosmo Crawley, Simpson's partner in the winning team of 1931, 1936 and 1937, and partner of John Pawle in the winning team of 1939 and 1946. He also won the Amateur singles in 1929.

The only professional of this era able to hold his own with this galaxy of talent – other than world champion Charles Williams, who had left Harrow for Chicago in 1923 – was Albert Cooper, who had learnt to play at Wellington under Walter Hawes. He was a mighty left-handed hitter. He won the Scott-Chad Cup for the Professional championship of the British Isles in 1932, and in 1934 he defeated Akers-Douglas for the British Open championship. Two years later he was defeated by David Milford, who went on to win the world title. Shortly before the war, he went as Rackets professional to Eton, where he kept the game alive in very difficult circumstances.

A professional of a slightly older generation who certainly deserves a mention is Charles Read of Queen's Club, where he started as a ball-boy at the age of thirteen in 1902. A year later he joined his uncle 'Judy' Stevens at Harrow, and here he learnt to play Rackets and squash rackets. At seventeen, he returned to Queen's Club as head Rackets professional, replacing Walter Hawes who had gone to Wellington.

He was successful at all three games he played. At Rackets, he was Professional champion from 1925 to 1932. In 1931 a competition was held for the professional title in which he beat C. Atherton of Cheltenham to reach the final. His opponent was Albert Cooper, who had beaten Jim Dear. In the final Read won by 3 games to 2. At squash, he was Professional champion from 1920 to 1929 and at lawn tennis from 1921 to 1928.

Arthur Whetton of Haileybury might well have been in the top rank of players had he not been killed in the Second World War. After the war, a new generation of talented Rackets players emerged. Competing for the world title were such amateur players as John Pawle, Geoffrey Atkins, James Leonard, Charles Swallow, Willie Surtees and Howard Angus. At British Open championship level were players such as Peter Kershaw, John Thompson, Richard Gracey and Martin Smith. These were the players who won the Amateur singles from 1946 to 1975, apart from 1950 and 1951, when Milford

Left to right: *David Milford, John Thompson, Peter Kershaw, Geoffrey Atkins.*

returned to show what an old dog could do. Most of them were also winners of the Amateur doubles, in such fine company as Bimby Holt, Ronnie Taylor, Tom Pugh and Charles Hue Williams.

Milford and Thompson had an outstanding record in the Amateur doubles, winning ten times between 1948 and 1959. Their nearest rivals were Bimby Holt and Ronnie Taylor, winners in 1947 and 1949, who ran them very close in five finals. In 1951, the match was so even that both sides ended up winning 84 points, although Milford and Thompson won by 4 games to 3.

John Thompson won the Amateur singles in 1954–55 and 1957–59, and won the doubles again in 1966 with Tom Pugh as his partner.

Thompson's fighting spirit – the mark of a champion – was called upon in two exciting finals of the Amateur championship. In 1957, he lost the first two games to Mike Coulman, won the next two and led 12–3 in the fifth. Coulman caught him and led 13–12; Thompson made it 13 all. Coulman again led 2–0 in the set to 3, but Thompson finally won the game 16–15, and with it the match and the championship, with a timely drop shot.

He endured an even worse situation in 1959 against J.M.G. Tildesley, who won the first two games 15–11, 15–0 and led 14–8 in the third. All seemed to be over

Silver statuette made by David Wynne for the author.

to everyone except John Thompson. He fought back to win the third game 17–16, the fourth game 15–13 and the final game 15–8. This is without doubt one of the best examples of the saying that a match is not lost until the last ball is played.

Michael Pugh was known and admired throughout the Public Schools for his energetic organisation of a 'Circus' – a group of his friends with whom he would tour the schools and give invaluable match practice to young players. He took the idea from Peter Eckersley, who had played against a few school second pairs before the Second World War. His first regular partner was C.G. (Tim) Toppin, and later Malcolm Burr. Other members of the Circus were his two sons, Tim and Tom, Roger Eckersley and Charles Cullen. Nothing gave him greater pleasure than the success of his two sons at Tennis and Rackets.

He was a man of taste – in claret as well as art. He was an early sponsor of the sculpture of David Wynne, also a useful Tennis player, and commissioned a head of Peter Latham. In 1960, David Wynne made a figure of a Rackets player for the author out of silver from his father's trophies; the model was Tom Pugh.

Two other outstanding pairs were Geoffrey Atkins

and Peter Kershaw (1953, 1961–62), and Richard Gracey and Martin Smith (1964–65, 1969–71). Another remarkable doubles player was Charles Hue Williams, with five victories to his credit with three different partners – James Leonard (1967–68), Howard Angus (1972–73) and Geoffrey Atkins (1974). He also earned a well-deserved victory in the Amateur singles in 1977.

Two players to emerge at this time were later to develop into world-class competitors. Willie Boone and John Prenn were in the winning pair for their respective schools, Boone for Eton with Mark Faber in 1968, Prenn for Harrow with Mark Thatcher in 1971. Prenn went on to win the Swallow Trophy for three successive years, 1974–76.

They first clashed in a major competition in the final of the Amateur singles in 1976 when Boone won a very close match by 3 games to 2. In the final game Prenn had a match point at 14–10 and three more at 14–13 before Boone clinched it at 17–14. The following year, Boone beat Prenn again in the semi-final by 3 games to 0, but in the final of the Louis Roederer Open, it was Prenn who beat Boone, by 4 games to 1.

They met yet again in the final of the Amateur singles in 1978, when Boone won another close match by 3 games to 2. They played off in April to decide who should be recognised as challenger to Surtees for the world championship. Prenn took the first leg 4–2; Boone won the first two games of the second leg easily, to level the match. The next two games were extremely close, but were eventually won by Boone, 17–14, 17–16. In the match, Boone won 113 points to Prenn's 110.

Prenn won the Amateur singles for the first time in 1979, beating Boone in the final, but Boone had his revenge in the Louis Roederer by 4 games to 1.

Prenn retained his Amateur title in 1980, beating Boone convincingly by 4 games to love in the final, and went on to win the Open championship again beating Boone, but more narrowly by 4 games to 2.

These two leading players presented a contrast in style. Boone was the mighty hitter with a formidably fast service. He was quite capable of overwhelming an opponent with the violence of his attack, and was a dogged fighter in adversity. Prenn, an outstanding stroke-player in the classical mould, hit the ball hard and low, and he had the ability to vary his service, which was a highly effective tactic. He invented a service of his own, the equivalent of the American twist lawn-tennis service, which won him many important points.

RACKETS TOURS

Following the very successful American tour of 1947, several more tours took place up to 1980. In 1953, Great Britain fielded a very strong side, comprising Kenneth Wagg (captain), David Milford, John Thompson and Geoffrey Atkins.

Before the international match, Milford and Thompson won the US Amateur doubles in Detroit and the Canadian doubles in Montreal, but Bobby Grant had shown what a formidable competitor he still was at the age of forty-one by beating Milford (3–0), Thompson (3–0) and Atkins (3–2) on successive days to win the Canadian singles. In the final, he had a great struggle with Atkins, who looked the likely winner when leading 10–8 in the final game. Atkins overall won 67 points to Grant's 64.

In the US singles, Grant continued on his triumphant path, beating Thompson (3–0) in the semi-final and Milford (3–0) in the final.

In the international match, Britain had a convincing victory over the USA by 5 matches to nil. Atkins, playing brilliantly, had a surprisingly easy revenge on Grant (3–0); Milford beat Stan Pearson (3–1); and

Thompson beat Clarry Pell (3–1). In the doubles, Milford and Thompson beat Grant and Pearson; Atkins and Wagg beat Dick Leonard and F.F. de Rham.

Atkins stayed on to compete in the Tuxedo Gold Racquet and had the satisfaction of a fourth victory over Grant (3–1).

In 1956, the international trophy was contested at Queen's Club, London. A powerful British team retained the trophy, winning by 4 matches to 1. Atkins was by that time resident in Chicago and played for the USA. He duly won the top singles honours, beating Thompson after a close match (3–2). Milford beat Charles 'Babe' Pearson (3–1), Mike Coulman beat Stephen Colhoun (3–0). Milford and Thompson beat Atkins and W. Wood Prince (4–1) and Bimby Holt and Ronnie Taylor beat Pearson and Wagg (4–1).

The 1960 tour was led by Dick Bridgeman, who unfortunately fell ill. The British team were further handicapped by the absence of David Norman as the result of a leg injury incurred in the final of the Canadian doubles. America won the international match by 5 matches to 2. The American team made an impressive start, winning the first three matches. Grant beat Mac Bailey (3–0), Peter Read beat Robin Allen

The international match of 1956. Standing (left to right): *Charles Pearson, Steve Colhoun, John Thompson, Bimby Holt, Kenneth Wagg, David Milford, Ronnie Taylor.* Seated: *Mike Coulman, Geoffrey Atkins.*

(3–1) and Atkins and Babe Pearson beat Tom Pugh and Bailey (3–0). Roddy Bloomfield gave Britain her first victory, beating Babe Pearson (3–2), but Atkins secured the match by beating Tom Pugh (3–0), giving the US a decisive 4–1 lead. In the two doubles matches that followed, Clarry Pell and Read beat David Scholey and Malcolm Burr (3–0), and Stephen Colhoun and Pearson were leading 2–1 against Bloomfield and Allen when they were forced to retire after Colhoun sustained an injury over his left eye from a ball that flew off his racket.

During the course of this visit, Tom Pugh won the Western American singles and, in partnership with Mac Bailey, the US and Western American doubles.

In 1962, another British assault again failed to reclaim the trophy, the USA winning by 5 matches to 2. On the first day, the US won two out of the three doubles matches, the only winning British pair being Kenneth Wagg and Dick Bridgeman, who beat Clarry Pell and Babe Pearson 3–1 after a fast and furious contest. In the singles, Bridgeman beat Pearson (3–1), but Peter Read beat Tim Pugh (3–1), Jimmy Bostwick beat Roger Eckersley (3–0) and Clarry Pell beat Julian Bevan (3–0).

In 1963, a Jesters Rackets team toured the USA. Miles Connell was captain, and his powerful team included Charles Swallow, Mike Coulman, Dick Bridgeman, Jeremy Hogben, Maurice Baring, M.S. Ross-Collins and Oliver Case. They won the international match by 8 matches to 1.

There was a visit to Canada in May 1967 to celebrate the centenary of the Montreal Racket Club. Eight leading British players were invited and all expenses were paid by their generous Canadian hosts. Pete Bostwick from New York won the singles, defeating James Leonard, Jeremy Hogben and Charles Hue

Dick Bridgeman.

Williams in so doing – a notable performance. The doubles were won by Richard Gracey and Martin Smith.

Another Jesters team toured America in 1973 and retained the trophy. Howard Angus was a member of the team but could not play in the international match which clashed with the US Tennis singles. The Jesters team consisted of Charles Hue Williams, J.K. Rogers, P.D. Rylands, A.C.S. Tufton, T.P. Halford, J.G.M. Walsh and J.N. Travis.

1980–2000

Although Rackets did not quite match Tennis for the number of new courts opened in these twenty years, there was a considerable increase in the number of people continuing to play after leaving school. Under the guidance of the Rackets committee, chaired successively by Garth Milne, Paul Nicholls, Charles Hue Williams and Sir Mervyn Dunnington-Jefferson, several new tournaments were introduced, there was a significant increase in the levels of sponsorship, and evening clubs thrived on school courts. This process was accelerated in 1989 by the appointment of

Brigadier Andrew Myrtle as the first full-time administrator of the Tennis and Rackets Association. In addition, a National League, the brainchild of Mick Dean, meant that competitive matches, latterly under a handicap system, became a regular feature of the evening clubs. Rackets has been consistently sponsored by Celestion Loudspeakers and Lacoste thanks to Dan and John Prenn, while other major supporters include Rank Xerox, Peel Hunt and Henderson Private Investors. A number of specific events have been sponsored by other individuals and firms.

In 1980, there were twelve schools with courts, six of them with two courts. A further six clubs made a total of twenty-four courts. Since then, four courts have been restored at Marlborough, Cheltenham, Newcastle and Queen's Club, and a new court has been built at St Paul's School, thanks to the generosity of an Old Pauline benefactor. Sadly, St John's College, Cambridge, decided to demolish the Portugal Place complex so that neither of the ancient universities has a Rackets court, and players depend for practice on the hospitality of Haileybury and Radley. Thus in 2000 there were twenty-eight courts in action in the UK.

The resurrection of the second court at Queen's Club was achieved due to the determination and drive of David Norman and with generous financial help from many devoted enthusiasts. It was named the Bridgeman Court to mark the dedication of Dick Bridgeman who did so much to promote Rackets post-war. The additional court means that there are much better facilities than there were before at the headquarters of the game. It is also used by Westminster School.

In the world championship, the years from 1980 to 1987 were dominated by the continued rivalry of John Prenn and Willie Boone. John Prenn defeated the holder, Willie Surtees, in 1981 by 6 games to 4 in a match played in New York and at Queen's Club. In 1984, he lost the title to Boone by 2 games to 7 in

David Norman was an effective chairman of the T&RA.

Montreal and at Queen's Club. Prenn had his revenge in 1986, winning by 8 games to 6 in New York and at Queen's Club.

In 1988, a new star arose in the Rackets court – James Male, the first ambidextrous and double-handed player in the game. John Prenn had decided to resign the world title for business reasons and a match was arranged between Male and Boone for the vacant title.

British world champions invited to Buckingham Palace in 1992: (left to right) James Male, Howard Angus, Geoffrey Atkins, Willie Surtees, John Prenn and Willie Boone.

Neil Smith, the elegant challenger, beat world champion James Male 4–2 in Chicago in 1999.

Male won the first leg, played in Chicago, by 4 games to 1. He narrowly won the first two games of the second leg at Queen's Club and, aged twenty-three, became the youngest world Rackets champion since Peter Latham, who won in 1887, aged twenty-two.

Male successfully defended his title in 1991 in Chicago and at Queen's Club, defeating Shannon Hazell by 6 games to 2; in 1993 in Philadelphia and at Queen's Club, defeating Neil Smith by 6 games to 5; and in 1995 in Chicago and at Queen's Club, defeating Neil Smith again, this time by 6 games to 2.

In 1999, a further challenge was arranged between the same two outstanding players in Chicago and at Queen's Club. Smith led by 4 games to 2 in Chicago, but unfortunately injury prevented Male from playing the second leg and Smith became the new world champion.

The outstanding new Rackets court at St Paul's was officially opened by Lord Aberdare on 20 January 2001. This coincided with the second leg of the world singles championship. James Male, the challenger, had defeated the holder, Neil Smith, by 4–1 in New York the previous week and by winning the two games required for outright victory he regained the title he had held between 1988 and 1999. The length of time it took to play these two games and the quality of play were a fitting tribute to the condition of the new court.

The Open singles has been dominated, not surprisingly, by the same players as the world championship. Between 1977 and 1986, Willie Boone and John Prenn contested the final eight times, Prenn winning on six occasions. Prenn was a fine tactician with an ideal match temperament. He never seemed to be under pressure, and his wide range of strokes made full use of the geometry of the court. There followed three epic victories by James Male over Neil Smith, repeated again in 1991 and 1996, but Smith had some consolation in winning against Shannon Hazell, Rupert Owen-Browne and Boone (twice) in the 1990s. Boone, who won on six occasions between 1979 and 1998, was narrowly beaten by Smith by 4 games to 3 in 1999. Boone's long run of successes was a tribute to his supreme fitness and his match temperament, although his ebullience led to difficult moments for the referee. Male won again in 2000 when he beat Peter Brake, the Queen's Club professional, by 4 games to 2.

Willie Boone's first appearance in an Amateur singles final was in 1976. Up to 1996 he appeared in twenty-two consecutive finals, two competitions having been held in 1985 and 1988, in January and December. The sequence must surely be a record for a national final in any sport, and he returned in 1998, winning on eight occasions in all. In the same period, John Prenn won five of his twelve finals, and James Male won on all eleven occasions in which he was a finalist.

The world doubles championship was inaugurated in 1990 with the expectation that challenges would occur every two years, alternating with the world singles challenge. John Prenn and James Male were the first winners, beating Neil Smith and Shannon Hazell by 8 games to 5 at Manchester and Queen's Club. Then in 1992, Smith and Hazell beat Prenn and Willie Boone by 7 games to 3 at Clifton College and at Queen's Club. They have since defended their title successfully on three occasions, Smith having moved from Queen's to New York, and despite the fact that Hazell had left Rackets to be a squash professional in the US. In 1993, they beat Prenn and Male by the narrowest of margins, the games being 7 all, 166 points to 160. In 1996, they beat the same opponents by the emphatic score of 5 games to love, but were hard pressed by Boone and Peter Brake in 1998, winning by 7 games to 6. Their success came from the combination of Smith's elegant stroke play down the side walls, and Hazell's fleetness of foot in retrieving and volleying up the front of the court.

The Open doubles began in 1981, and for the first five years was dominated by Willie Boone and Randall Crawley, whose persistence in return made him an ideal partner for Boone. John Prenn and James Male were equally dominant from 1986 to 1990, beating Boone and Crawley three times and Neil Smith and Shannon Hazell twice. Boone characteristically bounced back to win from 1995 to 1997, twice with Tim Cockroft, a rapidly improving player, and once with Peter Brake. The most remarkable result was in 1998 when Male, with a much younger partner, the left-hander Mark Hue Williams, beat the world champions Smith and Hazell by 4 games to 1. The success of this new partnership was confirmed in 1999 when they beat Jonathan Larken and Toby Sawrey-Cookson, the Clifton professional, in straight games; and in 2000, they beat Guy Barker and Alister Robinson by 4 games to 2, a repetition of the result in the Amateur doubles.

The pattern was similar in the Amateur doubles with Willie Boone and Randall Crawley successful from 1980 to1984 and again in 1986, and John Prenn and James Male winning from 1988 to1991 and in 1993 and 1995. Tim Cockroft, a sound unspectacular player in the forehand court, was successful four times in the 1990s, three times with Boone and once with Rupert Owen-Browne, a mighty but somewhat erratic striker of the ball.

A significant breakthrough for the younger generation of players came in 1999 when Guy Barker and Alister Robinson, who had won the Public Schools championship in 1983 for Marlborough, beat Boone and Mark Hue Williams by 4 games to 2; but in 2000 they lost by the same score to Male and Hue Williams, who

had entered this competition together for the first time.

During these twenty years, faster balls, more tightly strung rackets and warmer courts means that doubles at the highest level has become a breathtaking spectacle. There have undoubtedly been moments of danger when all four players have tried to seize the initiative by advancing up court to volley, but there have been no serious incidents, probably due to disciplined training at school. The role of the referee has become more difficult as the quicker players are able to retrieve shots that have passed their partner's attempts to volley, or to claim a let at the back of the court.

In the Public Schools doubles championship, Tonbridge was the dominant force, playing in nine of the twenty-one finals and winning six. Otherwise honours were well spread, with Harrow winning three times, Marlborough, Clifton, Rugby and Eton twice, and Wellington, Radley, Winchester and Haileybury once. In the same period, Tonbridge and Eton were the most successful schools in the colts and junior colts doubles, a tribute to their professionals, David Makey and Norwood Cripps, respectively.

In the Foster Cup for singles, success was confined to seven schools, with Tonbridge and Harrow winning five times, Radley and Rugby three times, Clifton twice and Eton and Cheltenham once. Winners on two

Play in the 1999 Open doubles at Queen's, which was won by James Male (bottom) and Mark Hue Williams (top left). Their opponents were Toby Sawrey-Cookson and Jonathan Larken (far right).

Andrew Myrtle, retiring Chief Executive of the T&RA, and Norman Rosser, chronicler of the game.

occasions were James Male (Radley), Johnny Longley (Tonbridge), who had the distinction of not losing a match at Queen's Club, in singles or doubles at all ages, Matthew Windows (Clifton), Richard Carter (Rugby) and Alex Titchener-Barrett (Harrow). All of these had successes in the doubles, and another prominent player was Rupert Owen-Browne (Tonbridge) who won the doubles twice and the singles once. Particularly noteworthy was the success of Jamie Stout in the Foster Cup 2000, just twelve years after Cheltenham reopened their court.

In 1993, the Faber family presented a cup in memory of Mark Faber, an outstanding games player, who had been in the winning Eton pair for three years from 1967 to 1969 and had played in the Foster Cup finals, winning in 1967 and 1969. The cup is awarded each season to the school with the best combined results in the singles and doubles tournaments, played at Christmas and Easter, points being awarded to semi-finalists and finalists, with weighting in favour of the doubles and the senior events. Rugby won in 1993, Eton from 1994 to 1997, Tonbridge in 1998 and 1999, and Harrow in 2000.

Professionals Ron Hughes (Malvern), Roger Crosby (Harrow) and Peter Ellis (Haileybury) retired after a lifetime of service to the game, while Mick Dean retired after over twenty years as Radley's professional. For Peter Ellis, retirement has been a relative term as he has continued to mark with great skill at many of the major events. Other long-serving professionals still in harness are Derek Barrett (Wellington), Norwood

Cripps (Eton), Robert Wakely (Marlborough), Peter Ashford (Winchester), Roger Tolchard (Malvern), Philip Rosser (Rugby) and David Makey (Tonbridge).

Although the prestige of Rackets remains high in the schools, the opportunities for practice have tended to diminish as demands for academic time increase and the major team games have claimed more time both for matches and practices. Thus the role of the masters-in-charge, in support of the professionals, has become more significant as they seek to protect the players, invariably good all-rounders, from excessive demands on their time. Among those who promoted the cause of Rackets, while assisting on court with enthusiasm and varying degrees of skill, were Mark Greenstock and Peter Warfield (Harrow), Norman Rosser, Andrew Rambridge and Andy Murtagh (Malvern), John Thompson (Marlborough), Ian Graham (Rugby), David Kemp and John Gibbs (Tonbridge), Chris Potter (Wellington) and Robert Turnbull (Haileybury). Karl Cook has played a major part in the revival of Rackets at Cheltenham, firstly as professional and latterly as master-in-charge.

Several families have made remarkable contributions to Rackets over the years and for two of them, the Grays and the Crosbys, this has continued into the twenty-first century. The Gray family influence began with Henry, William and Joseph, world champions between 1863 and 1887 except for three years. It included three generations of professionals at Rugby, spanning over a century – Joseph (1868–94), Harry (1894–1937 and 1939–46) and Peter (1936–39 and 1946–71) – and now Richard Gray's firm is the only manufacturer of Rackets rackets.

Equally remarkable is the Crosby family with four generations of professionals, pictured on page 240. Jim Crosby was at Whale Island, Portsmouth, from about 1890 to 1895 and then at Marlborough (1895–1922). His sons Jim (Winchester 1910–39) and Fred (Harrow 1922–62) followed him into the profession and Fred's descendents carried on the tradition. His son Roger was first assistant and then professional at Harrow from 1951 to 1996; grandson Martin was assistant at Harrow (1983–88) and is now the professional at Charterhouse. Surely no other game can boast such dedication from these and countless others.

In 1987, Bill Stephens, then secretary of the Tennis and Rackets Association, and the late James Knott Jr initiated a scheme whereby groups of players from the UK and the USA and Canada were to tour each other's country, visiting clubs and schools. The first tour took place in 1989 when a British team visited the USA. Two years later there was a return tour from America to Britain and this pattern has continued up to 1999 – six tours in all.

RACKETS IN THE USA AND CANADA

RACKETS HAS BEEN PLAYED in New York since the end of the eighteenth century. James Knox acquired property on Allen Street in 1793 and a few years later built a Rackets court. He had learnt to play in Halifax, where he had sought refuge during the Revolution. The court was 100ft long by 36ft wide, with no back wall but a line on the floor. There were two other lines across the court: one 30ft from the front wall with a circle in the centre, and another 80ft from the front wall. Service had to be delivered from the circle and had to fall between the 30ft and 80ft lines.

The balls were 'made of white woollen yarn dampened and wound over a piece of solid rubber about the size of a marble. They were covered with leather and sewed with different colors of silk, blue, yellow and scarlet.' (G.M. Rushmore). Liquor was free, champagne $2 a bottle and Havana cigars 5¢ each.

In the 1830s another court was built at the corner of Bowery and Broome Streets, run by Alexander Fink and known as the Butchers Club. Their best player was Elias de Forrest, known as Uncle Elias, but the court did not last very long.

Meantime, the Allen Street club had become immensely popular. Robert Knox, son of James, was the local champion until the arrival of Edward La Montagne from Montreal in 1848.

In 1845 the Broadway Racquet Club was built, inspired by Robert Emmet and designed by Richard T. Carman. It lay on the east side of Broadway between Prince and Houston Streets and included bowling alleys and a billiard room. The Rackets court was of the same dimensions as that in Allen Street. The professional in charge was Billey De Voe, the first American professional of whom any record exists.

The game was very popular and the club had some 200 members. The players, though keen, were not of a very high standard; the best among them were Robert Edgar, Edgar Newbold, Beverley Robinson, John A. Post and William J. Emmet. None of them was a match for Edward La Montagne.

Edward La Montagne was the outstanding amateur player of the 1840s and 1850s. Like other well-known players of the game since then, he was a wine merchant, representing the celebrated Bordeaux firm of Barton et Guestier, whose directors have always taken a keen interest in Tennis.

In 1854, La Montagne built the first covered court on 13th Street/Sixth Avenue, known as the Gymnasium Club. He was guaranteed a return of 7 per cent for four years on his investment. The court was 70ft x 30ft (10ft longer than standard) and had two galleries for spectators. The front wall was of polished stone, the side walls of cement and the floor of Georgia pine. The professional was Fred Foulkes, the American champion defeated by William Gray in 1867. The club was sold in 1868.

The popularity of Rackets soon spread to other American cities. On 25 November 1889 at 923 Walnut Street, the Racquet Club of Philadelphia was opened with two Rackets courts; and the Boston Athletic Club opened its doors in December of the same year with Tom Pettitt as head professional. In September 1893, the Chicago Athletic Association opened two courts in Michigan Boulevard and put Harry Boakes in charge.

In the winter of 1899/1900, the Tuxedo Club opened with a Tennis court and squash courts. The Rackets court, designed by Bickley, was not ready until 1902.

Edward La Montagne.

In 1903, a new court was opened at the Racquet and Curling Club of Detroit with a match between George Standing and Harry Boakes. This was another Bickley court of standard size. The first professional was George Healey.

Rackets grew rapidly in popularity in Boston, where a second court was added at the Tennis and Racquet Club in 1904, and four years later a third was built at the Randolph Club at Harvard. In Chicago, a second court was opened at the Illinois Athletic Association in 1906. This was unique in that the players had to enter it through a trap-door in the floor.

In 1909, a court was opened in St Louis, with Dave Gardiner, trained by Standing in New York, in charge. Two years later he was replaced by Frank Lafforgue, another of Standing's pupils. It was mainly thanks to Lafforgue's coaching ability that Joseph Wear and Dwight Davis won the Amateur doubles title for St Louis in 1914.

In 1909, two more courts were built at the University Club of Chicago, as well as four squash courts. Harry Boakes was put in charge with his son, Harry Boakes Jr, to help him. In Philadelphia the Racquet Club moved to its present building on 16th Street in 1907, with two Rackets courts, a Tennis court, five squash courts and one doubles squash court, the first in the United States.

During this period, two private courts were built – one by Eugene Higgins at Morristown, New Jersey in the 1880s, and the other by George Gould at Georgian Court, Lakewood, New Jersey about 1900. Frank Forester taught Jay Gould and his brother, Kingdon, to play Rackets at Lakewood.

Two post First World War events that took place in New York and Chicago are of great importance to the modern scene. Firstly, the New York Racquet and Tennis Club moved in 1918 to its present location at 370 Park Avenue, where it had two Rackets courts, two Tennis courts and five squash courts. Secondly, two courts were opened at the new Chicago Racquet Club on Schiller Street in 1923, and Charles Williams was invited over from England to take charge of them.

During the early years of the game in the United States, many fine players emerged; most of the professionals were recruited from England, but the amateurs were all home-bred. The first-known American champion was Fred Foulkes of New York, who played and lost to William Gray for the world championship in 1867. By the 1880s, the two outstanding players were Englishmen: Harry Boakes, at Quebec and later at Chicago (1893), and Robert Moore, at New York and later at Tuxedo (1900). They met for the Professional championship in 1883 and Boakes won. Nominally, he held the title until defeated by George Standing in 1893, but had he been in the United States rather than in Canada, he might well have been defeated before then by Tom Pettitt, another Englishman, trained in Boston and holder of the world title at Tennis from 1885 to 1896.

George Standing had come to the New York 43rd Street Club in 1892, and after defeating Boakes established himself as the outstanding player in America. In 1897, he challenged Peter Latham for the world championship, but was defeated by 8 games to 4 in a match played at Queen's Club and the New York Racquet and Tennis Club.

In 1890 the American Amateur championship was inaugurated, and for the first eight years shared by two outstanding players, B.S. de Garmendia (six) and J.S. Tooker (two). In 1898, the sequence was broken by a great Canadian player, F.F. Rolland.

The next great professional was a Scotsman, Jock Soutar, brought to Philadelphia by Frederick Tompkins in 1907. The story of his rivalry with Charles Williams has already been told. Soutar won in 1913 and 1922, but Williams had the last laugh in 1929.

B.S. de Garmendia.

Stanley Mortimer and Clarry Pell.

In the meantime, some outstanding amateur players had emerged. In the 1890s Clarence Mackay of New York was in the forefront of amateur players and, shortly after him, Lawrence Waterbury and Reginald Fincke. The latter was considered by some to be potentially the greatest Rackets player of all time and he was certainly able to defeat professionals as well as amateurs. Unfortunately, however, he had to give up after an accident in the court while still under thirty.

The years 1915 to 1933 were dominated by Clarence C. Pell and Stanley G. Mortimer. Their record speaks for itself – Pell was the Amateur singles champion twelve times and won the Tuxedo Gold Racquet fourteen times. Mortimer won the Amateur singles on four occasions and the Tuxedo Gold Racquet on three. Together they won the Amateur doubles nine times. Pell won the British Amateur singles in 1925, beating H.W. Leatham 3–0 in the final.

In the late Thirties, there emerged another outstanding amateur player, Bobby Grant III of New York, who had learnt to play Rackets at Eton. He won the American Amateur singles ten times despite four lost years of war when no competition took place. With

Clarence Pell Jr he won the doubles seven times. He won the Canadian singles on all eight occasions on which he competed. In 1953, he showed his tremendous ability against a strong team of British visitors, including David Milford, John Thompson and Geoffrey Atkins.

Grant was also a first-class Tennis player. In 1946 he achieved a double victory, winning the Amateur championships of both Rackets and Tennis, a feat accomplished previously only by B.S. de Garmendia in 1894 and Eustace Miles in 1900. He also won the Amateur doubles twice, in 1941 with Ogden Phipps and in 1960 with Alastair Martin.

Grant was the last great American player. Since then the Amateur championship has been won mostly by British-born players, working in America or visiting. They have included Geoffrey Atkins (seven times), David Norman (five times), Willie Surtees (nine times) and Howard Angus and James Leonard once each.

Ogden Phipps presented a cup for the Open championship of the United States in 1938 in memory of Clarence Pell – the Clarence Pell Racquet Cup. The first winner was Bobby Grant, who won it again in 1941, 1948 and 1950. Ken Chantler of Montreal was

Bobby Grant and Clarry Pell.

the first professional to win it in 1940, and again in 1957 and 1960. Albert (Jack) Johnson won it in 1959 and 1964; Jim Dear in 1962 and 1963.

Several amateurs have been doubles victors – Geoffrey Atkins (1958 and 1968), Tom Pugh (1967–68) and Pete Bostwick (1969–70) – but Willie Surtees surpassed them all by winning from 1971 to 1979.

As in India, Rackets was first played in Canada in military garrisons. It started towards the end of the eighteenth century in Montreal, Hamilton (Ontario), Quebec and Halifax, Nova Scotia.

It is believed that the Montreal Rackets Club was formed in about 1800 and it certainly existed in 1825 when a military map shows a court on the east side of Sanguinet Street, north of Craig Street.

The next court in Montreal was built in 1836 at the corner of St Peter and Craig Street. It was an open court of wooden construction, measuring about 34ft x 80ft. It was much used by officers of the garrison as well as pupils from neighbouring schools. Here Edward La Montagne learnt to play, and held the club championship from 1839 until he left for New York in 1852. He later described the court as open to the sky,

the walls and floor painted black. Small boys would gather around it to pick up the balls that now and then went over the walls.

A macabre story is told of this court. Major Erle, later General Erle of Majuba Hill fame, was struck in the eye and the eyeball fell at his feet. Clapping his hand to his face he turned to the gallery and said, with a smile, 'The ladies won't look at me now.'

One of the first champion players was Sir Hippolyte Lafontaine, who played with a Pittman racket, shaped like a Tennis racket.

In Quebec, an old open-air court is known to have existed in the Artillery Barracks, and a new one was built about 1851 at the rear of Palace Street. Here the Governor-General, Sir Edmund Head, used to play. The marker was Mahon, who later went to Montreal.

This court was burnt down in about 1861 and a new one built, originally near St Louis Gate but later moved to a site off Grande Allée. Here the marker was Harry Boakes, who later played such a magnificent match with Joseph Gray in New York.

In 1860, a court was built in Hamilton, Ontario, and initially was much used by civilians and military alike. It went out of use in 1883.

Two more courts were built in Montreal before the Montreal Racket Club court was opened in 1862 between Craig Street and Fortification Lane. This was a covered court with good natural lighting and remained in use until sold to the *Montreal Star* in 1870.

Many curious activities took place in these early courts, including boxing and rat-killing. 'The club professional would obtain a sackful of rats from the harbour from time to time and release them in the court. Whereupon members would watch from the gallery as their pet fox terriers were let loose, wagering on which terrier would kill the most rats.'

About 1875, the Montreal Racket Club moved to St George Street and engaged Mahon and his son from Quebec as markers until 1881 when Albert Bridger was invited over from England. This court was regulation size, 30 ft x 60 ft, but the back wall was not at right angles – the left receiving court was slightly obtuse, the right slightly acute. Exhibition matches were played here by Bridger and Boakes from Quebec. It was highly exclusive, with only thirty to thirty-five members. Prominent among them was F.M. David, a brilliant if somewhat erratic player, who had brought Bridger from England and who was responsible for raising the money and supervising the building of the present Concord Street court in 1889.

In a mistaken endeavour to improve the doubles

Celebrated Canadian amateur, David McLernon.

game, this new court was originally about 4 ft longer and 2 ft wider than normal, but in 1909 this was remedied with the aid of Bickley, and the court reduced to regulation size.

The earliest outstanding Canadian Rackets player was F.F. Rolland, the first winner of the Canadian Amateur championship in 1896 and the winner on seven other occasions. In 1898 he won the American singles, played that year in Boston, becoming the first of only two Canadians to have won this event. Apart from his skill as a player, he set a fine example of good sportsmanship and was an inspiration to many young players.

The Canadian championship – and the renowned hospitality of Canadians – has attracted many foreign visitors, especially from the neighbouring United States. The first visitor to win it was B.S. de Garmendia from New York in 1897, followed by Q.A. Shaw from Boston in 1898.

Rolland came back into his own in 1899, but Eustace Miles from England took the title in 1900.

Between the two world wars, the best Canadian amateur was Angus Cassils, who won the Montreal club championship every year from 1919 to 1930 except for 1923. He won the Canadian championship in 1920 and 1929, but mostly this was won by American visitors, especially Clarry Pell (first in 1914 and subsequently seven times) and Bobby Grant III (three times).

Since the Second World War, the best Canadian amateurs have been J.A. Rolland (winner of the Canadian championship in 1964 and thirteen times winner of the club championship) and David McLernon (winner of the Canadian championship 1970–72 and 1976, and eight times winner of the club championship). Mostly the Canadian Amateur championship has continued to be dominated by foreign visitors, British as well as American. Bobby Grant added five more victories, and the title has been won by Geoffrey Atkins (six times), David Norman (three), Willie Surtees (four), Willie Boone (three), John Prenn (eight), James Male (five) and Tim Cockroft (three) among others.

There has been a tradition of rivalry between Montreal and Boston, and in 1936 a handsome trophy was given for an annual match between the two clubs.

Rackets in North America was indeed lucky when the era of Grant, Pell and Atkins was succeeded by the arrival of Willie Surtees who lived first in Chicago and then in New York. He became world champion in 1972 and defended six times in the next ten years, bringing such great champions as Howard Angus, Willie Boone and John Prenn to North American shores. The idea of playing one leg of the world championship in the new world was firmly established. David McLernon of Montreal was a revelation during this period. He is the best North American born player since Bobby Grant, and he duelled often with Surtees.

The leading English players of the era came for a crack at Surtees, lured also by the North American formula for a Rackets weekend – black-tie stag night on Thursday, ball on Saturday, Rackets from Friday to Sunday, singles and doubles. In addition to the future world champions, other English tourists (and sometime residents) were David Norman, Charles Hue Williams, Garth Milne, Christopher Greene, Richard Bonsor, Andrew Beeson, the brothers Crawley and Nichols, Simon Davies, Tim Cockroft, Victor Cazelet, Rupert Owen-Browne, Nicholas Barham and William Maltby among others. The effect of these visits was to raise the standards and excite the appetites of North Americans for top-class Rackets. Plenty of them caught the bug. Dick Lightfine and Rob Wood of Chicago, Michael McMaster, Bart Sambrook and McLernon, of course, of Montreal, Dick Turner and Murray Sales of Detroit, Devens Hamlen of Boston, Peter Read and Edward Ulmann of New York, and Peter de Svastich of New York and Tuxedo, became homegrown winners of national amateur titles, albeit often in doubles with English partners.

The international flavour of the game gave birth to the first Quadrathlon, held in Montreal in 1976 – Rackets, golf, lawn tennis, and another game. It was a huge success and has been held roughly every ten years since then. The Queen's Club hosted the jamboree in 1986. In 1996, it was a Quintathlon (shooting was added) in Chicago and Detroit, and finally the millennium ended with the Queen's Quintathlon in 2000 to which over seventy North American Rackets players travelled.

North American Rackets owes a great deal to the wonderful professionals who have nurtured the spirit and skill of the game in the clubs. The doyens were Ken Chantler (Montreal), Jack Johnson (Chicago) and Jimmy Dear (New York). The next generation included Jimmy Burke (Boston), Mark MacDonald and John Cashman (Chicago), Steve Tulley (Montreal), Tom Greevy (Tuxedo), Eddie and Mike Noll and Rob Whitehouse (Philadelphia), Shannon Hazell (New York), Neil Smith (Chicago and New York) and James Beaumont (New York).

The clubs themselves were lucky to have guiding spirits who fostered the game at home and continentally via the North American Racquets Association. These included Michael Huband, Ron Kaulbach, Rick Hart and Tim Price in Montreal; Rob Wood, Rick Burkes, Ted Tieken and Davis Anderson in Chicago; Kevin Broderick, Tom Howe and Michael Goodell in Detroit; Tom Elliott and Louis Habina, Philadelphia; Kurt Graetzer, Greg Van Schaack and Peter de Svastich, Tuxedo; Devens Hamlen and Denis Walsh, Boston; Peter Read, Kevin MacGuire, Nick Gardiner, Kendrick de Koning, William Bristowe, Edward Novis, Guy Devereux and Edward Ulmann, New York.

The twenty-first century has dawned with a fine prospect in Jonathan Larken, Old Etonian, resident in New York, who in 2001 swept the US and Canadian Amateur singles and the US and Western Opens with wins in formidable company, earning the right to challenge for the world championship. The future looks bright as the game continues in high style on a wave of enthusiasm on the American side of the pond.

RACKETS IN INDIA

A SPLENDID BOOK, *Rackets in India* by Colonel A.R. Winsloe, CMG, DSO, late RE, was published in Bombay by the Times of India Press in 1930. This comprehensive account of the game in that country between the wars provides much information about contemporary rackets, balls, methods of building courts and running competitions; in the course of this, many interesting sidelights are revealed on the state of the game.

The book is dedicated to Major-General S.H. Sheppard, CB, CMG, DSO, who wrote a foreword. His knowledge dated back to 1892 when, he tells us, 'Polo, Cricket and Rackets were the leading games in India.' After the war of 1914–18, Rackets declined in popularity, partly because of the expense and partly through the rival attractions of lawn tennis, hockey and squash. He pays tribute to Colonel Winsloe for his great efforts to revive the game in India.

Colonel Winsloe devotes a chapter to the history of Rackets in India and how it had spread throughout the country in the wake of the British Army. He recalls that forty years earlier, 'the income of the average sportsman enabled him to play polo and Rackets in addition to going out pig-sticking and shooting.' When he wrote, costs had risen greatly, not least due to a 30 per cent customs duty on goods imported from England.

He writes of some seventy courts in total and a map showing their location is included as an appendix. These courts evidently varied tremendously in size and pace; some were considerably larger than standard; all were slower than their English counterparts. Some were covered, most open. The oldest were at Sangor (1821) and Madras (1831); the best at Bombay, Calcutta, Jubbulpore (all covered courts) and Rawalpindi (an open court). The Bombay court was slightly larger than usual (64ft x 32ft), the same size as the older of the two present courts at Harrow.

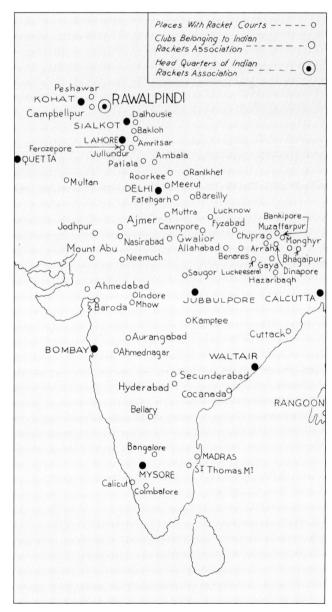

Rackets courts in India (from Rackets in India *by Colonel A.R. Winsloe).*

The court at Kohat (far left) *near Peshawar, Pakistan, in 1873.*

Several major tournaments were held, the first being the Bombay Gymkhana in 1885. The tournament in Rawalpindi started in 1901, the Northern Circars in 1903, Western India at Poona in 1904 and Central India at Jubbulpore in 1927.

Outstanding among players was Jamsetji, the Parsee marker at the Bombay court, who came to London in 1903 and defeated Gilbert Browne of Prince's Club for the world championship. In 1911, he lost the title to Charles Williams, the Harrow professional, who was sixteen years or so younger. Jamsetji was Professional champion of India from 1899 to 1917.

Of the amateurs, General Sheppard was outstanding, but Colonel Winsloe also mentions Colonel W.E. Wilson-Johnston, the aptly named Colonel A.J.H. Sloggett, Colonel J.G. Greig and R.J.O. Meyer. General Sheppard was the only Indian Army player to win the British Amateur championship and he also won the Army championship at Prince's in 1903, 1906 and 1921 – on this last occasion as a Major-General, at the age of fifty-one.

After the rules of Rackets, Colonel Winsloe writes of the balls and rackets, which he calls bats. Balls had evidently tended to get larger until standardised by the Tennis and Rackets Association some twenty years previously at about one inch in diameter and one ounce in weight. Balls in India were either covered with linen or leather, but both were affected by climatic factors, such as damp or excess heat. It is of interest that in England balls were apparently baked in the course of manufacture and had then to be allowed to cool down for twenty-four hours owing to the heat-retaining property of the wool in them. This wool content also made them appetising to the white ant, and the Colonel recommended keeping them in a linen bag.

It wasn't easy, he points out, to replace the woollen part of the core, since the old blue and red uniforms were no longer readily available and khaki was a poor substitute.

Rackets, too, deteriorated with climatic conditions in India. The Colonel recommends olive oil or linseed oil, and black rather than white gut. Attempts at producing a metal racket with metal strings had not succeeded.

After a chapter on the construction of courts, he lists them all, indicating in each case their location, size, whether open or covered, their ownership, the material of the walls and any special remarks. Among the latter are ferro-concrete doors at Rawalpindi and Jubbulpore, a door in the side wall at Bakloh, and a note of the court's location in Residency grounds at Hyderabad.

As an appendix, he lists results of the various championships as well as detailed specifications for the construction of courts.

There was an Army court at Rangoon in Burma; and another court very much on its own was at the Hurlingham Club, Buenos Aires. This court was built by polo players in the Argentine and was in use until about 1930.

HISTORY OF THE RACKETS BALL

THE EARLIEST KNOWN *Book of Racquets* by J.R. Atkins, published in 1872, describes in detail the characteristics of the ball in use at that time. It was made by J. Wilson of 17 Roman Road, Victoria Park, London, who appears to have been the main manufacturer of both rackets and balls.

The 'Wilson' ball as used in the latter half of the nineteenth century was smaller than the present-day ball. It had a diameter of between 1in and $1\frac{1}{8}$ins and weighed less than 1 oz or 28 gms. There is, however, some evidence that in the 1850s the ball was both larger and heavier.

The Wilson ball was made of compressed cloth cut into strips and soaked in water. When saturated, the cloth was rolled into a ball and secured with several coils of strong hempen thread. It was placed in a 'cup' made of iron or hard wood consisting of two hemispheres, and compressed in a screw-press. The resulting core was further wound with damp worsted thread with further pressings until it had reached the proper dimensions. The finished core was placed on a square of sheepskin (smooth side out) which had been dampened and stretched. The four corners were pulled up and secured with stout thread. The overlapping pieces were cut off and the four seams were stitched together in a similar way to lacing a boot. The finished ball would undergo further pressing and baking to harden and dry it.

From early in the twentieth century, racket ball manufacture passed to Jeffrey Maling of Woolwich. Edward J. Bailey later became director of the business and became the main supplier of fives and Rackets balls until 1952.

The 'Bailey' ball was similar in construction to the old Wilson ball, but was somewhat larger and heavier. Although its characteristics were inconsistent, in general it measured about 1.56 ins in diameter and weighed about 35 gms.

Examination of old Bailey cores shows that the inner cloth was almost exclusively made from soldiers' uniform material and in one or two cases the piping from uniform trousers has been found. Maybe a supply of out-dated uniforms was purchased by Malings as suitable material for the inner cores of Rackets balls.

The performance of the Bailey ball was variable and often it would either lose its shape or the stitching would come adrift after a rally or two. A really good yellow, well-baked ball was much sought after by the players and was a delight to use. On the other hand, a 'stone' or heavy, poor-bouncing ball gave no pleasure, but was useful to the server.

Fifty or more balls were often used in a match and many were discarded after a single rally. At that time, any player could discard a ball at will and it was not until the late 1950s that the present rule was introduced, permitting only the receiver to claim a new ball. The balls were the property of the club professional who usually held a stock of two or three gross. He would bounce out a good set of balls for an important match and keep the throw-outs for the lesser players. In the 1930s, the cost of a ball to the player was about threepence and after use the balls were sent back to Bailey for reconditioning and re-covering.

Sadly, during the Second World War, Maling's premises suffered considerable bomb damage and Mrs Bailey was a casualty in the air raids. After the war, Bailey, then in his seventies, carried on limited business at 96 Wellington Street, Woolwich, but sheepskin covers were no longer available. White linen adhesive tape was introduced in lieu and this could be easily removed and replaced at the court after use. By 1950, there was a serious shortage of Bailey balls. Existing stock at the courts had run down and Bailey was no longer able to produce new cores. In addition, makeshift repair by inexperienced hands had damaged cores beyond the point of reconditioning. Some of the school courts which had closed during the war found it very difficult to obtain balls and, as so often happens, necessity became the mother of invention.

In the early 1950s, John Thompson, the Rackets master-in-charge at Marlborough College, and Bill Gordon, who was appointed Marlborough Rackets professional in September 1951, began experimenting in making new Rackets balls. They were convinced that the secret of preventing loss of shape lay in finding a suitable material to make a solid inner core. They tried wood, ebonite and even glass marbles, but to no avail. The resulting worsted-wound balls neither had the correct bounce nor made the right sound.

In 1954, Dr J.C. Swallow (whose son Charles was at that time in the Charterhouse pair and in 1970 became British Open champion) provided some invaluable advice. He was a director and later chairman of the Plastics Division of ICI and he suggested that it might be worth trying polythene, a derivative of crude oil. During the war, Dr Swallow had headed a research team experimenting with polythene as an electrical insulator. The results of this work had figured in the development of RADAR equipment, which contributed so much to the UK war effort.

Polythene was produced after the war in 1¼in diameter spheres for medical use, to prevent the collapse of patients' lungs during surgery. Dr Swallow helped in procuring some of these spheres both for Marlborough and for Bill Hawes, the Charterhouse professional who was also experimenting with ball-making at the time. Hawes turned some polythene spheres on a lathe so that he could try cores of different sizes.

The first polythene balls were made at Marlborough and Charterhouse in 1954 with these 1¼in spheres. Adhesive tape covers were placed on the polythene core, which was then wound by hand with damp worsted, and two outer white tape covers were added. This produced a ball with encouraging characteristics. Unfortunately, the polythene cores tended to crack in play and the ball was too slow when cold and too fast when it warmed up with play.

The Tennis and Rackets Association had been kept informed of these experiments and they proposed that in due course each court in the country should be sent balls for trial. It was hoped to use the polythene ball for championships as soon as a suitable prototype was in production.

Bill Gordon ground down some cores to 1in diameter and these produced better playing characteristics and helped to reduce the pace of the ball

when warmed up. Meanwhile, Dr Swallow suggested that injection moulded polythene would be stronger. Craxford Mouldings Limited were approached and they agreed to produce injection moulded polythene spheres of 1in diameter and the Tennis and Rackets Association agreed to purchase the matrix mould. The first supply of these cores arrived at Marlborough towards the end of 1954.

The first use of the polythene-centred ball in a championship was in January 1955 for the Noel-Bruce Cup at Queen's. John Thompson produced a set of balls with the new 1in spheres, which were called T2. These had six inner tape covers and were wound with worsted with two outer tape covers. The ball was about 1.5ins in diameter and weighed about 29gms.

After the championship (incidentally, won by Thompson and M.C. Cowdrey for Tonbridge) a questionnaire was completed by the eighteen leading players and elicited the following comments:

Question	Yes	No	Generally satisfactory
Do you like the T2 ball better than the Bailey ball?	13	2	3
Is the ball too fast?	3	10	5
Is the bounce too high?	6	2	10
Is there too much variation when the ball is hot and cold?	15	2	1
Is the ball an improvement on any other in use since the war?	17	1	
Would you be prepared to use the T2 ball in the Amateur championship?	15	1	2

These generally favourable comments were received with some relief. The two main criticisms were that there was too much variation in pace with temperature, and that when warm the bounce was too high. For a brief period a ball-heater, consisting of a small box containing a 60-watt electric lamp and a shelf for the balls, was tried. This was placed in the gallery by the marker and enabled the balls to be warmed up before use. This reduced the variation in pace, but did not solve the problem of the high bounce. Although the T2 ball was suitable for adult play at the top level, it was too fast for schoolboys and the Public Schools championship.

Bill Gordon found that by adding additional inner tape covers, the pace of the ball could be reduced, and from then onwards a polythene-cored ball could in theory be made to suit any court.

In February 1955, the Tennis and Rackets Association set up a ball-testing sub-committee comprising Harry Altham, the Winchester master-in-charge, and Jim Dear, the senior playing professional at Queen's, to whom all makers were invited to send samples for testing. The G6 ball made by Bill Gordon at Marlborough won the day, and the Tennis and Rackets Association decided that the G6 ball should be used for the Public Schools championships in 1956 and 1957.

The problem of producing the G6 in sufficient numbers still had to be solved. Each hand-wound ball took at least half an hour to make and was very hard on the hands. Gloves had to be worn to prevent the worsted thread cutting the fingers. Between May 1955 and January 1956, Bill Gordon made 1000 G6 balls – some 500 hours' work. This should go on record as an outstanding feat of patience and dedication which undoubtedly did much to save the game from extinction during this critical period.

Despite this magnificent effort, the problem of production remained if all courts were to have adequate supplies of the new G6 ball. In the summer of 1955, Marlborough began experimenting with a winding machine. John Thompson produced a Heath Robinson contraption made from old film spool-winding apparatus found in a science laboratory cupboard. With the aid of a foot clutch made from an

Bill Gordon making Rackets balls.

old bicycle three-speed cable, he was able to wind a ball in fifteen minutes by turning the handle with his right hand, operating the clutch with his left foot and rotating the ball gradually with his left hand. This gave rise to thoughts of a mechanical power-driven winder, which would solve all problems.

At last help came from an unexpected quarter. Jim Hurn, captain of Wiltshire County Cricket Club at the time, was a talented mechanical inventor and he became interested in the notion of an automatic winding machine. Towards the end of 1955, he and a Melksham garage mechanic, Charlie Vines, produced the first prototype. There were initial problems in the timing of the rotation of the ball as winding proceeded, so that the thread did not build up on an axis. Eventually this was solved by trial and error and on 21 January 1956, Jim Hurn arrived at the Marlborough Rackets Court with the machine. Having set it up in Bill Gordon's room, Jim Hurn said, 'Right Bill, try that. If it works, let us have it back and we'll put in permanent bearings.'

Since then, this fantastic machine has wound some 41,000 Rackets balls. It can wind two balls in seven minutes and after forty-four years is still going strong. It has never been back for permanent bearings! The problem of supply was solved and Bill Gordon set to work in earnest.

In 1956, the G6 ball was officially adopted as the championship ball throughout Great Britain. In 1963, the North American Rackets Association also recognised it. The G6 was almost indestructible – it kept its shape indefinitely, the bounce was consistent and there was little variation with temperature.

In the late 1950s, terylene thread replaced worsted, as it was stronger and could be wound dry. Terylene was in turn superseded by nylon, which has similar properties. The original G6 had a diameter of 1.5 ins and a weight of 28 gms. Thus it was slightly smaller and lighter than the old Bailey ball and fewer rackets were broken. One ball lasted at least half a game, and this all-round economy greatly reduced costs.

However, although the G6 was such a success, there were some problems with the core, which eventually cracked. This, combined with the need to reduce production time, led Bill Gordon in the early 1980s to change from the 1in moulded core to a 1⅛ins core turned on a lathe from an extruded rod of polythene. This increase in core size reduced the winding time considerably.

In 1992, Bill Gordon, at the age of seventy-nine, finally retired and his son Nigel took over production of the G6 ball. After thirty-seven years and over 32,000 balls, Rackets owes Bill Gordon an enormous debt of gratitude for his dedication to the game.

Since then, some minor, but important, changes have been made to the ball, mainly in the method of manufacture. Responding to requests for balls of different speeds, Nigel Gordon has introduced four balls of varying specification. These can be tailored to suit an individual court, primarily by altering the core size. Currently under development is a new coating for the winding. This should extend the life of the ball by reducing the damage done when replacing the covers. Despite the original winding machine's longevity, a new machine has been made to replace it, eventually.

Peter Ashford started making balls when he became the professional at Winchester in 1974. His ball is used for the Public Schools singles and doubles championships and has been adopted by many schools. He has a mechanical rolling machine and turns the polythene centres himself, so that the balls are essentially hand-made. Peter Ashford can make at most five balls in an hour.

Right *High stakes. The ball used at Manchester on 20 April 1887 in the match for £100 a side between Harry Gray and Peter Latham. Gray won 4 games to 2.*

Below *Old sewn Bailey balls and stages in the manufacture of the modern polythene-centred G6 ball.*

PART III

TENNIS AND RACKETS COURTS AROUND THE WORLD

A tense moment in the 1999 Open doubles championship at the Queen's Club. Both Tennis and Rackets have entered the twenty-first century with an impressive array of fine players.

AIKEN TENNIS CLUB

A VERY LONG WAY from other US Tennis centres, the court at Aiken (near Augusta, on the Georgia/South Carolina border) has depended mainly on winter visitors from New York, both amateur and professional. The court and the club building seem to be unchanged since their construction in 1902, except that a fan has now been installed for summer players – a temperature of 100 degrees at eight in the morning being a little too much to take.

When Mark Devine took over as professional in 1995 there were only fifteen regular players. Now there are fifty, and they include three remarkable juniors. Camden Riviere has already won the British Under-12 and Under-14 championships quite convincingly, and at the age of twelve (in the year of publication) has a handicap in the low 20s. If he continues this progress, Devine tips him as likely to be the youngest world champion in the game.

Seth Kopald is the same age and has been playing for just a year, but is ready for tournaments. He is the grandson of Bobby Goodyear, who has been the club president for at least twenty years and is reported to be in good shape to run for another twenty. Finally, Claire Voegele, at the age of ten, was showing an eye for the ball such as no other junior Devine had seen for years.

At the other end of life's scale is Dr A. Calhoun Witham, who at the age of eighty still took four hours of lessons a week and has won more of Aiken's small internal tournaments than any other player.

The club hosts two championships of international importance, the Aiken handicap doubles in November (for players of thirty and over) and April (thirty and

Dr A. Calhoun Witham, still going strong.

The remarkable young Camden Riviere, with president's daughter Ginny Goodyear and Mark Devine.

under). Most of the great players of the time have entered, from Norty Knox and Pierre Etchebaster to Julian Snow. Among leading professionals who have taken part in exhibition matches and clinics at Aiken in recent years are Chris and Steve Ronaldson, Mike Gooding, Lachlan Deuchar, Ruaraidh Gunn and Jonathan Howell. Devine himself, who began his career at Leamington in 1986, is still among the world's leading players and with a handicap of +4 is the top-ranked player in the US.

When the court was built (under the sponsorship of William C. Whitney), it joined an older club already equipped with bar and billiard room, the centenary of which was celebrated on the court in 1998 with a party attended by 150 people. That might never have happened: in 1937 the court was sold to a local garage, but a group of Tennis enthusiasts refused to lie down and bought it back.

Etchebaster's engagement as the professional at Aiken had a profound influence on the game of Tennis. He trained three students of the Aiken Preparatory School there, each of whom later became world Tennis champion – Norty Knox and the brothers Bostwick, Pete and Jimmy.

Aiken professional Mark Devine, watched closely by his doubles partner, Nick Wood.

Party time on New Year's Day 2000. Left to right, back row: Duncan Rutherford, Jim Geddes, Woody Millen; second row: Bill Blalock, Howard Hickey Jr, Dr Dieter Voegele; third row: Alan Corey, Bud Herbruck, Tiger Riviere, Bob Harrington, John Haddon, John Shealy, Dr Harry Shealy, Dr F.M. Durst, Ash Milner, Bobby Goodyear, Fred Wright, Albert Bostwick; front row: Lou Papouchado, George Handy, Charlie Bostwick, Dacre Stoker.

BALLARAT

COMPLETED IN 1984, when it was opened by Rear Admiral Sir Brian Murray, Governor of Victoria, the Tennis court at Ballarat is slower than the others in Australia and takes good 'cut'. The grille is unusually large, and new lights installed in July 1999 make it one of the best-lit courts in the world. Its creation is largely due to local businessman John Gilbert, who lives in a mansion next to the club.

Though relatively small, it gained early prestige by the introduction in 1985 of the Ballarat Silver Racket, an event that has attracted many of the world's outstanding players. Winners have included Chris Ronaldson, Lachlan Deuchar, Chris Bray, Jonathan Howell, Frank Filippelli and Julian Snow.

Ballarat staged the world ladies' singles and doubles championships in 1997, at which the British players Penny Lumley and Sue Haswell were dominant. Jo Edwards and Laura Fowler lead the local ladies, and in Wendy Whitehead the club boasts one of the few lady presidents in the world.

Among other home players, Wayne Spring has won the Amateur championship no fewer than ten times and Steve Virgona and Andrew Fowler went on to become professionals. The current pro is Brett McFarlane.

Three presidents and a governor: (left to right) *James Cartledge (Hobart), Paul Wheeler (Melbourne), John Abraham (Ballarat) and H.E. Sir Brian Murray (Victoria).*

Opened in 1984, the court at Ballarat is said to take good cut.

Head professional Brett McFarlane.

LE JEU DE PAUME DE BORDEAUX

THIS TENNIS CLUB has been in existence since 1788, when M. Peres Duvivier, a rich Martiniquan, built a court in the rue Rolland to satisfy the Duc d'Artois, who intended to spend some time in Bordeaux. The first known court in the town, however, existed in 1460 and bore the name of Talbot.

John Talbot, Earl of Shrewsbury, was appointed Lieutenant of Aquitaine by Henry VI and in 1429 directed the siege of Orleans. He and his son were killed in battle when fighting on behalf of the Barons of Aquitaine, faithful to the English king, against the forces of Charles VII of France. Talbot is buried in Winchester Cathedral.

The French Revolution ruined the Duvivier family. The court was sold to a firm of carpet makers and had ceased to be used for Tennis by 1827. Fifty years later, after periods as a concert hall and then an auction room, it was bought for 53,000 francs by an enthusiast, M. Duroy de Suduiraut, who restored it.

In so doing, he reversed the court so that the dedans was more conveniently situated at the end which had previously been the grille. This meant an alteration to the tambour and may explain the curious construction of the wall at the top, which has been retained in the new court, built in 1978. The new court is situated in Merignac, a pleasant suburb of Bordeaux.

Among the annual competitions are the Coupe Duroy de Suduiraut (the club championship), the Raquette d'Or and the Raquette d'Argent (for French players only), and the Coupe de Bordeaux, open to amateurs of any nationality. This has been won by some distinguished foreign players, including Edgar Baerlein, Lord Aberdare and Howard Angus (five times). John Ward won in 1982 and 1985, before Julian Snow captured it in 1987 and held it for ten years.

Alongside the Coupe de Bordeaux is the Edouard Kressmann Trophy tournament, an international handicap event for the over fifties, played in memory of a remarkable connoisseur of the game and initiated by his son Roland. There is also an unusual team competition (two singles and a double) for the Coupe de Noel, in which all entrants are listed by ability, and the worst paired with the best.

Robert Fahey serves on to the boarded penthouse at Bordeaux.

Among the club's strongest players in recent years have been Jean-Guillaume Prats and Christophe Chueka. In the year 2000, the club championship was won by Charles Blanchot, brother of the current president and son of a former president. On a wider front, the club staged the French National Open in 2000, which was won by Marc Seigneur.

The club organized the 1988 bicentenary of Jeu de Paume in Bordeaux, staging a fortnight of memorable festivities and tournaments, including a dinner on the court attended by the then Lord Mayor of Bordeaux, Jacques Chaban-Delmas.

Right *Bordeaux president Henri Blanchot congratulates Wayne Davies as he receives the runner-up prize at the French Open.*

Below *There has been a tennis court at Bordeaux since 1460. This one was built in 1978.*

BOSTON
THE TENNIS AND RACQUET CLUB

DURING THE PAST QUARTER-CENTURY, the Tennis and Racquet Club has recovered from dire financial straits, revitalized in time for its second century. Founded early in the 1900s, the club enjoyed great social prominence through the first half of the twentieth century, no doubt partly due to the desirable location of its magnificent building. No expense was spared in its construction. The entrance hall was finished in Caen stone, and it had a staircase of marble and wrought iron, and a panelled ceiling.

Highly talented members won many national titles in the early years, particularly on the Rackets doubles court. However, Boston names have seldom reached the honours boards since the Second World War, the most notable exception being the all-Boston 1948 Amateur Tennis final, when E. Mauran Beals beat Charles H. Stockton.

The passing of the founder members, together with the residential drift out of the city centre, deprived the club of its financial base. John Bigelow, Treasurer during the 1960s, recalls Christmas-time board meetings when the Governors, entertained to 'free' dinner and cocktails, received his recitation of the club's sad financial plight with riotous laughter and covered most of the deficit by passing the hat.

That tactic failed in the following decade and despite personal loans and a mortgage on the building, disaster loomed. In 1978 a small cadre of members, led by Devens Hamlen, took over the club building and assumed responsibility for its debts. In 1986 the club became a tenant in a portion of the refurbished building. Subsequent renovations have included a new international squash court and an expanded royal dedans.

Boston's imposing edifice: no expense spared.

Hamlen also proved to be the club's most resilient Rackets player, winning many singles and doubles titles over four decades of play. John Prenn's nephew Alexis won several singles titles while a student at Boston University, and successfully partnered Dick Brickley at doubles. They won the Western Open in 1984. During the 1990s Rob McLane and David Mead dominated the domestic scene.

Henry Wheelwright, a Boston patron in the seventies and eighties.

Devens Hamlen: successful player, president and landlord.

Denis Walsh, also known as the Prince of Nara, expounding at a club dinner, and holding the attention of John Prenn.

Dick Brickley, a prominent player for over two decades.

James 'Jimmy' Burke, for fifteen years the Tennis and Rackets professional.

Hamlen, Brickley and McLane have shone on the Tennis court too, but not as brightly as Jeff Randall who won seven singles titles. Jeremy Wintersteen won the club singles in 1999 and 2000. In doubles, Brickley has appeared in an astonishing nineteen finals in twenty-two years, winning eleven with various partners. Phil Stockton, another title winner at both games, is the grandson of one of the club's founders, as was his doubles partner, C.T. Russell III.

In the past thirty years the club has invited, included and embraced (with varying degrees of success) women into its collective bosom. Significant players have been Nancy Brickley in the seventies, Lisa Tutrone, Mimi Coolidge and Sheila Reilly in the eighties and Brenda Sabbag in the late nineties.

Both games received a considerable fillip with the arrival in 1978 of Barry Toates as professional. He won the US Open Tennis title in 1979, and had a substantial effect on the standard of play at the club. He was succeeded by Mike Reilly and then, for the past fifteen years, by another former US Open Tennis champion, Jimmie Burke, a gifted player and teacher. After twenty years as president (and landlord) of the club, Devens Hamlen stepped down in favour of Bob Hurley, a veteran of the US club scene. Recognizing that the club's main appeal is to young city-based singles – men and women – he has tried to broaden its membership by instituting family-friendly practices, both social and athletic, that feature weekend events for parents and children. Plans are currently under way to add two more squash courts.

The founders of the club were usually looking for an escape from what they perceived as the day-to-day cares of the world. Today, members view it as just one more item in the schedule of their busy lives. It is a friendly and accessible place, poised to meet the new century.

BRISTOL & BATH

ALTHOUGH THE BRISTOL & BATH TENNIS CLUB was founded in December 1985, it was another twelve years before they had a court of their own. During that time, competitive home fixtures were played at the Hardwick House court, the club having obtained a corporate membership by courtesy of Phoebe, Lady Rose. They also put on special events and coaching days at Hardwick in order to promote the game generally and to enhance membership. As a result of these activities, the club built up a total membership of over 200 from all over the country and abroad, before opening their own premises.

The club was founded on the desire of a few enthusiastic players in the Bristol area to restore the court in Bath or alternatively to establish a new court in the locality. The inaugural meeting was held under the chairmanship of John Barford on 5 December 1985.

It was clear that the Bath Court, probably the only surviving eighteenth century court in the country, was not going to be available because the Trust who ran an industrial museum in the building were unwilling to relinquish occupation. So the club concentrated on procuring a site in the Bristol area and efforts were focused on land owned by Clifton College, Bristol.

After several years and a number of abortive investigations, Clifton College kindly offered a site at

Above and below *Kevin King, first professional at Bristol & Bath, serving in the newly opened court.*

the Beggar Bush playing fields, about a mile west of the main campus over the Clifton suspension bridge. The site was occupied by some old workshops and the provision of land for the court was conditional on the club providing new workshops.

John Bretten, chairman at the time and a member of the inaugural committee, and Michael Jones, the secretary, formulated detailed plans and a financial strategy. Planning permission was obtained, after a long battle, in autumn 1994, and at this stage the building costs of the court were estimated at £404,000. This was shortly before the national lottery came into operation in January 1995, and Bristol & Bath were among the first applicants for a grant to submit detailed proposals.

In August of that year the club was told that its application had been agreed in principle, and the grant was formally confirmed in May 1996. The final costings amounted to £565,000 plus VAT; the lottery contributed £353,000 and the balance was raised by the club, mainly through selling fully transferable twenty year memberships.

The first ball was struck in December 1997 and the court was officially opened by the Earl of Wessex on 14 February 1998. There are extensive club rooms, some of which overlook the court at first floor level, providing an unusual viewing area. There are television camera viewing points and, unusually, fire doors leading from the court to the exterior so that social functions can be held on the court in safety. Provisions have also been made for an electronic scoreboard.

The club secured Kevin King as the first professional, and such was the enthusiasm that in the third week of November 1998, less than a year after play began, all 98 hours of court time were filled. Since then the club has continued to grow, attracting the majority of its members from newcomers to the game, and thus meeting one of its principal aims of widening participation in Real Tennis in the West Country.

Left *Another court, another commemorative racket: the Earl of Wessex with chairman John Bretten at the club's official opening, 14 February 1998.*

Below *Sue Haswell (left) and Charlotte Cornwallis in one of the exhibition matches at the official opening ceremony.*

THE BURROUGHS CLUB

STATE-OF-THE-ART ARCHITECTURE and Tennis have come together in the new Millennium Court at the Burroughs Club on the Middlesex University's Hendon campus, which was opened by the Earl of Wessex on 16 January 2000. An approach to Peter Luck-Hille by the University's Dean of the Business School, Professor David Kirby, led to a Grant Agreement between the University and The Luck-Hille Foundation, a charitable body, in September 1998. Building work began in October.

Right *Frank Filippelli, head professional at the Burroughs Club Millennium Court, with James Male (left) after winning the Professional doubles in January 2000.*

Below *Ground-breaking at Hendon – Professor Michael Driscoll (left), Vice-Chancellor of Middlesex University, sharing the shovel with Peter Luck-Hille.*

Above *Steve Virgona, assistant professional and one of the most talented players of the new generation.*

Below *Play during the inaugural match on the new court in January 2000.*

Peter Luck-Hille had a very influential role in the whole design and construction process; he largely led the project on behalf of the Foundation and the University. Pringle Richards Sharratt were appointed architects, Ian Sharratt as principal and Miranda MacDonald as job architect, and following lengthy research, a design philosophy evolved and construction techniques developed.

The court is the first to use a new light-management system to diffuse natural light and produce enough artificial light to meet televisual levels without glare. The walls above the play line are made of a translucent system, Kalwall, imported from Boston, which allows about 20 per cent of the light through without the light source being identified.

The roof is eliptical, with glazing along the full length of the court on the north side. The light entering through these glazed units is reflected on to the remaining underside of the roof, producing a very even diffused light. The walls are of re-enforced concrete and the playing surfaces are coated with a newly developed Armourcoat plaster with a high resin content.

New technology has even entered the penthouse. Older courts that rely on wood for their structural strength suffer in time because wood moves and the penthouse lines become distorted. The new court uses an inverted steel 'T' section believed never to move under normal stresses of weight and temperature. The roof boards are of maranti, said to be a more stable alternative to oak, but the most significant feature is the angle at which the roof is set.

Forcing the return of serve has become increasingly popular among leading players, shallow penthouse roofs playing into their hands. By increasing the angle of the roof to produce a steeper penthouse, spinning serves are given greater weight, thus perhaps restoring advantage to the server.

Other niceties of the new court include underfloor heating, roof ventilation, a sophisticated video system and an electronic scoreboard in the grille.

CAMBRIDGE UNIVERSITY

B Y THE END OF THE SIXTEENTH CENTURY, most Cambridge colleges had their own Tennis courts, but they gradually fell out of use. By the beginning of the nineteenth century only Pembroke's survived, giving its name to Tennis Court Road. In 1853, the Wellington court was built in East Road, and both courts were used by the University until their demise at the end of the century. The annual match against Oxford began in 1859 – just three years after the establishment of a regular Boat Race.

The first of the two Clare and Trinity courts, modelled on the Tuileries court in Paris, was built in 1866 at a cost of nearly £3,000; the second was added in 1890 for £2,232, under the supervision of William C. Marshall, who had been responsible for the Queen's Club courts. The roof of the second court was opened up in 1913, giving overhead light to supplement the customary side windows.

The outbreak of the First World War led to their temporary closure. Appeal funds saved them in 1919 and 1929, but in 1933 the 1890 Tennis court was converted into four squash courts. At the same time, electric lighting was installed in the old court, the walls and floor were painted white and orange balls were

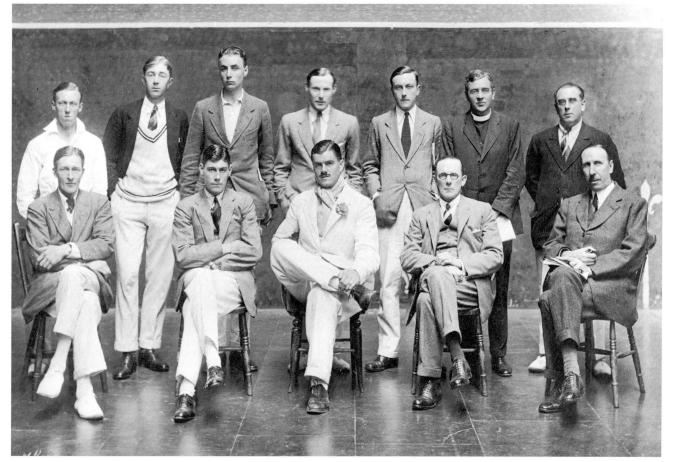

A distinguished Cambridge group including father and son professionals Eric Twinn (back row right) *and Arthur* (back row left), *former Amateur champion Dugald Macpherson* (centre back), *Billy Ross-Skinner* (centre front) *and the historian and former Queen's Club secretary E.B. Noel* (front right).

used in an attempt to improve visibility. The experiment was not a great success and the original colour was restored in 1960.

Only six professionals have been in charge during more than a century, each an outstanding contributor to the success of the game at Cambridge. John Phillips, son of the Duke of Wellington's former professional at Stratfield Saye, was appointed manager in 1866 (at a salary of 25 shillings a week), and reigned until 1882. He was succeeded by his assistant, Jim Harradine, who took on his nephew, Arthur Twinn, as a boy assistant in 1893. Twinn took over in 1909 and in 1921 was joined by his son Eric, and they remained together until the outbreak of war in 1939.

Bill Tutt was in charge from 1945 to 1956, followed by Brian Church in 1958. He was responsible for training many of today's professionals, including Barry Toates (Melbourne), Adam Phillips (Hatfield) and Andrew Knibbs (Newmarket); but the outstanding trainee was Chris Bray (Petworth), who

Right *...but usually open for play – the popular and long-serving Cambridge professional Brian Church.*

Below *The first of the two Clare and Trinity courts, built in 1866.*

rose to be second in the world rankings. Church also trained a large number of first-class amateurs, the most eminent being Howard Angus, Amateur champion 1966–82 and world champion 1976–81 – the only amateur to have won the world titles at both Tennis and Rackets.

Kees Ludekens is now the head professional, assisted by Kate Leeming and Mark Hobbs. He encouraged the growth of the game in Cambridge to such an extent that the court was in use for fifteen hours a day almost every day of the week, and in 1998 the committee launched an appeal to fund the restoration of the 1890 court to Tennis. It was opened for play a year later.

Left A leading Cambridge University player in recent years, Mark Howard was Amateur singles runner-up in 1996.

Below Kees Ludekens (right), Cambridge professional, with Marc Seigneur (left), winner of the 1999 Browning Cup, played at Cambridge, and runner-up Andrew Knibbs. Simon Stokes, the Club committee member in charge of the restoration of the second court, looks on.

CANFORD SCHOOL

CANFORD'S FIRST TENNIS COURT is mentioned in a 1541 document describing the 'Cituation of the house and manor of Canford':

The tenys playe: itm thar is a tenys playe buylded of tymbr and bords standing sowth and north and it jonyth to the sowth est corner of the forsaid bed chamber havyng a wyndow lowkyng owt of the chambr in to the tenys playe and the flore of the saime playe is of hard stone that came owt of purbeke and it contz in length xxiiiijvj ffowt and in bredith xxiij ffowt but the bords and timbr warke is in great decay.

After 1776, the medieval buildings (apart from 'John o'Gaunt's kitchen', which still stands) were replaced by a mansion, and this was greatly enlarged after Sir John Josiah Guest bought the Dorset manor in 1845. It was the second baronet, Sir Ivor Bertie Guest, later Lord Wimborne, who in 1879 had both a Tennis and a Rackets court built in the grounds. *The Times* attended the opening:

The floor is of slabs of Yorkshire flag, each 7ft. by 4ft. and 4ins. thick, laid on dwarf walls, so as to secure ventilation and prevent sweating. There are no windows, but the court is beautifully lit from above by skylights 16ft. deep, running on either side of the ridge the whole length of the roof, and completely preventing the possibility of shadow. The distinguishing feature of the court, however, is due to the attention which has been paid to ventilation, which is secured by Louvre ventilators placed over the tie- rods of the roof at either end. Openings fitted in the same manner are made in the main wall above the play line. The result of the care and attention bestowed upon every detail of the court was seen in the admiration expressed by all the players on each day of a most trying week, and so far experience has shown that that admiration was not misplaced.

The Tennis court was renovated in 1913 and a new floor installed, but the Rackets court fell into disrepair (it was converted into two squash courts in 1962).

Canford School was founded in 1923, in the final years of the resident professional, Edward 'Ted' Johnson. His eldest son, Edward Junior, taught the game to a handful of boys, and they played their first match against a team from Queen's Club in November 1925.

During the 1930s, the fixture list was extended and the master-in-charge, W.S. Strain, devoted much time to taking boys in his car to play in other courts. G.H.Holman arrived as professional in 1933, and in 1935 W.D.Whiston became the first Canfordian to win

Canford's outstanding old boy, Spike Willcocks.

a Tennis blue at Cambridge. No competitive play was possible during the war, as American servicemen occupied that part of the school near the Tennis court.

The roof, which had been restored in 1935 through the generosity of Lord Aberdare and others, was battered in the war, and severe gales continued to take their toll. Strain and, briefly, Holman worked on after the war to revive the game, and the court was much restored in 1952.

By then, J.T.Hankinson had taken over as master-in-charge, and Malcolm Taylor, the school's cricket professional, had been trained at Lord's to move into Tennis. He was replaced in 1969 by Hampshire's former Test cricketer Derek Shackleton, who, the records say, 'received some basic instruction at Lord's and soon became a competent marker.'

Darcy Steed, who had served Canford since his boyhood, spent his final ten years before retirement as master-in-charge. He gave way to John Boys in 1973,

the golden jubilee of the school's foundation, which was marked by the complete re-decoration and re-equipment of the dedans by the Old Canfordian Society. The centenary of the court, in 1979, was celebrated with exhibition matches between several leading players.

In 1980, Boys and his headmaster, M.M. Marriott, realised that the school could not support a full-time professional unless the court was opened to outside players. Rob Bartlett, trained by Chris Ronaldson at Hampton Court, was appointed with authority to make part of his living by forming a club for local enthusiasts, who would pay subscriptions and court fees. It was an immediate success, and membership now stands at 120. Bartlett left for the new court at Ballarat, Victoria, in 1982, but not before he and one of the boys, J.S.M. Trice, had been sponsored in a twenty-six-hour marathon to raise money for improved lighting.

Adam Pyne, the assistant professional.

Steve Ronaldson, a tower of strength as the professional since 1982.

He was succeeded at Canford by Steve Ronaldson, brother of Chris, under whose long tenure of office both the club and the school have developed greatly, hosting several national events and establishing the annual ladies' doubles tournament. A series of assistants have given excellent support, including such talented players as Mike Gooding, Adam Phillips and Austin Snelgrove, who in 1997 went on to become the first professional at the new Prince's Club in Washington, with which the Canford Club is now affiliated.

Over the years, the Club have funded many improvements to the Tennis facilities, including comfortable furniture in the dedans, which is now partitioned from the court; a kitchen area with limited bar availability; and a small changing room with a shower for the steadily increasing number of ladies who play.

The school team, while inevitably varying in strength, have maintained a busy fixture list, which notably includes the Hatfield House weekend at Canford, for decades a major social event.

When John Boys retired (after thirty-three years), his successor as master-in-charge, Rick Raumann, twice took boys to the States, playing at New York, Philadelphia, Tuxedo and Washington. Several boys have won national junior titles in various age groups and some have gone on to be full-time professionals.

Outstanding among the Old Boys is James 'Spike' Willcocks, who at twenty-three became the second-ranked British amateur. He and B.J. Ronaldson brought the Henry Leaf Cup to Canford in 1998 and 1999, and Canford School confidently expect their eighty-year-old reputation as a nursery for Tennis talent to extend far into the future.

CHARTERHOUSE SCHOOL

Although the school's greatest days of Rackets lie largely in the past, Charterhouse retain an honoured place in the history of the game. One of the four entrants in the first Public Schools championship of 1868, they reached five finals in the eight years from 1887 to 1894, winning three, and won every one of their five finals from 1906 to 1914.

Charles Swallow, the finest player produced by Charterhouse.

Their very earliest Rackets years were significantly disadvantaged. There was a court of some kind in the corner of their cricket ground in central London in the early nineteenth century, and two new open courts had been built by the 1860s, but one possessed only one side wall, the other none at all. They drew Eton (the eventual winners) in the 1868 contest, lasted seventeen minutes and won seven points.

They did not enter again until 1878, by which time the school had moved to Godalming, Surrey, and boasted (from 1877) two covered courts. The covering must have been on the scanty side, for a writer in the school magazine of 1881 deplored 'the occasions on which the court is so wet as to be worse than useless'. Nearly fifty years passed before it was decided to re-roof the No.1 court, but while the work was in progress a storm flooded the court and ruined the floor. In 1939, extensive repairs were carried out and the floor partly re-laid but not sufficiently far forward, resulting in the two-paced floor of today – a considerable advantage to the home team.

The first outstanding player at Charterhouse was probably F. Dames Longworth, who later won the UK Amateur singles three times. He was the school's first string in 1881, and must have watched a remarkable exhibition match played there in 1879 by four of the Gray brothers. Walter, the school's resident pro, who challenged for the world title in 1888, partnered Henry (Cambridge), who had been world champion 1863–66. They were beaten by Joseph (Rugby), the reigning world champion, and George (Haileybury), the only one of five brothers not to be world champion. The fifth and greatest, William, had died at Eton four years earlier at the age of twenty-nine.

Dames Longworth returned to the school as a master in 1886, and had an electrifying effect on the game there, inspiring his pupils to the Public Schools final ten times in the next twenty-eight years. They won in 1888, 1893, 1894 (Vane Pennell and Edward Garnett in both 1893 and 1894), 1906, 1909, 1910 (H.W. Leatham and H.A. Denison, who two years later won the UK Amateur doubles), 1912 and 1914.

Leatham, who returned to Charterhouse as the school doctor, had a distinguished court record. He won the Amateur doubles six more times, in partnership with the Hon. C.N. Bruce (later Lord Aberdare), and was Amateur singles champion in 1914 (beating Edgar Baerlein in the final) and 1924. At Cambridge, he played against Oxford for three years at Rackets and two years at Tennis, winning all his matches, singles and doubles, in both sports. His predecessor at Charterhouse, Vane Pennell, also became an excellent Tennis player, taking the Amateur singles title from Eustace Miles in 1904.

Dames Longworth retired from his post in 1921, and it was more than thirty years before the school had cause for serious Rackets celebration. Then came the greatest player in their history, and one of the greatest in the world, Charles Swallow. He was in the first Charterhouse pair for three years, winning the Foster Cup in 1955 and leading them to the championship in 1956. He won all his matches for Oxford against Cambridge from 1959 to 1961, and won the Amateur doubles with his University partner, J.M.G. Tyldesley, in 1960.

Swallow first won the Amateur singles in 1964, taking the title 3–2 from Geoffrey Atkins. In the same year he challenged him for the world championship, losing 5–7 at Queen's Club. Swallow went on to be Amateur champion in 1966, 1968 (the year in which he and J.J.M. Hooper secured the Old Carthusians' only victory in the Noel-Bruce Cup) and 1969. He lost the Open singles final to James Leonard in 1967, but beat him for the title in 1970. Then he attacked Atkins for the world again, going down 3–6 over the two legs in Chicago and at Queen's. In 1997, Charles Swallow succeeded David Norman as Chairman of the Tennis and Rackets Association.

Bill Hawes was the professional who coached Swallow through his school years. One of the famous Rackets-playing family (the son of Walter), Hawes served Charterhouse with inspiring enthusiasm and untiring devotion for thirty-three years after the war. His predecessors included Walter Gray (twenty-five years), Gilbert Browne (twenty-two years) and Jack Giles (fourteen years). Steve Tulley stayed for eleven years after Hawes, and Martin Crosby (son of R.J., grandson of F.J.) has run the show since 1988.

Considerable improvement to the courts and galleries has been effected over the past twenty years, including replacement of the roof, a lighting overhaul

Old Carthusians Nigel Pendrigh and James Acheson-Gray, who won the Bathurst Cup for Britain in 1999 with Julian Snow.

Martin Crosby (left) *has successfully nurtured the game at Charterhouse since 1988.*

and installation of a powerful heating system that has significantly increased the pace of play. Crosby's successful nurturing of the game is reflected in the healthy competition that exists in all age groups for places in the teams – despite the siting of the courts at the bottom of a steep hill.

Mike Grindy reached the final of the Public Schools colts singles in 1999, and in the past decade two Old Carthusian pairs (James Acheson-Gray with Rupert Lawson, and Tim Drayson with James Hamblin) have been in the final of the Milne Hue Williams Under-24 doubles competition.

Tennis players have done well, too, Acheson-Gray and Nigel Pendrigh winning the Henry Leaf Cup for Charterhouse twice, as well as the Amateur doubles in 1994, when they beat Julian Snow and Mike

McMurrugh in the final. They were also members of the Bathurst Cup side that beat Australia at Leamington in 1997 and at Hobart in 1999.

On his arrival, Martin Crosby set up the Charterhouse Monks Rackets Club. It has flourished with regular fixtures against the school, Queen's Club, Harrow and Marlborough, as well as representation at various weekend events, undertaking a North American tour in 1995 and the hosting of touring clubs from the US.

The Rackets Professional singles championship was staged at Charterhouse in 1992, when Neil Smith beat Shannon Hazell, and the UK leg of the world championship challenge between Smith and James Male was due to be held there in 1999, until injury to Smith prevented it.

CHELTENHAM COLLEGE

Two open-air Rackets courts were built in 1852, on the site of the present English department and kitchens, and the first singles championship was held in 1858. Two covered courts were completed, on either side of the gymnasium, in 1864; and four years later the College was one of four schools contesting the first Public Schools' doubles tournament at Prince's Club, London. George Gray, of the famous Rackets family, was appointed part-time professional in 1870, and Albert Wright took on the job with great success in 1896.

Soon after the First World War, K.S. Duleepsinhji, later to be known as one of England's great batsmen, briefly attended the College and proved to be a phenomenal Rackets player. He was the singles champion for each of his three years as well as the doubles champion (with different partners), and in 1922 the Cheltenham first pair won every school fixture.

The game declined thereafter, and in 1939 it expired. During the war the whole gymnasium block was requisitioned by the War Office, and subsequently one court became the maintenance department's workshop and the other was divided for various uses (including badminton).

Nearly fifty years later, thanks to the efforts of headmaster Richard Morgan, the east court was re-opened for play, and it remains one of the fastest and truest courts in the world. Karl Cook, who had been trained by Shannon Hazell at Clifton College, was appointed the professional, the school came back on to the competitive circuit, and the Cheltenham Gold Racquet was instituted.

As part of the school's 150th anniversary

Cheltenham's gymnasium block, with the 1864 Rackets courts at each end.

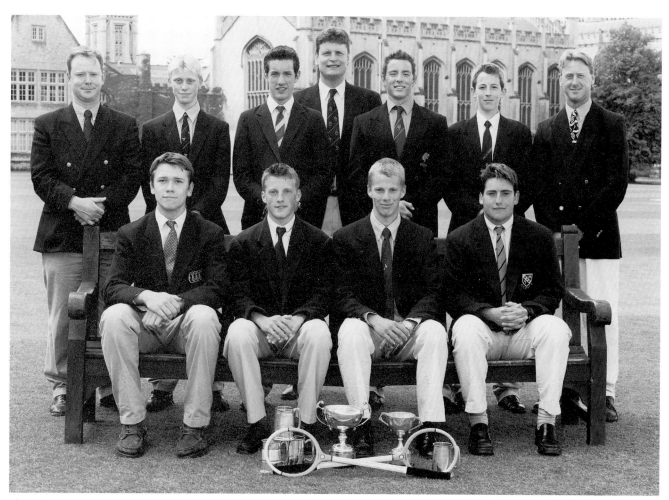

The college party that toured the USA in autumn 1999. Back row (left to right): *A.M. Durston (master), Alex Coldicott, Ben Snell, K.A. Cook (master), James Hayes, Jamie Stout, Mark Briers (professional).* Seated: *Ed Shaw, Graeme Tyndall, Michael Stout, Richard Howell.*

Sam Fairbairn (left, Cheltenham) on his way to winning the 1996 Renny Cup against Chris Wilson (Harrow).

celebrations, the Professional championship was held there in 1991 – won, appropriately, by Shannon Hazell. Eight of the Club players toured North America in 1994, after which Karl Cook had to retire from the pro's job, as he was appointed a housemaster.

Former Worcestershire and Durham cricketer Mark Briers, then the cricket pro, got a taste for the game in 1994, and took over the following year. He and Karl Cook, as master-in-charge, formed an effective partnership – one eager to learn, the other reluctant to let go.

The season 1999–2000 proved to be a memorable one. College hosted the British professional championships, toured North America notching up some impressive performances in New York, Tuxedo Park, Philadelphia and Montreal, had a Foster Cup finalist, Graeme Tyndall, and a Renny Cup winner, Michael Stout. Together these two were runners-up in the Public Schools doubles championship, and James Stout and Alex Coldicott won the colts doubles.

An impressive start was made to the 2000–01 season, with an all Cheltenham Foster Cup final, James Stout beating Alex Coldicott, and Dan Hall winning the junior colts singles.

THE RACQUET CLUB OF CHICAGO

THE ONLY CLUB IN NORTH AMERICA with two Rackets courts (as well as what was a Tennis court, now used for indoor lawn tennis), Chicago has an even prouder boast – one member succeeded another as world Rackets champion. Between them the two residents – Geoffrey Atkins and Willie Surtees – held the title for a quarter of a century (interrupted by Howard Angus in 1973 and 1974), and one leg of every world championship match between 1967 and 1977 was played on the No.1 court there.

Atkins had won the title in 1954, before he settled in Chicago, and defended it successfully in Chicago and at Queen's against James Leonard (1967) and Charles Swallow (1970). At the same two clubs, Surtees beat Angus for the title in 1972, lost it to him

the next year, won it back in 1975 and kept it (5–0) in 1977. Then he left for New York, where he played the first leg of his 5–0 win in 1979 against Willie Boone.

Though there have been no subsequent triumphs quite as glorious, Chicago holds its rightful place as one of the world's great clubs. Five world championship matches have been held in the re-built No.1 court, one of the fastest in the world – Boone against James Male in 1988; Shannon Hazell beating Neil Smith in the eliminator in 1990 to challenge Male; and Male defending in 1991, 1995 and 1999, when he lost the title to Smith.

The US Open was held at the club in 1986, 1990 and 1998, and a host of domestic tournaments held in recent years have included nine Western Opens and

Entertainment Chicago-style to celebrate the first leg of the 1999 World Rackets Challenge between James Male and Neil Smith.

Davis Anderson, a major contributor to the success of Chicago Rackets over the past thirty years.

Willie Surtees, a Chicago member and former world champion.

three US Amateurs. In December 1982, Chicago hosted a tournament to celebrate the twenty-fifth anniversary of the North American Racquets Association, to which the top sixteen players in the world were invited. All but Surtees were able to compete, and Boone beat John Prenn in the final.

The weekend was not solely dedicated to athletic endeavour. On the Friday evening, cocktails were served on the tennis court, accompanied by a string quartet from the Chicago Symphony Orchestra. Dinner was served in the No.2 Rackets court, with the club's new general manager carrying in the crown pork roast with the musical support of three members of the orchestra's brass section, stationed in the gallery.

Similar lavish offerings filled the weekend (no expense was spared), but the manager hastened his own demise when he subsequently transformed a traditional Thursday evening buffet into a 'Mexican Night', with the normal exquisite salads replaced with rice and beans.

Further proof that Rackets itself is not given a disproportionate share of the club's resources came ten years later, when six bands scattered throughout the

Geoffrey Atkins (left), world champion 1954–72, with Neil Smith who became the new champion in Chicago in 1999.

building helped to celebrate the club's seventieth anniversary (during which a number of minor injuries were attributed to excessive enthusiasm in the line dancing). A similar shindig saw out the seventy-fifth in 1997.

The major influences on Rackets in Chicago over the past thirty years have been Davis Anderson and Rob Wood, both former presidents of NARA, the late William Wood Prince Sr, Ted Tieken, Peter Dunne, Keene Addington and Jack Borland.

Whispered suggestions that the club does not need two Rackets courts, and that one might be converted into an international squash court, have been dismissed largely because of the major advantage Chicago holds in attracting so many events to the club, where the effort to maintain and improve the facilities is constant.

The second court used to be so dark it was known as the dungeon, and on one hung-over Sunday morning, Surtees was in danger of losing his US Amateur semi-final because of the difficulty he had in finding the ball in the gloom.

The Racquet club was officially opened in October 1924, with Charles Williams leaving Harrow to be the head professional. Five years later, on his own court, Williams regained the world championship from Jock Soutar, to whom he had lost it in 1913. When Williams died in 1935, Mike Petroskey took over, to be followed by Tony Bertolotti (1947) and Albert (Jack) Johnson in 1972. Mark McDonald, who has been at the club since 1970, became head pro in 1985 and is assisted by John Cashman, who came from Philadelphia in 1988 for what was going to be a two-year stint.

The Tennis court, completed in 1922, was converted for lawn-tennis use in 1936, during the Great Depression and the concurrent absence of a professional. It is of regulation playing area, but inevitably in a cramped enclosure. Several proposals to restore it to its original purpose have been met with opposition from the many users of the facility. However, a solution may be at hand. In 1999, the club bought an adjoining apartment building, and a committee is investigating various architectural and economic alternatives, which include establishing a proper lawn tennis enclosure on the new site and converting the current court back to Tennis. It is too early to tell whether that will be feasible, but many members hope so, knowing that Tennis tournaments would bring another element of excitement and interest to the club.

CLIFTON COLLEGE

CLIFTON'S RECENT RACKETS HISTORY was brilliantly embellished by the achievements of Matthew Windows, the most talented player of his generation. For four consecutive years he swept the Public Schools mantelshelf of its trophies – in 1987 the Jim Dear Cup (Under-15), in 1988 the Incledon-Webber (Under-16), and in 1989 and 1990 the Foster Cup – only the second Cliftonian to win it, and only the seventh player to retain it.

Meanwhile, Windows and Justin Crane proved almost invincible doubles partners throughout their schooldays. In 1990, they brought the championship to Clifton for the first time – at the 101st attempt! – beating Eton in the final. For only the second time in history, the same four players contested the final in March 1991 (Alex Smith-Bingham and Jonathan Larken for Eton). By that time, Windows had beaten Smith-Bingham in two successive Foster's finals, and it was no surprise that the Clifton pair triumphed again.

Not for the first time in the history of the game, cricket claimed a young man who might have gone on to be a great Rackets player. After reaching the semi-finals of both the Amateur and the Open

Matthew Windows: champion at Under-15, Under-16, Under-21 and Under-24, twice winner of the Foster Cup, twice Public Schools doubles champion with Justin Crane.

Toby Sawrey-Cookson, the Clifton professional.

Jeremy Potter, all-round sportsman who developed a passion for Tennis late in life.

championships in 1998, Windows devoted himself to batting for Gloucestershire.

The College has had a Rackets court since 1884, entered the Public Schools championship in 1886 and first reached the final in 1895. Among their most remarkable players was H.H. Lonquet-Higgins, who was in the school pair for four years before the First World War, and the gifted all-rounder R.C. Riseley. After playing for Clifton, he was first string for Oxford for four years, winning the Varsity singles in 1935, 1936 and 1937 (each time beating J.H. Pawle, later to be four times Amateur champion) and the doubles in 1934, 1935 and 1937. While still an undergraduate, Riseley reached the Amateur singles final, losing to David Milford, the world champion.

At Tennis, he won the Varsity singles in 1935 and 1936, and the doubles in 1934, 1935 and 1936. He won the MCC Gold Racquet in 1950, and twice reached the final of the Amateur singles, taking the title in 1955 against Peter Kershaw, his former Oxford Rackets partner.

The College next reached the Public Schools doubles final in 1936, and were there again in 1941, when the extraordinary Jeremy Potter was in the pair. This talented and enthusiastic games player (hockey, cricket, squash, lawn tennis as well as Rackets) was also head boy at Clifton and became a celebrated writer, historian and publisher. In 1994, he produced a scholarly historical work, *Tennis and Oxford*, inspired by the fact that by then he had become entranced by the game. He came to it late, but nevertheless had considerable success in veterans' tournaments in his sixties. Shortly before he died in 1997, at the age of seventy-five, he wrote a biography of Clifton's first headmaster, John Percival, whose son was in that first Rackets pair of 1886.

Among the line of Clifton professionals, Bertie Barnes (1900–50) was outstanding as a player and a character. To mark his retirement, he partnered R.P. Keigwin in a match against the school pair. Keigwin, coached by Barnes, had been in the Clifton pair in 1901 and 1902, and their combined ages amounted to

Clifton's highly successful evening club, The Boasters, every January stage a weekend event (this one was in 1999) that combines Tennis and Rackets.

141 against the school pair's thirty-four, but experience carried the day.

In 1965, Terence Whatley took over, after the early death of George Ferguson, and considerable success ensued. J.P. Willcocks won the Incledon-Webber Cup in 1968, D.G. Parsons in 1969 and 1970, D.R. Gordon in 1971. Willcocks and Parsons lost the championship final of 1971 to Harrow (Mark Thatcher and John Prenn), and in 1972, Parsons became the first Cliftonian to win the Foster Cup.

Whatley himself did well enough, winning the Professional singles 3–1 against Norwood Cripps in 1980; and his 1994 successor, Toby Sawrey-Cookson, a contemporary of Matthew Windows, won the same title in 1999 – and, incidentally, beat Windows in the Open semi-final of 1998, having in the previous round inflicted the first defeat for ten years on world champion James Male.

Both Whatley and Sawrey-Cookson have inspired the evening club, the Clifton Boasters, to substantial achievements in the National League and enthusiasm for overseas tours. In 1985, they visited New York, Tuxedo Park, Detroit and Chicago; and in 1988 Montreal, Boston and Philadelphia.

DETROIT RACQUET CLUB

IN RECOGNITION of the revitalisation of the club as a Rackets destination, a ninetieth anniversary celebration was staged in May 1992. Distinguished guests included Edward F. Ulmann and former world champion Willie Surtees, and a week of Rackets, golf, tennis and sailing was capped with a formal dinner on the court.

The game had lain fallow for a while at Detroit, and was rejuvenated largely through the efforts of John O'Brien and his brother Joseph. They attracted a much-needed infusion of energy to the court, in the shape of players such as Thomas P. Howe, Robert Thibodeau Jr., William Goldsmith, Ronald Birgbauer and Michael Goodell. Howe was the best of these and has remained so, as the perennial winner of the club championship.

Nine club members undertook a tour of the Rackets courts of England in 1994, an exhausting ten-day ordeal that was highly successful socially and resulted in a dramatic improvement in court performance. It was the following year that Howe won the Murray Sales singles title, the first time a Detroit member had won a nationally sponsored tournament since Sales himself – who trained Howe – took the title

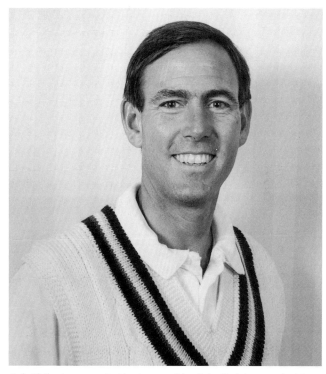
Bob Thibodeau sports the impeccable style that has made him one of the favourites of the international Rackets scene.

in 1970. Sales, an outstanding player, twice held the US Amateur doubles and three times the Canadian doubles.

That year of 1995 was also the first of the Detroit Racquets Club's Amateur Rackets Fellowship, whereby a player trained at a public school plays as a guest of the club for three months during his gap year. The following year, Detroit hosted the second leg of the American Quintathlon, a competition involving five days of Rackets, squash, golf, tennis and shooting, complemented by numerous dinners.

Joseph Bickley built the Detroit court in 1903, and it remained an open one until 1912, when it was glazed over, electric lighting installed, and the walls renovated by Bickley at a cost of $3,800. There is a notably splendid gallery capable of accommodating more than 100 spectators. The first national championship to be played there was the Amateur singles in 1951 – the first time it had been held outside

Michael Goodell displays the blazing serve that led him to the finals of the 1999 US Open doubles.

Norb Madison (left) *and Tom Shumaker take a break during the Millennium Quintathlon.*

President Ted Turner, steadying hand at the helm, helped guide the club into the new millennium.

New York, Boston or Philadelphia – and they staged the US doubles two years later, when David Milford and John Thompson of Britain beat a high-class field.

National championships are allocated to courts on a rotating basis by the North American Racquets Association, and Detroit host either the Western Open, the Pell Cup, the Bertolotti Cup, the US Amateur singles and doubles, or the Kendrick Cup. The last named, for novices, was presented in the mid 1950s by a Detroit club member, Charles Kendrick. His Rackets was often played in the company of Charles Johnson, and the pair were affectionately known as 'Chuck' and 'Chick'.

As well as their internal club championship, the club instituted the Detroit Racquet Club Invitational in 1977, to increase competition between players from Chicago and Detroit.

ETON COLLEGE

Eton launched themselves on the Rackets world in spectacular fashion. They won the first two Public Schools team championships in 1868 and 1869, though their first courts were not built until 1866. They were runners-up for the next three years, and in the first eighteen years of the championships failed to reach the final just four times. Those first courts, which were replaced in 1903, were said to be adequate, but slow, with the service line lower than it is today.

Great start though that was, the achievement was eclipsed more than a century later by an astonishing result in the Foster Cup, the Public Schools singles contest. All four entrants from Eton reached the 1998 quarter-finals, and all four won – a clean sweep for the Cup that caused many an old Etonian chest to swell with pride.

Their first outstanding player was C.J. Ottaway, who played in both the College's early triumphs. It is said that he never lost a match for Eton or Oxford where he won the University singles three times and was in the winning doubles pair four times in successive years. By the end of the century, Eton had produced one of the great names of these games, Edgar Baerlein, later to be Amateur champion of Rackets nine times, and of Tennis thirteen times.

The two 1902 courts are still regarded as among the best in the country, and helped the College win the Public Schools championship again in 1905. They were, incidentally, upgraded when the Old Etonian Racquets and Tennis Club contributed to the installation of modern lighting in 1973, as well as improved changing facilities.

Eton's next golden period came in the 1920s, when they won three times and (up to 1931) played in nine finals. Among the successful players of that period were Ronny Aird, later to become secretary and then president of the MCC, and the formidable combination of Kenneth Wagg and Ian Akers-Douglas, who won the Amateur doubles three times. Akers-Douglas also played in eight Amateur singles finals, winning three of them, and in 1933 beat Lord Aberdare for the Open title.

The brilliant young American Bobby Grant III played first string in 1929 and 1930, later dominating the Rackets scene on the other side of the Atlantic for seventeen years. In 1947, he was surprisingly beaten in a match to decide who played Jim Dear for the world title.

Four Eton pairs reached the schools final in the 1940s (only once during the war years was the competition not played), and in 1944 the pair were Anthony Ward and Richard Greenwood, both of whom subsequently gave unstinting service to Rackets and Tennis as administrators as well as players. Ward

Old Etonian Tom Pugh, for twenty-five years an outstanding doubles player, performs on his own with equal success a little later.

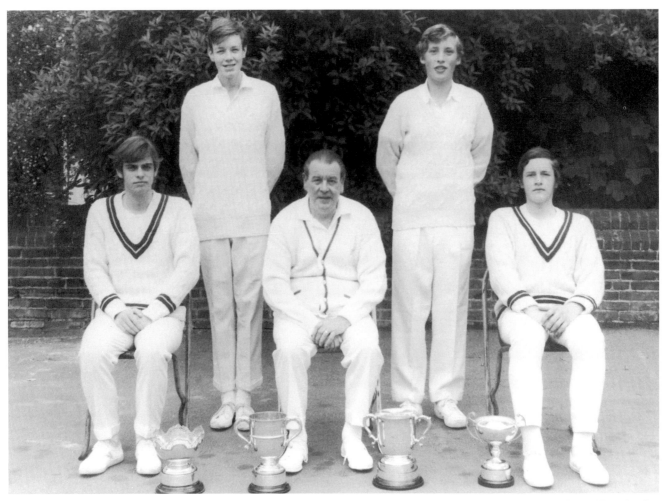

Ronnie Hawes (centre), *with outstanding 1968 pupils Mark Faber* (front left) *and Willie Boone* (right), *who won the Public Schools championship; and J.E. Pease* (back left) *and Robin Drysdale, who won the Angus Cup.*

became Chairman of Queen's Club, and Greenwood was for many years Hon. Treasurer and Membership Secretary of the Tennis and Rackets Association.

Twenty-seven years after their last Public Schools triumph, Eton hit the button again, winning seven times between 1955 and 1970, every one during the reign of the outstanding professional Ronnie Hawes, who established a wonderful rapport with the boys. His coaching and encouragement led to the development of some of the finest Rackets players of the era. They included Tom Pugh (1955), who won the Amateur doubles with John Thompson in 1966 and with Willie Boone from 1975 to 1977. Pugh twice won the US Open and the Tuxedo Gold Racquet (1966 and 1967), and he had victories in the US doubles (with Mac Bailey) and the Canadian doubles (twice with Boone), as well as the Canadian singles.

An even finer player led the Eton pair in 1958 – James Leonard. He later played Geoffrey Atkins for the world championship twice, was Open champion from 1967 to 1970 and four times Amateur champion, and three times won the Amateur doubles (once with Charles Swallow and twice with Charles Hue Williams). His partner in that Eton victory was David Norman, whose achievements were also spectacular. Norman was five times US Amateur and once US Open champion. He was champion of Canada three times in singles and four in doubles, and later he was an inspiring Chairman of the Tennis and Rackets Association.

Garth Milne was another of Eton's successes, in 1960 becoming the first player to win the Foster Cup two years in succession, and the next year taking the doubles championship with Brian FitzGerald. Then came the three Faber brothers, a rare family whose father, Julian, led Winchester to the Public Schools trophy in 1935.

Michael was in Eton's winning pair in 1963 and 1964, and the youngest, David, reached the final in 1979. Between them came the most remarkable Faber,

Mark. He equalled the Public Schools record by being in the winning pair three times, 1967, 1968 and 1969, playing with Lord Richard Wellesley, Willie Boone and Andrew Milne. He won the Foster Cup in 1967 and 1968, and went on to take the University singles and doubles for Oxford three times from 1970. After his tragically early death, his family presented the Association with the Mark Faber Cup, which rewards consistency and depth in school competition. In recent years, it has been won by Eton four times in succession.

Boone became one of the world's greatest players, and remained so for a remarkably long time. Between 1976 and 1986 he played in eleven consecutive Amateur singles finals, winning five of them. Eight years after that he won the Amateur singles and doubles and the Open doubles all in the same year, by then skipping lightly through his forties. He first won the British Open singles in 1979, and was heading for middle age when he won it again in 1995.

Following Mark Faber's three Public Schools

Left Public Schools championship winners in 1963, Robert Pilkington and Michael Faber, with Ronnie Hawes.

Below Eton's most celebrated player, Willie Boone, makes a delicate enquiry of the referee on the way to winning the 1998 Amateur doubles with James Male.

Four Etonians filled the 1995 Foster Cup semi-final places: (left to right) Patrick Wigan, Neal Bailey, professional Norwood Cripps, Dominic Palmer-Tomkinson and Guy Smith-Bingham. Between them the four also won the doubles and the second-pairs championships.

Charles Hue Williams congratulates Norwood Cripps on Eton winning the Mark Faber Cup for the fourth successive year, in 1997. Roger Crosby, the Harrow Rackets professional, applauds.

doubles wins, Robin Drysdale (later to play Davis Cup tennis) led Eton to a fourth successive win in 1970, the year in which he also won the Foster Cup. It was twenty-five years before Eton won it again. That was the stunning year when the College made a clean sweep of the quarter-finals, and Neal Bailey, Patrick Wigan, Guy Smith-Bingham and Dominic Palmer-Tomkinson fought it out for the Foster Cup. This was the only singles trophy that had so far eluded the master-professional, Norwood Cripps, during his seventeen years at the school. Bailey took the prize, beating Smith-Bingham in the final. Smith-Bingham, whose elder brother Alex also reached the Foster final, won the Under-15 Public School singles in his first two years at Eton. In 1997, he and Hugo Loudon (unseeded) won the Public Schools final, losing only one game throughout the competition.

The long line of outstanding players who joined Eton as professionals must take much credit for the school's gilded history in the game. Ronnie Hawes and Norwood Cripps have been mentioned, but among the others were three world champions – William Gray, who began the line in 1868, Cecil 'Punch' Fairs in 1875, and Jim Dear twice, from 1951 to 1952 and from 1972 to 1979.

Mark Hue Williams has followed his father into the top ranks of the game.

FALKLAND PALACE

BUILT IN 1539, this is the oldest existing Tennis court in the world, and also the only active open-air court. It is a Mecca for visiting players from all over the globe, who relish the opportunity to play on a court with no dedans, no tambour and no roof! For those who enjoy giraffe serves, the sky is the limit – literally.

King James V of Scotland built the court as a *jeu quarré*, as opposed to a court *a dedans*. Instead of a dedans it has four lunes (square openings) in the wall behind the server and an ais in the corner diagonally opposite the grille; all of these score winning points. There are no line galleries, entry to the court being by two doors on either side of the net at chase-the-door, and the penthouse roof has a pitch roughly ten per cent steeper than usual.

The floor, consisting of thick paving slabs, has been relaid twice, in 1628 and in the 1890s. There have been several restorations, the most important being that by the third Marquess of Bute near the end of the nineteenth century. By then the building had fallen

The Queen's Club provided a sweet chestnut tree to mark the 450th anniversary of Falkland's Royal Tennis court in 1989. Left to right: *Peter Wordie, long-time club member and co-author of* The Royal Game; *Douglas Bremner of the National Trust for Scotland; Major A.B. Cran, club chairman 1988–98; Elisabeth Woodthorpe; Jemma Cordery of the National Trust for Scotland; Ewan Chalmers, club member.*

The oldest existing court in the world, and the only active, open-air court, Falkland has four lunes in the server's wall instead of a dedans.

into a sad state and needed excavation of the floor, a complete rebuild of the penthouses and total re-plastering of the walls, without which the court would probably not be usable today.

It reopened with a match involving Sir Edward Grey, later to become Foreign Secretary. Since the Second World War, the National Trust for Scotland has maintained the Palace, and it is thanks to them that the court is in its present excellent condition. The Queen has visited the court twice, in 1958 (her first sight of Tennis) and in 1991.

In 1989, the 450th anniversary was celebrated by staging a tournament that brought together players from Australia, Belgium, France, Holland and the US, as well as several from English courts. Prince Edward honoured the tournament with his presence, and played in a doubles match partnered by Sally Jones. A temporary roof raised over the court guaranteed a week of brilliant sunshine which, coupled with the majestic surroundings, created a special and unforgettable atmosphere. The event was won, fittingly perhaps, by a team from the Falkland Palace Club, and the trophy is displayed in the exhibition room at the court.

There is play on the court all the year round, Scottish weather being not nearly as bad as is reputed. Visitors may be pleasantly surprised to find there is no booking system and no time limit to matches. The small number of local players regard it as 'tennis heaven'.

JEU DE PAUME DE FONTAINEBLEAU

R EOPENED IN 1990 after many lost years, the *jeu de paume* of the royal palace in Fontainebleau, built by King Henry IV of France in 1601, claims to be the world's oldest enclosed Tennis court. With its outsized dimensions of 31.20 by 13.60 metres, it is also the largest, and its penthouse roofs are the highest and most steeply pitched.

It is a quirky, endearing, unheated, great old barn of a place, and until its renovation in 2000 its notoriously uneven floor of hard limestone blocks created a gloriously unpredictable bounce that brought many a modern professional to woe and gnashings of teeth.

As if all that were not enough, it is a part of France's public domain, as open to tourists as are the museum, gardens and salons of the royal palace itself. As a result, gawping visitors commonly wander in and out of the galleries, chatting loudly, often snapping photos and invariably placing their innocent faces perilously close to the netting. All in all, Fontainebleau is a special, even a unique court.

From 1601 until the French Revolution in 1789, the same family, the descendants of Nicolas Dupont de Compiegne (a companion in arms of Henry IV) occupied the concierge's lodgings near the court, drawing their revenues by renting rooms to players. Kings and future kings played there, and as early as

'A quirky, endearing old barn of a place': this is the largest, and oldest, enclosed court in the world.

223

1607 the personal physician of the future Louis XIII noted that the five-year-old Dauphin 'took volleys and played a good backhand'. Saint-Simon recorded that Louis XIV enjoyed strolling over to the court on rainy days to watch the best athletes play the game 'at which he had earlier excelled himself'.

In August 1702, a terrible fire broke out in the nearby Pavilion des Armes, threatening the entire palace. To save the royal apartments and chapel, fire fighters razed roofs to make fire breaks, and directed the flames to the *jeu de paume* and the orangerie. This sacrifice was repaired thirty years later, when a new roof was installed and the present limestone floor laid.

Although its physical aspect changed very little, the court was used only sporadically after the Revolution. The game was very much 'out' for the firebrands, just as many a noble head would be 'off' if caught playing, and it was 1812 before the court was repainted and put back into playing shape for the (very brief) imperial enjoyment of Napoleon I.

No Tennis event at Fontainebleau throughout the nineteenth century was more remarkable than the exploit of Edmond Barre, who walked from Paris (forty-three miles) in ten hours and immediately took

Left *Anthony Scratchley, the current Fontainebleau professional.*

Action in the reopened court.

Young girl with shuttlecock by Jean Baptiste Simeon Chardin, 1699–1779

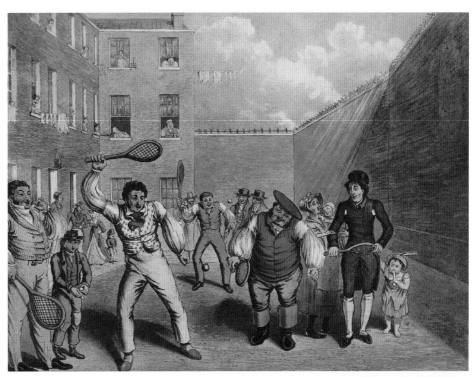

Right *Rackets at the King's Bench Prison*

Below *Rackets at the Fleet prison*

Left *The Tennis court at Versailles, painted by Boilly*

Below *Hampton Court*

Right *Tennis at Fontainebleau*

Below *The chateau and gardens of Fontainebleau from the south*

Left *The International Tennis Club of Washington (Prince's Court)*

Below *The Dinner Match at Leamington by Anthony Hobson*

on and beat his strongest challenger. The indefatigable Barre went undefeated for thirty-three years.

Use of the court was ceded to the club Le Sport de Fontainebleau in 1870, but there was less and less play there as the new rage, lawn tennis, grew in popularity. During the First World War it was painted white and turned into a physical therapy unit for wounded soldiers of the French army, and after the war the American Art School took it over for the piano masterclasses of Nadia Boulanger.

It was the mid 1980s before the building began the return to its true purpose, when a group of local enthusiasts formed the Cercle du Jeu de Paume de Fontainebleau. They persuaded the city administration to join the Ministry of Culture and a few honorary founding members – notably Lord Aberdare and Richard Duvauchelle – in a vast project to restore the court to its original splendour.

In an official ceremony awash with champagne and graced by the presence of Prince Edward, who whacked a few balls and pronounced himself satisfied, the court was reopened in the autumn of 1990. The leading Fontainebleau player Olivier Michel won the Raquette d'Or in 2000, beating Guillaume Ruault of Paris in the final. The current professional is Anthony Scratchley and the President of the Cercle is Rudolph Chelminski.

Rudolph Chelminski, President of the Cercle du Jeu de Paume de Fontainebleau.

GREENTREE

At the beginning of the new century the Greentree Court in Manhasset, New York remains one of Court Tennis's most cherished venues.

Previously a private court on the Whitney family property, the court as well as the house, grounds and contents are now controlled by the Greentree Foundation. John Hay 'Jock' Whitney, who passed away in 1982, and his wife Betsy Cushing Whitney, who died in 1998, created the Greentree Foundation to further their charitable and philanthropic aims. For many years Clarence C. 'Clarry' Pell kept the court in active use on behalf of the Whitney family with regular weekend play, along with the well-known Greentree weekend competition for the Payne Whitney Cup. It was a great loss to his family, the game of Court Tennis, and all of the Greentree players when Clarry Pell died in 1998. After that, Peter DiBonaventura ably conducted the affairs of the Greentree tennis court until

Greentree, Long Island: 'The most beautiful court in the world.'

Jack Hickey, Greentree's popular Court Tennis director, alongside the court.

the United States Court Tennis Preservation Foundation took over its operation in 1999.

The great traditions of the court are continuing apace. The members of the committee for Tennis at Greentree – Peter DiBonaventura, Charles T. Johnstone, Peter Guernsey and William F. McLaughlin Jr – are working with the long-time professional, and now Court Tennis Director, Jack Hickey, to foster steady and active play on the court, hold the annual Whitney Cup tournament and encourage the development of the game.

Two important women's Tennis events were held at Greentree in the 1999–2000 season, the Anne Boleyn and the US women's singles and doubles championships. Both were extraordinary successes for the women's game and for Greentree, as well.

Notably, the 1999 Whitney Cup tournament was won for the first time in many years by the Greentree team. It was a hard-fought and much-appreciated victory for the home team. From the ongoing Whitney Cup competition to the emerging women's and juniors' events, and with the able assistance of Jack Hickey, Greentree hopes to showcase Court Tennis at its magnificent best for many years to come.

Jock Whitney.

HAILEYBURY

THE DECADE OF THE 1970s was a golden era for Haileybury Rackets, with a succession of very talented players pressing for places in Haileybury teams. John Dawes, Robin Hollington, Robert Gradon, Peter Barber, Paul Hearn, Robert Wakely and William Hollington all won events at Queen's. Richard Ellis, son of Peter Ellis, had an outstanding record, with seven wins at Queen's – twice in colts doubles (1974 with William Hollington and 1976 with Peter Wallis), colts singles in 1975, senior doubles with Wallis in 1978 and the Foster Cup three times in 1977, 1978 and 1979. Richard went on to represent Oxford at Rackets, Tennis and

cricket and played for Middlesex in Mike Brearley's side.

In 1980, M.I. Tentori won the level singles and in 1982 S.W.D. Heck and R.R.N. Bonallack won the Peter Gray Cup. The following year, T.R. Symonds and J.M. Dawes won the second pairs event.

In the 1990s, T.P. Faulkner won the Renny Cup in 1991 and a gifted left-hander, Rob Walker, reached the finals of the Jim Dear Cup in 1990, the Incledon-Webber Cup in 1991 and, with P.D. Stafford, the Peter Gray Cup in 1991. Walker's partnership with David Cruickshank has been the outstanding Haileybury pair in recent years. Together they won the colts doubles in

Peter Ellis flanked by his 1978 Public Schools champions Peter Wallis (left) and his son Richard.

Senior doubles winners 1993, Rob Walker (left) and David Cruickshank.

Peter Ellis, the greatly admired Haileybury professional for thirty-three years, was also a most respected marker in the game.

The over 40s singles final, November 1999. Howard Angus, Haileybury's Rackets professional and former world champion, discusses fitness after a narrow defeat against another former world champion Willie Boone, several years his junior.

1992, the senior doubles in 1993, but lost in the final the following year to Rugby. Walker has, at Oxford, set a record of five successive doubles wins in the Varsity Match, and is a blue at Tennis as well.

Duncan Stahl, son of the international squash player Chris Stahl, reached the finals of the Renny Cup in 1993 and the Foster Cup in 1994, and the all-rounder Richard Palmer got to the finals of the Jim Dear Cup and Incledon-Webber Cup in 1993 and 1994 respectively.

In 1996, Haileybury's idiosyncratic, droll and greatly admired professional, Peter Ellis, retired after thirty-three distinguished years as Rackets and cricket coach at the college. His famous one-liners enliven any Rackets gathering and caused many a Professional Rackets Association meeting to come to a halt with laughter. Draws for the Schools championships are not quite the same without him. However, he continues to mark many matches at Queen's and is reluctant just yet to hand on the mantle of world's best marker to younger pretenders such as Derek Barrett, Professional at Wellington, or his own pupil Robert Wakely, the Professional at Marlborough. Peter was succeeded as professional at Haileybury by Howard Angus, the left-handed former world champion, a late recruit to the ranks of Rackets professionals.

HAMPTON COURT, THE ROYAL TENNIS COURT

NO TENNIS COURT IN THE WORLD has a history as richly royal as this one, and it is more fully documented elsewhere in the book. Suffice it to say here that one English king built the court, another rebuilt it, three renovated it, one painted it white and turned it into a drawing room, and Christopher Wren used it as a timber store – and all of that before 1720. In 1903, Edward VII consented to become its Patron, as has every monarch since.

The first of its world championships was held in 1885, when Tom Pettitt took the title from George Lambert. By then the windows on both the west and east sides had been glazed, and soon afterwards the habit of darkening the floor with bullocks' blood was discontinued in favour of black paint.

By 1896, there was a cash crisis, and an annual subscription was introduced. Despite the club ceasing to function during the First World War it flourished well enough for heating and lighting to be installed before the next war, during which the court suffered major bomb damage.

P.A. (Tony) Negretti ran the club almost single-handed after the war, filling the posts of Hon. Secretary and Hon. Treasurer from 1947 until 1973, when the club was reconstituted. He handed over to an active committee in what became known as the

The court was built, rebuilt and renovated by a succession of English kings.

'Palace Revolution', after which the lights were replaced, members redecorated the court and Negretti was elected President.

Howard Angus, who had taken the world championship from E.L. Scott in 1976, successfully defended it against him at Hampton Court in 1977, and beat off, by 7–0, the challenge from Chris Ronaldson in 1979, losing it to him at Queen's Club in 1981 (Angus retired injured when behind 5–1).

Ronaldson had by then become the Hampton Court professional, perhaps the most brilliant player to do so. He joined in 1979, after serving Oxford, Melbourne and the Sun Court at Troon, and soon had the court running at full capacity (some 5,000 court hours a year). New competitions were inaugurated (including the Seal Salver for those over fifty, where the handicap is on age only) and a club ladder was started. It was not long before the club could not cope with the flood of applications for membership, leading to the introduction of an entrance fee and a waiting list.

Only the eleventh head professional at the court since 1820, Ronaldson needed top-class practice to maintain his status as world champion. This led to first Wayne Davies and then Lachlan Deuchar working at the Royal Tennis Court, in the latter's case for six years, providing a feast of good tennis and coaching second to none. Ronaldson defended his world title at Hampton Court in 1983 against Wayne Davies, whom he again beat (at Queen's) in 1985 – the year,

World champion Chris Ronaldson, only the eleventh head professional at Hampton Court in 180 years.

incidentally, in which the Hampton Court floor was painted red.

The club hosted the Amateur singles in 1982, 1983, 1984 and 1996, and the British Open in 1987, when Davies, having just taken the world title from Ronaldson, lost to Deuchar. In 1983, the inaugural Billy Ross Skinner Invitation Mixed Doubles was held on the court, and it was played there for the next sixteen years. Meanwhile the club's Field Trophy team, infected with success and enthusiasm, were victorious in 1980 and for eleven of the next thirteen years.

A new tournament was created in 1998, the Dresdner Kleinwort Benson Classic for the world's top eight professionals. It was won by Nick Wood, who had just left Hampton Court after ten years as assistant to take over at Holyport; for the following two years it was won by world champion Robert Fahey. The 1999 ladies' world championships were held at the club, when the reigning champion, Penny Lumley, defeated RTC's Sue Haswell in the final in three close sets.

Annual competitions held within the club include

Lesley Ronaldson, a major influence in the development of ladies' tennis.

Nick Wood (second right), *winner of the first Dresdner Kleinwort Benson Classic, played at Hampton Court in 1998, together with* James Male (left), *Frank Filippelli* (second left) *and Chris Bray.*

the Camm Cup (for the level singles championship), the Savage Trophies (doubles), the Lathom-Browne Cup (handicap singles) and the De Laszlo Bowl (handicap doubles).

The Keeper's house, built in 1636, extended in the mid nineteenth century and lost after the death in 1883 of the last Keeper, Major William Beresford, was recovered and refurbished in 1993. It provided club rooms, a professionals' workshop, and an admirable flat for the head professional. Ronaldson's two sons, Ivan and Ben, now work as his assistant professionals.

In 1989 the Queen granted permission for a second Tennis court to be built and a detailed investigation of the possibilities began. The club wanted to build within the confines of the Palace, close to the existing Stuart court, and such sensitive siting required approval of several national and local authorities. Ministerial approval was given in 1997, and planning permission granted at the end of May 1999.

HARBOUR CLUB

TENNIS FORMS A SMALL but lively part of this luxurious club, opened in 1993 on the site of the old Fulham power station, on the north bank of the Thames. It boasts swimming pools, lawn-tennis courts both indoor and outdoor, and a gymnasium. The premises are spacious, sparkling and highly attractive.

Close to central London, the club is frequented by celebrities galore.

Former world number one Lachlan Deuchar manages the court, which is situated underground and inevitably lacks height. His first full-time professional was Kees Ludekens, who left for Cambridge in 1996. Among the professionals to work at the Harbour since then are Brad Dale, Mike Gooding, Olivier Michel and Stefan King. The full-time post is now held by Marc

Marc Seigneur, current professional and a competitive match player.

Lachlan Deuchar, Tennis manager at London's luxurious Harbour Club.

Seigneur, who regained the French Closed championship in 1997 and won the Browning Cup (the British professional singles handicap tournament) in 1999. He beat Andrew Knibbs (Newmarket) 6–4 6–3 in the final.

The club is an unashamedly commercial enterprise, and the Tennis players enjoy a remarkable width of sponsorship both for internal competitions and for their teams in national championships. In 1996, Lachlan Deuchar was able to call on Nick Wood and Nigel Pendrigh to join him in winning the National League, while he himself won the Professional singles and the Masters, and lost in the finals of the British and US Opens.

There is a substantial caucus of active club members, many of them new to the game, who keep the Tennis court busy throughout the year. Simon Kverndal has so far been outstanding among them. The Category F Open championship for handicaps of 50 and over was held there in 1999, drawing a record entry of twenty-eight.

Right *Lachlan Deuchar* (right) *with Jonathan Howell having won the Professional doubles in 1995.*

The court has an enviably consistent playing surface.

HARDWICK HOUSE

THE FIRST TENNIS COURT at Hardwick House, near Pangbourne, Berkshire, was built in 1897 by Charles Day Rose. In 1907 he built a second nearer the house – supposedly for greater convenience – and the original slowly fell into disrepair. All that remains is the external architecture of the building. It is notable that Charles Rose was also able to entertain his guests with Eton fives and Rackets. While both of these courts are severely delapidated, the former is in relatively better repair and behind it you can still see the outline of the Rackets court.

The 1907 court remains one of the few in the world to be privately owned and the Rose family remain enthusiastic and generous supporters of the game.

The first recorded match at Hardwick House involved the Hon. Alfred Lyttleton, H.E. Crawley, E.F. Newton and Charles Rose himself. It was supervised by the professional Edward Gray, from Prince's Club, and attracted the attention of *The Times*:

> *. . . Altogether the work seems to be nearly as perfect as human foresight and sagacity can make it and reflects the greatest credit on the builder. If we must find fault (and no criticism is good without a little spice of that kind) we should object to the extreme high finish of floor and walls, the object having been obviously to obtain an extremely quick surface. This no doubt has been secured – but is that an advantage?*
>
> *The idea has probably come into the young Tennis world from that of Rackets, where quickness is the paramount point. It is not so in Tennis, which is sufficiently difficult with less rapid surfaces. But the difficulty used to be of another sort, involving more skill and less of the slap-bang slash-and-smash style of the present day. It seems a pity to alter the game in that direction!*

In 1898 the court staged a match between world champion Peter Latham and Cecil 'Punch' Fairs, two players who between them held the world championship from 1895 to 1912. The same pair

A painting by the Hon. Neville Lytton, showing him at the hazard end in a match against Charles Rose, the grandson of the founder, at Hardwick.

Phoebe, Lady Rose, generous chatelaine of Hardwick House, with Tennis enthusiast the Earl of Wessex.

played the opening match in 1901 on Rose's new court at Suffolk House, Newmarket, to which Latham had been lured away from Queen's Club. Sir Charles, as he then was, moved Latham in 1907 to the new court at Hardwick House, Edward Gray having left for Brighton. The noble proprietor and his star employee played the opening match on 14 December, Latham so skilfully controlling the play that Sir Charles won the second set 6–5. The two of them played several times a month for the next three or four years.

Thereafter enthusiasm waned and entries in the Hardwick House match book are spasmodic. Some illustrious names appear in the late 1930s (including that of Latham in 1938, when he was seventy-five years old), but it was not until the 1980s that Tennis took a firm hold again. The creation of The Friends of Hardwick House Tennis Court, largely by David Weston and Adrian Snow, enabled the latter to repair the court, install lighting and create changing room facilities in the grille penthouse.

The Friends have a full fixture list, including inter-club competitions, and thanks to the goodwill of the Rose family, other clubs and visiting players use the court from time to time. While there is no formal lease

Kate Leeming, always a most welcome visiting professional to Hardwick House.

between the club and the estate, there is a licence to occupy which is capable of being renewed with the agreement of both parties.

HARROW SCHOOL

Harrow's two Rackets courts were built exactly a century apart. The first opened in February 1865, at a cost of about £2,000; the second, the 'Crosby' court, in September 1965, after £33,455 had been spent. Not all of that sum was for the actual building work, though that did prove a problem. No courts had been built since Haileybury's in 1908, and the firm of Bickley, with its expertise in court construction, no longer existed.

Bickley's patent was discovered in the New York Public Library, and H.G. Harbour, one of the Bickley plasterers, provided some first-hand information, but there remained the difficulty of trying to suit modern materials to an old formula. Great credit is due to Charles Swallow who stage-managed the project, to the architect, Robert Bostock, and the builder, Donald Jones of T. Jones and Son, for accomplishing the task so successfully.

The original proposal and the offer of a most generous contribution towards the cost of a second Rackets court came from Old Harrovian Geoffrey Simmonds in 1963. More than 300 contributors followed his example.

The first professional, George Smale, coached the Harrow pair to win the Public Schools championship in 1871, and from then until 1888 Harrow dominated the championship, winning thirteen of their fifteen finals. Walter Gray, from the famous Cambridge cricket family, took over from Smales in 1872 (occasionally playing cricket for Middlesex at the same time), and

Harrow – Roddy Bloomfield (left) and Christopher Strang to the fore – beat Marlborough – Neil Marr (left) and Peter Anderson – in the final of the Public Schools doubles championship in 1954.

when he left for Charterhouse in 1877 no resident professional was appointed until 'Judy' Stevens came from Prince's Club in 1885.

By this time the Crawley family had begun their march through Rackets history. First, three brothers played in winning pairs before the end of the nineteenth century – Ernest in 1883 (he later won the Amateur Tennis title three times), Eustace in 1885–6, and Stafford in 1895. He was the father of Cosmo, who played in the Harrow pair for three years with his cousin Leonard, and of Aidan, who was in the pair that reached the final in 1926.

Aidan's two sons both played for the school for two years, Andrew in 1964–5 and Randall in 1967 (when the pair lost 3–4 to the Eton pairing of Lord Wellesley and Mark Faber) and 1968. Randall Crawley subsequently formed an almost unbeatable partnership with Willie Boone (ex-Eton), dominating the British Open doubles through the 1980s. As celebrated a player as the Crawleys was Percy Ashworth who, after being in the winning Harrow pair of 1887, went on to win the Amateur singles in 1890 and the Amateur doubles seven times – four

Harry Foster collects a cup from Christopher Holdsworth Hunt, managing director of Peel Hunt plc, for winning the Under-24 singles championship. He previously won the H.K. Foster Cup in 1992.

times with H.K. Foster and finally, in 1909, with Edgar Baerlein.

The school continued their triumphant progress to the end of the nineteenth century and beyond, winning six of their eight finals between 1890 and 1903. They did not reach the championship final again until 1925, when they won, as they did in 1931 and 1932, on both occasions with Roger Pulbrook in the pair (in 1933 he was still there, but they lost to Rugby).

No public school has won the championship more often than Harrow, and though their domination of the game had expired, Harrow continued to be successful after the war. Geoffrey Simmonds and Robin Treherne-Thomas won in 1947, Derek Taylor and Tom Pigott in 1948 and Christopher Strang and Roddy Bloomfield in 1954. Roddy Bloomfield also won the H.K. Foster Cup in 1954.

Success then became spasmodic, with a sixteen-year gap until Thatcher and Prenn won in 1971. It was another twelve years before David Dick and Steven Seagrave won in 1984 and fourteen before Tom Dunbar and Rupert Wilcox did it in 1999. John Prenn meanwhile had gone on to become one of the great players of the game, winning the Swallow Trophy (Under-24 singles) three times, the Amateur singles four times and the British Open a record six times (on each occasion beating Willie Boone in the final).

Alex Titchener-Barrett won the H.K. Foster Cup in 1996 and 1997, a fine achievement.

Roger Crosby, Harrow's professional for thirty-four years, took over from his father, Fred, who had been there since 1922. Grandfather A.J. Crosby (left) is seen here with his three sons, Jim, Fred and Arthur.

A century as Rackets professionals was celebrated by Crosby family representatives Roger (left) and son Martin (right) at a Queen's Club presentation in 1995.

Harrow have won the doubles championship more often than any other school. In 1999, their third successive year in the final, Tom Dunbar (left) and Rupert Wilcox, beat Tonbridge 4–1. John Eaton, Harrow professional, is with them.

Though the doubles prize so often eluded the school, they hit another golden era for singles in the 1990s. Charles Danby won the Foster Cup in 1991, Harry Foster in 1992, Alex Titchener-Barrett in 1996 and 1997, and Tom Dunbar in 1999. Titchener-Barrett's record is remarkable: the only Harrovian to win the Foster Cup twice, he appeared in eight consecutive Queen's Club finals, including four wins at Under-15.

Peter Warfield, a former England rugby international, has been master-in-charge of Rackets since 1985 and his enthusiasm has influenced the game greatly. But no name is more securely attached to Harrow's success than that of Crosby. Two of them, father and son, between them spent over eighty years there as Rackets professionals.

Fred Crosby arrived in 1922 and Roger, at first his assistant, took over from him in 1962, retiring in 1996. Both were excellent motivators and great characters, exuding friendliness, and it is no wonder the new court was named the Crosby court. John Eaton is now the head professional. Roger's son Martin worked as assistant professional at Harrow from 1983 to 1988 before becoming the professional at Charterhouse.

Harrow's Thursday Rackets Club (which for two years ran on a Wednesday evening) has been notably successful, and was the forerunner of several similar clubs based at other schools. Most members are local people with a lawn-tennis or squash background. The general standard has risen, and the spirit and level of enjoyment of the friendly matches between clubs is high. The Harrow Hammer has become a popular event each October, attracting entrants from all the other evening clubs.

HATFIELD HOUSE

DURING THE STRONG REVIVAL of Tennis in the Victorian era, it became fashionable for the aristocracy to add courts to their country houses. The court built at Hatfield House in 1842 by the second Marquess of Salisbury is a typical example, and the Cecil family used the Hertfordshire court exclusively for nearly 100 years. It was inaugurated with a match between Lord Salisbury and the Rector of Hatfield, the Rev. F.G. Faithfull.

The fifth Marquess was probably the most accomplished player of the family, with a particularly fast overhead serve. He represented Oxford University (as Lord Cranborne) in 1914, and continued to play at Hatfield House until the closure of the court after the outbreak of war in 1939.

The court was used as a furniture store throughout the war and for several years afterwards, until in 1955 three local enthusiasts, Dick Granville, Francis Tufton and Norman Oliver, persuaded Lord Salisbury to let them form a club. They raised £600 for cleaning and refurbishing the court, and added electric light (fed by a coin meter).

No resident professional was appointed until Kevin King came in 1982, though an unbroken line of professionals had served Hatfield from its beginning until the Second World War. They included three of the famous Lambert family. The founding father, Joseph (John) Lambert, was there from 1849 until his death in 1905 at the age of ninety-one.

He continued playing until well past eighty, and was first assisted and then succeeded by his youngest son, Charles. (Another of the brothers, George, was world champion from 1871 to 1885.) Jack Groom took over on Charles's death in 1915, to be followed when he

Hatfield's court, built by the second Marquess of Salisbury in 1842, was used as a furniture store in the Second World War. The picture was painted by J.C. Skinner in 1992.

went to Lord's in 1924 by one of Joseph Lambert's grandsons, Alfred.

A draft of an 1842 letter from the second Marquess throws fascinating light on the duties and rewards of the marker in those days. Lord Salisbury was writing to the father of Charles Phillips, the first professional at Hatfield:

I have been making some inquiry as to the payment of Tennis markers and from the best consideration I can give the subject I propose to give your son if it suits him 12s. a week and lodging and firing. That he should receive 3d. per set for marking and 6d. per set for playing with those gentlemen in the neighbourhood to whom I give permission to play in the court which I shall do by ticket (and to mark for the company in my house.) I shall of course expect your son to repair the rackets and balls and to keep the court in good order. But there will still be a great deal of spare time upon his hands and I wish he had some employment which would lead to his advantage and keep him out of idleness. I would suggest to you for example, what I believe many markers are in the habit of doing, his

Julian Snow and James Acheson-Gray receive the 1999 Amateur doubles trophy from Lord Charles Cecil at Hatfield.

Howard Angus (left) won the Bridgeman Cup (UK over-50 Amateur singles) against John Ward (right) at Hatfield in 1999. Also pictured are John Ritblat and Colin Dean.

The Tufton family's association with Tennis goes back seven generations, to Lord Thanet in 1801. Four of them played for two hours at Hatfield in 1993: brothers Anthony (Lord Hothfield) and Nicholas (left) won eighteen games. So did father and son Francis and Edward (right).

learning to make Tennis shoes, which would probably be a source of considerable profit to him, or in short any other sedentary occupation which would not take him off the premises.

In 1987, the sixth Marquess generously granted the club security of tenure, enabling them to make substantial improvements to both the court and the off-court facilities. The club room, the pro's shop, a ladies' changing room and heating generally were among the vital considerations, for which costs doubled and redoubled as the planning stage went on.

Finance was at last secured, and work began in August 1988. It was progressing well when, one month into the three-month contract, the builder died. Fortunately, his wife decided to keep the work force together to complete the contract, under the supervision of Michael Beare, and the end result was very satisfying.

These developments benefited the membership greatly, and enabled the club to stage major tournaments, as well as to hold modest social functions. The 150th anniversary of the opening of the court was celebrated in July 1992; in 1994 major structural repairs were carried out by the Estate; and the following year the club formed itself into a limited company, which enabled it to enter into a formal lease with the owner.

Among the most significant of recent professionals, after Kevin King, were Jiannis Hrysicos (from Ballarat), Matty Hayward (Hobart), Mike Gooding (after six years in New York) and the current incumbents, Adam Phillips and Jonathan Dawes. The most successful player among them was Mike Gooding, who during his time at Hatfield (1993–96) won the French Open, challenged for the world championship and with Chris Bray achieved the Open doubles Grand Slam – the French, British, American and Australian titles within a twelve-month period.

Over the years many members of the club have achieved considerable success. Anthony Tufton (now Lord Hothfield) was Amateur champion in 1964 and Amateur doubles champion 1962–64; William Hollington won the Under-24 singles three times (1979–81); James Male, while still a Hatfield member, won the Amateur singles (1990) and the Amateur doubles three times (1979, 1989 and 1990).

Over-age tournaments have seen notable Hatfield success, particularly for Colin Dean, a latecomer to the game and the club Captain from 1984 to 2000. He won the world over-50 singles and doubles in 1990, and the world over-60 doubles with Sam Leigh in 1996. He also won six consecutive British over-50 singles titles (1985–90), the British over-50 doubles twice (1989 and 1990) and the British over-60 doubles twice (1995 and 1998).

Among occasional Hatfield players, John Ward has had prodigious success in over-age events having won eight British over-50 doubles titles (three with Sam Leigh), two world doubles titles (over-40 and over-50) and five British over-50 singles titles. Former world champion Howard Angus rejoined Hatfield when he took up a coaching post at Haileybury College, and he has now won the British over-50 singles four times and the doubles twice with Sam Leigh.

Hatfield has a large active membership and as well as normal play between members holds a number of internal competitions, hosts three or four national tournaments each year, and competes in various national team events. Hatfield reached the final of the Inter-club championship for the Field Trophy twice and won the Inter-club team handicap tournament in 1986. The club enters three teams in the National League: they won Division 1 in 1993, 1994 and 1995, and Division 3 in 1999.

They also nurture their less advanced players, known as the Hatfield Angoras (a high class of rabbit) and for many years, matches have been arranged for them too. They are always centred around lunch, which may be quite lavish and is often very sociable. That tradition continues today, although these days the matches are likely to be mixed-ability and often mixed-sex.

Adam Phillips narrowly lost an exhausting and decisive match in the 1998 National League Division I final against Paul Tabley (Holyport).

Jonathan Dawes, seen here (right) after a match with Ivan Ronaldson, is now a professional at Hatfield. He has learned much about teaching from his father Peter, the long-established professional at Seacourt.

HOBART TENNIS CLUB

AUSTRALIA'S OLDEST TENNIS COURT was completed in 1875, on the site of the first brewery in Hobart, Tasmania. Samuel Smith Travers, who had learned the game at Oxford, used for his building the plans and specifications of the court at James Street, off London's Haymarket, that existed until the mid nineteenth century.

The original floor was of paving stones, but these became uneven over the years and in 1932 half-an-inch of concrete was laid over them. This served the club well for more than fifty years, but major maintenance had to be carried out in 1993. Due to rising damp, and a stream that literally flowed underground, the floor had to be ripped up and the present excellent concrete surface laid.

The court was originally for the exclusive use of Smith Travers, who had brought with him from England an experienced professional in Thomas Stone – a man recruited by the Melbourne club when their court opened in 1882. For the next hundred years, the most notable matches at Hobart were played between the professionals of these two clubs, prime among them Woolner Stone of Melbourne (son of Thomas) and Percy Finch.

A remarkable man, Percy Finch assisted the Hobart professional at the age of twelve, in 1900, and became professional at fourteen, serving the club until he died in office in 1965 in his seventy-eighth year. He had little professional tutelage in Tennis, and learned the game largely from the club's first-class amateurs. He became world class himself, and was the Australian Professional and Open Champion from 1932 to 1947. In 1964 he was elected the first life member of the club.

A much later highlight was the annual battle for the Australian Open title between Barry Toates, who came to Hobart in 1967 from Cambridge University, and Chris Ronaldson of Melbourne. Toates held the title from 1968 until Ronaldson, later the world champion, beat him in 1976. Toates completely dominated the Tennis scene during that time, and revitalized the game in Hobart before moving to Boston in 1976.

On the occasion of the club's centenary in 1975, Pierre Etchebaster planted a grape vine (now flourishing over the outside pergola), and the

The entrance to the Hobart club.

Governor of Tasmania, Sir Stanley Burbury, presented the club with the Governor's Cup. Frank Willis of Manchester beat Toates in the first final. The Cup has been contested by leading international players several times since, with Graham Hyland of Hobart winning it three times and Chris Ronaldson twice. In 1999, it was taken by another world champion, Robert Fahey.

Thomas Stone became Hobart's first professional in 1875.

Percy Finch in 1930. He worked at Hobart from the age of twelve and died in office at seventy-seven.

Hyland was engaged as an apprentice under Toates, but left for the New York Racquet Club. He came back in 1981, not as a professional but to his farm outside Hobart. He remained one of the country's leading players. Lachlan Deuchar became the head professional in 1979, moved to Hampton Court in 1981, and was succeeded by Alistair Curley, who had learned the game as an amateur under Chris Ronaldson at Troon. He retired from professional tennis in 1989, giving way to former Melbourne amateur Tim Heughan, who moved to Holyport in 1993.

Robert Fahey, who succeeded him, had been assistant to Curley for two years before travelling overseas to improve his game. He had been an outstanding prospect from his first days as a player (Tasmanian Open lawn-tennis champion at the age of seventeen), and by the time he returned as head professional in 1993 he was one of the world's leading players and about to challenge for the world title.

He met the reigning champion, Australian Wayne

Davies, in Hobart for the first leg of the match in March 1994 and took it 7–1. Two weeks later in New York he became, aged twenty-five, the youngest world champion for eighty years. Fahey defended the title successfully in 1995, 1996, 1998 and (again against Wayne Davies) in February 2000. He has brought to Hobart its years of greatest glory and finest Tennis, even after leaving the club's employment in 1996 to study for an economics degree. He was succeeded as professional by the former Tasmanian badminton player, Brad Dale.

Among the many distinguished amateurs at the club the Butler family, descendants of the founder, stand out. The Championship Racquet, the club's premier tournament, was won nine times up to 1902 by C.W. Butler and twelve times between 1911 and 1932 by C.T. Butler. A fourth-generation descendant of Smith Travers, C.C.A. Butler, took the championship in 1973, but by then the club game was being dominated by David Martin (seven wins) and

Robert Fahey, youngest world champion for eighty years, with the trophy at Hobart in 1994.

Julian Snow (left), captain of the British team who beat Australia 3–2 to take the 1999 Bathurst Cup in Hobart. Brad Dale (centre) was the marker, and Mike Happell was, at the time, Australia's leading amateur.

Jim Wilkinson (eleven). Over the past twenty years, Graeme Bradfield has eclipsed all records with thirteen Championship Racquet wins.

Substantial numbers of female players took their first steps into the limelight in the 1970s, among them Judy Clarke, often champion of the club and the first world champion. The annual ladies' match between Hobart and Melbourne is named in her honour. Leading players of recent years have included Jane Hyland, Barbara Baker and Julianne Drewitt. Sumptuous new changing rooms for women, among other improvements to club facilities, were installed in time for the ladies' world championship of 1991.

For internal competitions, the club is divided into five grades, the last introduced in 1983, as membership continued to grow. A championship for each grade is held annually, as well as several handicap competitions, a junior girls' championship, a schools pennant and the annual Tasmanian Open and Tasmanian Handicap tournaments, both well patronized by members of the other Australian clubs.

An affiliated University of Tasmania Real Tennis Club was formed in 1997, and already boasts over thirty members. The growth in the number of clubs means that there are significant additions to the calendar, including events against Ballarat, Sydney, Romsey and Melbourne. The traditional keen rivalry persists between Hobart and Melbourne for the Percy Finch Inter-club Trophy, won 9–0 by Hobart in 1999 and 7–2 by Melbourne in 2000.

In late 2000 Tony Blum was taken on as assistant professional to Brad Dale.

HOLYPORT

Now THE HOME of the Royal County of Berkshire Real Tennis Club, the court at Holyport House was built for the owner, Sam Heilbut, in 1889. After initial trouble with the foundations, it proved to be one of the finest courts in the country with spacious dedans and changing rooms and an adjoining swimming pool. Weekend parties were frequent until Mr Heilbut's death in 1913.

His successor, Major H.M. Martineau, continued to run the court, even though he was more interested in cricket. During the Second World War, troops were billeted in the house and played basketball in the court; it was also used for skating. In 1950, the Holyport Tennis Club was formed by Max Heilbut and Leslie Crispe, and the support of Hubert Martineau and his daughter, Mrs Janne Cahill, and of more than fifty

Max Heilbut, a descendant of the original owner of Holyport House, formed the Tennis club in 1950.

members, enabled necessary repairs to be made and electric lighting to be installed.

The court reopened with a match between Alistair Martin, then the British and US Amateur champion, and his American compatriot Albert Johnson, a professional at Queen's Club. Later the legendary Pierre Etchebaster played exhibition matches there against Lord Aberdare, and it was at Holyport in 1954 that Jim Dear took his first step on the way to the world title by beating Henri St Germain of Bordeaux.

In 1985, Holyport House was sold and converted into a nursing home. The court was bought by a consortium consisting of Colin Lumley, Bryan Morrison, David Pearl and Chris Ronaldson. The roof was repaired, the changing rooms refurbished and the

Spike Willcocks receives the Amateur singles runner-up award from Bryan Morrison at Holyport in 1999. Julian Snow, the winner, and Charles Swallow look on.

The celebration by past and present professionals at Holyport in January 2000 to mark Chris Ronaldson's fiftieth birthday: the picture shows (back row) Arnaud Domange, Jerome Fletcher, Lesley Ronaldson, Steve Ronaldson, Ben Ronaldson, Jonathan Howell, Lachlan Deuchar, Gerard Eden, Charles Crossley, Kevin King, Ivan Ronaldson and Adam Pyne; (middle row) Kate Leeming, Kees Ludekens, Peter Dawes, Paul Tabley, Andrew Davis, Steve Brockenshaw, Mick Dean, Stefan King, Chris Bray, Marc Seigneur and Alan Oliver; (front row) Colin Lumley, Chris Ronaldson and Barry Toates.

Built in 1889, the court was the scene of frequent parties.

Spectator comforts at the Royal County of Berkshire club.

court brought up to championship standard, which entailed the building of a new side penthouse.

The new Club opened for play in September 1986, with Kevin King as the enthusiastic professional and Lesley Ronaldson as manager. Holyport was transformed from a quiet tennis backwater into a busy modern facility, largely used by local residents who previously knew little of the game. Nick Wood, one of the world's leading players, became head professional in August 1998, and Jo Iddles started as his assistant two years later.

For many years Holyport has been the home of the British Professional singles championship, and finals have been played before crowds of more than a hundred. The National League, now boasting nearly fifty teams, was inaugurated at Holyport and played there for the first few seasons. Run as a members' club which leases the court from the owners, Holyport has a distinctive character and an active social programme. It is also proud of the fact that the club champion for the past eight years is Penny Lumley, the world champion and the outstanding female player of this or any other generation.

Nick Wood took over as Holyport professional in 1998.

THE HYDE TENNIS CLUB

RESTORED AND RE-INVIGORATED nearly seventy years after it was last used for Tennis, this old court came back to the game in 1998, the resident cows having been evicted and hay bales relocated. Joe Gundry, grandson of the man who had it built in 1883, gave the court and a parcel of land to the care of the Bridport and West Dorset Sports Trust; National Lottery and other generous funding arrived; the side and grille penthouses, demolished by the American Army, were rebuilt; and John Gundry, the great-grandson, took up the honorary secretaryship in time to welcome the Earl of Wessex to the re-opening ceremony.

The pretty little village of Walditch, a mile or so outside Bridport, is the most improbable location for a

Right The court as a cowshed!

Below The Earl of Wessex, who opened the new club, receives Honorary Life Membership from its chairman, Cleeves Palmer. Lord Aberdare, Lord Digby the Lord Lieutenant of Dorset, John Gundry the Hon. Secretary and Richard Salt, Chairman of the Bridport & West Dorset Sports Trust, look on.

The Hyde court re-opened for play in June 1998.

Tennis club. The court stands next to the Victorian Gothic country home of its creator, Joseph Gundry, who played for Oxford in 1859 and whose racket still hangs in the lobby.

Mark Coghlan took on the challenge of running a club with only four known players, and soon attracted enough beginners to warrant a second professional, Mark Hammersley. Between them they have nurtured an atmosphere of enthusiasm and enjoyment that would be envied by many. In its third season, the club has some 175 members and a busy fixture list with twenty-five events.

JESMOND DENE

THE REVIVAL OF TENNIS at Jesmond Dene, just outside Newcastle, is one of the success stories of the past twenty years. This beautiful old court, with its unusual rose windows, was built in 1894 for the owner of Jesmond Dene House, Sir Andrew Noble. He used it until he was over eighty, and the tradition continued through his four sons and three grandsons. Apart from the first few months, Edgar Lambert was the professional there until 1928, when he was succeeded by his son Charles, who was born in the professional's house adjoining the court and was of the fourth generation of that great line of Tennis professionals.

The fortunes of the court had been at a low ebb since the First World War, when it had been used for the making of airship gasbags and water ballast bags, and in 1931 the Noble family sold the estate, which was taken over by Newcastle City Council. The court was adapted for use as two badminton courts, and the lease was held by the Northumberland Badminton Association, though occasional Tennis play continued.

Lord Hothfield was instrumental in founding the Jesmond Dene Tennis Club in 1981, but the playing hours were severely restricted – Wednesday and Thursday were completely devoted to badminton, and there could be no Tennis on the court after 7 p.m. on Monday, Tuesday and Friday. Nevertheless, the club committee of Kiwi Craig, Ed Nicholl and Tim Bull held regular competitions, among them an open

Jesmond Dene's imposing structure, with its rare rose windows, was built in 1894.

Above *John Duns, an energetic worker and player for Jesmond Dene.*

Right *Freddy Such, instrumental in the club's revival.*

Play in the renovated court.

Lord Hothfield and Richard Skinner (standing) are Jesmond Dene stalwarts. In front are former court manager Paul Hetherington and trustee Alan Douglas.

amateur tournament for the Jesmond Dene Cup. Julian Snow was an early winner.

By the time the court's centenary dinner was held, in October 1994, there was no professional and little money in the kitty, and no more than ten hours of Tennis were being played in a week, most of those booked by Freddy Such and John Duns, but a change of fortune was on the horizon. The breakthrough came in 1997 when the club, with the help of keen member Mrs Annie Douglas, found alternative venues for the badminton players. When the court returned exclusively to the purpose for which it was built, proper restoration took place, Anthony Scratchley became the professional and lovingly improved the floor. When he left to take up a position in Bordeaux, Paul Hetherington managed the court and enthusiasm rose again. There is now a membership of eighty and court hours average more than thirty a week under new professional Peter Patterson.

LAKEWOOD, THE GEORGIAN COURT

In the 1880s, the charming little town of Lakewood in the pines area of south central New Jersey was a well-known health resort and winter paradise for the wealthy. By the 1890s, Lakewood was a resort for the rich and famous. In the early 1890s, George Jay Gould began to consider moving to a country place where his children would enjoy fresh air and beautiful countryside. In 1896 he purchased a 150 acre tract of land in Lakewood and engaged the famous New York architect Bruce Price to design a lavish country estate, which became known as Georgian Court.

In 1898, Gould and Price added Bachelor's Court, now known as the Casino. The building featured an indoor polo field and stables, bowling alleys, squash courts, swimming pool, guest rooms, a trophy room and a formal dining room. But most important of all, the Casino featured a Rackets court and a Tennis court, where George's son Jay would learn the royal and ancient game of Court Tennis. Jay was coached by Eustace M. Miles, a British Tennis champion, and by Frank Forester of the Prince's Club, London. He is reputed to have exhibited a natural talent early in his career and he quickly became known for his railroad service as well as his ability to lay down a chase. He became the Amateur champion of the US in 1906 and retained the title until 1925. The court at Georgian Court is historically significant, both for nurturing arguably the greatest amateur player the world has ever known and for its unique setting and history.

The former estate of George Jay Gould and his family is now listed in the registry of the National Register of Historic Places and has been designated a National Historic Landmark. In 1925, the Sisters of Mercy acquired the Gould estate and founded Georgian Court College, a Catholic arts college for women that offers a co-educational evening and graduate programme for students of all faiths. The college is vibrant, forward thinking and supports diversity and academic excellence. Georgian Court College serves 2,400 day, evening and graduate students of all backgrounds.

The imposing entrance to the Casino.

After active use during the Gould years, the Tennis court at Georgian Court College has been dormant since 1924 – but that is about to change! Plans have been formulated to revive and restore the court where Jay Gould first learned the game.

Edward J. Hughes, at that time president of the United States Court Tennis Association (USCTA), held several meetings with the college in the early

Above *The Gould Casino tennis court.*

Right *Jay Gould was US Amateur singles champion eighteen times.*

1980s to discuss reviving the court, and again in 1997. In October 1999, discussions reopened between Georgian Court College and United States Court Tennis Preservation Foundation (USCTPF) board member John W. McNamara, a former president of The Racquet Club in Philadelphia. Those discussions continued over the next twelve months and have resulted in the New Jersey Historic Trust, Georgian Court College and the USCTPF dedicating funds to renovate the Jay Gould Court. Architectural estimates and plans have been completed and it is hoped that the work will commence in the first half of 2001 and be completed by the middle of that year. Arrangements will be made through the USCTA so that students at the college will be able to take Tennis lessons. Should there be enough interest displayed by the students, the college is prepared to issue credits towards a degree course.

In addition, it is anticipated that various USCTA tournaments will be held at Lakewood annually and that overseas touring teams visiting the United States will be invited to play on the Gould Court. It is also planned that some intercity matches between clubs in the USA will be played at Lakewood.

Members of the USCTA, the Preservation Foundation and Georgian Court College are devoted to seeing the court preserved and fully restored. Stylistically it is a typical example of Court Tennis architecture set within an unusual and highly original sports facility. Historically however, the association of this space with Jay Gould, one of the most revered legends of the sport in the United States, is of great significance. For members of the USCTA and the USCTPF, the opportunity to play their sport here is tremendously exciting.

LEAMINGTON TENNIS COURT CLUB

Unique in Britain in that it is still a gentlemen's club with a Tennis court, rather than a Tennis club, the Leamington Tennis Court Club was conceived in 1844 and built in 1846. The small group of Warwickshire gentlemen who formed it wanted somewhere to meet and socialize in addition to the hunting field and each other's houses, and the town had nothing that approximated to the clubs in London's Pall Mall.

To be able to play Tennis there was an agreeable adjunct, but one that at the time was probably not used as much as the billiard room or the card tables.

With the disappearance of the older Tennis clubs such as those in James Street, Haymarket, Prince's in Knightsbridge and Prince's in Brighton, Leamington claims to be the oldest purpose-built Tennis club left in the world. It is also interesting that the first lawn-tennis club was formed in Leamington, and one of the real Tennis club's members, Harry Gem, has as good a claim as anyone to being the inventor of lawn tennis.

Essentially a gentlemen's club with a Tennis court, Leamington's ambience is far from spartan. This is the bar.

Above *Some of the active members in typically sociable mode after a match with the Hamsters.*

Right *A fine portrait of the Reverend Herbert Green, the club chairman 1917–33.*

Leamington's first membership list was probably its most distinguished. It contained several titled gentlemen (the heirs to the earldoms of Warwick and Aylesford were among the founders), three Members of Parliament, several high-ranking military and naval officers, and one or two famously hard-living eccentrics.

In spite of the social and economic changes of the late nineteenth century, including the lessening of the status of such spa towns and the difficulties suffered by land-owning members during the agricultural depression, Leamington survived its moments of crisis and continued to prosper. At that time, all the members were gentlemen – they did not work in trade or, with a few notable exceptions, in the professions. In the club's first days, a noble lord blackballed a prominent doctor, and no lawyer was allowed to join until the next century.

By that time, outdoor sports had become nationally organized and Tennis lost some of its pre-eminence. The court was refurbished in 1898 but there was not a great deal of play on it, and the average age of members was increasing. The club's original open Rackets court had been enclosed but nevertheless fell into disuse and in 1921 was converted into two squash courts. In 1939, they were sold to the printing works next door.

The court was closed during the war and rented out as a furniture depository. The vote to re-open it in 1947 was carried by a narrow majority thanks to the persuasive powers of Michael Pugh. Many of

Julian Snow receives the Bathurst Cup from Lord Apsley, heir to the present Earl, when Britain won it at Leamington in 1996. Peter Bromwich, chairman of the club, is on the right.

the older members had by then lost interest in playing.

The court survived, but it was thirty years before new lights were installed and the club became an increasingly popular venue for national tournaments. The goodwill thus built up manifested itself when serious dry rot was discovered in 1986 and £100,000 was needed immediately. It was raised by members and friends of the court, at home and overseas.

Like most provincial Tennis clubs, Leamington cannot draw on the pool of playing talent that is available in London. Nevertheless, the club has an enthusiastic playing membership who particularly enjoy the domestic tournaments – accompanied, as ever at Leamington, with betting on the result, thus perpetuating the tradition of raffish behaviour.

Such tournaments were made immeasurably more popular by the handicap system developed at Leamington, and adopted and refined by the Tennis and Rackets Association. The use of a handicap to bring about an evenly matched contest between players of differing ability is almost as old as the game itself. It goes back to the time when gentlemen club members wanted to bet on matches between professionals from different clubs, but needed to ensure that both sets of backers were in with a chance, even when one of the players was clearly superior to the other.

A handicap agreed for such a one-off situation was a simpler matter than framing a handicap for a tournament involving entrants of widely differing ability from several clubs. Although handicap tournaments for professionals began in 1921, the system was somewhat hit-and-miss until 1966 when Charles Wade, the Tennis captain at Leamington, tried to improve it for the club's open tournament.

It remained unsatisfactory until 1979 when Wade, with the help of his brother Ian and Chris Ronaldson (then the world champion), came up with the idea of allocating each player a number that reflected his ability – the lower the better, as in golf – and a simple

Kevin Sheldon, Leamington's professional, acknowledged as an excellent teacher of the game.

Charles Wade, inventor of the now internationally accepted Tennis handicap system.

subtraction would indicate the handicap that should be used for each match.

More than a decade passed before the system reached its final shape. The Tennis and Rackets Association adopted it in the mid-1980s, and appointed Charles Wade chairman of what is now the Handicapping and Ranking Sub-Committee. The development of the system now in use has proved a major boon to Tennis and has had an impact on the game, in relative terms, comparable to the introduction of handicapping in golf.

Of the club's many professionals, the most distinguished was probably the first, Edmund Tompkins, who left in 1849 and became world champion in 1862. His assistant, Frederick Foulkes, learned to play Rackets on Leamington's open court and later emigrated to Canada and became the North American champion. The present professional, Kevin Sheldon, has served the club much longer than any of his predecessors.

A book about the club, *The History of the Leamington Tennis Court Club 1846–1996*, was written by Charles Wade and published to mark the club's sesqui-centenary in 1996.

Lord's, Marylebone CRICKET CLUB

In 1898, only sixty years after the first Tennis court was built at Lord's cricket ground, the court was demolished. W.G. Grace was still playing at the time and two summers earlier 30,000 spectators had somehow crammed into the ground to see the Australian Test. Something had to go. The Rackets court (built in 1844) went, too, and the Mound Stand was erected. All was not lost however, the purchase of the freehold of an adjoining property, in Grove Road, providing space to replace both the Tennis and Rackets courts and also to build a squash court.

The floor of the old Tennis court, which had been re-paved in 1866, was moved to the new one, the more worn flagstones being used near the net. The cost of the buildings, exclusive of heating and cementing, was agreed at £8,110; on top of that the specialist Joseph Bickley charged £100 for the floor of the Rackets court and £250 each for the walls of both courts. The squash court was built in Portland cement.

Eight months was the proposed completion time, but there was a long delay due to a legal action brought by the tenant of the property next door, who

The original court at Lord's, built in 1838, was demolished in1898. The building included facilities for wining and dining.

obtained an injunction for Ancient Lights and trespass to a party wall. The action was ultimately settled out of court, but it was not until 1 January 1900 that the new courts were opened.

Even then the problems were not over, and Bickley was called back to remedy defects in the walls and floor of the Rackets court. A new door also had to be fitted. Sadly, there was little play in the Rackets court after the First World War and a squash court was built within it with a magnificent gallery.

During the building hiatus, both Prince's Club and Hampton Court offered hospitality to Lord's members, and the 1899 Gold and Silver Racquet prizes were played at Prince's. This ancient Tennis competition, open only to members of the MCC between 1867 and 1896, was won seventeen times in those years by J.M. Heathcote and twelve times by the Hon. Alfred Lyttelton. In the thirtieth year of the prize, Sir Edward Grey became the first man to break their domination.

Two of the game's greatest and most memorable professionals, Jack Groom and Henry Johns, successively presided over the court for more than fifty years in total. Groom trained at Prince's and assisted at Hatfield House from 1907, returning there after the war before coming to head the team at Lord's in 1924. He was one of nature's gentlemen, whose Cockney good humour helped him mix on easy terms with everyone. He was a fine player, running Edgar Baerlein close for the Open championship in 1931 and winning it the next year, and a wonderful coach, taking as great an interest in less able players as he did in the best.

During the Second World War, a bomb fell immediately behind the courts, destroying Groom's home and removing the roof of both courts. Groom and his family moved with difficulty into the professional's rooms between the two courts and remained there for the duration. Largely thanks to his efforts, corrugated iron was obtained to cover the Tennis court and he and the Clerk of the Works installed it – a typically practical action that probably saved the court. The Rackets court, however, was beyond repair by the end of the war and was converted into the Memorial Gallery in 1953.

Henry Johns took over in 1954 and remained in charge until 1975. He had first come to Lord's in 1936 after training at Prince's and spending two years with the Cazalets at Fairlawne. He was a masterly player on the Lord's court (champion of the world there, Jim Dear used to say), an excellent coach and a delightful personality. He trained many young professionals and was an outstanding marker, handling many of the most important matches of his time.

The portrait of Henry Johns was painted by Anthony Hobson to honour his retirement in 1975.

Tennis also owes him a special debt of gratitude for making new balls after the war, which may have saved the game from a slow death.

Henry Johns was succeeded by David Cull, whom he had trained and who was still in charge at the end of the century. Mark Ryan and Chris Swallow were his assistants.

During the 1980s the hallowed and venerated bathrooms were demolished – the baths themselves were preserved and incorporated in the new men's changing rooms – and a ladies' changing room was added. In the same period, the MCC Weekend was introduced. Doubles are played over three days on a handicap basis in two groups against the clock (for the Mason-Sharp and Osborn Parker Cups), preceded on the Friday night by a dinner – a heavily subscribed and popular part of the Tennis calendar.

Christopher Swallow and Mark Ryan, the assistant professionals at Lord's, (far side of the net) *faced up to Chris Bray and Nick Wood in the 1999 British Open doubles.*

Lord's celebrated the centenary of their 'new' court with a dinner in the Long Room in January 2000.

David Cull was guest of honour at a dinner held to mark his twenty-fifth year as senior professional. Drinking a toast to him are Robin Sligh (left) and Lord Kinnoull.

Also established in recent times is the Henry Johns Cup, which enables the annual doubles handicap competitions to be held, as with the singles competitions, in two groups. It joins the long-running and popular handicap competitions for the Ronnie Aird Cup, the W.H. Ollis Cup and the D.P. Henry Cup. Towering above them all, the battles for the Gold and Silver Racquets go on, among the most prestigious competitions of the modern game.

The possibility of a second Tennis court is being discussed, the result of the continuing enthusiasm for the game at Lord's. Now that the MCC has changed its rules to admit female members, there may soon be a broader Tennis-playing membership.

MALVERN COLLEGE

OF ALL THE FAMILIES whose names appear on the Rackets roll of honour, none surely should be inscribed more firmly than that of Malvern's famous Fosters. The Rev. Henry Foster was the housemaster whose energy and enthusiasm led to the building of both the College's courts, next to his house, in 1881 and 1903. No doubt he also had some influence on the fact that his seven sons and four daughters all played the game.

In all but five of twenty-one years (from 1889 to 1909) there was a Foster, and sometimes two, in the Malvern pair for the Public Schools championship – and in one of those years Malvern did not enter. Three times in that period the College won the title – in 1892 with young Henry (always known as Harry) K. Foster

H.K. and W.L. Foster, members of a remarkable Rackets-playing family.

and brother Wilfrid; in 1900 with Basil Foster and William Evans; in 1908 with another two Fosters, Maurice and Neville.

Harry was the outstanding player of the brood, and it is after him that the Public Schools singles championship trophy is named. He went on to reach the Amateur singles final the year after he left school, and then to win it for the seven years after that, twice demolishing in the final as fine a player as Eustace Miles by three sets to love, and once beating brother Wilfrid by the same margin.

In 1904, ten years after his first Amateur singles triumph, Harry reached the final again. He played the holder, the brilliant young Edgar Baerlein. Harry reckoned, knowing that he was not as fast as he had been, that he would have to hit Baerlein off the court in three sets if he were to win, and embarked on a flood of furious hitting. It worked.

The remarkable Harry (who also played cricket for Worcestershire) won the Amateur doubles eight times between 1894 and 1903 with a variety of partners including brothers Wilfrid and Basil. The latter was himself Amateur champion in 1912 and 1913, and won the doubles five times, once with Harry and once with Wilfrid. Some family!

Between the wars Malvern won the championship three times, in 1920, 1936 and 1937. Desmond Manners recorded what may be a unique achievement – he played in the school pair for five successive years (1934–38) and reached the final in three of them, winning twice with Nigel Beeson. Manners also won Malvern's Prichard Racquet Trophy five times.

The courts were closed in 1940, suffered war damage and were not reopened until 1954. It was twelve years before Malvern reached the final again, beating Radley for the title, but from 1973 to 1977 the school pair played in five consecutive finals. They won three of them – in 1974 with the Nicholls brothers, Mark and Paul; in 1975 with Paul Nicholls and Martin Tang; and in 1977 with Philip Rosser and Andrew McDonald.

Mark Nicholls also won the Foster Cup in 1973 and 1974 – a period of extraordinary success that was due, in large measure, to the outstanding coaching ability of

Philip Rosser and his partner Andrew McDonald, who won the Public Schools doubles championship in 1977, together with professional Ronnie Hughes.

Ronnie Hughes, the Malvern professional from 1956 to 1986. After Malvern, Mark Nicholls won the Army championship five times, and Paul took the Swallow Trophy (Under-24 open singles) four times from 1979 to 1982.

Among many other Old Malvernians to prosper on the Rackets court, prime position is held by Mark Hubbard, who won the Swallow in 1997 and beat the world champion, Neil Smith, in the semi-final of the professional singles championship in 1999. Hubbard and Anthony Scammell won the Leonard Cup (Under-21 open doubles) in 1994 and the Milne Hue Williams Cup (public school old boys Under-24 doubles) in 1997.

Three Old Malvernians are currently schools Rackets professionals – Hubbard is at Radley, Philip Rosser at Rugby and Roger Tolchard came back to Malvern in 1984.

Other professionals at the College have been Walter Gray (from 1891), Johnny Laker (1895), Stewart Green (1925) and Frank Young (1953). Of the masters-in-charge since the war, the most formidable name is that of Norman Rosser who ran Rackets there from 1955 to 1983. He remains one of the national pillars of the game.

Both finalists in the 1998 Renny Cup were from Malvern – Tom Bomford (right) beat Jonathan Thompstone 3–1.

Since 1989 a flourishing evening club, the Malvern Mavericks, has developed under the guidance of Bruce St L. Burnett. Matches are played regularly against the Clifton Boasters, the Marlborough Magicians and the Cheltenham and Cotswold Club. The Mavericks reached the final of Division 2 of the National League five times in six years recently without becoming champions.

Old Malvernians won the Milne Hue Williams Cup for the first time in 1997 – Mark Hubbard (left) and Anthony Scammell with Roger Tolchard, the College professional.

MANCHESTER TENNIS AND RACQUET CLUB

FEW RACKETS COURTS have had so short a life as the first pair built in Manchester. With funds raised after a public meeting in Manchester Town Hall, a site was bought in Miller Street, at the corner of Blackfriars Street and Chapel Street, Salford, where two courts were built. They opened in May 1876 with a match featuring three of the Gray professionals, Joseph (from Rugby), Walter (Charterhouse) and George (Haileybury), and Tom Attread of Prince's Club, London.

Little more than a year later, the club was gone, compulsorily acquired by the London and North-Western Railway Company. Another site was found, in Blackfriars Road, Salford, and one Rackets court, one Tennis court and a bowling alley were built. They changed the name of the club to include Tennis and opened in December 1880. The club premises stand on the same spot today, little changed but for the addition of a squash court, built in 1925.

Amateur championships were held at the club for Rackets (1878–82) and Tennis (1883–87), and a Professional Tennis championship from 1888 to 1894, won four times by Peter Latham (later the world

The exterior of the original Manchester club.

273

Frank Willis dressed informally before preparing for the testimonial dinner held in his honour. Left to right: *David Holt, Richard Christmas, Geoffrey Piggott, Frank Willis, Peter Kershaw, Michael Thomas and His Honour Judge Simon Fawcus.*

champion). Inter-club Rackets matches were also played, Manchester beating the Liverpool Racquet Club in every year but one from 1892 to 1911.

The Amateur Tennis singles championship for the Queen's Club Cup was first played at Manchester in 1922, after Queen's ceded its right to organize it, and has been played there several times since. The winner in 1922 was the greatest of all Manchester amateurs, Edgar Baerlein – one of the world's greatest players of both games. His record is so astounding it merits careful reading.

Baerlein first won the national Rackets singles title in 1903 and twenty-eight years later, at the age of fifty, he beat Jack Groom for the first British Open Tennis championship. Within those twenty-nine years, Baerlein took the Amateur Tennis singles thirteen times and the Rackets singles nine times (despite the interference of the First World War). He also won the MCC Gold Racquet (for Tennis) ten times in eleven years, losing the 1930 final to Lord Aberdare, but reversing the result the following year. Eleven times he

brought the Bailey Cup for inter-club Tennis doubles to Manchester, and six times he won the Amateur Rackets doubles.

Baerlein was not the first Manchester member to win the Amateur Rackets title. Percy Ashworth took it in 1890, and subsequently reached the final four times. He won the Amateur doubles seven times (four times with H.K. Foster, and once with Baerlein).

As Baerlein began (almost imperceptibly) to fade, Manchester's Lowther Lees bloomed. He won the Amateur Tennis singles eight times between 1928 and 1946 (with another World War removing six annual opportunities), and took the title from Baerlein in 1931. Quite astonishingly, there was not one Amateur Tennis singles final between 1912 and 1937 in which either Baerlein or Lees (or both) did not play. Lees's record of eleven Amateur Tennis doubles wins includes seven as Baerlein's partner.

Lees lost the 1948 Tennis Amateur singles final to Peter Kershaw, the third of Manchester's outstanding players and another in Baerlein's mould, with equal

Steve Brockenshaw (right), *Frank Willis's successor, with Rod McNaughtan, the assistant professional.*

The Tennis players have established a special link with the club at Bordeaux, to which they presented a stained-glass window, and they have also toured in Australia and the US. The Melbourne club presented the Blackfriars/Sherwood Trophy in 1992 for matches between the two clubs, and it has been played for several times at both clubs. Manchester won the initial match, thanks to their greater experience at doubles, but the Australians soon caught up. Regular matches have also been played against Philadelphia, home and away, and in 1997 Manchester were runners-up in the Percival Cup competition there.

The club hosted the Tennis Varsity Match from 1996 to 1999. It was won by Oxford every time, but in 1999 there was a nail-biting contest. At the end of normal play, the score stood at three matches each and they played a deciding double. It went to 5–5 before Oxford won.

Spike Willcocks, one of their outstanding players, won the Manchester Gold Racquet in 1998.

Among the club's recent professionals have been George Cooke (1949–1971), Graham Stephens, Derek Barrett and Frank Willis, an outstanding Tennis player who served the club from 1971 to 1977, and again from 1986 to 1999. When he retired for health reasons, he was given a testimonial dinner on the court. Willis won the Field Trophy four times and was British Open champion from 1967 to 1970, when he was beaten by Howard Angus, as he was in the next three Open finals. Willis challenged George Bostwick

facility for both games. His triumphs began at Rugby, where he won the 1934 Public Schools Rackets championship with Raymond Lumb. Kershaw played Tennis for Oxford against Cambridge for three years and Rackets for two years, in every match winning his singles and doubles. He won the Amateur Rackets singles in 1939 and the doubles three times with Geoffrey Atkins. He won the Amateur Tennis singles twice and the doubles seven times. With Robert Riseley as his partner, he never lost a doubles match.

Peter Kershaw was not content with his service on the court. He joined the club as an undergraduate in 1933, was honorary secretary from 1951 to 1978 (the position his father Harold held from 1909 to 1949), and then became president for three years. Incidentally, his uncle, G.G. Kershaw, won the Amateur Rackets doubles with Baerlein in 1914 and 1920.

Among the Manchester competitions, the annual Gold Racquet weekend, instituted in 1966, has proved very popular with the leading players of both games as well as with gourmets.

Steve Brockenshaw cutting the ball to a length.

A testimonial dinner was held on the Rackets court in March 2000 for Frank Willis, one of the greatest of Tennis professionals, who served Manchester for twenty years.

for the world title in 1969, losing by eight sets to eleven in New York and Manchester.

On Frank's retirement, Steve Brockenshaw joined as senior professional. This completed a nice circle as Steve had been introduced to the game by Frank via the squash court, and joined as his assistant in 1985. He left to become senior professional at Moreton Morrell in November 1990 and his return is welcomed by all.

The assistant professional is Rod McNaughtan who joined aged sixteen in 1996. A good player, he has matured immensely by shouldering some of Frank's duties and generally holding the fort. He was also introduced to the club via playing squash with a club member.

MARLBOROUGH COLLEGE

MORE THAN SIXTY YEARS after being converted into three squash courts, Marlborough's 1901 Jubilee Court was restored to Rackets in 1988, thanks to the generosity of the Ledger Hill Investment Company. The work was carried out in memory of an Old Marlburian, A.E.L. Hill (1901–1986).

The College's first court, an open one, was built on the site of the present Memorial Library in 1860, but had to give way to new classrooms in 1899. Meanwhile, the first closed court was built in 1881, the gift of A.H. Beesly (first housemaster of Summerfield), to whom Marlborough Rackets owes a greater debt than to any other individual. Renovated in 1913, it proved to be one of the very best in the country.

The College's third court, the Jubilee, was the gift of Old Marlburians in 1901 and was built alongside the Beesly Court. Sadly, it was always too slow, and this was the court that turned to squash in 1925, and has now been restored.

Marlborough's first outstanding player was Eustace H. Miles. He never played Rackets for the school and concentrated on Tennis when he arrived at Cambridge. Nevertheless, he won the Amateur Rackets singles championship in 1902, and the doubles four times.

His Tennis record was extraordinarily good. He won the Amateur singles nine times between 1899 and 1910, losing twice in the final. He also won the MCC Gold Racquet fifteen times between 1897 and 1913, only once failing to reach the final. Among the great amateurs in Tennis, he indisputably succeeded J.M. Heathcote and Alfred Lyttelton as king of the game, preceding the legendary Edgar Baerlein.

John Thompson and David Milford, the two Marlborough School masters who won the Amateur doubles championship ten times in twelve years.

Miles made a considerable contribution to the literature of both games, his best-known book being *Racquets, Tennis and Squash*, published in 1902. Aside from that, he was a vegetarian, a teetotaller and the purveyor of some rather eccentric theories about games.

In the early days, the school could not afford the services of a professional. It was not until 1895 that A.J. Crosby was appointed, and he served the school for twenty-seven years. To him goes the credit for the first two victories in the Public Schools championship, in 1901 and 1919. Crosby was a distinguished local citizen and was Mayor of Marlborough twice. Three of his four sons – Jim, Fred and Arthur – and one grandson (Roger, at Harrow), and one great-grandson Martin at Charterhouse became Rackets professionals.

In 1928, one of the immortals of the game, D.S. Milford, arrived on the Marlborough staff and was immediately a tremendous asset to Rackets at the College. He first won the Amateur singles in 1930, took the title seven times before 1952, and held the Open championship from 1936 until it was revived after the war. During the same period, he held the

Guy Barker, who narrowly beat Ali Robinson in the H.K. Foster Cup final.

world championship, beating Norbert Setzler 7–4 in 1937.

His doubles prowess was even more remarkable. After taking Marlborough twice to the Public Schools championship as master-in-charge, he first won the Amateur championship with P.M. Whitehouse in 1938. After the war, he began his remarkable, record-setting partnership with John Thompson, winning the Amateur doubles title ten times in twelve years.

A Tonbridge boy, Thompson joined the Marlborough staff in 1946 and guided the school's Rackets for several decades (as well as becoming British Open champion in 1959 and Amateur singles champion five times). Apart from that, Rackets owes him a considerable debt for his untiring efforts (in conjunction with Bill Gordon, the College professional from 1951) in developing a polythene-centred ball, without which Rackets might not have survived.

Gordon nursed three winning pairs to the Public Schools championship (two of them containing Mike Griffith, who won the Foster Cup in 1961 and later became the Sussex cricket captain). Gordon was succeeded in 1980 by Robert Wakely, whose success has been just as solid (nineteen Public Schools finals, singles and doubles, in twenty years).

Two of his boys have proved to be among the best Rackets players in the history of the College. Alister Robinson and Guy Barker contested an all-Marlborough Foster Cup final in 1987 (Barker winning narrowly), after they had just lost the Public Schools doubles to Tonbridge (whom they beat 4–0 the next year). The same players have each subsequently appeared in the Amateur singles final, and in 1999 they beat Willie Boone and Mark Hue Williams 4–1 to become the Amateur doubles champions.

John Thompson is still fully involved in the game, pictured here in 1999, watching a match from the Queen's pressbox.

Ali Robinson, runner-up in the 1999 Amateur singles, receives his champagne from David Norman, while winner James Male watches.

The school's outstanding pair of recent years – Ali Robinson (left) and Guy Barker with professional Robert Wakely and the trophy for winning the 1988 Public Schools doubles championship.

ROYAL MELBOURNE TENNIS CLUB

MELBOURNE'S CENTENARY in 1982 was marked by Australia winning the Bathurst Cup for the first time. Having beaten the US 3–2, they disposed of Great Britain by 4–1. The result gave considerable impetus to the celebrations, and foreshadowed the expansion of enthusiasm for the game in Australia, where the two long-established Tennis clubs of Hobart and Melbourne have now been joined by three others.

Melbourne's first court was opened in April 1882 by the Governor of Victoria, the Marquess of Normanby. Thomas Stone (then the Hobart professional) was engaged to run the club on a salary of £250 and ten per cent of the gross receipts. By 1886, the club was in financial crisis and threatened with closure, a disaster averted by the generosity of the landlord who agreed to reduce the rent to £250 a year. The club thereafter flourished to such an extent that it was able to buy its freehold in 1896. Queen Victoria awarded the club what must at the time have been seen as the ultimate accolade – permission to use the prefix 'Royal' in its title.

The south court at Melbourne, one of the two courts in the new club building, was opened in 1974, replacing the one built in 1882.

Taking part in the celebrations that followed the 1998 world championships were (left to right) *Graham Hyland, Ted Cockram, Alistair Curley and Mike Garnett.*

Gerald Patterson and Woolner Stone.

Thomas Stone gave long and devoted service to Melbourne over many years, even offering to forgo his salary after the outbreak of war in 1914 when interest in Tennis waned and receipts dropped alarmingly. Members rallied round, and although his salary was reduced to £150, the club was saved again.

When Stone died in 1924 at the age of eighty-five, he was succeeded by his son Woolner who faced a crisis aggravated by the Second World War, from which the club escaped by the skin of its teeth. By that time, a swimming pool and a squash court had been added, but the latter was of sub-standard size and another had to be built later. In 1932, lady members were admitted to play squash.

There was very little play in the court in the post-war period. Even the competition for the Melbourne Gold Racket, held every year since 1882, did not resume until 1965 except in the Melbourne Olympic year of 1956 when it was won by Lord Aberdare. In 1957 the club was offered to the Melbourne Cricket Club, who fortunately refused it; in the nick of time the members themselves put up the money and secured its future.

The gradual recovery of the club began then, and an additional squash court was built in 1960. In 1964

Barry Toates, senior professional and always a big draw as a player.

The world championship was played at the club in March 1998. Seated (left to right): Barry Toates (head professional), Frank Filippelli (professional), Chris Butler, Brad Dale (professional at Hobart), Dr Richard Travers (Vice-President), John Abdallah, Julian Snow (challenger), Robert Fahey (world champion), Gina D'Ettorre, Mike Garnett (Australian Royal Tennis Association), Adam Mickelburough, Russell Sievers (President), Tony Poolman, Ted Cockram, Tony Rayward and Philip Barker.

the President, Dr Stewart Bastow, tragically died on court, and in the same year the less-surprising death of Woolner Stone occurred, at the age of eighty-eight. He had stayed loyally with the club through many financial and other vicissitudes, and at his death had been employed there for sixty-seven years, forty of them as the Tennis professional.

Despite the disadvantage of not being able to afford to engage his successor, the club edged firmly ahead. The Gold Racket was revived in 1965 and the Silver Racket in 1968. The Percy Finch Racket, a new competition between the Melbourne and Hobart clubs, named after the long-serving Hobart professional, was instituted in 1965.

In 1971, the club received an offer to buy the original property on Exhibition Street for A$675,000. It was accepted, and a new site bought at Sherwood Street, Richmond, for A$131,000. New buildings were designed, and a tender of A$312,000 accepted for the construction. Chris Ronaldson, then at Oxford, was appointed manager and professional, and the new club, with two Tennis and two squash courts, was opened by Lord Aberdare in 1974. It has changed little since then, although the decline in popularity of squash (which never really took on) meant that one of the courts could be converted into a gymnasium (downstairs) and a meeting room (upstairs).

Ronaldson's successful reign – his matches against Barry Toates of Hobart drew many spectators – ended when he left for Troon in 1978. Since then several outstanding professional players have passed through, including Lachlan Deuchar, Wayne Davies, Paul Tabley, Frank Filippelli and Colin Lumley.

Among the leading amateurs of the club, J.B. Box dominated the early years, winning the Gold Racket from 1882 to 1894, and again in 1899. C.H. Mollison took it fifteen times between 1903 and 1923. Richard Searby, who won the Gold Racket in 1965 and 1966, played for Oxford University in 1953 and 1954, and his brother Michael for Cambridge in 1955 and 1956. Together, they entered the Henry Leaf Cup competition, representing Geelong, and the Bathurst Cup in which Australia competed for the first time.

G.G. Hiller won the Gold Racket every year from 1968 to 1973, and again in 1975, and E.W. Cockram took it six times in the 1980s. The outstanding player subsequently has been Mike Happell who has contested thirteen finals since 1984 and won ten of them. Another fine amateur player is Chris Sievers.

Over-age tournaments have been extremely popular and heavily contested. Many fine players from the past have continued their competitive playing because of them, and some have hurtled into the game with great success at an advanced age. The late Vernon Mursell, who had played squash for many years, took up Tennis with zest in 1985 at the age of sixty-three and created something of a record by winning four world titles – over-fifty and over-sixty singles, over-fifty doubles (with Chris Butler) and over-sixty doubles (with Harry White).

The International Teams Event, restricted to players over fifty, was first played at Leamington in 1996 and won by Britain. Now formally recognized as being for the Ted Cockram Trophy, it was played at Melbourne in January 1999 and won by Australia; however, it was regained by Britain in Paris in November 2000. The club members, numbering some 600, are well serviced by five professionals headed by Barry Toates with the assistance of Paul Tabley, Robert Fahey (world champion), Andrew Fowler and Parke O'Dwyer. During the year 2000, Robert Fahey achieved the lowest ever handicap of +13.8. By winning the British Open at Queen's Club in November, he achieved the grand slam in the same year that he successfully defended his world championship crown at Melbourne.

In one of the finest Tennis matches seen, Robert Fahey (right) retained his world championship in 1998 by beating Julian Snow (left) 7-4. Between them is marker Adam Mickelburough.

THE MONTREAL RACKET CLUB

COURTS GALORE seem to have been built in various quarters of Montreal throughout the nineteenth century (including an open wooden one in 1836). The club was founded around 1800 but their first recorded professional marker, Johnny Mahon, was appointed as late as 1875. Albert Bridger from England served from 1881 to 1915, during which time the present court was built on Concord Street (1889).

Most remarkable of all their pros was Ken Chantler. His fifty years of service to the game was celebrated with a testimonial dinner on court in 1978. A superb Rackets player, Chantler won the Junior Professional championship at Queen's Club in 1928, came to Montreal in 1929, won the US Open in 1940, 1957 and 1960, and beat Bobby Grant III to win the North American Open in 1947. Jim Dear beat him 8–1 in the subsequent world title match.

Steve Tulley came from Charterhouse to take up the mantle in 1988, returning to England in 2000 to launch the Rackets programme at St Paul's School in London.

Among the club's outstanding amateurs, David McLernon's name is celebrated for his domination of the game in the late 1960s and throughout the seventies (and he was still winning the club doubles in 1998 and 1999, with Karel Nemec). Over the past decade McLernon has been supplanted by Bart Sambrook, more often than not the winner of both singles and doubles titles.

The Montreal Club has always been at the heart of Canadian Rackets, and the last weekend of January is reserved for the Canadian Amateur championships, which attract players from the US and the UK as well as from all over Canada. The weekend is the highlight of the year for the North American Rackets Association as well as for the club. Bryce Maher, the resident steward/manager who works tirelessly for the club

Ken Chantler, 1910–94.

Bart Sambrook, club champion.

Timothy Price, President of the Montreal Racket Club.

Geoff Heward in fine form.

Ron Kaulbach – another winner.

throughout the year, spends Thursday to Sunday on the premises, sleeping when he can on a vacant sofa.

The club has a good international reputation, too: in 1999 twenty members played at the Detroit weekend, and in 2000 twenty-three members, with thirteen partners, went to London for the UK Millennium Quintathlon.

Over the past twenty years, there have been significant physical changes at the club. The downstairs cubbyhole of a bar has been replaced with a fine wood and brass bar, with refrigerators, and there is another bar upstairs in the President's Lounge. The cellar, where once there was nothing, has been converted into a wine cellar for the club, and members are allowed to keep their private stock there, too. There is also a huge humidor of fine cigars.

David McLernon (left) dominated for a decade and more. With him here is David Norman, who is a past winner of the Canadian doubles and singles.

MORETON MORRELL

FEW TENNIS CLUBS, say the members here, can boast such a high percentage of handicappers below twenty, or such an imposing ambience in which to play. The court was built in 1905 by Charles Tuller Garland, an American citizen who later served with the British Army in the First World War and was the owner of Moreton Hall, the entrance gates of which face those of the court.

The Garlands trace their descent from the Garlands of Essex, whose coat of arms is displayed on the façade of the court building, while C.T. Garland's initials are incorporated in the mosaic floor within. Now part of Mid-Warwickshire College, a few miles south of Leamington, the Hall (neo-William and Mary) and the estate were bought on Garland's death by Col. R.J.L. Ogilby, whose coat-of-arms is in the court itself.

The court was acquired by Major James Dance MP in 1949, and with the help of many supporters

The beautiful exterior to the court. The centre of social activities, now luxuriously refurbished.

Action in the court, acknowledged for its consistency of bounce.

including Mr Garland's three daughters and Lord Willoughby de Broke, the Moreton Morrell Tennis Court Company was formed in 1963 to acquire the building and the surrounding grounds.

In 1913 *The Field* described the court building as being ahead of any other in the country 'in luxury of appointment', and you can still see why. Over the moulded archway leading to the playing area is the bas-relief 'Mercury and Pandora', by the neo-classical sculptor John Flaxman RA, and elaborate cornices and pilasters decorate the dedans. In the 1970s the outer dedans, separated from the inner by sliding screens, was provided with a wood-burning stove for the comfort of patrons.

The first professional at Moreton Morrell was the legendary E.J. (Ted) Johnson, brought up by his father, for fifty years Lord Wimborne's professional at Canford, to do the job properly. Young Ted's first posts were at Prince's Club and Tuxedo Park, but when Charles Garland built this court Ted came home, at the age of twenty-five, and stayed right there until he died in 1970, aged ninety-one.

The inaugural match was between Johnson and Peter Latham, five times world champion, and in 1908 Ted played Punch Fairs for the world title at Brighton, losing 2–7. He later challenged Fred Covey for the championship. When the challenge was not taken up, Johnson was entitled to claim the title by default. Typically, he declined to accept an honour for which he had not fought.

Tom Granville, Moreton Morrell amateur turned professional.

Andrew Hamilton, chairman of the Tennis Committee.

By all accounts, he was the perfect professional – a player of exemplary style and strength, a man of charm and modesty, and a relentlessly efficient and devoted coach and marker. He spent more than seventy years in the game – and when he talked of having played before His Royal Highness, he was referring to the man who became King Edward VII.

Struggling to keep afloat during the difficult 1970s, the club was deeply indebted to the hard work of Sir Richard Hamilton, the Honorary Secretary, whose translations of Albert De Luze's *La Magnifique Histoire du Jeu de Paume* and Pierre Barcellon's *Regles et Principes de Paume* are important additions to the game's rich literary history. Sir Richard, Roland Owen-George and Dr Anthony Hobson (well-known for his portraits of Henry Johns and Howard Angus, and for 'The Dinner Match', which hangs in the bar at Leamington) organised two appeals for ongoing restoration work and were instrumental in the appointment of Jonathan Howell as full-time professional in 1978.

Despite his tender years, Howell (only the second professional at the court in seventy-three years) rejuvenated the club, encouraging new members and fostering improved playing standards. The world invitation singles and doubles were held at the court in 1980, a tournament that culminated in the memorable final between Chris Ronaldson and Frank Willis. At two sets all and five-all, Ronaldson saved match point by hurling himself to the floor to scoop a ball from the tambour. The match ended with Ronaldson beating a worse-than-a-yard chase laid by Willis.

By then on course to become one of the world's leading players, Howell moved on to Bordeaux in 1982. Among subsequent professionals were Andrew Davis, Steve Brockenshaw and the current professional Tom Granville, who used to play at the club as an amateur.

In the early 1990s, the original Bickley floor and parts of the external structure began deteriorating at an alarming rate, and the club had to raise £100,000 for repairs. The fact that the work was completed and paid for by 1998 was a considerable achievement, and tribute not only to the energy of the members, but to the warmth with which the club is regarded by players across Britain.

The leadership of David Willoughby de Broke, whose first tuition on the court was from Ted Johnson in the late 1950s, has given the club great confidence for the future. The Tennis committee, chaired by Andrew Hamilton, presides over a hive of tournament activity, and some excellent amateurs have come along in the past twenty years, notable among them Sally Jones who was ladies' world champion in 1993.

NEWMARKET & SUFFOLK REAL TENNIS CLUB

O PENED IN 1901 and closed in 1923, this court remained out of Tennis use for seventy years. When the centenary of the inaugural match is held, in June 2001, it will have been in play for just twenty-five of its one hundred years. However, that is cause enough for celebration.

The court was built by Joseph Bickley for Sir Charles Rose at enormous cost – £6,000 compared with, for instance, the second court at Cambridge, built at around the same time for £2,000. It was the first to incorporate all the features of a modern court, and was the second of Sir Charles's three courts, the other two both being at Hardwick House (1896 and 1907). Its playing characteristics are often compared with those of the Bickley court at Moreton Morrell.

The first two professionals were the greatest players of their day, and both world champions: Peter Latham (1901) and Cecil 'Punch' Fairs (1908). On Sir Charles's

Mark Coghlan (now at Hyde) and Kevin Sheldon play a Professional singles handicap match at Newmarket.

Chris Bray (left) was the winner of an exhibition match with Nick Wood (right) at Newmarket, attended by a record crowd. In the centre is Newmarket professional Andrew Knibbs.

Left to right*: Gordon Kerr, runner-up in the club's open singles competition; John Burnett, co-owner of the club and a semi-finalist; Chris Hollingsworth, co-owner, presenting the cup; and Duncan Hughes, the winner.*

death the court did not remain with the Rose family, and in 1923 it was converted into a garage workshop.

Its restoration, master-minded by John Shneerson, was completed in 1995, when it was opened as a privately owned club run for members. Kevin King and John Dawes were the professionals. They worked hard to achieve success, but running a new club in a small town was not easy and financial problems caused the court to be put on the market again in 1998.

Three local players (Chris Hollingsworth, Alex Riley and John Burnett) bought it, formed a new club and made substantial improvements, installing central heating, a kitchen, better showers and a new viewing area behind glass through the hazard galleries from within the club Room. Membership costs were reduced, which increased court usage, and now eight internal club competitions are held.

In 2000, Newmarket won Division Four of the National League, professional Andrew Knibbs playing with Duncan Hughes and Barry Coupe. In 1999, the club ran a two-court handicap doubles competition in conjunction with Cambridge University, as their contribution to raising funds for the restoration of the second court at Cambridge. Entrance fees produced £2,000, and a number of contributors were attracted to the successful fund-raising dinner at Trinity that weekend. A joint three-court competition is now a possibility, but the club's main hope is that the next hundred years will be less barren than the last.

NATIONAL TENNIS CLUB, NEWPORT

THE NATIONAL TENNIS CLUB was formed in 1980 when the original court, destroyed by a series of fires in 1945 and 1946, was rebuilt, retaining the floor and some of the walls.

The original court – designed by McKim, Mead and White, built by contractor David Perkins of Boston, and completed in 1880 – was situated alongside the lawn-tennis courts of the Newport Casino Club, which was created by the publisher James Gordon Bennett as an alternative to the Newport Reading Room. The first professional, Englishman Tom Pettitt who had been the assistant in Boston, remained at Newport as head professional for forty-six years. He was succeeded by Dan Kenney who presided until the 1945 fire. After that, the court lay in disrepair until 1979. Then the reconstruction project commenced, due to the efforts of Clarry Pell Jr, Jack

Slater, Sammy Van Alen and Allison Danzig. The first balls of the new era were struck by Clarry Pell, Philip Stockton, Alistair Martin and Lord Aberdare, and the official dedication of the court took place during the inaugural Tiffany Cup tournament in August 1980. This tournament, the longest running at the club, is now named after founder and former club president Clarry Pell.

The first professional at the reopened club was Barry Toates who, like Tom Pettitt, was English and had come from Boston. Barry developed the initial core membership and schooled them in the proper form. He was succeeded as head professional in 1987 by George Wharton. The club has been fortunate to have had many qualified assistants, including Jacques Faulise who has been the winter assistant for fifteen years.

Left to right: *Tim Chisholm (New York head professional), George Wharton (National Tennis Club head professional), Charles Johnstone (United States Court Tennis Association president) and Morris Clothier (US amateur champion).*

The National Tennis Club has been considered the official court of the United States Court Tennis Association (USCTA) since its restoration in 1980. As the game has grown, new institutions have been formed, including the United States Court Tennis Preservation Foundation (USCTPF), to provide complementary organization and funding for the public enjoyment of this unique amateur game. As the National Tennis Club has matured, so have its congenial relationships with the International Tennis Hall of Fame (ITHOF), the owner of the court and beautifully manicured grounds; with the USCTA, the ruling body for the game in the United States; and with the USCTPF, with its important charitable and educational mission in support of the game.

The court was originally primarily a summer court, but as the membership has grown to more than one hundred, play is now year round. The club has hosted the Bathurst Cup, the Van Alen Challenge, U.S. national championships and many interclub events. Creativity has been the hallmark of scheduling. There are active night leagues and extensive junior programmes. The club is one of the busiest in the United States, averaging sixty hours per week in bookings.

Since the club reopened it has been ably led by Presidents Jonathan Isham, Barclay Douglas, Clarry Pell, James Wharton and Jonathan Pardee, each of whom has seen the club through various stages of growth. Without their dedication, the National Tennis Club would not be the success it is today.

The distinctive Clarence C. Pell weathervane which overlooks the centre court at the International Tennis Hall of Fame.

Members on court during the Opener, the traditional start of the season.

New York,
THE RACQUET AND TENNIS CLUB

ONE OF THE MOST FAMOUS clubs in the world, New York's Racquet and Tennis Club stands on Park Avenue, dwarfed by surrounding skyscrapers. Two fine Tennis courts and one Rackets court are on the third (US fourth) floor, and a second Rackets court has been converted into a doubles squash court.

This is the club's third site. After a court on 13th Street closed in 1868, the city had no Rackets facility until 1876 when the Racquet Court Club was opened at 55 West 26th Street. The new club had two Rackets courts, each with two galleries, one above the other. In 1882, Robert Moore from Prince's Club was engaged to take charge of the courts, and he was joined two weeks later by Albert Wright, trained at Cambridge by H.J. Gray. In 1890, the club changed its name to the Racquet and Tennis Club and moved to a new site at 27 West 43rd Street where there was one Rackets court and one Tennis court. A second Rackets court was added in 1904.

The club moved to its present site in 1918. The architects of this magnificent building were McKim, Mead and White and, as usual, the construction of the courts was supervised by Bickley. Apart from its prestigious club rooms and a great many other facilities, the club houses one of the world's great sporting libraries.

A Rackets championship was inaugurated at the club in 1876, the first winner being Edward La Montagne who learned to play in Montreal. In 1914, Clarry Pell claimed his first victory; he went on to win the championship every year up to 1932 and again in 1935. Robert Grant III, who learned to play the game at Eton, won the championship in 1937 and from 1939 to 1941. Later, serving in the navy, he survived the sinking of an aircraft carrier by the Japanese. After the war, he won the club championship from 1946 to 1949. He was also a talented Tennis player, winning the club championship in 1948.

Clarry Pell Jr followed in his father's footsteps and won the club Rackets championship from 1950 until 1956. The winner in 1957 and from 1960 to 1963 and

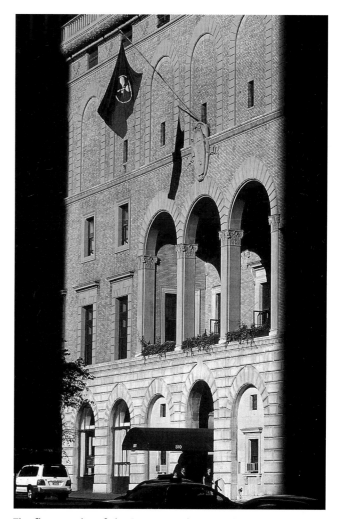

The fine exterior of the Racquet and Tennis Club.

again in 1972 was Peter B. Read. His victories were interrupted by Geoffrey Atkins (1958 and 1959) and George H. (Pete) Bostwick who won for eight consecutive years from 1964 to 1971. From the beginning of the 1970s to the end of the century, multiple winners of the club championship were led by William Bristowe (six times), R.A. Pilkington (four times) and E.F. Ulmann, Kevin MacGuire and William Maltby (three times each).

In the club doubles Pell Snr was outstanding, winning the President's Cup five times in partnership with Stanley G. Mortimer. Read and MacGuire likewise won the trophy five times, from 1979 to 1982 and again in 1986. Other multiple champions have been Peter de Svastich, Robert Power and Robert Pilkington.

The front wall has been replaced twice, the last time with the aid of Armourcast of England. It now looks destined for a long life. The incandescent lights have been replaced with metal halide lamps which give just as good light but are substantially more economical.

On a wider stage, William Surtees defeated Willie Boone 4–0 in New York in the first leg of the world singles in 1979; in 1981 Surtees beat John Prenn 4–2 in the first leg in New York but lost the match at Queen's; and in 1986 Boone defeated Prenn 4–3 in the first leg. The world doubles, inaugurated in 1990, have been played three times in New York – 1993,1996 and 1998. In each match Shannon Hazell (the club professional 1983–85) and Neil Smith (club professional 1993–98) held their title, defeating James Male and Prenn the first two times and Boone and Peter Brake on the third occasion. Smith took the Open singles seven times in the 1990s.

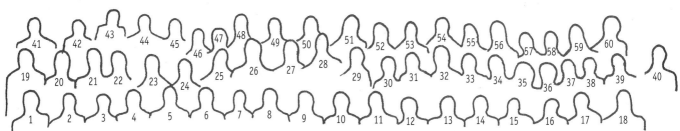

J.J.S. Larken won the national Amateur singles in 1998, and in 2001 swept four major North American singles titles – the US and Canadian Amateurs and the US and Western Opens. Based on this record, he has submitted a challenge for the world championship. In the Amateur doubles, E.F. Ulmann was victorious eight times in the period from 1978 to 1994, three times with Surtees and five times with Boone.

The club Tennis championship was started in 1892, and for the first four years was won by B.S. de Garmendia, a fine all-round athlete who also won the Rackets championship six times. The Tennis championship was dominated from 1901 to 1917 by Joshua Crane Jr (nine wins) and Charles E. Sands (eight). From 1920 to 1939 the outstanding Tennis players were C. Suydem Cutting (winner 1920–25), Hewitt Morgan (1926 and 1928–31), Jimmy Van Alen (1932–33) and Ogden Phipps (1934–37).

The arrival of Pierre Etchebaster at the club in 1930 gave Tennis-playing members the opportunity to be coached by one of the greatest masters of the game in Tennis history, and they made full use of it. Alastair Martin first won the club championship in 1939, but war service intervened, and he next won it in 1949 and

The second leg of the challenge match for the Tennis world championship was played at New York's Racquet and Tennis Club on 14, 16 and 18 March 1994. Robert Fahey, the challenger, beat Wayne Davies 6–0, 6–5, 6–2, 6–3, 6–5, 5–6, 6–4, 6–4, 4–6, 5–6, 6–0, 1–6, 6–2.

1. K. Jacobs	7. J. Knott	13. Mrs V. Phillips	19. P. Tabley	25. J. Jensen	31. K. King	37. J. Faulice	43. J. Pardee	49. S. Edmonds	55. E. Cabillon
2. D. Endres	8. J.D. Soutter	14. R. Boenning	20. H. McVickar	26. R.G. Manice	32. R. Adams	38. Mr Davies	44. P. Meares	50. A.M.C. McCormick	56. P. Guernsey
3. W. Simonds	9. R. Fahey	15. T. Phillips	21. R. Magowan	27. S.G. Smith	33. J. Russell-Carter	39. A. Curley	45. R. Travers	51. W. Rand Jr	57. J. Ashman
4. H. McMorris II	10. G.H. Bostwick Jr	16. Mrs P. Phillips	22. O.H. Soutro	28. S. Abernethy	34. G. Wharton	40. N. Smith	46. Mrs R. Travers	52. J.K. McCall	58. Mrs Wheeler
5. R. Brickley	11. W.F. Davies	17. D. Phillips	23. D. Newman	29. E.F. Wagner Jr	35. Mrs G. Wharton	41. N. Vohr	47. Mrs Bergland	53. T. Greevy	59. E. Wheeler
6. E. Hughes	12. Mrs W.F. Davies	18. A. Jacobs	24. J. Shockett	30. Mrs E.F. Wagner Jr	36. Mrs J. Faulice	42. J. Wharton	48. R. Bergland	54. L. Habina	60. N. Pendrigh

In the professionals shop: (left to right) *Neal Vohr, Yasser Xamel and James Beaumont.*

Wayne Davies, head Tennis professional from 1982 to 1996 and a former world champion, in action on the Racquet and Tennis Club court.

1952, followed by a remarkable victory in 1965. He won the doubles twenty times in succession from its inauguration in 1949 to 1968 with ten different partners.

Robert L. Gerry Jr was the most successful singles player of the 1940s, winning from 1940 to 1947 and in 1950 and 1951. After that, the championship was dominated by those great American players who featured on the world championship scene – Norty Knox (1953–58), Jimmy Bostwick (1959–60) and Gene Scott (1970–78).

Wayne Davies, from Australia, was head Tennis professional from 1982 to 1996, and the club greatly benefited from his reign as world champion. He wrested the title from Chris Ronaldson at Queen's in 1987 and successfully defended it at New York in 1988, 1989, 1991 and 1993. Considered unbeatable at New York, Wayne agreed in 1994 to defend against Robert Fahey in two legs – the first at Hobart, where he lost by seven sets to one, and the second in New York where he almost redeemed himself, winning four of the first five sets before eventually succumbing.

Scott won the national Amateur singles ten years out

of eleven between 1974 and 1984. Subsequently Morris Clothier, the transplanted Philadelphian, won the national singles six times (1987–92). G.R. Jones, a leading doubles specialist, won the national doubles title six times between 1986 and 1992, twice with Kevin McCollum and four times with Clothier.

Over the last twenty years, Clothier has had the finest record in the club singles championship, winning every year but one from 1988 to 1999. He also excelled in the club doubles with seven victories in the period 1989–97, the last three times with Charles Johnstone, president of the United States Court Tennis Association.

A number of dedicated professionals have served the club. They include Jack and Alfred White, Frank and Arthur Forester, Jack Hammond, Walter Kinsella and Norbert Setzler in the earlier years, followed by Frank Blow (1902–48), Norbert Setzler (1920–42), Raymond Johnson (1921–42), William White (1927–61), Tony Bertolotti (1929–42), Pierre Etchebaster (1937–74), Mike Petroskey (1946–65), Albert 'Jack' Johnson (1951–59), Charles Petroskey (1951–79), Frank 'Bunny' Gannon (1959–73), Joe O'Donnell (1962–72), Jim Dear (1970–72), Tommy Greevy (1973–79), Graham Hyland (1979–82), Wayne Davies (1982–96), William Simonds (1996–99) and Tim Chisholm (since 2000).

In August 1992, the club was honoured with a visit by Crown Prince Naruhito of Japan. HRH Prince Edward, the Earl of Wessex, visits and plays on occasion. In addition, the club regularly hosts touring sides, notably in recent years from Royal Melbourne, the MCC, Leamington and the Savile Club.

Willie Surtees and Edward Ulmann, three times US Amateur Rackets doubles champions, and twice US Open doubles champions.

THE ORATORY

The first Tennis court to be built in the UK for more than eighty years opened at The Oratory School, near Reading, in the final week of 1989. Since it was of modern construction, it was possible to introduce several novel features: the placing of fourteen glass panels in the playing surface of the court, thus increasing the number of potential spectators; the inlaying of court markings into the floor, thus saving time and money because the court does not have to close for re-marking lines; and the omission of natural light (and leaks) by the use of profile sheeting. The court relies on electricity.

It was when The Oratory began playing cricket against Beaumont School at Lord's that they first became aware of Tennis, but it was not until David Weston became a school parent that the playing of Tennis there became a reality. Adrian Snow, the headmaster at the time, was persuaded to allow the boys to be introduced to the game and coached in it at Hardwick House, not far away at Pangbourne.

Mark Eadle, then the young assistant at Oxford University, gave his time freely to the boys, and it was not long before more wished to play than could be accommodated at Hardwick. With the help of Ron Womersley, an Oratory teacher, boys were also taken to the court at Oxford University.

The Oratory had moved during the war from its

Right *Adrian Snow, Oratory headmaster 1972–88, whose vision came so successfully to life.*

Below *All present and correct at the opening of the new Royal Dedans and Club Room, December 1999.*

Above *The first court to be built in the UK for eighty years was opened in 1989.*

Right *Mark Eadle has become a most able professional.*

home at Caversham to Woodcote House, some eight miles north, a fine site with virtually no facilities. Considerable constructional development took place during the headmasterships of Father Adrian Morey (1952–67) and Adrian Snow (1972–88), one of the consequences of which was that the sporting facilities had become sufficiently attractive for people outside the school to want to use them.

It was clear to Adrian Snow (now the chairman of the Friends of Hardwick House Club) that Tennis was a good game in itself, and one which could be played by pupils for almost the rest of their lives (unlike most other sports); and that it could also be a source of additional finance. The school's governing body accepted this line of argument and a Tennis court was included in the sports centre which was about to be constructed at Woodcote in 1988. Adrian Snow had been the contractor for many building projects at the school and when he retired as Headmaster he continued, as Warden and Managing Director of Oratory Construction, to supervise all aspects of the creation of the Tennis court. The first game on the court was played, appropriately, between David Weston and Adrian Snow. The current headmaster, Clive Dytor (2000–), a keen player and supporter of Real Tennis, continues to encourage Oratorians to participate in the game.

As its first professional, the school was lucky to recruit Jonathan Howell, at the time in his eighth year at Bordeaux. He was attracted not only by the prospect of participating in a new court, but also in returning to England to play cricket and coach the school XI. Against some expectations, the use of the court by outside personnel took off, and it was not long before Howell needed an assistant. Mark Eadle was available, and the partnership has been an unqualified success. The court is given near-maximum usage, visited by players from all over the world, and The Oratory Real Tennis Club is thriving.

Professional Jonathan Howell has created enormous interest in the game at The Oratory.

OXFORD UNIVERSITY

ALTHOUGH THERE WERE TENNIS COURTS in Oxford in the fifteenth century, the first known University court was built by Christ Church around 1545. The present court at Merton Street was built about 1798. It was preceded on the same Postmaster's Hall site by one dating back to a lease of 1595.

The lease was held by the Wood family from 1608 to 1758 when it was taken on by Edmund Tompkins of Waterperry, the first of a substantial family of Tennis players. In the time of Edmund Tompkins III, the court was rebuilt in its present form (except for the floor, which was not re-laid until shortly before the First World War). He left for Brighton in 1836, by which time the lease was held by Thomas Sabin.

The Tompkins returned in 1866 in the form of Edmund IV, who came to Oxford when London's James Street court closed. He brought with him that court's dedans benches, which remain at Oxford today, and in due course the lease passed on to his son-in-law, J.H. Dickinson, and then to his son, R.C.E. Dickinson.

After the Second World War, there was no resident professional at the University until Peter Ellis arrived from Queen's Club in 1961. The reign of Peter Dawes, who came from Lord's in 1965, was particularly successful, and his wife proved an expert re-coverer of Tennis balls. Chris Ronaldson, then a promising lawn-tennis player, took over when Dawes left for Seacourt in 1972 and stayed for two years before going to the new court at Melbourne. He was followed at Oxford by Mick Dean, Mike Flanagan, Steve Ronaldson, Jerome Fletcher and Alan Oliver. A former Oxford United trainee professional footballer with no Tennis experience, Mark Eadle was taken on as assistant and took to the game so well that he moved on to Holyport.

Kees Ludekens, an enthusiastic young player at Ballarat, came to Oxford and stayed for five years, doing much to raise the profile of the Varsity match as well as starting the women's Varsity matches in 1992. He left for Cambridge in 1994 when Andrew Davis (from Leamington and Moreton Morrell) joined Oliver as joint head professional.

The University has had a succession of strong sides in the past decade, rarely being beaten by Cambridge. James 'Spike' Willcocks, the former Canford schoolboy, has been the most prominent player both as undergraduate and post-graduate. He worked on his game so successfully that he reached the highest standard ever achieved by a player still at university

Sartorial splendour – Alan Oliver, joint head professional.

Lord Willoughby de Broke, celebrated Tennis enthusiast and benefactor, spoke at the 1995 Quatercentenary dinner.

A dinner at Brasenose helped to celebrate 400 years of Tennis at Oxford.

Oxford continued their domination of Varsity Tennis with a 5–1 win over Cambridge at Manchester in 1997. Alan Oliver is in the centre, and joint head professional Andrew Davis is second from the right.

(handicap +2, and the second-ranked amateur in Britain).

Off the court, many have worked hard to maintain the game and its facilities. In 1965, the Unicorn Club was founded to support the courts and it flourished under the guidance of Sir Peter Gretton, bursar of University College, and since 1978 under a succession of long-serving chairmen. In the early 1990s the Oxford University Tennis Foundation was formed to raise and manage funds for the benefit of the game, with John Cook, Martin Mercer and Lord Willoughby de Broke as trustees.

Accumulated funds from the Unicorn Club, augmented by an appeal led by Brigadier Hugh Browne, former bursar of Oriel College, led to major improvements to the Club building. A new long lease was negotiated with Merton College, the landlord, and the new clubhouse was officially opened by Lord Aberdare in September 1997.

The 400th anniversary of Tennis in Oxford was marked in 1995 by an international inter-club tournament, and a book, *Tennis and Oxford* by Jeremy Potter, was published at the same time, with all proceeds going to the appeal.

PARIS
SOCIÉTÉ SPORTIVE DU JEU DE PAUME ET DE RACQUETS

ONE TENNIS COURT remains in this city where once there were hundreds. Contemporary accounts at the end of the sixteenth century estimate the number wildly, three writers plumping variously for 250, 1,100 and 'more than 1,800'. Historians generally settle for the fact that there were at least 500, all of which have disappeared.

As late as 1907, the two courts at the Tuileries (built in 1862 and 1882) were converted into an art gallery. They were replaced the following year by two second-floor courts in rue Lauriston, one of which became four squash courts in 1927. At the survivor, there is still considerable life, and in 1998 a European Masters tournament was held to celebrate its ninetieth anniversary. It was contested by eight professional champions and was won by Nick Wood (then of Hampton Court) who beat Chris Bray (Petworth) in the final.

In the first major victory of his career, Nick Wood beat Chris Bray 6–2, 6–4, 6–2 to win the 1998 European Masters in Paris. Left to right: Chris Bray, Mme Pernigo, Nick Wood, sponsor Gianbattista Pernigo, Club President Gerard Welker and professional Laredo Massip.

Charles Lesueur, formerly at the Tuileries, was the new courts' first maitre paumier in 1908, succeeded on his death in 1916 by Ferdinand Garcin. His father, Seraphim, had been head professional at the Tuileries, and his great-uncle had managed the court at Fontainebleau. Young Garcin was a stylish player in the great French tradition, but not a strong man physically. This led to his 7–4 defeat by Cecil 'Punch' Fairs in the world championship of 1906, played at Brighton. Pierre Etchebaster took over from Garcin at Paris in 1925, and had become world champion by the time he went to New York in 1930.

Two annual competitions were inaugurated at the Tuileries in 1899 (and continued at rue Lauriston) – the Raquette d'Or and the Raquette d'Argent, to which was later added the Raquette de Bronze, all confined to French residents. The Coupe de Paris, open to amateurs of any nationality, was instituted in 1910 and has since been won by many of the world's leading players.

The Raquette d'Or was won in 2000 by Olivier Michel (Fontainebleau) who beat Guillaume Ruault (Paris), the former holder, in four sets. The Raquette d'Argent, which is confined to players who have not won the Raquette d'Or, was won in 1999 by Charles Blanchot (Bordeaux). The Raquette de Bronze was created to give an opportunity to players at handicaps over 35, and in 1998 and 1999 was reserved to players under twenty-five. It was first won by Ivan Ronaldson, then at Fontainebleau. In 2000 the competition was again opened to players of all ages and in the final Cyrille Philippe beat Nicolas Dumon, both from the home club.

The Coupe Gould Eddy, now considered to be the French Amateur doubles championship, was launched in 1923 and has been an annual fixture since 1997.

Rue Lauriston during the 1978 Bathurst Cup. Jean Borotra (left), *three times Wimbledon champion, meets fellow Basque and former world Real Tennis champion Pierre Etchebaster for the first time in thirty years. Roddy Bloomfield* (centre) *was playing for the British team.*

The club has held ladies' international handicap tournaments since 1991, and they draw some twenty-four players to Paris each year.

In the year 2000, Paris hosted the Ted Cockram Trophy, a competition for over-fifties begun in Australia in 1999, as well as the Bathurst Cup, which was won by Great Britain. The competition for the Bathurst Cup was held at rue Lauriston in 1978, when Britain beat France 4–1 and the US 3–2; and in 1987, when Australia beat France 4–1 and then lost 0–5 to Britain.

Right *Paris member Baptiste Roussillon in play.*

Below *France's 1999 Bathurst Cup team in Hobart.* Left to right: *Xavier Masip, Denis Grozdanovitch, Gerard Welker, Tim Batten, Charles Blanchot, Sylvain Elalouf.*

PETWORTH HOUSE

RECENT RESEARCH suggests there have been as many as six Tennis courts at Petworth House, the earliest of them (probably two) existing in the late sixteenth century. There is an entry in the household accounts of 1588–89 for £4 2s. 2d. for plastering and paving Tennis courts. This record of more than 400 years of play is exceeded only at the royal palaces of Hampton Court and Falkland. Some historians suggest that King Henry VIII may well have built courts at Petworth even earlier. The house and park were given to Henry VIII in 1535 by the sixth Earl of Northumberland for somewhat obscure reasons, but Queen Mary returned Petworth to the Percy family in 1557.

The interest of the Percy family in Tennis was maintained. The ninth Earl spent the years 1605–21 in the Tower of London (under suspicion of complicity in the Gunpowder Plot), but during this time he made plans for building work to be done on his release. These included a Tennis court to be built at Syon House, Isleworth, but a condition of his subsequent release was that he must not venture more than thirty miles from Petworth House.

The court in 1909.

His Clerk of Works drew up what became known as 'The Petworth List' in 1615. It consists of the names and dimensions of fourteen London courts. A reproduction of the list and a contemporary map showing the positions of the courts is on display at the Petworth court in the magnificent cabinet presented to the club by Mike Corby in 1998.

The third Petworth court appears to have been built 'in the Cichen yarde' and was probably thatched – in 1654 Nicholas Paige was paid 'for layeing on eight loads of straw on the Tennis Court att 5.0s Lo.' The dimensions of this court as noted in *The Percies of Petworth 1574–1632* are difficult to reconcile. The main wall was said to be 94ft long, the gallery wall 97ft and the penthouse 101ft.

It now seems unlikely that the Duke of York (later James II) played on this court. The eleven pages of expenses incurred by the Duke for Tennis, which are in the Petworth House archives, almost certainly refer to play on the court at St James's Palace, which was built in 1617. The individual charges are nonetheless interesting – three shillings a set for the court, one shilling and sixpence for a dozen balls and sixpence a set for the marker. Rackets were five shillings each, shoes were the same price, a pair of socks cost half-a-crown (a bit steep!) and 'hire of a pair of drawers for Mr Howard to play in – sixpence'. The brothers George and Henry Howard were later the fourth and fifth Earls of Suffolk.

A new court was built at Petworth House in 1700, sited somewhere in the Carpenters' Yard (now known as the Estate Yard where the present court stands). Presumably the roof of this court proved to be too low for towards the end of 1791 recorded items of expenditure include making sashes and frames 'a story higher' and 'Raising the Tennis Court House', as well as 'Getting out and carrying up a stairs at ye Tennis Court'.

Kevin Sheldon wins the 1988 Browning Cup. Left to right: *Captain Coote, Lord Egremont, Kevin Sheldon, Lady Egremont, Colin Lumley (runner-up) and Bob Baveystock.*

Even after all this work, the court (which served as the town's courthouse in 1795) was moved in 1797, literally stone-by-stone, to a new site at the north end of the house. In the process, a rare omission was corrected. The 1700 court had no 'door' gallery. In the new court (the fifth) a 'door' was installed and payment of 1s. 6d. was made to 'Willm. Nightingale for turning two columns for the tennis court'.

Among the keen players at this time was Mr Socket, Rector of Petworth and tutor to Lord Egremont's children. He noted playing with the Duc de Berry from Paris, but 'was disappointed and could give him 30'. A plan in the county archives shows this court (which measured 90ft by 30ft) fitted up for 'an eating room' in January 1822.

Finally, the court was rebuilt yet again in 1872, back to somewhere near the original position in Carpenters' Yard. A damp floor brought trouble this time; the earlier courts had been supported on arches and did not experience that problem. Joseph Bickley was brought in to remedy the situation in 1903. He made detailed recommendations for major work around the foundations but in the event seems only to have been required to stain the floor and paint the lines for £25.

Chris Bray, resident professional and world-class player.

Playing in the new millennium at Petworth – 9.00 a.m. on 1 January 2000. Back row: *Hugh Smorfit, Julian Francis, Martin Fairbarns (secretary), Alan Chalmers, Martin Paterson, Harvey Rawlings.* Front row: *Brian Rich, David Godfray (chairman), Bill Yeoman, Anthea Mearns, Carolyn Armstrong-Smith.*

Not surprisingly, rising damp continued and in 1908–09 Bickley was back to tackle the foundations. At the time, he suggested laying large hot-water pipes in a trench below the net to help keep the floor dry and assist ventilation. The work was not done, and condensation in the winter months which frequently meant closure of the court has since been eliminated with extra heating.

The court was well used through the early years of the twentieth century, especially by the third Lord Leconfield, and in 1918 Harry Lambert, second son of George, was engaged as the professional. He was succeeded by Emil 'Frank' Latham, son of world Tennis and Rackets champion Peter Latham. Tennis at Petworth House did not recover from the Second World War until 1959 when Andy Dawson inspired the revival of the court as an independent club, with the assistance of the National Trust and Lord Egremont. It was reopened in April 1960 but was without professional help until George Cooke came to live on the estate following his retirement from fifty years' service at Manchester.

Failing health prevented him playing, but he offered great encouragement by coaching any player who needed his advice, and worked tirelessly to maintain the court and its surroundings. He died in 1978, much loved by all who came in contact with him, and his wife continued to be a pillar of strength around the court.

The Browning Cup, a handicap competition for professionals, was revived and played at Petworth in 1974. It was won after a gruelling three-hour match by Mick Dean of Oxford (rec.15 and a bisque) playing against Norwood Cripps (owe half 30). The Amateur doubles came to Petworth in 1977, Alan Lovell and Andrew Windham beating Howard Angus and David Warburg.

Restoration of the dedans and ancillary rooms had by then created much-improved facilities for the players, and in 1978 the floor of the court was repainted, the second or possibly third time the Portland stone slabs had been painted since they were laid in 1872.

The arrival of Chris Bray in June 1988 provided the club with a world-class player and coach. Trained under Brian Church at Cambridge, Bray was assistant to Peter Dawes at Seacourt until coming to Petworth. His achievements on court since then have been spectacular – Open singles champion of Britain, Australia, France and the US, Professional singles champion of Britain and the US, and fourteen Open doubles titles across the world.

THE RACQUET CLUB OF
PHILADELPHIA

Many of North America's finest players of Rackets and Tennis have been members of this club, which was formed in 1889 with a clubhouse on Walnut Street and two Rackets courts. Although the club did not hold an internal championship until 1901, it soon inaugurated the inter-club doubles competition, and in 1899 hosted the first US Amateur doubles championship. The next year, Philadelphia staged a magnificent exhibition doubles match between Britain's Peter Latham (the world champion) and Eustace Miles (US Amateur champion) on one side, and on the other America's George Standing (twice runner-up to Latham) and Tom Pettitt (former world Tennis champion). The British pair won by four games to three.

The remarkable British professional Frederick C. Tompkins, youngest of John Tompkins's seventeen children, came to the club in 1904. He was trained at Prince's Club and then worked at Stratfield Saye and Malta. In 1907 the club moved to new premises in South 16th Street, where there were two Rackets courts (one later converted to squash) and one Tennis court. To help him, Tompkins brought over two more British pros, Jock Soutar and Cecil Baldwin.

By this time the club had some excellent Rackets players – Hugh Scott and George Brooke won the US Amateur doubles in 1902; Scott won it six more times with other partners; Brooke won the Amateur singles in 1904 and the club championship six times. Then came two players with exceptional gifts. Jay Gould

The world Rackets championship of 1913. Charles Williams (seated fourth from the left), one of the lucky survivors of the Titanic disaster, versus Jock Soutar.

The players at Manchester during the club's 1996 tour. Left to right: (standing) *Val Sauri, Andy Kinzler (Tennis chairman), Ed Reitmeyer, Peter Willis, Henderson 'Woozie' Supplee, John McNamara (tour organizer), Harry Hare, Bill Schwarze, Vin Maiello;* (kneeling) *Bill McLaughlin and Mike Noll (Tennis professional).*

joined the club in 1909 and Joseph Wear in 1916, from St Louis. They held the Philadelphia Rackets singles title between them alternately from 1916 to 1921 and won the US Amateur doubles together in 1920 (Wear also won it in 1914 and 1917), but at Tennis, Gould was supreme.

He won the British Amateur singles in 1907 and 1908, took the world championship from George Covey 7–1 on the Philadelphia court in 1914, and won the US Open in 1919 and 1921, on the second occasion beating his own club's professional, Jock Soutar, at that time the reigning world Rackets champion. Between 1906 and 1925, Gould won the US Amateur Tennis singles eighteen times – that is, on every occasion the contest was held; between 1909 and 1932, he won the US Amateur doubles nineteen times (six of them with Wear), failing only three times to take the title.

Of the many families whose names grace the club Rackets honours board, the Pearsons were perhaps the most remarkable. Stanley W. Pearson Sr won the club singles six times and the doubles eight times; Stanley W. Jr won the club singles for ten consecutive years after the Second World War and the doubles four

John McNamara (left) and Bill McLaughlin.

Left to right: *Rob Whitehouse, head professional; Rob Fahey, winner of the 1999 US Open; Andy Kinzler, Tennis chairman; and Sam Howe, US Open chairman.*

times, once with his brother C.B. Pearson. Nationally, Stanley W. Sr won the US Amateur doubles with W. Coxe Wright (twice US Tennis champion) in 1932; Stanley W. Jr won the US Amateur singles in 1952 and the doubles with C.B. in 1956 and 1957; and C.B. won the US singles in 1957 and the doubles with C.C. Pell Jr in 1959.

The name of Van Alen echoes through American Tennis, largely because of the great service rendered to the game as first president of the USCTA by William L. 'Sammy' Van Alen. As players alone, the family can hardly be ignored, though concentration is needed to sort out one from the other.

Sammy's peak was probably before the Second World War when he won the US Amateur doubles with his brother J.H. Van Alen of New York, but he survived well enough to win the Philadelphia Club singles in 1940 and 1948 and the doubles with his son, J.L. 'James' Van Alen in 1962. James won the club singles five times between 1966 and 1978, and with his

brother William L. Jr won the club doubles four times and the US Amateur doubles in 1967.

When Frederick Tompkins retired as the club head professional in 1936 after thirty-two years' service, he was succeeded by Jock Soutar, one of the great Rackets players of all time and world champion from 1913 to 1929. So powerful and accurate was his service that the one-service rule was introduced in the US. On his retirement in 1949, the club post went to Jimmy Dunn who had started as a boy under Tompkins in 1928. ('You'll never make it,' said Tompkins. 'You're Irish, you're a redhead, and you're a southpaw.')

Shortly afterwards Dunn broke his left arm and switched to playing right-handed. He reached the finals of the US Open Tennis singles from 1956 to 1964, losing four times to Albert 'Jack' Johnson and twice to Jimmy Bostwick; he won the US Open doubles six times and the US professional singles five years running. At Rackets, Jack Johnson saw him off again in the US Open finals of 1959 and 1964.

Dunn was a Philadelphia professional for fifty years, giving way in the mid-1980s to Ed Noll. An affable personality with a populist view of Tennis and a thorough knowledge of the club's traditions (having served as a professional there earlier), Noll halted the declining interest in the game by encouraging the younger members to take it up, and by increasing the number of tournaments and the size of the draws to make sure there was plenty of action for them.

A succession of vibrant chairmen of the Tennis Committee played a major part in this revival of enthusiasm. Bill Shettle, John McNamara (an expatriate Briton), Bill McLaughlin and Andy Kinzler each extended the frontiers, and McNamara in particular showed his international flair by organizing team Tennis tours to Britain and France.

Kinzler, the current chairman, most notably promoted junior Tennis at the club, reviving the dormant junior tournaments and being instrumental in establishing the US National Junior Singles. In 1992, that contest, which has been played at the club since its inception, attracted six players, all from Philadelphia; in 1999, there were more than thirty entrants, from Britain as well as the US.

Now recognized as the centre of junior Tennis in America, the Racquet club's young members dominate the US Junior Nationals. Drew McGowan won the title for the first three years, then Gabe Kinzler took it five times from 1995. Andy and Gabe Kinzler won the Father and Son Doubles in 1995 and 1998 and Dick and Barney Tanfield won it in 1999 and 2000.

Ever since the Jimmy Dunn years, the Racquet club has been known for the long tenure of their athletic staff and for their commitment to training young professionals. Like many other Philadelphia professionals, Ed Noll was introduced to Tennis as a young assistant from nearby East Falls, and during much of his time as the club professional was assisted by two more from East Falls, Mike Noll and Rob Whitehouse. In 1998, Ed Noll stepped out of the court to become general manager of the club, and Rob Whitehouse is now head professional.

PRESTED HALL

DREAMS DO SOMETIMES COME TRUE. Here in rural Essex, the drive and passion of one man has brought to life a dream that would not be out of place in a collection of fairy stories. In Feering, on a site previously earmarked for a golf course, an hour by train from the City of London, Mike Carter has created the only pair of Tennis courts to be built in the northern hemisphere in the twentieth century, and the only privately funded courts in Britain since 1905.

Mike Carter had his first taste of Tennis as a Cambridge undergraduate in the 1960s. He was immediately addicted and determined to build a new court that would be accessible to a new generation of players, and one that would break the somewhat élitist image to which the scarcity of courts had inevitably led the game.

Frustrated by planning authorities when he tried to build a court near his home at Ipswich, Mike found Prested Hall, a sixteenth century mansion halfway between Chelmsford and Colchester and close to the main A12 road. He converted the house to a hotel with eleven en suite bedrooms and planning permission for a further forty but was turned down for a lottery grant for the Tennis courts – the Sports Council felt that the game had recently had its fair

At the launch in June 1999 – Charles Swallow (left) and Andrew Myrtle from the T&RA with Trish Dawson.

Prested Hall.

Above *Pro-am doubles runners-up John Evans, amateur (left) and Marc Seigneur, professional at the Harbour Club (centre) with founder of the club Mike Carter at Prested in October 1999. Mike Carter must be congratulated on his magnificent achievement in building two such superb courts.*

Left *Two of the game's leading ladies played on opening day – Penny Lumley (right) and Sue Haswell.*

share of funding, with the successful applications for a new court at Bristol and the restoration of an old one at Bridport.

In April 1998, the foundations were laid with Mike Carter as Foreman of Works, chief labourer and machine driver. By December the first court was pretty much ready, and by the end of the year the former assistant professional at Melbourne, Adam Mickelburough, flew into Heathrow with his family, ready to coach new members. The second court (now the No.1 court), with a glass grille wall, was finished in June 1999 and Prested was officially opened over the weekend of 26–27 June.

A clutch of champions from the Tennis and Rackets world were among those in attendance – Andrew Myrtle and Charles Swallow from the Tennis and Rackets Association, Howard Angus, Chris and Lesley Ronaldson, Penny Lumley, Sue Haswell and Ralph Howe. A Ton-up doubles tournament (won by Mike Carter and Chris Ronaldson) ran alongside handicap events. In October the pro-am doubles were held at

Prested, and in November the over-forty-five, fifty-five and sixty-five championships were held there. Many British clubs have visited Prested, as have groups from Ballarat, Melbourne and Washington.

As well as a large and comfortable club room, spacious changing rooms and the hotel facility alongside, Prested has some most unusual features – a large viewing area behind the glass grille wall, and no chase lines on the floor of the courts. These are replaced by half-yard stripes of alternating colours, so that most calls are 'worse than' something (if blue), or 'better than' something (if green). Only occasionally do exact yard or half-yard chases occur.

A high-tech gymnasium was opened in April 2000, three new Astro lawn-tennis courts in October 2000, a health and beauty treatment centre in November 2000, and the Hall is up and running as a hotel, with facilities for weddings and other functions. A 25 metre indoor swimming pool is under construction.

By the end of its second season the club had over 100 members, mostly local and active, and many of whom had never played Tennis before.

Prested professional Adam Mickelburough (left) *with Martin Fairbarns and John Burnett.*

THE QUEEN'S CLUB

LONDON'S HEART OF RACKETS AND TENNIS for more than a century, the Queen's Club (known universally as Queen's) was founded in 1886 under the patronage of Queen Victoria, built on market garden land in West Kensington and opened in 1887. The amateur championships of both games were created there, and since 1888 nearly all the major national Rackets championships (including those of the Public Schools, from which most of Britain's great players have risen) have been played there.

In Victorian times there was a vast choice of sports for members. There were Eton fives courts, a running track, and pitches on which cricket, rugby, soccer, hockey and lacrosse were played. Croquet and billiards were available, of course, as well as lawn tennis, roller skating and (briefly) ice skating; and for a while, with difficulty, even golf.

Two squash courts were added in 1904, two more in 1924, and in 1926 one of the original two Rackets courts was converted into two more squash courts.

Among the great professionals who have served Queen's are several world champions: Charles Saunders (Tennis) and Charles Williams (Rackets), and two men who won the world titles of both, the phenomenal Peter Latham and Jim Dear. Somewhere near the bottom of the list of paid hands is Dan Maskell, who rose from

Left to right: *Mark Agate, Dudley McDonald, Sir Mervyn Dunnington-Jefferson (chairman of the T&RA Rackets committee) and Alexander Anton. Dudley McDonald and Sir Mervyn Dunnington-Jefferson have been pillars of strength in the organization of Tennis and Rackets events at Queen's.*

being a ball-boy to become, at seventeen, the first junior professional Rackets champion. Efforts to persuade him to stay in that game failed when he beat Charles Read for the professional lawn-tennis championship, and went off to Wimbledon.

Norwood Cripps, an outstanding Tennis player, served as senior professional until he went to Eton in 1979. He was succeeded by David Johnson from Lord's who is still doing a first-class job there. Among his talented assistants have been Neil Smith (later world Rackets champion), Peter Brake (now head Rackets professional) and Andrew Lyons.

Today the club is a wholly owned subsidiary of the Lawn Tennis Association who also have their headquarters there, as does the Tennis and Rackets Association, and Racket sports are the focus of the club's attention.

During the past twenty years, a major development and building programme has been carried out. This has included the restoration of the second Rackets court to its proper purpose (now named the Bridgeman Court),

A man for all games and all seasons – the ubiquitous secretary of Queen's Club, Jonathan Edwardes.

Champagne celebrations after the 1995 championships – Willie Boone in the foreground, Charles Hue Williams and James Male plus families.

Above *Garth Milne (centre), who organized the spectacularly successful Quintathlon in 1986, surrounded by the competitors.*

Left *James Male – Rackets amateur, Tennis professional – is now one of the world's top Tennis players.*

the refurbishment of both Tennis courts and the dedans areas, the creation of a Tennis and Rackets museum and the rebuilding of the Rackets gallery, damaged by fire in 1979. Funding for all this work (more than £300,000) was raised by the Tennis and Rackets Association under the dynamic leadership of the chairman, David Norman.

Meanwhile, scarcely a step was missed in the pageant of excitement provided by the two games at Queen's. Week after week through the long seasons, players and spectators alike have revelled in matches of sometimes unbelievable quality. Among those of the greatest historic as well as passionate significance were the emergence of James Male as the Open singles champion in 1987, ending the decade-long domination of the final by Willie Boone and John Prenn. Male's ambidexterity was, at the time, astonishing and undoubtedly secured his wins over Boone and, in the final, Neil Smith.

Male was then twenty-three and only a year later devastated Boone 6–1 in the world final, the second leg of which was played at Queen's. Two weeks after that he

Above *A nail-biting business – masters-in-charge and Andrew Myrtle, the T&RA's chief executive, at a crucial point in a schools championship match.*

Right *Major Domo – Reg Routledge, former Queen's house manager and a most knowledgeable tennis historian.*

retained his Open title, blowing away Prenn 4–1 and Smith, again, in the final 4–0. A wind of change had clearly roared through Rackets.

In 1991 Male and Prenn, by then British Open doubles champions for five years, lost that title to the young professionals Neil Smith and Shannon Hazell in what many in the gallery rated the greatest doubles match ever played. The score was 15–2, 7–15, 15–12, 13–18, 15–4, 12–15, 15–12. Dan Maskell happened to be there. 'Fabulous,' he wrote to David Norman the next day. 'I still find it hard to believe that four men could play so wonderfully for so long.' Maskell timed it, with his precision, at 2 hours 52 minutes; most of us reckoned three hours was close enough.

In May 1992, Julian Snow become the first amateur to win the Laurent-Perrier Tennis Masters at Queen's. Well established as the game's leading amateur player, Snow beat Robert Fahey in the semi-final and Chris Bray, the Petworth professional, with disappointing ease in the final. Two years later, with Fahey approaching his peak, Snow was eliminated 12–7 by the Australian

Above *Masters-in-charge and schools Rackets professionals meet during the 1998 Public Schools singles championships.*

Left *Professional doubles – David Johnson anxiously watching Peter Brake's railroad service.*

on his march to become the youngest world champion yet.

In what Norman Rosser called 'one of the best matches ever seen at Queen's', James Male held off another Rackets assault by the elegant Neil Smith to hold his world title in 1993. Smith had taken the first leg 4–2 in Chicago, and then went 5–2 up at Queen's. With a stunning display of double-handed battery, Male took the next (and last) four games.

Male's first Rackets defeat in a major tournament for ten years was one of the club's shocks of the 1990s. In the 1998 Open singles he lost his quarter-final to Toby Sawrey-Cookson, 14–17 in the fifth game. The young Clifton professional met forty-seven-year-old Willie Boone in the final and did not win a single game.

There is one more rising star to note on a Queen's Tennis court – in November 1998 the twenty-year-old Australian Steve Virgona had a surprising win over world champion Rob Fahey in the Open singles, 2–6, 3–6, 6–1, 6–1, 6–2. He then defeated Mike Gooding in the semi-final and took two sets off Julian Snow in the final.

Queen's may be renowned for such superb competitors as these, but at heart it is a club like any other, albeit in a more sumptuous setting than most. The sponsored Queen's weekends continue to flourish, and grass-roots members can compete for three handicap events at Tennis (the Haycraft, Broadwood and Druce Cups), while there are two competitions for club-standard Rackets players, the Parker Vase and the Queen's Club Cup, as well as the David Watkins Trophy. This is an annual event named after the man who was largely responsible for the now widely used handicap system for Rackets, which is service-ratio driven.

Young Rackets players enjoy the benefits of subsidized membership, introduced by the Tennis and Rackets Association in 1982 in conjunction with Queen's and other clubs, which allows school leavers to continue to play at greatly reduced cost.

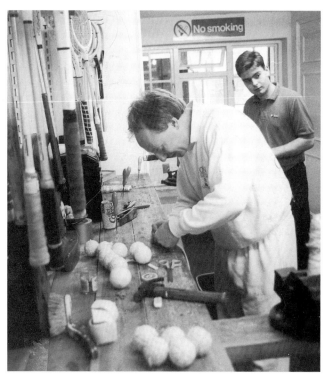

Right *David Johnson, Queen's senior Tennis professional, at work with assistant Andy Lyons.*

Below *Last gasp – left to right: Willie Boone, Charles Hue Williams, John Prenn and James Male.*

In the club's centenary year of 1986 and again in 2000, as part of the millennium celebrations, Queen's hosted a quintathlon in which many North American players took part. The first one – the first ever held in this country – was organized by Garth Milne and the second by John Prenn. Both comprised a demanding schedule of social activities as well as competition in Rackets, Tennis, lawn tennis, squash and golf. Both were memorably successful.

The administration of so complex a club has never been an easy matter. Even in the rural days when a few grazing horses and sheep dotted the grounds, the board of management had problems to solve. In 1893, for instance, they decreed that nursemaids should not be allowed on the premises, but then they had to decide how to distinguish between a nursemaid and a nursery governess. In 1895 they considered a proposal to take a six-month option to buy the All-England Lawn Tennis and Croquet Club at Wimbledon for £30,000. The proposal was not realized.

Between 1914 and 1928 the secretary at Queen's was the celebrated Tennis historian E.B. Noel. In 1945 Dickie Ritchie returned from war service to find the club heavily damaged and the finances badly wounded too. He saw it through the difficulties and survived in the job for thirty years. When Jonathan Edwardes, an enthusiastic and successful Rackets player, took over as club secretary in 1980, he was faced with a long period of building and development problems, but by the end of that decade a resurgence of interest and activity was obvious.

The club has devised a successful system of committees for each sport, the members of which are drawn from the general committee, the members and the management. The Tennis and Rackets Association chairmen, first the late Dick Bridgeman and then David Norman, shaped, with the club's help, the new and splendid facilities that Queen's now offers the players of these captivating games.

RADLEY COLLEGE

ACKETS AT RADLEY made little impression on the outside world until after the First World War, but in the past twenty years the phenomenal achievements of two Old Radleians, James Male and Julian Snow, have more than made up for the school's rather slow start. Though there had been a court at Radley since 1885, it was 1922 before a pair reached the Public Schools final and 1930 before the prize was won.

A taste for the game was established when in 1855 the Warden had wing-buttresses built on to the clock tower, forming four courts in which the game of bat-fives became popular. In 1864, an acrostic appeared in the school magazine, appealing for funds for a Rackets court:

R   *Radleians old to us be kind*
A   *And money for our racquets find,*
D   *Do all of you some gold disburse*
L   *Long hidden in your private purse.*
E   *Each one may well some trifle spare*
I   *In slight remembrance of the care*
A   *And pains, which you all met with here,*
N   *Nor think your money ill-bestowed*
S   *Since it's a debt you long have owed.*

Eventually sufficient money was raised (£964) for a court, and a pair entered the championship in 1887. Real progress was made when Bertram 'Brahms' Abraham, from Prince's Club, became the professional in 1911, and he gave devoted service to Radleian Rackets until 1948. He drew his richest reward when P.I. Van der Gucht and W.H. Vestey beat the Eton pair 4–1 in the 1930 final – the only Radley success until Male and Snow won the championship without conceding a game in 1982.

Ronnie Lay had joined Abraham as his assistant in 1925, later marrying his daughter, and in 1948 he succeeded his father-in-law. Before retiring in 1971 he had coached two pairs to the Public Schools final – Dexter and Dipple in 1953 and Rogers and Osborne in 1966.

Mick Dean, who reached his peak as an outstanding Tennis player in the 1980s, joined the teaching staff in 1978 and took charge of Rackets until December 1998. The professional's post was then filled by Mark Hubbard, who had won the Under-24 Rackets singles

in 1998 and in his first month at Radley enjoyed the rare accolade of beating Neil Smith in the Professional singles, later losing the final to Toby Sawrey-Cookson.

It was in Mick Dean's time that Male and Snow came to the fore. Male, the elder of the two, took the first glittering steps by winning the Public Schools Under-16 prize (the Incledon-Webber Cup) in 1979. In 1980 and 1981 he won the H.K. Foster Cup, losing only one game throughout the two years' matches; in 1982 he and Snow brought the Public Schools doubles trophy back to Radley (not one game lost), and at the end of that year Snow won the Foster.

There was little doubt that the pair of them, individually or in harness, were going to make a tremendous impact wherever they used their talents. Male, the more forceful and relentlessly determined player, immediately stormed the Rackets world. He won the Swallow Cup (Under-24 singles) in 1984, 1985 and 1987 (he did not enter in 1986); he reached the final of the British Open in 1985 and won it in 1987, 1988 and 1989, each time against Neil Smith; and in 1988, at the age of twenty-three, beat Willie Boone for the world championship by 6 games to 1, the youngest player to do so since Peter Latham in 1887.

It was not surprising that Snow, the young master of

Julian Snow – absolute domination of amateur Tennis.

James Male – a formidable Rackets champion.

court craft, turned early to Tennis. In 1985, he won both the Under-21 and the Under-24 titles, keeping his Rackets hand in by winning the Under-24 doubles with Neil Smith. In 1986, Snow won the Manchester Gold Racquet for Tennis, beating James Male in the final. Male had discovered such relish for the game that in 1987 he beat Snow for the Manchester Gold Racquet and then joined him to win the Amateur doubles.

That was the year in which Snow began his absolute domination of the amateur Tennis scene by beating Howard Angus in the Amateur singles final. He won that title for eleven of the next twelve years, losing only in 1990 when Male beat him in the final. In 1997, he won the US Open (and the doubles with Male) and in 1998 the British Open. After eliminating both Chris Bray and Mike Gooding for the world challenge, he lost it 7–4 to Robert Fahey in 1998. Throughout the years, he has scooped up almost countless doubles titles, the most interesting of which have been his Open Tennis wins with Male in 1997 and 1998.

Through the 1990s, James Male played Rackets to a level unattainable by the rest of the world. He beat off world challenges from Shannon Hazell and Neil Smith (twice), before surrendering the title in 1999 after an ankle injury sustained in the first leg of Smith's third challenge. Male was reeling in singles titles at will – the Amateur eight times, the Open another four times and in January 2001 he won back the world championship against Neil Smith. At Tennis, Male turned professional in 1999, immediately winning the singles and, with Frank Filippelli, the doubles.

Understandably, Radley College has felt considerable pride in these achievements, not least when in 1985 Snow, Male and Thane Warburg brought the Henry Leaf Cup to Radley for the first time in history, breaking an eleven-year run by the Wykehamists.

ROMSEY

NEWEST OF AUSTRALIA'S five Tennis clubs, this innovative building in the State of Victoria was the dream of vigneron and architect Gordon Cope-Williams. Opened in 1999, it is impressive in the extreme, with a complete glass grille wall, and is built in the style of an aisled barn, which gives the court, its central feature, an air of lightness and space.

Surrounding the court, but under the same roof, are the subsidiary and fascinating features of the complex. To the north is the 'cellar door' wine sales, overlooking the vineyard (mostly chardonnay and pinot); and there is a lounge room from which

Right *The lounge at Romsey. The club also has a vineyard, wine cellar and cricket oval.*

Below *Newest of Australia's five Tennis clubs, Romsey's innovative complex was opened in 1999.*

Large areas of glass wall provide superb viewing.

spectators may look through the glass wall. Upstairs, there is more viewing to be had through the glass above the grille penthouse. To the south are the members' rooms, including bar, billiard room and mezzanine area with glass wall for viewing.

To the east, behind the main wall, are the changing rooms, gymnasium and administration offices (with more viewing above). To the west are the banqueting hall, restaurant and kitchens.

The main walls of the court are a light battleship grey, and in keeping with Australian tradition the grille has a caricature – not of a monk this time, but a somewhat provocative portrait of a fifteenth century lady tennis player, Margot of Hainault. The club soon attracted 150 members, and engaged Robert Bartlett as professional. The inaugural Romsey Open was staged in 2000 and restricted to the world's top eight players. In the final, Robert Fahey won a high-class match with England's Chris Bray.

To support the increasing membership at Romsey, the club took on an assistant professional, Jacob Potts, in late 2000.

Players in an exhibition match at Romsey to mark the opening of the court included (left to right) *world champion Robert Fahey, Royal Melbourne professional Paul Tabley, Romsey professional Robert Bartlett, Royal Melbourne head professional Barry Toates and Ballarat head professional Brett McFarlane.*

RUGBY SCHOOL

HERE IS A RACKETS RECORD that will take some beating – Rugby produced three players who between them held the world championship for thirty-four out of forty-four years. Rugby's great men were David Milford (1937 to 1947, without a challenge); Geoffrey Atkins (1954 to 1972, unbeaten through five challenges); and Willie Surtees, who took the title in 1972, lost it to Howard Angus in 1973, won it back in 1975 and held it comfortably until John Prenn beat him in 1981. Surprisingly, of the three only Surtees won the Foster Cup, though Milford was twice in pairs that won the Public Schools championship.

Rugby played in four of the first eleven championship finals, winning in 1870 despite the handicap of the school court (built in 1864) being considerably above standard size. A second court was added in 1883.

For more than 100 years there was a Gray in charge of Rackets at Rugby. Joseph Gray, who held the world championship for ten years, served from 1868 to 1894. He was succeeded by his son Harry (1894 to 1937), during whose time Rugby won the championship six times and played in eleven finals.

Among his pupils (who included Milford and Atkins) were the remarkable Simpson brothers. The older of them, C.F.B. Simpson who was killed in the First World War, held the extraordinary record of playing first string for Rugby for five years (1907–11). He reached the Public Schools final in 1908 and won it in 1911 with W.H. Clarke. It was at Oxford that his brother J.C.F. (later Sir Cyril) hit the heights, winning the University singles three years running (1920–22) and the doubles twice. He went on to become Amateur singles champion (1926–28) and Open champion (1929–32), as well as six times Amateur doubles champion.

Harry Gray sent both his sons, Peter and Ronald, to Rugby. Peter was captain of Rackets in 1930 and Ronald in 1932–33, reaching the schools final with Raymond Lumb the first year and winning it with him the second. Lumb was joined by Peter Kershaw in 1934 and won again. Kershaw, a fine player at both games, was a member of the winning pair of Old Rugbeians in the Noel-Bruce Cup twelve times (three with Lumb, eight with Milford and once with Atkins); and was in the winning trio in the Henry Leaf Cup – the Tennis competition for old boys – an amazing fourteen times.

Of all Rugbeians, Geoffrey Atkins took all-round ability to the greatest heights. As well as his run

Geoffrey Atkins reigned supreme as the world Rackets champion for seventeen years.

Richard Carter (left) *with Robin Hicks, winners of the Public Schools doubles championship in 1995.*

Richard Carter reached the final of the schools doubles three times.

as world Rackets champion, Open champion and Amateur champion, Atkins was also Amateur Tennis champion in 1960, 1962 and 1963.

Harry Gray, who trained him at Rackets, first retired in 1937 and was succeeded by his son Peter; however Harry returned in 1939 for seven years, covering the war period. Peter Gray saw seven pairs through to the Public Schools championship final, winning in 1938, 1939, 1952 and 1965 (with Willie Surtees as first string). Surtees also took the Foster Cup that year, as had two earlier pupils of Peter Gray, J.M.G. Tildesley (1954) and J.L. Cuthbertson (1958). Gray's own son Nigel played for the school in 1962–63.

Philip Rosser is now the Rugby professional. Though triumphs may have been less frequent lately, the school reached the championship final for three consecutive years in the 1990s. Richard Carter played in all three with different partners, winning in 1994 with C. Richards and in 1995 with R. Hicks. This last pair did not lose a game until meeting Eton in the final, whom they beat 4–2. The annual tournament at Queen's Club is still the highlight of the year for Rugby's Rackets players.

ST PAUL'S

ST PAUL'S SCHOOL, founded in 1509 by Dean Colet in the shadow of the medieval cathedral, moved to West Kensington in 1884 and from there in 1968 to a 42 acre riverside site in Barnes, where there are now 790 pupils in addition to 440 at the Preparatory School, Colet Court. An anonymous benefactor marked the new millennium by providing funds for the building of a Rackets court and for the employment of a professional. Steve Tulley arrived from Montreal to launch the sport at the school, and St Paul's has thus become the first school whose pupils are predominantly day boys to make Rackets available.

Right *Steve Tulley, St Paul's first professional.*

Below *The exterior of the St Paul's court.*

The St Paul's court is based on the No. 1 court at Queen's Club. The architects, Barnsley, Hewett and Mallinson, have combined the elements of a traditionally constructed court from one hundred years ago with up-to-date technology. The court walls, for example, are one and a half bricks thick with a soft mortar, but the internal finish is modern. Instead of the 40mm thick traditional Bickley formula, a 20mm thick render was used. The exact composition of the original is lost and would not have complied with current health and safety legislation. The render used is more environmentally friendly and, we are told, can withstand the force of a sledgehammer.

The position of the court and the link to the sports

James Male(left) regains his Rackets world championship title from Neil Smith in the second leg at St Paul's.

hall and five galleries are designed to encourage interest in the game. At first-floor level is a stand for up to seventy spectators. At ground level, the door to the court is glass to aid teaching and allow a view into the court for the resident professional, whose room faces it.

The building is positioned so that mature trees are retained. At low level, polished blocks have been used and at high level western red cedar boarding has been chosen as it blends with the landscaping and provides texture, colour variation over time and low maintenance cost.

On 20 January 2001, the court was officially opened when the school hosted the second leg of the world singles Rackets championship. The very high quality of the court was immediately apparent.

It took the match contender, James Male, just two games to regain his title from the defending champion Neil Smith, but the games were keenly fought and included many long rallies. To the delight of over seventy spectators, the two players agreed to play a further two games for a crate of champagne, which James Male also won.

Within the school, Rackets has attracted so many pupils that Steve Tulley, the professional, hardly has enough hours in the day. In time, St Paul's aims to compete at the very top levels and the High Master is determined to support the sport so that all pupils who wish to play may do so.

After the match, Lord Aberdare, President of the Tennis and Rackets Association, unveiled a plaque dedicating the court to the memory of E.P.C. 'Pat' Cotter, classicist, bridge writer and sportsman, who taught at St Paul's from 1928 to 1965.

The day ended in magnificent style with a celebration dinner at the Queen's Club, sponsored, as had been the match, by the generous benefactor.

RMA SANDHURST

U P TO THE MID 1990s, Rackets flourished in the Army, where the game had been encouraged from its early formative years. By 1911, there were courts at all the main depots, including Aldershot, Chatham, Colchester, Portsmouth, Shorncliffe and the Curragh (Co.Kildare). The Army introduced the game to Canada and to India, where in 1930 there were some seventy courts.

The Royal Military Academy is credited with the first building of a closed court – by 1806 there were two courts at Woolwich, one covered and one open, at either end of the main block. The whole block was

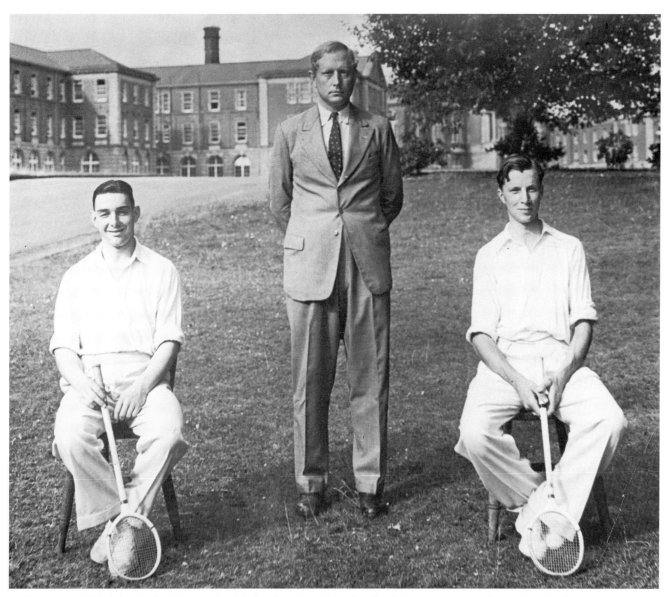

Andrew Myrtle (right) *in the Sandhurst pair with Pat Mesquita. Brigadier Myrtle became the best Army player in the post-war years. Standing is Major W.K. Hedley.*

A time for nostalgia during the Sandhurst Cup. Left to right: Derek Barrett (the Wellington professional), Lt Col Malcolm MacLagan and Mike Bolton, a former Army Rackets champion.

General Tim Toyne Sewell presents the Regimental Doubles Trophy to the Army Air Corps pair of Captain Paul Tennant (left) *and Major James Illingworth.*

demolished in 1859 and two new courts built. At about the same time, the fives court at the Royal Military College, Sandhurst, was converted into a Rackets court.

The present Sandhurst courts were built about 1877, and two years later the first RMA v. RMC match was played – an annual encounter (except for war years) until about 1926. By 1940, the courts were being used for military purposes. One was restored in 1948 (by which time the two colleges were amalgamated into the RMA, Sandhurst), but the other is now used as a lecture theatre.

New strip lights were installed in 1978 and an invitation doubles competition for the Sandhurst Cup was inaugurated, which proved very popular. It is still played, over an April weekend, when Wellington College allow the Army the use of their court and thirty to forty military and civilian players take part. However, the change of emphasis in the Officer Cadet intake at Sandhurst has led to boys from non Rackets-playing schools predominating, which has meant that few Rackets players are now joining up.

At the time of writing, the future of the court is in some doubt. It needs extensive maintenance, and in the current economic climate funding is hard to justify for a facility that is so little used.

A dwindling band of enthusiasts still fiercely compete for the Army championships, held at Queen's Club in February. Among the finest players of recent years have been Barry Aitken (Royal Logistic Corps), Christopher Braithwaite (Light Dragoons), Alex Finlayson (Queen's Royal Lancers), David Reed-Felstead (Royal Horse Guards), Stephen Segrave (Irish Guards) and two from the Army Air Corps, James Illingworth and Paul Tennant.

They follow in the footsteps of the outstanding Army player of the past fifty years, Andrew Myrtle, who won the singles championship seven times – as a Second-Lieutenant in 1955, a Captain in 1960, 1961 and 1962, a Major in 1964 and 1965 and as a Colonel in 1976. He was a Brigadier when, in 1977, he played for the third time in the winning inter-regimental doubles pair with Tim Toyne Sewell for the King's Own Scottish Borderers.

Many of the star names of Army Rackets also appear on the Tennis trophies. Some talented and keen players on the Staff Course at Shrivenham have injected new blood into the game, and a substantial fixture list is maintained. Home matches are played on Lady Rose's court at Hardwick House.

Major Iain Park-Weir presenting the Real Tennis Cup to Major Andrew James (Grenadier Guards) at Canford in 1998. Also pictured is the runner-up, Colonel Barry Aitken.

SEACOURT TENNIS CLUB, HAYLING ISLAND

THERE CAN HARDLY BE a more unusual and unexpected sports complex than this. The Tennis court in this south coast oasis was built in 1911 by J.F. Marshall, a talented player, at a cost of £10,000. The club was formed in March 1966 with no more than twenty Tennis and badminton enthusiasts. By the end of the year there were seventy-eight members and today there are more than 1,200. The club boasts, in addition to the original court, a Rackets court, four squash courts, two badminton courts, two all-weather and floodlit lawn-tennis courts, a fitness gym, a sports hall that is used as a fencing salle and a petanque area, as well as recently refurbished bar, restaurant and changing areas.

Marshall, who won the MCC Gold Prize in 1914, sunk the court three feet into the ground to avoid too

At the heart of the 1966 Seacourt revival were (standing) *Paul and Nick Danby and* (seated) *John Parker, Ned Danby and Francis Snell.*

obtrusive a building. It opened in June 1911 with a match between the former world champion Peter Latham and the man who had taken the title from him, Cecil 'Punch' Fairs.

The surprising factor of that opening day was that the match that followed was a mixed doubles – a very mixed doubles, involving the two finest amateur players of the day, Eustace Miles and the Hon. Neville Lytton, partnering G.H.K. Bone and Mrs Lytton (later Baroness Wentworth). The lady was said to be a formidable opponent who practised with her own professional. He happened to be Fred Covey, at the time the best Tennis player in the world after Latham and Fairs.

This unusual promotion of a female Tennis player set a standard that Seacourt has never lost. In 1913 the club launched a handicap competition for ladies, and in 1978 the first Ladies' Open was staged there and has often been played there since. One of the leading female players in the world, Alex Garside, is a Seacourt

member, competes in the club's annual Silver Racket competition and has represented Seacourt in the Field Trophy team. With Sally Jones, Alex Garside won the world doubles in 1989 and 1991, and in 1994 won the British Open and French Open singles titles. Her many doubles titles include the British Open (nine times), the French Open and the Australian, US, French and Scottish championships.

When the original Seacourt owner died after the Second World War, the property was bought by Charles Sylvester, who repaired the court after war damage and started a social club. Demolition threatened in the early 1960s, but in 1966 Ned Danby, Francis Snell and John Parker formed the Seacourt Tennis Club Ltd and acquired the court for the shareholders. Paul and Nicky Danby joined the Board later.

The Rackets court, added in 1980, included a glass door. Derek Barrett served as professional from 1969

Judith Lytton, a Tennis player of championship class.

Ivan Snell led the victorious Field Trophy team in 1990.

Mixed doubles tournaments are well established at Seacourt. Bryn Sayers and Alex Garside receive their prizes from sponsor Carolyn Armstrong-Smith at the Wineflow Mixed Doubles.

to 1970 when Peter Dawes took over. He has made a significant contribution to the club's success and has taught many assistants who are now club professionals, including Danny Jones, who joined him at Seacourt in 1991. Danny Jones won the Silver Racket in 1995 and 1996, and with Chris Bray represents Seacourt in Division One of the National League. All the members of the successful Field Trophy team learned their Tennis at Seacourt. Captained by Paul Weaver since 1992, and with Ivan Snell playing at No. 1, they reached three finals before beating Hampton Court for the Trophy at Bristol in 1999. Juniors have done very well too, winning several Under-16 national tournaments.

In 1998 Paul and Nicky Danby and John Parker stood down as directors of the company. Mrs Jenny Paterson was elected chairman and managing director, the first time that position has been held other than by a member of the Danby family.

Charles Swallow makes a presentation to Peter Dawes at the dinner held in his honour by the T&RA Council on his retirement in 2000 after twenty-five years as Chairman of the Real Tennis Professionals Association.

SYDNEY,
MACQUARIE UNIVERSITY

Tennis came to Australia's most populous city when this court opened in October 1997. The financial involvement of former world champion Wayne Davies and his family was crucial in finding the necessary funds – more was needed after the opening when it was found necessary to rebuild both the floor and the main wall.

As part of the opening celebrations, Australia challenged Britain to compete for the Vice-Chancellor's Trophy. There was a narrow win for the home side (Robert Fahey, Frank Filippelli, Graham Hyland and Wayne Davies) against Julian Snow, James Male, Mike Gooding and Nick Wood. The following year the club hosted the Australian Open singles, in which Fahey beat Filippelli in the final.

Robert Lawton (left), the man who inspired the University to act, seen here with Rob Dery (President of the club) and competitors Rob Fahey and James Male.

Tennis comes to Sydney – the opening celebrations in 1997 performed by Federal Minister for Health Dr Michael Wooldridge, a well-known Tennis identity.

The court is light and airy, with pale green walls.

Credit for motivating and nurturing the plans to build this court goes to Robert Lawton, the Executive Officer at the University. With no experience of the game, he was inspired by what he saw at Melbourne and Hobart, and worked hard to obtain university approval for the complex.

The court is light and airy, with pale green walls. There is no bandeau as such, just a metal piping edge, and perhaps uniquely the ball basket is in the middle of the trough. Among the club's best players are Robert Angell, Rob Dery, Tony Happell and Peter Meares – all former Melbourne members before work took them to Sydney.

In early 2001, the clubrooms were enhanced considerably with the installation of a mezzanine floor above the dedans – thus providing magnificent viewing for spectators.

The head professional is Simon Kinniburgh.

Peter Meares, one of the best club players.

TONBRIDGE SCHOOL

T̶HOUGH TONBRIDGE has only one Rackets court (opened in 1897), it is located in the heart of the school. This has enabled boys of all ages to snatch occasional moments on the court at all times of the day, and over the years this has proved a great advantage.

Since David Makey took over as professional in 1983, Tonbridge has won a total of thirty-five Public School titles, more than any other school. Three different pairs won the doubles championship in three consecutive years, from 1985 to 1987, and in 1987 all four Tonbridge pairs reached the finals of their various age groups, winning three of them.

Some outstandingly talented boys have enriched the teams over the past twenty years. Adrian Spurling,

Right *Rupert Owen-Browne won the Foster Cup in 1984 and the Under-24 singles in 1989.*

Below *David Makey stepping forward to receive his runner-up prize after Peter Brake (Queen's Club) retained his professional singles title at Tonbridge in 1997.*

Lord Aberdare (left) *with Lord Cowdrey, who had a brief but distinguished Rackets career.*

beaten by Julian Snow in the Foster Cup final of 1982, won it in 1983, and with Rupert Owen-Browne brought the doubles championship back to Tonbridge. Owen-Browne reached five Public Schools finals and won four of them, including the Foster Cup in 1984 and the doubles championship in 1985 partnered by Simon Davies.

Jonathan Longley, between 1984 and 1987, was the first and remains the only boy to win the main six Public Schools tournaments – the Under-15 and Under-16 singles and doubles, the Foster Cup (1985 and 1986), and the doubles championship (1986 and 1987) – eight titles and never a defeat at Queen's.

During the 1990s, Dan Cherry reached five national finals and won three of them, including the Public Schools doubles with Jamie Parker, who reached the second-pair final in his first year, having played Rackets for only two terms. Jamie Parker played in a further six national finals in his school career, winning five of the six majors and being unable

to compete in the sixth because of a school cricket tour.

Makey, a newcomer to Rackets in 1980, spent two years at Malvern learning from Ron Hughes – a master teacher with a master pupil. Rackets at Tonbridge pre-Makey had been in the hands of the Hull family since before the First World War, and that by extraordinary chance. James Hull was a friend of Walter Hawes of Wellington College, who introduced Hull's elder son, Charles, to the game and then took him on as his assistant.

After three years Charles Hull moved to Prince's Club, and in 1913 he accepted a post as squash professional on the Titanic. Hawes persuaded him not to go, and in May 1914 he was appointed professional at Tonbridge. A year later he joined the Army, and by then he had bullied his younger brother, Arthur, into assisting him. Charles lost a leg in the war, and Arthur took over as senior professional in 1920. He remained there for the next forty-eight years.

Jamie Parker (left) *reached seven schools finals at Queen's, winning five. He beat Ned Cazelet (Eton) to take the 1998 Foster Cup.*

Charles Swallow presents the 1998 Public Schools doubles trophies to Jamie Parker. He was partnered by Dan Cherry.

Tonbridge first entered a pair for the Public Schools championship in 1878, but failed to reach the final until John Thompson and Peter Pettman took them there in 1937, followed by Colin Cowdrey and John Campbell in 1951. The first Tonbridge victory came in 1957 from Miles Connell and Peter Rylands (who had won the Foster Cup in 1956).

Cowdrey had a distinguished, if brief, career in Rackets before cricket claimed him completely. He played first string for Oxford in 1952, 1953 and 1954, winning all his matches against Cambridge, and in 1952 – only one year after school – faced Geoffrey Atkins in the Amateur singles final. He three times helped Tonbridge win the Noel-Bruce Cup (1953,

1955 and 1957) in partnership with John Thompson, a player of exceptional skill.

Five times Amateur and once Open champion in the 1950s, Thompson was held in even greater awe for his performances on the doubles court. Playing with David Milford, he took the Amateur doubles ten times between 1948 and 1959, and then again with Tom Pugh in 1966. As well as his Noel-Bruce victories with Cowdrey, Thompson won it four times with Richard Gracey, thus getting the Tonbridge name engraved on the trophy seven times in nine years. Gracey then formed a stunning partnership with Martin Smith (another Amateur singles champion), winning the Old Boys' Cup every year from 1969 to 1974.

THE TUXEDO CLUB

THE OLDEST TENNIS COURT still in continuous use in the US, located at Tuxedo Park, New York State, was opened in 1899. It has the unusual feature of a grille that resembles a winning gallery, being covered with a net to which a bell is attached. The court is located in a magnificent building by the lake, not far from the main clubhouse. There is also a Rackets court, and ample changing accommodation. The club itself was founded in 1886, and is the first in the US to produce its own uniquely decorated racket, designed in green with gold club symbols and the year of origin.

Eustace Miles, the British Amateur champion, supervised the building of the court, and he persuaded Robert Moore to come over from England to take charge. Moore, who by this time had a large family, had to buy a pony and cart to provide transport to and from the village. He stayed at Tuxedo for twenty years, and takes much of the credit for teaching Rackets to Clarence Pell and Stanley Mortimer, who between them dominated the American game between 1915 and 1933.

The two professionals to give the longest service in the club's history are 'Bunny' Gannon from the New

Spike Willcocks holds the Tuxedo Gold Racquet 2000, after beating Mike Happell 6–2, 6–3, 6–5 in the final. Left to right: Tom Greevy (head professional), Harry McVickar (co-chairman of Court Tennis and Racquets committee), Spike Willcocks, Mike Happell, Philip R. Mengel (co-chairman of Court Tennis and Racquets committee and match referee).

Tennis professional Tom Greevy, here with Spike Willcocks, has been at Tuxedo Park for more than thirty years.

The front entrance to the Tennis court, the oldest in the US still in continuous use.

York Racquet Club (1922–59) and the present incumbent, Tom Greevy, who has been there since 1967. He has been very active in motivating old and new players and controlling the many tournaments held every year. In recent years he has initiated both a junior and a ladies' programme, the latter resulting in Tuxedo's first ladies' invitational event.

The principal competitions at the club are the Gold Racquets for both games. The prize in each case is a miniature gold racket, greatly coveted by the leading players, especially as a player who wins the trophy three times may retain it – provided he pays for a replacement. This condition has proved to be a serious deterrent, but apparently not for the first Tennis winner.

Charles Sands won that Gold Racquet tournament in 1903, 1904 and 1905, and away the prize went. It was not seen again for ninety years, when his heirs found it in the attic of his former house on Sand's Point, Long Island. They graciously returned the trophy to the club, where it holds a prime place in the trophy cabinet. Between 1989 and 1998, the prize was won five times each by Morris Clothier of the US and Nigel Pendrigh from Petworth.

Clarence Pell, whose name is now attached to the US Open Championship Rackets trophy, won Tuxedo's Gold Racquet every year from 1914 to 1927 except in 1924, when Stanley Mortimer beat him. Four times in the 1990s Pendrigh was the winner, with Guy Devereux taking it in 1998 and 1999.

Among other competitions are the Spittoon and Cuspidor Cups, which used to be consolation singles trophies for Rackets and Tennis, but are now given to the winners of a doubles competition. Less coveted is the 'Empty Helmet' award. This can be made at any time of the year and is given to a player who shows a lack of intelligence – one who forgets, for example, to take his bisque. More than fifty players are now actively involved in Tennis at Tuxedo, where national fixtures as well as domestic tournaments are frequently held.

INTERNATIONAL TENNIS CLUB
OF WASHINGTON

WHEN PRINCE'S COURT OPENED on 11 October 1997, it was the first Tennis court to be built in the US since Chicago's was completed in 1922. Three hundred friends of the game attended, including representatives of eight American and six British clubs, and the air of effortless grace that lay over the opening ceremony belied the ten-year struggle that had gone into the building of the court.

The driving force was Haven N.B. Pell, son of Clarence Pell, who won the US Amateur Rackets singles in 1958 and the doubles eight times, and who much later became an enthusiastic and highly competitive Tennis player. Haven Pell put together a group of Tennis-playing Washingtonians who spent three years planning and organizing the building of a court at a private school, before a last-minute demand scuttled the effort; and another three abortive years transferring the attempt to a small Washington college.

Their determination survived these disappointments, and the breakthrough came when it was decided to build the facility under the auspices of the United States Court Tennis Preservation Foundation, which is dedicated to developing players and introducing the game to a wider public.

'Court tennis in America was traditionally played in private, all-male, all-white clubs,' Pell said, 'and we wanted to broaden horizons. We specially wanted to stimulate interest among women and young players.'

An ideal site was found at the Regency Sport and Health Club in McLean, Virginia, six miles from Washington. The club closed one of its many indoor tennis courts to make room for Tennis. More than 200

The court's unique main wall is 18ft high and made of glass.

The view from the penthouse across Prince's court and beyond.

Situated six miles outside Washington, at McLean, Virginia, the court was opened in October 1997 and soon attracted visitors from the UK.

donations were received from across the Tennis-playing world, and the $650,000 facility was financed.

The organizing committee included Frederick H. Prince, without whose generous support the project would not have been possible, and the court soon became known as Prince's – a gesture also towards the famous Tennis and Racket clubs built in the Knightsbridge area of London in the nineteenth century. The unique feature of the new court is an eighteen-foot-high main wall made of plate glass, which gives spectators an unrivalled view of play – and a particularly thrilling one when the best of players are forcing off the wall at 100 m.p.h.

Prince's began with a membership of fifteen, but by the second season there were fifty and the club hosted the National 'C' and 'D' Championships. Students from St Albans and Potomac schools played regularly on weekday afternoons, and a firm core of women took up the game. In February 1999, the first Ambassadors' Cup was held there, with three of the world's top ten professionals in the field of eight. Mike Gooding, from the UK, beat Mark Devine (Aiken) in the final.

The first annual club dinner, in May, also formed a farewell party for Austin Snelgrove, who had come from Canford School, England, to be the club's first professional. He was succeeded by Tim Johnson, the lawn-tennis coach at St Albans school, who has generated great enthusiasm for the game among its students.

Leading young players include, most notably, Bradley Allen, who at the age of fifteen won the UK 16-and-under championship, and a year later the Under-18 – an amazing accomplishment for one who had taken up the game less than a year before his first tournament in Britain. The young man also won Prince's first club championship, beating in the semi-finals none other than Haven Pell, who counted it as vindication for the endless hours he spent working to bring Prince's off the drawing board.

'Had I known at the outset how hard it would be,' he said, 'I might never have started. But then I would never have seen the look of pride in the eyes of my father when he first saw the court. He was eighty-six,

Haven N.B. Pell (right) was the driving force behind the first Tennis court built in the US since 1922. At the opening he presented a memento to his father, former Rackets champion Clarry Pell, who died the next year.

in failing health, and had only seven months to live. I also would not have had the privilege of losing to a fifteen year old who has the potential to become one of America's greatest players.'

WELLINGTON COLLEGE

RACKETS AT WELLINGTON received an early boost when in 1867 Captain and Mrs Compton presented a challenge cup, to be contested annually. It was decided in 1870 that the winner of the cup should receive an additional prize of £2 – a rash decision that was swiftly rescinded, to be substituted by 'four dozen practising balls for the use of the two finalists before the Haileybury match'.

Wellington first competed in the Public Schools championship at Prince's Club in 1871, and first won the title in 1891. G.J. Mordaunt and R.H. Raphael, who had lost to Harrow the previous year, faced the redoubtable Foster brothers of Malvern in the final, H.K. and W.L., and beat them 4–2.

George Smale was the school's professional at the end of the century ('One of the greatest teachers of

Derek Barrett, the long-serving Wellington professional, seated between O.J. Rigby and M.H.L Griffith-Jones in the party that visited Detroit, Chicago and Montreal in 1998. Left to right: F.W.T. Beer, T.H.C. Burns, M.E.T. Briers, J.B. Lyon and C.M. Oliphant-Callum, the master-in-charge.

play,' said Eustace Miles of Smales) and he was succeeded in 1902 by the first of the great Hawes family, Walter. His extraordinary coaching ability led to championship wins in 1907 (again against Malvern, and another Foster brother), 1913, 1921 (with Lowther Lees in their pair, later to win the Amateur Tennis singles eight times) and 1926.

Left Colin Haycraft won the Public Schools Rackets championship in 1946, partnered by J.E.L. Ainslie. Scholarly publisher and witty raconteur, he became an enthusiastic Tennis player in the eighties.

Below Bob Mulliken, flanked by his 1980 Public Schools doubles championship winners, the brothers James and Andrew Mallinson.

In 1933 a bath with a geyser was installed at the court, the Rackets Book recording that 'Visitors may now soak their tired limbs in a tiled bathroom concealed behind a rubber curtain.' Only boys in the VIII were allowed to use it, however, and they had to supply their own towels. Three years later a new front wall was put in the court, the scaffolding standing in tubs filled with sand, and plasterers working continuously by the light of acetylene lamps. Walter Hawes, meanwhile, worked on re-surfacing the upper parts of the side walls.

The game continued to thrive during the war, and by 1944 there were fifty or sixty boys playing. Walter's son Ronnie returned from the war and took over from his father as Rackets professional, and immediately the school won the Public Schools doubles championship again, beating Harrow 4–1 in 1946. Ronnie's service to Wellington was as devoted and as skilled as his father's, and there was universal regret when he left for Eton in 1953, though not before he saw T.L. de Mesquita win the Foster Cup.

Peter Willey was the master-in-charge at the time, and reported the remark of a school governor – 'Glad to see you're taking over, Willey. Teach 'em how to stop hard balls – make 'em all the better at stopping hard bullets.'

In 1956, Wellington was fortunate to acquire the services of Jim Dear. The playing ability of this former world champion could not be doubted – and he held the British Professional championship from 1946 to 1974. He proved to be an admirable coach of teenagers, and did wonders in improving the standard of play at the school. G.B. Trentham won the Foster Cup in 1963, and C.N. Hurst-Brown in 1969.

Then Dear went to New York, and was followed at Wellington by Bob Mulliken from Dartmouth. He served Wellington splendidly, and was rewarded by the brothers Mallinson winning the Public Schools championship in 1980. The following year he had to retire, through ill-health, and his place was taken by Shannon Hazell, who was trained at Clifton and won the Under-24 singles in 1983–84. Later he won the Professional singles and challenged James Male for the world title in 1991.

By then he too had left for New York and was succeeded by Derek Barrett, then at Manchester. Chris Potter had two spells as master-in-charge, very successful and popular periods, and the atmosphere he engendered has been maintained by his successor, Charles Oliphant-Callum. Barrett was still there in 2000, and has seen the College win four championships and appear in twelve other finals. After Walter Hawes, he has become Wellington's second longest-serving professional.

WINCHESTER COLLEGE

THE MOST STARTLING ACHIEVEMENT in Winchester's 130 year Rackets history was to win the Public Schools doubles three years running twice in nine years. The first hat-trick (1943–45) inspired an Old Wykehamist, K.O. Hunter, to pay for lighting to be installed in the old court; the second (1949–51) set what was then a unique record, with Mike Coulman playing in all three triumphant pairs. A rare family double was pulled off too, with Giles Myrtle in the 1944 and 1945 pairs, and his brother Andrew playing in 1950 and in 1951, in which year they also beat Oxford and Cambridge in the same week.

Only Eton and Harrow have a better record in the game than Winchester, who reached the championship finals in 1874 and 1875 and first won it in 1904, with Clarence Bruce (later Lord Aberdare) as first string. The first court at the school was built in 1871 at the expense of the headmaster, the Rev. George Ridding. A second court was added in 1910, both of them built under Joseph Bickley's supervision, but the new one had to be re-surfaced in 1929 and had a new front wall in 1968. Lighting was installed in 1934.

Some of Winchester's success in Rackets must be ascribed to a series of outstanding masters-in-charge and professionals. The school was criticized in 1875, despite their successes, for being the only Rackets-playing school that did not employ a professional. They sent for Frederick Andre, an odd character intriguingly described by A.N. Palmer in his *Winchester 1900–1905*:

> *Always on the move, always with a grievance, always combining gloom and humour, and given to muttering devastating asides concerning even the most distinguished of our visitors, Andre was a typical Cockney. He was short and spare of figure; his face, with its scrubby dark moustache, expressed absolutely nothing but disillusionment and a determination not to be optimistic. His progress was a perpetual jog-trot. Even in the street he trotted, in the court he kept up a continuous shuttle, but always in the right direction, so that he rarely had to hurry, while as for running – I don't suppose he stretched his legs once a fortnight. If your ears were sharp enough to catch, if you had the key to his rapid, unending Cockney mumblings, he was an admirable teacher. But better still than his precept was his practice. He was a beautiful player with a model style, free and compact, graceful and devoid of flourish.*

Longest serving of all the Winchester professionals was Guy Padwick, who was Jim Crosby's assistant from 1925 to 1939, and thereafter senior professional until 1975. He coached nine winning pairs during his fifty years, including all the hat-trick victors, three winners of the Public Schools singles in five post-war years, and the triumphant championship outsiders of 1953. That

Julian Faber (right) and Anthony Kingsley, winners of the Public Schools championship of 1935.

Peter Ashford, head professional at Winchester for twenty-five years, with Nick Hall (left) and Matthew Segal, 1992 Public Schools *championship winners.*

was when the unseeded partnership of Richard Whatmore and David Lowe beat the holders, Rugby, in the first round and Radley, with Dexter and Dipple, in the final.

The Nawab of Pataudi played in the finals of 1958, losing to the powerful Etonian pair of James Leonard and David Norman, and 1959, when he and Christopher Snell beat Eton 4–3. And then, still in Padwick's time, along came Howard Angus.

Though he won the Foster Cup in 1962, Angus was never in a championship-winning pair at Winchester, and indeed never dominated the world of Rackets as he did, for so many years, the world of Tennis. Angus won the Amateur Tennis singles in 1966, the year he left Cambridge, and won it for another fourteen consecutive years. In those fifteen finals, he conceded only six sets.

Alan Lovell took the title from him in 1981, but Angus regained it – for the last time – in 1982. Accompanied by Lovell and, for eight years, by Peter Seabrook, Angus led the Old Wykehamists to eleven successive Henry Leaf Cups from 1974. He had already had a major hand in four other Leaf wins while Lovell was still at school. Lovell and Seabrook, incidentally, won the Public Schools Rackets championship for Winchester in 1972, without conceding a single game.

Meanwhile, at an even higher level of play, Angus held the British Open Tennis singles from 1970 to 1979, and was the world champion from 1976 until Chris Ronaldson beat him in 1981.

Various fates conspired to frustrate Angus in his attempt to emulate Peter Latham and become only the second player to hold the world championships of Rackets and Tennis at the same time. He was the Amateur singles champion of Rackets from 1972 to 1975, and won the British Open six times between 1971 and 1978. But though he played in four world championship finals against Willie Surtees, his only win was in 1973, before he held the Tennis title.

For the past twenty-five years, Peter Ashford has been head professional at the College. In that time Winchester has won all the available cups except the Foster – last brought home by Angus, and before him by M.D. Scott (1951), Andrew Myrtle (1950) and J.D. Thornton (1947). Ashford nursed the rise of an exceptional pair of players in Nick Hall and Matthew Segal, who won the Public Schools doubles in 1992, the colts doubles in 1990, and the junior colts doubles in 1988. Hall beat Segal both for the colts and junior colts singles titles. Between 1990 and 1999,

Alan Lovell who won the Public Schools Rackets doubles with Peter Seabrook and later won the Amateur Tennis singles.

Winchester reached the semi-finals of the doubles championship five times.

The out-of-school evening club at Winchester has been operating with considerable success for nearly thirty years. The Wykeham Rackets Club was formed in 1971 to encourage Old Wykehamists and others in the locality to play the game. They met on a Wednesday; in 1974 the Monday Club grew from them, the first real town rather than old boys club to be so formed.

Numbers fluctuate, students coming and going from Southampton University, but the regular membership has been consistent and long-lasting, and often has the benefit of Peter Ashford's participation. In 1995 and in 1999 the Monday Club won Division II of the national Henderson League, and members regularly attend other club competitions. A Rackets tour to the US was much enjoyed in 1996, visiting Detroit, Philadelphia, Tuxedo Park and New York.

DISUSED COURTS

Rackets and Tennis courts that have fallen into disuse, and even disappeared altogether, nevertheless deserve their place in the history of the games.

BUCKHURST

Believed to be the only private Rackets court in existence, though no longer in use, it was built in 1857 on the estate of Earl de la Warr in East Sussex. A brass plate in the gallery notes that it commemorates the capture of Sebastopol in the Crimean War. It was built by Colonel Lord West, who commanded the 21st Royal North British Fusiliers during the siege and in 1869 succeeded his father as sixth earl.

During the Second World War it was requisitioned by the Army, and later used for storing logs. It was restored in 1963 and a match was played by Cosmo Crawley, Julian Faber, Bimby Holt and Charles Swallow.

UNIVERSITY CLUB OF CHICAGO

When the club moved in 1909, it was to a building that contained two Rackets courts. That year Harold F. McCormick, a member of the club, won the US Amateur singles, and he later donated a court to the University. It was used by scientists in the Second World War to house an atomic reactor and, incorrectly, came to be known as the 'Atomic Squash Court'.

Professionals were engaged throughout the club's history, but in 1984 the court was converted to a fitness centre, and in 1994 four squash courts were built.

DARTMOUTH, ROYAL NAVAL COLLEGE

Most Rackets courts in naval establishments were closed or converted to squash courts by the end of the First World War. The exceptions were those in Malta (destroyed in the Second World War) and the two at Dartmouth. A Royal Navy singles championship was played there between 1919 and 1939, and briefly at Queen's Club after the war. The game was revived at Dartmouth in the mid-1950s and Bob Mulliken was appointed professional in 1957 but interest waned when he left for Wellington in 1969. One court was used for badminton.

UNIVERSITY CLUB OF DETROIT

A Rackets court was built for the club in 1931 and remained in excellent condition for forty-five years. The number of players declined, and in the late seventies it was converted for badminton, basketball, volleyball and a game called pickleball.

EASTON NESTON

The longest Tennis court in England was built on Sir Thomas Fermor-Hesketh's estate in Northamptonshire in 1887, on the foundations of one dating back to the early seventeenth century. The game could be watched from the comfort of the adjoining smoking room, and the penthouse gallery was well furnished with armchairs, bookcases and the like.

Sir Thomas's son, the first Baron Hesketh, converted the court so that it could be used for the Victorian sport of Sphairistike, which came to be known as Sticky and gave way to lawn tennis as we know it. Hesketh removed the penthouses and the tambour, and badminton was later played on it.

GIBRALTAR

The Rackets court on the Rock, built about 1890, was used by members of the garrison. Between the wars, the Royal Navy used it for an annual match between the Mediterranean and Atlantic Fleets. W.H. Hoare was the professional there for more than forty years but interest fell away after the Second World War. The court was restored later and staged European Open championships in 1978 and 1979, won by Willie Boone the first year and John Prenn the next. The court has deteriorated since the British Army garrison left the Rock.

LAMBAY ISLAND

This open Tennis court was built by Cecil Baring, later the third Baron Revelstoke, off the coast of Ireland in 1922. Rainwater was 'squeegeed' into the ball trough, which served as a drain leading to the sea. The other main hazard was seagull droppings. Floor and walls were whitish, and the balls were coloured dark green to make them visible.

The court, which still stands, has a penthouse and galleries on both sides, that on the main wall occupying about half the length of the court and having the shape of a long bay window.

The walls with which the bay ends are angled, and from about chase three in the middle of the court, it was possible to strike the ball on to the main wall above the penthouse so that it rebounded into the winning gallery opposite. The obstacle of that penthouse greatly restricted boasting against the main wall, off which it was almost impossible to play a stroke into the dedans.

ROSSALL SCHOOL

Two Rackets courts were built here as part of a sports complex opened in 1883 during the headmastership of the Rev. H.A. James, who had come from Marlborough in 1875. In 1904, for the first and last time, a pair represented the school at Queen's Club.

The courts deteriorated under the weather, maintenance costs were too high, and the game faded out in 1923. Squash courts now occupy the space.

STRATFIELD SAYE HOUSE

The first Duke of Wellington built a Tennis court for his two sons in 1830 on the site of Lord Rivers' riding school in the north of Hampshire. The Duke's butler,

Phillips, became the professional. The Duke later built a court at Cambridge, and Phillips' son John became the professional there.

The Stratfield Saye court fell into disrepair early in the twentieth century. The seventh Duke demolished it but the walls still stand.

SUN COURT, TROON

This is the unhappiest of stories of a lost Tennis court. Built on a private estate in 1905, it fell into disrepair in the 1930s and formed part of a naval gunnery school during the war. Restoration on an historic scale took place after the house (by then a hotel) was bought by Alistair and Jill Breckenridge, and it re-opened for Tennis in October 1969.

Chris Ronaldson arrived from Melbourne as the professional (succeeded by Walter Gregg and then Mike Gooding), and there was a solid fixture list. The first Scottish Open was held there in 1980, and again in 1981, 1984 and 1988.

Meanwhile the hotel had been sold for conversion to a nursing home, with a specific clause in the missives of sale that Tennis was to continue as long as there was reasonable demand. This did not satisfy a small group of players, who succeeded in getting all the buildings on the site listed.

Tennis was played until early 1991, but the listing severely hampered the new owner's plans for the site. When attempts to have the listing lifted failed, the owner barred entry to the court. It stands empty.

WESTMINSTER SCHOOL

Before the end of the eighteenth century, the school's Little Dean's Yard had been cleared, and a primitive form of Rackets developed against the blank wall of the dormitory. It was played with a long-handled wooden bat, and probably resembled the game played in the Fleet prison.

A science block was built in 1903–05 which contained a Rackets court, and in 1908 Westminster entered a pair for the Public Schools championship. The game survived through the First World War, and another pair contested the championship in 1920, but they seem to have been the last to represent the school. By 1934, fives courts occupied the Rackets space.

THE TENNIS AND RACKETS ASSOCIATION

THE INCREASE in Tennis and Rackets activity over the last twenty years has laid a growing burden on the governing body of both games – the Tennis and Rackets Association.

Dick Bridgeman was chairman from 1979 until his untimely death in 1982. He was a prime mover in the drive to develop both games after the war and his efforts were enormously successful. He instituted the Young Professionals Fund in 1959 and later the Tennis and Rackets Charitable Trust which now bears his name. When the second Rackets court was restored at the Queen's Club in 1988, it was named the Bridgeman Court in his memory. For over twenty-five years he was ably supported by Richard Greenwood who, at various times, was joint honorary secretary, honorary treasurer and honorary membership secretary. Richard Greenwood was given a special award in 1991 for his invaluable voluntary contribution to the Tennis and Rackets Association.

For many years Nicholas Smith has acted as honorary secretary of the Trust, which has paid out some £200,000 to thirty-two different clubs and educational establishments to help finance the training of Tennis and Rackets professionals and the restoration or building of courts. His behind-the-scenes activity, as well as his legal advice, has been of great service.

Dick Bridgeman was a difficult act to follow but David Norman's energy and experience proved equal to the task. He recruited the indefatigable Bill Stephens as full-time secretary with an office at the Queen's Club, and set in train a thorough review of the Association's affairs. His dynamism, hard work and perseverance led to a growth in the membership, an increase in the number of competitions and the further development of both games. He oversaw the raising of over £350,000 which enabled the Queen's Club to rebuild the second Rackets court, refurbish both Tennis courts, establish a Tennis and Rackets museum, refurbish the dedans and provide new rooms for the professionals. This resulted in a new fifty-year agreement between the Tennis and Rackets Association and the Queen's Club regarding the use of these outstanding Rackets and Tennis facilities. Charles Wade was commissioned to report on all aspects of the Tennis and Rackets Association and a fundamental restructuring of the Association followed, with redefined roles for the Council and two games committees under the co-ordination of a chief executive. The Association's rules were re-written with four members of the Council and six members of each games committee directly elected by the members.

David Norman appointed Brigadier Andrew Myrtle as chief executive and secretary in 1989. Brigadier Myrtle's experience in the army, his knowledge of both games, his capacity for hard work and his popularity with everyone, players and spectators, made him the ideal person for the post. It was not long before he took over as membership secretary and treasurer from Richard Greenwood. Bill Stephens continued to edit the Annual Report and Newsletter until 1995 when Brian Dowling undertook the task; Dudley McDonald was director of development and of the Young Professionals Fund until handing over to Andrew Myrtle in 1992.

Shortly after the reorganization, the Association approached the Sports Council with a four-year plan for the development of both games. In the event, two four-year plans were accepted, for 1994–98 and 1998–2002, and the Sports Council agreed annual grants of between £10,000 and £25,000, totalling some £115,000 over the eight years. The grants enabled the Tennis and Rackets Association to employ a Tennis Court Development Officer (Adrian Snow) and a Training Officer (Henry Macintosh). Adrian Snow, with the aid of a brochure he has produced on Building Real Tennis Courts, has about twenty potential developers on his books. Henry Macintosh has the task of overseeing the training of the Tennis professionals in conjunction with the Real Tennis Professionals Association (RTPA). The grants also enabled the Tennis and Rackets Association to encourage more young Tennis players and to employ a part-time membership secretary.

In March 1997, after a most successful tenure as chairman, David Norman handed over to Charles Swallow, a world-class Rackets player, a good Tennis player and an experienced administrator.

Following on the Wade report, the institution of two main games committees has proved a success, with outstanding contributions from their chairmen. From 1979 to 1992, Alan Lovell was a most hard-working chairman of the Tennis committee, showing foresight and providing inspired leadership during his thirteen years in the post. Then Colin Dean gave six years of selfless service, and was followed in 1998 by Julian Snow.

Garth Milne succeeded Howard Angus as chairman of the Rackets committee in 1979, followed in 1983 by Paul Nicholls. In 1988, Garth Milne returned as joint chairman with Charles Hue Williams; in 1990, Charles Hue Williams was sole chairman and he made a significant contribution during his total of twelve years of office. Sir Mervyn Dunnington-Jefferson Bt took over in 2000. The Association is indebted, not only to the chairmen and members of these two committees but also to those who serve on the various sub-committees.

After serving with distinction for twelve years, Chief Executive Andrew Myrtle retired in January 2001. James Wyatt was selected to take his place and is proving a most able successor.

The Real Tennis Professionals Association was formed in 1975 with Peter Dawes as its chairman; he remained in that post for twenty-five years, giving devoted service, and, as chairman, sitting on the Tennis committee and on the Council. He was succeeded by Jonathan Howell in 2000. The Professional Rackets Association (PRA) was formed in 1919. Roger Crosby was chairman from 1981 to 1996, sitting on the Rackets committee and on the Council, as does his successor David Makey.

SPONSORS

The Tennis and Rackets Association is immensely grateful to its sponsors. Without their generous help, there would be nothing like the increase in the popularity of both games. The first major sponsor of Tennis was Unigate who were involved for three years from 1979. They were succeeded in 1982 by George Wimpey PLC, thanks to the chairman Clifford Chetwood (now Sir Clifford). A very keen Tennis player, he is the president of the Hampton Court club. Wimpey were most generous in their sponsorship and the increased funds available for the top competitions resulted in a significant improvement in the standard of play. For four years during the Wimpey sponsorship Tennis was also sponsored by Rank Xerox, thanks to chairman Sir Derek Hornby.

From 1994 to the present day, the British Land Company PLC have taken over from George Wimpey as the major sponsor of Tennis. They have been enormously supportive thanks to the personal interest of their energetic chairman, John Ritblat, a keen player of both Tennis and Rackets. A number of specific events have been sponsored by individual firms who deserve our sincere thanks.

Rackets has been equally fortunate in receiving the generous support of a number of sponsors and they are detailed on page 162.

THE PRESS

It is not easy to obtain good coverage in the national press for minority sports and credit should be given to those who have managed to persuade editors to give space to Tennis and Rackets. Christina Wood and her husband, Lainson Wood, reported on both games for the *Daily Telegraph*. After his death in 1957, Christina Wood continued to cover both games, except for a short period in the sixties when Tony Winlaw reported on Rackets. On her death in 1981 Rob McLean took over for six years until Norman Rosser became the Rackets correspondent; Tennis was covered by Sally Jones and a number of freelance journalists. Christina Wood's opposite number on *The Times* was Roy McKelvie; Bill Stephens took over from him from 1983 to 1990.

On the Rackets front, John Thompson made considerable contributions to *Country Life* in particular until he retired in the mid nineties and was succeeded by Norman Rosser. David Frost wrote for the *Guardian* over many years as did Richard Cooper for the *Observer*. Norman Rosser has continued to report on Rackets in the *Daily Telegraph*.

Sally Jones was the Tennis and Rackets correspondent of *The Times* for several years. She is now employed by the Tennis and Rackets Association but continues to write for *The Times* and some journals. David Hunn has written outstanding features on Tennis and Rackets in *The Sunday Times* and *Observer*. Sara Metherell writes features on Tennis for *Country Life*.

On television, a one-hour programme devoted to Tennis was broadcast on Channel Four in 1992; and three one-hour programmes were presented by the Earl of Wessex for Ardent Productions in 1995. The Earl of Wessex has been a strong supporter of major Tennis events. He is a keen player and is an honorary member of the Tennis and Rackets Association.

CHAMPIONSHIP
RECORDS

TENNIS

	Winner	Runner-up	Score	Venue
1740	Clergé			
1765	Raymond Masson			
1785	Joseph Barcellon			
1816	Marchisio	Philip Cox	James Street	
1819	Philip Cox	Amédée Charrier	James Street	
1829	Edmond Barre	Philip Cox	James Street	
1862	Edmund Tompkins	Edmond Barre	6–4 (retired)	James Street
1871	Edmund Tompkins	*resigned*		
	George Lambert	*claimed*		
1885	Tom Pettitt	George Lambert	7–5	Hampton Court
1890	Tom Pettitt	Charles Saunders	7–5	St Stephen's Green, Dublin
1890	Charles Saunders	*claimed*		
1895	Peter Latham	Charles Saunders	7–2	Brighton
1898	Peter Latham	Tom Pettitt	7–0	Brighton
1904	Peter Latham	Cecil Fairs	7–5	Brighton
1905	Cecil Fairs	Peter Latham	5–1	Queen's & Prince's
1906	Cecil Fairs	Ferdinand Garcin	7–4	Brighton
1907	Peter Latham	Cecil Fairs	7–3	Brighton
1908	Peter Latham	*resigned*		
	Cecil Fairs	*claimed*		
	Cecil Fairs	Edward Johnson	7–2	Brighton
1910	Cecil Fairs	Fred Covey	7–6	Brighton
1912	Fred Covey	Cecil Fairs	7–3	Prince's
1914	Jay Gould	Fred Covey	7–1	Philadelphia
1916	Jay Gould	*resigned*		
	Fred Covey	*claimed*		
1922	Fred Covey	Walter Kinsella	7–3	Prince's
1923	Fred Covey	Walter Kinsella	7–3	Prince's
1927	Fred Covey	Pierre Etchebaster	7–4	Prince's
1928	Pierre Etchebaster	Fred Covey	7–3	Prince's
1930	Pierre Etchebaster	Walter Kinsella	7–1	Prince's
1937	Pierre Etchebaster	Ogden Phipps	3–1 (retired)	Tuxedo
1948	Pierre Etchebaster	Ogden Phipps	7–2	New York
1948	Pierre Etchebaster	J.P. Dear	7–4	New York
1949	Pierre Etchebaster	Ogden Phipps	7–1	New York
1950	Pierre Etchebaste	Alastair Martin	7–0	New York
1952	Pierre Etchebaster	Alastair Martin	7–2	New York
1955	Jim Dear	Jack Johnson	11–10	New York & Queen's
1957	Jack Johnson	Jim Dear	7–3	Queen's
1959	Northrup Knox	Jack Johnson	7–2	New York
1966	Northrup Knox	Ronald Hughes	7–0	New York
1968	Northrup Knox	Pete Bostwick	7–3	New York
1969	Pete Bostwick	Frank Willis	11–8	New York & Manchester

table continues

	Winner	Runner-up	Score	Venue
1970	Pete Bostwick	Jimmy Bostwick	7–1	New York
1972	Jimmy Bostwick	Pete Bostwick	7–2	New York
1974	Jimmy Bostwick	Howard Angus	7–5	New York
1976	Howard Angus	Gene Scott	11–4	New York & Queen's
1977	Howard Angus	Gene Scott	7–2	Hampton Court
1979	Howard Angus	Chris Ronaldson	7–0	Hampton Court
1981	Chris Ronaldson	Howard Angus	6–1 (retired)	Queen's
1983	Chris Ronaldson	Wayne Davies	7–4	Hampton Court
1985	Chris Ronaldson	Wayne Davies	7–1	Queen's
1987	Wayne Davies	Chris Ronaldson	7–4	Queen's
1988	Wayne Davies	Lachlan Deuchar	7–1	New York
1991	Wayne Davies	Lachlan Deuchar	7–4	New York
1993	Wayne Davies	Lachlan Deuchar	7–6	New York
1994	Robert Fahey	Wayne Davies	9–5	Hobart & New York
1995	Robert Fahey	Wayne Davies	6–2 (retired)	Hobart
1996	Robert Fahey	Wayne Davies	7–1	Melbourne
1998	Robert Fahey	Julian Snow	7–4	Melbourne
2000	Robert Fahey	Wayne Davies	7–0	Hobart

BATHURST CUP

International Competition

In Paris eight game sets were played up to 1927

	Winner	Runner-up	Score	Venue		Winner	Runner-up	Score	Venue
1922	Great Britain	France	5–0	Queen's	1951	Great Britain	France	4–1	Paris
1923	USA	France	3–0	Paris	1954	Great Britain	France	3–0	Bordeaux
	Great Britain	USA	3–2	Paris	1955	Great Britain	USA	4–1	Queen's
1924	USA	Great Britain	3–1	Queen's		Great Britain	Australia	3–0	Queen's
1925	Great Britain	France	5–0	Paris	1957	Great Britain	France	5–0	Paris
1926	USA	France	3–0	Prince's	1958	USA	Great Britain	3–0	Queen's
1927	USA	France	3–1	Paris	1960	USA	Great Britain	3–2	Queen's
1928	USA	France	3–0	Queen's	1962	Great Britain	France	4–1	Paris
	Great Britain	USA	3–0	Queen's	1966	USA	France	5–0	Paris
1929	Great Britain	France	3–0	Paris	1969	Great Britain	Australia	4–0	Melbourne
1930	Great Britain	USA	5–0	Queen's		USA	Great Britain	3–2	Tuxedo and New York
1931	USA	France	3–1	Paris					
	Great Britain	USA	3–1	Paris	1975	Great Britain	Australia	5–0	Melbourne
1932	Great Britain	USA	3–0	Queen's		Great Britain	USA	5–0	Melbourne
1933	USA	France	3–2	Paris	1978	Great Britain	France	4–1	Paris
	Great Britain	USA	3–0	Paris		USA	Australia	5–0	Paris
1934	France	USA	3–2	Queen's		Great Britain	USA	3–2	Paris
	Great Britain	France	3–0	Queen's	1980	Great Britain	France	5–0	Lord's
1937	Great Britain	France	4–0	Paris	1982	Australia	USA	3–2	Melbourne
1938	Great Britain	France	3–0	Queen's		Australia	GB	4–1	Melbourne
1939	Great Britain	France	5–0	Paris	1983	Great Britain	France	5–0	Bordeaux
1947	Great Britain	France	3–2	Paris		Great Britain	Australia	4–1	Bordeaux
1948	USA	France	5–0	Queen's	1984	Australia	USA	3–2	Newport Rhode Island
1949	USA	France	3–2	Paris					
	USA	Great Britain	3–2	Paris		Great Britain	Australia	4–1	Newport Rhode Island
1950	Great Britain	France	5–0	Queen's					
	Great Britain	USA	3–1	Queen's					*table continues*

	Winner	Runner-up	Score	Venue		Winner	Runner-up	Score	Venue
1985	Australia	USA	3–0	Hobart Tasmania	1991	Australia	France	3–2	Melbourne
	Great Britain	Australia	4–1	Hobart Tasmania		Great Britain	USA	5–0	Melbourne
1986	Great Britain	France	5–0	Queen's		Great Britain	Australia	4–1	Melbourne
	USA	Australia	4–1	Queen's	1992	Australia	France	3–2	Bordeaux
	Great Britain	USA	3–1	Queen's		Great Britain	Australia	5–0	Bordeaux
1987	Australia	France	4–1	Paris	1994	USA	France	3–0	Newport
	Great Britain	Australia	5–0	Paris		Great Britain	USA	3–2	Newport
1988	Australia	USA	5–0	Ballarat	1996	Australia	France	5–0	Leamington
	Great Britain	Australia	3–2	Ballerat		Great Britain	USA	5–0	Leamington
1989	Great Britain	France	5–0	Philadelphia		Great Britain	Australia	5–0	Leamington
	USA	Australia	3–2	Philadelphia	1999	Australia	France	5–0	Hobart
	Great Britain	USA	3–2	Philadelphia		Great Britain	USA	4–1	Hobart
1990	Australia	France	3–2	Queen's		Great Britain	Australia	3–2	Hobart
	Great Britain	Australia	5–0	Queen's	2000	Great Britain	France	4–1	Paris
						Australia	USA	5–0	Paris
						Great Britain	Australia	4–1	Paris

UNITED KINGDOM

THE PRINCE'S CLUB SHIELD
For the Open Championship (Challenge)

	Winner	Runner-up	
1931	E.M. Baerlein	W.A. Groom	3–2
1931	E. Ratcliff	E.J.G. Johnson	3–1
1932	W.A. Groom	E. Ratcliff	7–1
1934	L. Lees	W.A. Groom	7–1
1935	L. Lees	W.A. Groom	7–2
1938	J.P. Dear	L. Lees	5–1
1950	R. Hughs	H.D. Johns	5–3
1951	J.P. Dear	R. Hughes	
1952	R. Hughes	H.D. Johns	5–3
1662	J.P. Dear resigned		
1962	R. Hughes	D.J. Warburg	5–1
1967	F. Willis	R. Hughes	4–3 (retd)
1968	F. Willis	H.R. Angus	5–2
1970	H.R. Angus	F. Willis	5–2
1972	H.R. Angus	F. Willis	7–5
1975	H.R. Angus	F. Willis	7–6
1976	H.R. Angus	F. Willis	7–2
1979	H.R. Angus	C.J. Ronaldson	7–0*

*H.R. Angus beat C.J. Ronaldson in a combined challenge for the British Open and world championships. He relinquished the Open Championship so that it could become an annual event.

THE OPEN SINGLES CHAMPIONSHIP
(Annual)

	Winner	Runner-up	
1979	H.R. Angus	C.J. Ronaldson	3–0
1980	C.J. Ronaldson	A.C. Lovell	3–0
1981	C.J. Ronaldson	W.F. Davies	3–2
1982	C.J. Ronaldson	G.J. Hyland	3–2
1983	C.J. Ronaldson	L. Deuchar	3–0
1984	C.J. Ronaldson	W.F. Davies	3–2
1985	C.J. Ronaldson	W.F. Davies	3–2
1986	L. Deuchar	C.J. Ronaldson	3–1
1987	L. Deuchar	W.F. Davies	3–2
1988	L. Deuchar	C.J. Ronaldson	3–0
1989	L. Deuchar	C.J. Ronaldson	3–0
1990	L. Deuchar	J.P. Snow	3–0
1991	L. Deuchar	R.L. Fahey	3–2
1992	J.P. Snow	C.J. Bray	3–0
1993	J.P. Snow	R.L. Fahey (retd)	0–1
1994	J.P. Snow	L. Deuchar	3–1
1995	R.L. Fahey	L. Deuchar	3–0
1996	M.H.J. Gooding	L. Deuchar	3–1
1997	C.J. Bray	R.L. Fahey	3–0
1998	J.P. Snow	S. Virgona	3–2
1999	J.S. Male	M.H.J. Gooding	3–1
2000	R.L. Fahey	C.J. Bray	3–0

OPEN DOUBLES CHAMPIONSHIP

	Winners	Runners-up			Winners	Runners-up	
1971	R. Hughes and N.A.R. Cripps	H.R. Angus and N.W. Smith	3–2	1986	W.F. Davies and L. Deuchar	C.J. Ronaldson and M.F. Dean	3–1
1972	F. Willis and C. Ennis	C.J. Swallow and N.A.R. Cripps	3–0	1987	W.F. Davies and L. Deuchar	N.A.R. Cripps and P.G. Tabley	3–1
1973	C.J. Swallow and N.A.R. Cripps	F. Willis and C. Ennis	3–0	1988	W.F. Davies and L. Deuchar	J.B.K. Howell and K. Sheldon	3–0
1974	C.J. Swallow and N.A.R. Cripps	F. Willis and C. Ennis	3–0	1989	W.F. Davies and L. Deuchar	J.B.K. Howell and K.Sheldon	3–0
1975	C.J. Swallow and N.A.R. Cripps	H.R. Angus and D.J. Warburg	3–2	1990	W.F. Davies and L. Deucher	R.L. Fahey and A.P. Meares	3–0
1976	F. Willis and D.W. Cull	C. Ennis and M.F. Dean	3–1	1991	C.J. Bray and M.H.J. Gooding	L. Deuchar and P.G. Tabley	3–2
1977 April	A.C. Lovell and N.A.R. Cripps	F. Willis and D.W. Cull	3–1	1992	L. Deuchar and W.F. Davies	F.J. Filippelli and J.S. Male	w/o
Dec	A.C. Lovell and N.A.R. Cripps	F. Willis and D.W. Cull	3–0	1993	C.J. Bray and M.H.J. Gooding	J.P. Snow and N. Wood	3–0
1978	A.C. Lovell and N.A.R. Cripps	C.J. Ronaldson and M.F. Dean	3–0	1994	C.J. Bray and M.H.J. Gooding	W.F. Davies and L. Deuchar	3–0
1979	A.C. Lovell and N.A.R. Cripps	C.J. Ronaldson and M.F. Dean	3–0	1995	R.L. Fahey and F.J. Filippelli	C.J. Bray M.H.J. Gooding	3–2
1980	A.C. Lovell and N.A.R. Cripps	B. Toates and F. Willis	3–0	1996	C.J. Bray and M.J. Happell	L. Deuchar and M.H.J. Gooding	3–2
1981	C.J. Ronaldson and M.F. Dean	W.F. Davies and L. Deuchar	3–2	1997	J.S. Male and J.P. Snow	R.L. Fahey and M.H.J. Gooding	3–0
1982	A.C. Lovell and N.A.R. Cripps	C.J. Ronaldson and M.F. Dean	3–0	1998	J.S. Male and J.P. Snow	R.G.A. Gunn and S. Virgona	3–0
1983	C.J. Ronaldson and M.F. Dean	C.J. Lumley and L. Deuchar	3–1	1999	R.G.A. Gunn and S. Virgona	J.P. Snow and J.S. Male	3–1
1984	L. Deuchar and W.F. Davies	C.J. Ronaldson and M.F. Dean	3–1	2000	C.J. Bray and N. Wood	J.P. Snow and T. Chisholm	3–2
1985	L. Deuchar and W.F. Davies	C.J. Ronaldson and M.F. Dean	3–0				

OPEN INVITATION TOURNAMENT

	Winner	Runner-up	
1965	R. Hughes	J.P. Dear	3–0
1966	F. Willis	N.A.R. Cripps	3–0
1967	F. Willis	G.W.T. Atkins	3–1
1968	H.R. Angus	F. Willis	3–2
1969	F. Willis	H.R. Angus	3–2
1970			
Jan	H.R. Angus	F. Willis	3–1
Nov	F. Willis	D.W. Cull	3–1
1971	N.A.R. Cripps	F. Willis	3–1
1972	F. Willis	N.A.R. Cripps	3–0
1973	N.A.R. Cripps	F. Willis	3–1
1974	H.R. Angus	N.A.R. Cripps	3–2
1975	C. Ennis	N.A.R. Cripps	3–2
1976	H.R. Angus	N.A.R. Cripps	3–2
1977	H.R. Angus	N.A.R. Cripps	3–0
1978	C.J. Ronaldson	H.R. Angus	3–2

AMATEUR SINGLES CHAMPIONSHIP

Queen's Club Cup

Championship of Queen's Club 1888, Amateur championship since 1889
Played at Manchester 1922, 1926, 1931, 1947, 1951, 1964; Lord's 1946, 1958

	Winner	Runner-up			Winner	Runner-up	
1888	J.M. Heathcote	Sir E. Grey	3–1	1938	Lord Aberdare	W.M. Ross-Skinner	3–0
1889	Sir E. Grey	E.B.C. Curtis	3–1	1939	W.D. Macpherson	L. Lees	3–1
1890	E.B.C. Curtis	Sir E. Grey	3–1	1946	L. Lees	W.D. Macpherson	3–1
1891	Sir E. Grey	Lord Windsor	scratched	1947	Lord Cullen	P. Kershaw	3–0
1892	H.E. Crawley	Sir E. Grey	3–2	1948	P. Kershaw	L. Lees	3–0
1893	H.E. Crawley	Sir E. Grey	3–2	1949	O. Phipps (USA)	W.D. Macpherson	3–0
1894	H.E. Crawley	Sir E. Grey	3–2	1950	A.B. Martin (USA)	W.D. Macpherson	3–1
1895	Sir E. Grey	H.E. Crawley	3–2	1951	P. Kershaw	D.J. Warburg	3–0
1895	Sir E. Grey	H.E. Crawley	3–0	1952	Lord Cullen	R.C. Riseley	3–2
1896	Sir E. Grey	H.E. Crawley	3–2	1953	Hon. M.G.L. Bruce	P. Kershaw	3–0
1897	J.B. Gribble	H.E. Crawley	3–1	1954	Hon. M.G.L. Bruce	P. Kershaw	3–2
1898	Sir E. Grey	H.E. Crawley	3–0	1955	R.C. Riseley	P. Kershaw	3–1
1899	E.H. Miles	J.B. Gribble	3–1	1956	Hon. M.G.L. Bruce	D.J. Warburg	3–0
1900	E.H. Miles	J.B. Gribble	3–0	1957	Hon. M.G.L. Bruce	D.J. Warburg	3–2
1901	E.H. Miles	J.B. Gribble	3–0	1958	N.R. Knox (USA)	Lord Aberdare	3–0
1902	E.H. Miles	J.B. Gribble	3–0	1959	D.J. Warburg	J.D. Whatman	3–2
1903	E.H. Miles	V.H. Pennell (retd)	2–0	1960	G.W.T. Atkins	D.J. Warburg	3–1
1904	V.H. Pennell	E.H. Miles	3–2	1961	D.J. Warburg	G.W.T. Atkins	3–0
1905	E.H. Miles	V.H. Pennell	3–0	1962	G.W.T. Atkins	D.J. Warburg	3–0
1906	E.H. Miles	Jay Gould (USA)	3–1	1963	G.W.T. Atkins	D.J. Warburg	3–1
1907	J. Gould (USA)	V.H. Pennell	3–0	1964	A.C.S. Tufton	D.J. Warburg	3–2
1908	J. Gould (USA)	E.H. Miles	3–1	1965	D.J. Warburg	A.C.S. Tufton	3–2
1909	E.H. Miles	Hon. N.S. Lytton	3–1	1966	H.R. Angus	D.J. Warburg	3–1
1910	E.H. Miles	Hon. N.S. Lytton	3–2	1967	H.R. Angus	D.J. Warburg	3–1
1911	Hon. N.S. Lytton	E.H. Miles	3–1	1968	H.R. Angus	D.J. Warburg	3–0
1912	E.M. Baerlein	Hon. N.S. Lytton	3–0	1969	H.R. Angus	D.J. Warburg	3–1
1913	Hon. N.S. Lytton	E.M. Baerlein	3–2	1970	H.R. Angus	A.C.S. Tufton	3–0
1914	E.M. Baerlein	J. Crane (USA)	3–0	1971	H.R. Angus	R.B. Bloomfield	3–0
1919	E.M. Baerlein	V.H. Pennell	3–2	1972	H.R. Angus	R.B. Bloomfield	3–0
1920	E.M. Baerlein	E.A.C. Druce	3–0	1973	H.R. Angus	A.C.S. Tufton	3–0
1921	E.M. Baerlein	C. Suydam Cutting (USA)	3–0	1974	H.R. Angus	A.C. Lovell	3–0
				1975	H.R. Angus	A.C. Lovell	3–0
1922	E.M. Baerlein	W. Renshaw	3–1	1976	H.R. Angus	J.D. Ward	3–0
1923	E.M. Baerlein	V.H. Pennell	3–2	1977	H.R. Angus	A.C. Lovell	3–2
1924	E.M. Baerlein	Hon. C.N. Bruce	3–1	1978	H.R. Angus	J.D. Ward	3–0
1925	E.M. Baerlein	Hon. C.N. Bruce	3–0	1979	H.R. Angus	A.C. Lovell	3–0
1926	E.M. Baerlein	Hon. C.N. Bruce	3–0	1980	H.R. Angus	A.C. Lovell	3–1
1927	E.M. Baerlein	Hon.C.N. Bruce	3–1	1981	A.C. Lovell	H.R. Angus	3–0
1928	L. Lees	R.H. Hill	3–2	1982	H.R. Angus	A.C. Lovell	3–0
1929	E.M. Baerlein	L. Lees	3–1	1983	A.C. Lovell	H.R. Angus	3–0
1930	E.M. Baerlein	W.C. Wright (USA)	3–0	1984	A.C. Lovell	M.F. Dean	3–0
1931	L. Lees	E.M. Baerlein	3–0	1985	A.C. Lovell	H.R. Angus	3–2
1932	Lord Aberdare	L. Lees	3–2	1986	A.C. Lovell	J.P. Snow	3–2
1933	L. Lees	Lord Aberdare	3–1	1987	J.P. Snow	H.R. Angus	3–0
1934	L. Lees	Lord Aberdare	3–0	1988	J.P. Snow	I.E.G. Snell	3–0
1935	L. Lees	Lord Aberdare	3–0	1989	J.P. Snow	M.J. Happell	3–1
1936	L. Lees	C.M.N. Baker	3–0	1990	J.S. Male	J.P. Snow	3–0
1937	L. Lees	R.H. Hill	3–0				*table continues*

	Winner	Runner-up			Winner	Runner-up	
1991	J.P. Snow	A.J.W. Page	3-0	1997	J.P. Snow	N.J.J. Pendrigh	3-0
1992	J.P. Snow	A.J.W. Page	3-0	1998	J.P. Snow	N.J.J. Pendrigh	3-0
1993	J.P. Snow	N.J.J. Pendrigh	3-0	1999	J.P. Snow	J.P. Willcocks	3-0
1994	J.P. Snow	N.J.J. Pendrigh	3-0	2000	J.P. Snow	J.P. Willcocks	3-0
1995	J.P. Snow	N.J.J. Pendrigh	3-0	2001	J.P. Snow	M.C. Howard	3-0
1996	J.P. Snow	M.C. Howard	3-0				

AMATEUR DOUBLES CHAMPIONSHIP

Inter-club doubles to 1953

Bailey Cup

1920–22	E.M. Baerlein and W. Renshaw (Manchester)	1961	Lord Aberdare and J.D. Whatman
1923	Hon. C.N. Bruce and R.H. Hill (Queen's)	1962–64	A.C.S. Tufton and J.W. Leonard
1924	J. Gould and C. Suydam Cutting (Paris)	1965	W.T. Vogt and E. Newbold Black IV
1925	E.M. Baerlein and W. Renshaw (Manchester)	1966	D.J. Warburg and R.L.O. Bridgeman
1926	L. Lees and M. Woosnam (Manchester)	1967–70	D.J. Warburg and H.R. Angus
1927	J. Gould and W.C. Wright (Philadelphia)	1971	*no competition*
1928	L. Lees and M. Woosnam (Manchester)	1972–74	D.J. Warburg and H.R. Angus
1929–31	E.M. Baerlein and L. Lees (Manchester)	1975	J.A.R. Clench and A.C. Lovell
1932–33	Lord Aberdare and W.D. Macpherson (Queen's)	1976	H.R. Angus and D.J. Warburg
1934–37	E.M. Baerlein and L. Lees (Manchester)	1977–79	A.C. Lovell and A.G. Windham
1938	Lord Aberdare and W.D. Macpherson (Queen's)	1980	H.R. Angus and R.D.B. Cooper
1939	Lord Aberdare and R.C. Riseley (Queen's)	1981	A.C. Lovell and M.F. Dean
1946	L. Lees and P. Kershaw (Manchester)	1982	P.G. Seabrook and J.D. Ward
1947–49	W.D. Macpherson and Lord Cullen (Queen's)	1983–86	A.C. Lovell and M.F. Dean
1950	R.C. Riseley and P. Kershaw (Oxford)	1987	J.P. Snow and J.S. Male
1951	P. Kershaw and M.A. Pugh (Manchester)	1988	A.C. Lovell and M.F. Dean
1952–53	P. Kershaw and R.C. Riseley (Oxford)	1989–90	M.J. Happell and J.S. Male
1954	Lord Cullen and Hon. M.G.L. Bruce	1991–93	J.P. Snow and M.E. McMurrugh
1955–56	P. Kershaw and R.C. Riseley	1994–95	J.R. Acheson-Gray and N.J.J. Pendrigh
1957	Hon. M.G.L. Bruce and Lord Cullen	1996	J.P. Snow and S.P. Howe
1958	A.B. Martin and N.R. Knox	1997–2000	J.R. Acheson-Gray and J.P. Snow
1959	Lord Aberdare and J.D. Whatman	2001	J. Willcocks and A. Hombrecher
1960	N.R. Knox and W.E. Lingelbach Jr		

MCC PRIZES

Gold and Silver Racquet Cups
For members of MCC only 1867–96; J.B. Gribble Cup presented to winner of Gold Racquet from 1904

	Gold Racquet	Silver Racquet		Gold Racquet	Silver Racquet
1867	J.M. Heathcote	J. Marshal	1877	J.M. Heathcote	R.D. Walker
1868	J.M. Heathcote	G.B. Crawley	1878	J.M. Heathcote	C.E. Boyle
1869	J.M. Heathcote	Hon. C.G. Lyttelton	1879	J.M. Heathcote	C.E. Boyle
1870	J.M. Heathcote	Hon. C.G. Lyttelton	1880	J.M. Heathcote	Hon. A. Lyttelton
1871	J.M. Heathcote	Hon. C.G. Lyttelton	1881	J.M. Heathcote	Hon. A. Lyttelton
1872	J.M. Heathcote	Hon. C.G. Lyttelton	1882	Hon. A. Lyttelton	J.M. Heathcote
1873	J.M. Heathcote	Hon. C.G. Lyttelton	1883	J.M. Heathcote	Hon. A. Lyttelton
1874	J.M. Heathcote	G.B. Crawley	1884	Hon. A. Lyttelton	J.M. Heathcote
1875	J.M. Heathcote	R.D. Walker	1885	Hon. A. Lyttelton	J.M. Heathcote
1876	J.M. Heathcote	R.D. Walker	1886	J.M. Heathcote	B.N. Akroyd

table continues

	Gold Racquet	Silver Racquet		Gold Racquet	Silver Racquet
1887	Hon. A. Lyttelton	J.M. Heathcote	1949	W.D. Macpherson	R. Aird
1888	Hon. A. Lyttelton	A.J. Webbe	1950	R.C. Riseley	W.D. Macpherson
1889	Hon. A. Lyttelton	Sir E. Grey	1951	W.D. Macpherson	R.C. Riseley
1890	Hon. A. Lyttelton	Sir E. Grey	1952	W.D. Macpherson	Hon. M.G.L. Bruce
1891	Hon. A. Lyttelton	Sir E. Grey	1953	D.J. Warburg	Hon. M.G.L. Bruce
1892	Hon. A. Lyttelton	H.E. Crawley	1954	Hon. M.G.L. Bruce	D.J. Warburg
1893	Hon. A. Lyttelton	Sir E. Grey	1955	Hon. M.G.L. Bruce	P. Kershaw
1894	Hon. A. Lyttelton	Sir E. Grey	1956	Hon. M.G.L. Bruce	D.J. Warburg
1895	Hon. A. Lyttelton	Sir E. Grey	1957	Hon. M.G.L. Bruce	D.J. Warburg
1896	Sir E. Grey	Hon. A. Lyttelton	1958	Lord Aberdare	D.J. Warburg
1897	E.H. Miles	Sir E. Grey	1959	P. Kershaw	D.J. Warburg
1898	E.H. Miles	H.E. Crawley	1960	D.T. Warburg	P. Kershaw
1899	E.H. Miles	Sir E. Grey	1961	D.J. Warburg	P. Kershaw
1900	J.B. Gribble	Sir E. Grey	1962	D.J. Warburg	Lord Aberdare
1901	E.H. Miles	Sir E. Grey	1963	D.J. Warburg	P. Kershaw
1902	E.H. Miles	Sir E. Grey	1964	D.J. Warburg	A.C.S. Tufton
1903	E.H. Miles	Sir E. Grey	1965	D.J. Warburg	A.C.S. Tufton
1904	E.H. Miles	Sir E. Grey	1966	H.R. Angus	D.J. Warburg
1905	E.H. Miles	H.E. Crawley	1967	H.R. Angus	D.J. Warburg
1906	E.H. Miles	Maj. A. Cooper-Key	1968	H.R. Angus	D.J. Warburg
1907	V.H. Pennell	E.H. Miles	1969	H.R. Angus	A.C.S. Tufton
1908	E.H. Miles	E.B. Noel	1970	H.R. Angus	A.C.S. Tufton
1909	E.H. Miles	W.M. Cazalet	1971	H.R. Angus	A.C.S. Tufton
1910	E.H. Miles	Capt. R.K. Price	1972	H.R. Angus	A.C.S. Tufton
1911	E.H. Miles	Maj. A. Cooper-Key	1973	H.R. Angus	A.C.S. Tufton
1912	E.H. Miles	Maj. A. Cooper-Key	1974	H.R. Angus	R.D.B. Cooper
1913	E.H. Miles	Maj. A. Cooper-Key	1975	H.R. Angus	A.C. Lovell
1914	J.F. Marshall	Capt. R.K. Price	1976	H.R. Angus	A.C. Lovell
1919	E.A.C. Druce	Capt. R.K. Price	1977	H.R. Angus	A.C. Lovell
1920	Capt. R.K. Price	E.A.C. Druce	1978	H.R. Angus	A.C. Lovell
1921	E.M. Baerlein	E.A.C. Druce	1979	H.R. Angus	A.C. Lovell
1922	E.M. Baerlein	Hon. C.N. Bruce	1980	H.R. Angus	A.C. Lovell
1923	E.M. Baerlein	Hon. C.N. Bruce	1981	A.C. Lovell	H.R. Angus
1924	E.M. Baerlein	E.A.C. Druce	1982	H.R. Angus	A.C. Lovell
1925	E.M. Baerlein	R.H. Hill	1983	A.C. Lovell	H.R. Angus
1926	E.M. Baerlein	Hon. C.N. Bruce	1984	A.C. Lovell	J.D. Ward
1927	E.M. Baerlein	Hon. C.N. Bruce	1985	A.C. Lovell	H.R. Angus
1928	E.M. Baerlein	Hon. C.N. Bruce	1986	A.C. Lovell	J.D. Ward
1929	E.M. Baerlein	Hon. C.N. Bruce	1987	A.C. Lovell	J.D. Ward
1930	Lord Aberdare	E.M. Baerlein	1988	A.C. Lovell	J.D. Ward
1931	E.M. Baerlein	Lord Aberdare	1989	J.D. Ward	J.D. Ward
1932	Lord Aberdare	W.D. Macpherson	1990	M.J. Happell	J.D. Ward
1933	Lord Aberdare	R. Aird	1991	N.J.J. Pendrigh	A.J.W. Page
1934	Lord Aberdare	R. Aird	1992	A.J.W. Page	N.J.J. Pendrigh
1935	L. Lees	Lord Aberdare	1993	N.J.J. Pendrigh	M.C. Howard
1936	L. Lees	Lord Aberdare	1994	N.J.J. Pendrigh	M.C. Howard
1937	Lord Aberdare	W.D. Macpherson	1995	N.J.J. Pendrigh	H.R.P. Jarvis
1938	R.H. Hill	W.D. Macpherson	1996	N.J.J. Pendrigh	M.C. Howard
1939	W.D. Macpherson	R. Aird	1997	J.P. Snow	M.C. Howard
1946	W.M. Ross-Skinner	W.D. Macpherson	1998	J.P. Snow	N.J.J. Pendrigh
1947	W.D. Macpherson	R. Aird	1999	J.P. Snow	J.R. Acheson-Gray
1948	W.D. Macpherson	R. Aird	2000	J.P. Snow	J.P. Willcocks

PROFESSIONAL SINGLES CHAMPIONSHIP

Lees-Scott-Chad Cup

1937	J.P. Dear (Prince's Club)	1988	W.F. Davies (New York)
1952	R. Hughes (Manchester)	1989	C.J. Ronaldson (Hampton Court)
1954	J.P. Dear (Queen's)	1990	L. Deuchar (unattached)
1962	R. Hughes (Malvern)	1991	L. Deuchar (unattached)
1966	F. Willis (Manchester)	1992	C.J. Ronaldson (Hampton Court)
1976	F. Willis (Manchester)	1993	L. Deuchar (Harbour Club)
1979	F. Willis (Unattached)	1994	L. Deuchar (Harbour Club)
1980	C.J. Ronaldson (Hampton Court)	1995	L. Deuchar (Harbour Club)
1981	C.J. Ronaldson (Hampton Court)	1996	W.F. Davies (unattached)
1982	C.J. Ronaldson (Hampton Court)	1997	L. Deuchar (Harbour Club)
1983	C.J. Ronaldson (Hampton Court)	1998	C.J. Bray (Petworth)
1984	C.J. Ronaldson (Hampton Court)	1999	S. Virgona (Holyport)
1985	L. Deuchar (Hampton Court)	2000	N. Wood (Holyport)
1986	C.J. Ronaldson (Hampton Court)	2001	R.L. Fahey (Melbourne)
1987	C.J. Ronaldson (Hampton Court)		

PROFESSIONAL DOUBLES CHAMPIONSHIP

	Winners	Runners-up	
1982	P.L. Dawes and K. Sheldon	C.J. and S.J. Ronaldson	2–1
1983	P.L. Dawes and K. Sheldon	L. Deuchar and J. Fletcher	2–1
1984	C.J. and S.J. Ronaldson	L. Deuchar and J. Fletcher	2–0
1985	C.J. and S.J. Ronaldson	C. Lumley and K. Sheldon	2–0
1986	L. Deuchar and J. Fletcher	C.J. and S.J. Ronaldson	2–0
1987	L. Deuchar and J. Fletcher	C.J. and S.J. Ronaldson	2–0
1988	C.J. and S.J. Ronaldson	C.J. Lumley and M.H.J. Gooding	2–1
1989	L. Deuchar and J. Fletcher	C.J. and S.J. Ronaldson	2–1
1990	P.A.B. Brake and C.J. Bray	N. Wood and A.P. Meares	2–0
1991	C.J. Bray and C.J. Lumley	A.J.M. Phillips and K.R. King	2–1
1992	L. Deuchar and R.L. Fahey	C.J. Ronaldson and S.J. Ronaldson	2–0
1993	M.J. Devine and K. Sheldon	C.J. Bray and J.B.K. Howell	2–1
1994	L. Deuchar and R.L. Fahey	C.J. Bray and M.H.J. Gooding	3–1
1995	L. Deuchar and J.B.K. Howell	C.J. Bray and M.H.J. Gooding	3–2
1996	C.J. Bray and M.H.J. Gooding	N. Wood and A.J.M. Phillips	3–1
1997	L. Deuchar and M.H.J. Gooding	N. Wood and A.J.M. Phillips	3–1
1998	C.J. Bray and M.H.J. Gooding	J.S. Male and R.G.A. Gunn	3–0
1999	C.J. Bray and M.H.J. Gooding	R.G.A. Gunn and S. Virgona	3–1
2000	F.J. Filippelli and J.S. Male	N. Wood and A.J.M. Phillips	3–0
2001	C.J. Bray and N. Wood	F.J. Filippelli and M.H.J. Gooding	3–0

THE UNITED STATES

OPEN SINGLES CHAMPIONSHIP

1919	J. Gould	1979	B. Toates*
1921	J. Gould	1980	C.J. Ronaldson*
1951	A.B. Martin	1981	G.J. Hyland*
1956–59	A.B. Johnson*	1982–83	W.F. Davies*
1960–62	J.F.C. Bostwick	1984	C.J. Ronaldson*
1963	A.B. Johnson*	1985	W.F. Davies*
1964	R. Hughes*	1986	C.J. Ronaldson*
1965	A.B. Johnson	1987	G.J. Hyland*
1966	G.H. Bostwick Jr	1988–90	W.F. Davies*
1967	J.F.C. Bostwick	1991–92	L. Deuchar*
1968	G.H. Bostwick Jr	1993	R.L. Fahey*
1969–70	J.F.C. Bostwick	1994–95	W.F. Davies*
1971	G.H. Bostwick Jr	1996–97	J.P. Snow
1972	J.F.C. Bostwick	1998	C.J. Bray*
1973–77	E.L. Scott	1999	W.F. Davies*
1978	J.J. Burke Jr*	2000–01	R.L. Fahey*

* Denotes Professional

OPEN DOUBLES CHAMPIONSHIP

1959	A.B. Martin and R. Grant III	1983	B. Toates* and F. Faulderbaum
1960	J.P. Dunn* and W.I. Forbes Jr	1984	L. Deuchar* and K. Sheldon*
1961	G.H. Bostwick Jr and J.F.C. Bostwick	1985	J.J. Burke* and P. Clement
1962	J.P. Dunn* and W.I. Forbes Jr	1986	W.F. Davies and P.E. de Svastich
1963	N.R. Knox and A.B. Martin	1987	G.J. Hyland* and D.J.S. Collins
1964–67	J.P. Dunn* and W.T. Vogt	1988	W.F. Davies* and P.E. de Svastich
1968–70	G.H. Bostwick Jr and J.F.C. Bostwick	1989	L. Deuchar* and P.E. de Svastich
1971	A.B. Martin and E.L. Scott	1990	R.L. Fahey* and A.P. Meares*
1972	S.P. Howe III and E.M. Noll*	1991	W.F. Davies* and L. Deuchar*
1973	R.J.B. Bijur and L.C. Dominguez	1992–93	J.P. Snow and R.L. Fahey*
1974	S.P. Howe III and E.L. Scott	1994–95	C.J. Bray* and M.H.J. Gooding*
1975–76	J.F. Sammis III and R.W. Tuckerman	1996	J.P. Snow and N. Wood*
1977	N.A.R. Cripps* and C.J. Ronaldson*	1997	J.P. Snow and J.S. Male*
1978	O.M. Phipps and E.L. Scott	1998	R.G.A. Gunn* and S. Virgona*
1979	E.L. Scott and B. Toates*	1999	J.P. Snow and J.S. Male*
1980–81	O.M. Phipps and G.J. Hyland*	2000	J.P. Snow and N. Wood*
1982	O.M. Phipps and W.F. Davies*	2001	C.J. Bray* and N. Wood*

*Denotes Professional

AMATEUR SINGLES CHAMPIONSHIP

1892	R.D. Sears
1893	F. Warren
1894–95	B.S. de Garmendia
1896	L.M. Stockton
1897	C.R. Fearing Jr
1898–99	L.M. Stockton
1900	E.H. Miles
1901–04	J. Crane Jr
1905	C.E. Sands
1906–09	J. Gould
1910–17	J. Gould
1920–25	J. Gould
1926	C. Suydam Cutting
1927	G.D. Huband
1928–29	H. Morgan
1930	Lord Aberdare
1931–32	W.C. Wright
1933	J.H. Van Alen
1934–37	O.M. Phipps
1938	J.H. Van Alen
1939	O.M. Phipps
1940	J.H. Van Alen
1941	A.B. Martin
1946	R. Grant III
1947	E.M. Beals
1948–49	O.M. Phipps
1950–56	A.B. Martin
1957-58	N.R. Knox
1959	J.F.C. Bostwick
1960–63	N.R. Knox
1964	J.F.C. Bostwick
1965–69	G.H. Bostwick Jr
1970	J.F.C. Bostwick
1971	G.H. Bostwick Jr
1972	J.F.C. Bostwick
1973	H.R. Angus
1974–78	E.L. Scott
1979	R.E. Howe III
1980–84	E.L. Scott
1985–86	K.B. McCollum
1987–88	M. Clothier
1989	M. Happell
1990–91	M. Clothier
1992	J.P. Snow
1993	T. Chisholm
1994	N.J.J. Pendrigh
1995	T. Chisholm
1996–99	N.J.J. Pendrigh
2001	J.P. Snow

AMATEUR DOUBLES CHAMPIONSHIP

1909	J. Gould and W.H.T. Huhn
1910	G.R. Fearing Jr and Joshua Crane
1911–17	J. Gould and W.H.T. Huhn
1920–24	J. Gould and J.W. Wear
1925	C. Suydam Cutting and F. Cutting
1926	J. Gould and J.W. Wear
1927–29	J. Gould and W.C. Wright
1930	F.P. Frazier and G.W. Wrightman
1931–32	J. Gould and W.C. Wright
1933	G.R. Fearing and W.C. Wright
1934–39	W. Rand and O.M. Phipps
1940	J.H. Van Alen and W.L. Van Alen
1941	O.M. Phipps and R. Grant III
1946–47	E.M. Edwards and W.E. Lingelbach Jr
1948	O.M. Phipps and A.B. Martin
1949–50	A.B. Martin and R.L. Gerry Jr
1951	A.B. Martin and E.B. Martin
1952	F.X. Shields and O.M. Phipps
1953–54	F.X. Shields and A.B. Martin
1955	W.L. Van Alen and F.H. Griffin Jr
1956–57	A.B. Martin and N.R. Knox
1958–59	N.R. Knox and S.H. Knox III
1960	A.B. Martin and Robert Grant III
1961	N.R. Knox and S.H. Knox III
1962	A.B. Martin and W.T. Vogt
1963–65	N.R. Knox and O.M. Phipps
1966	A.B. Martin and S.T. Vehslage
1967	J.L. Van Alen and W.L. Van Alen Jr
1968	N.R. Knox and W.F. Talbert
1969	J.F.C. Bostwick and G.H. Bostwick Jr
1970–71	N.R. Knox and A.B. Martin
1972	N.R. Knox and E.L. Scott
1973	G.H. Bostwick, Jr. and J.F.C. Bostwick
1974	R.E. Howe III and S.P. Howe
1975	E.L. Scott and R.E. Howe III
1976	P.W. Clement and W.M. Shettle
1977	N.R. Knox and O.M. Phipps
1978	R.E. Howe III and W.J.C. Surtees
1979	R.E. Howe III and O.M. Phipps
1980	N.R. Knox and J.F.C. Bostwick
1981–82	O.M. Phipps and E.L. Scott
1983	G.H. Bostwick and R.E. Howe
1984–85	G. Bell Jr and P. Clement
1986–87	G.R. Jones and K.B. McCollum
1988	H. Bunis and P.E. DeSvastich
1989–91	M. Clothier and G.R. Jones
1992–94	R.E. Howe and J.P. Snow
1995	M. Clothier and T. Chisholm
1996	N.J.J. Pendrigh and P. Clement
1997	J.P. Snow and R.E. Howe
1998	S. Aldrigh and N.J.J. Pendrigh
1999	R. Devens and J. Capello
2000	R.E. Howe and J.P. Snow

FRANCE

COUPE DE PARIS

1910	C.E. Sands
1911–13	Hon. N.S. Lytton
1914–20	Capt. R.K. Price
1921–25	E.M. Baerlein
1926–27	Hon. C.N. Bruce
1928	W.C. Wright
1929	L. Lees
1930	Marquis R. du Vivier
1931	W.C. Wright
1932–35	Lord Aberdare
1936	Marquis R. du Vivier
1937	R.H. Hill
1938	Lord Aberdare
1947	Lord Cullen
1948	R. Aird
1950	F. Alvarez
1962	D.J. Warburg
1976	H.R. Angus

OPEN NATIONAL

1993	R.G.A. Gunn
1994	R. Nicholson
1995	M. Seigneur
1996	I.O. Ronaldson
1997	M. Seigneur
1998	I.O. Ronaldson
1999	D. Grozdanovitch
2000	M. Seigneur

COUPE DE BORDEAUX

1909	B.H. Seward	1962	J.W.T. Wilcox
1910–11	W. Bazin	1963	M.H.L. Bowler
1912–13	P. Deves	1964–65	H.R. Angus
1914 & 1920	Capt. R.K. Price	1966	J.Q. Greenstock
1921	E.M. Baerlein	1967	A.F. Goulty
1922–23	R.K. Price	1968	D.J. Sloan
1924	P. Deves	1969	M. Peuvrel
1925–26	Comte R. du Vivier	1970	H.R. Angus
1927–28	F. Blanchy	1971	R.J. Potter
1929	Comte R. du Vivier	1972	M. Peuvrel
1930	F. Blanchy	1973	Y. Faugère
1931	Marquis R. du Vivier	1974	A.C. Lovell
1932	Comte F. du Vivier	1975–76	B. Sarlangue
1933	Capt. G.N. Scott-Chad	1977	H.R. Angus
1934	Lord Aberdare	1979	H.R. Angus
1935–37	Marquis R. du Vivier	1980	B. Sarlangue
1938	M. Dupont	1981	W. Hollington
1947–50	F. Alvarez	1982	J.D. Ward
1951–52	M.A. Pugh	1983	A.C. Lovell
1953	G. Blanchy	1984	R.C. McKenzie
1954	D.J. Warburg	1985	J.D. Ward
1955	M.H. Searby	1986	M.J. Happell
1956	N.F. Robinson	1987–96	J.P. Snow
1957	W.E. Rawson-Shaw	1997	N.J.J. Pendrigh
1958	B.H.I.H. Stewart	1998	J.P. Willcocks
1959	M. Faugère	1999	C. Blanchot
1960	N.W. Smith	2000	I.E.G. Snell
1961	Hon. A.C.S. Tufton		

RAQUETTE D'OR

1899–1900	C.E. Sands	1959	M. Faugère
1901	W. Bazin	1960	R. Diani
1902	A.F. de Luze	1961–62	J. Strauss
1903–04	W. Bazin	1963	M. Peuvrel
1905	A.F. de Luze	1964	A.G. Lawrence
1906–07	W. Bazin	1965	M. Peuvrel
1910–11	W. Bazin	1966	L.M. Ravet de Marbaix
1912	P. Devès	1967	M. Peuvrel
1913–14	W. Bazin	1968	J. Strauss
1920	P. Devès	1969	H. Faugère
1921–22	J. Worth	1970	J. Strauss
1923	P. Devès	1971–72	M. Peuvrel
1924	D. Lawton	1973	C. Ricard
1925–29	Comte R. du Vivier	1974	R.D.B. Cooper
1930–32	F. Blanchy	1975–84	B. Sarlangue
1933	Marquis R. du Vivier	1985–88	D. Grozdanovitch
1934	A.J. Drexel Biddle Jr	1989	C. Chueka
1935–37	Marquis R. du Vivier	1990–91	D. Grozdanovitch
1938	L.J. Aslangul	1992	C. Chueka
1945–46	F. Alvarez	1993	D. Grozdanovitch
1947	H. Cruse	1994–95	J.G. Prats
1949–51	F. Alvarez	1996	D. Grozdanovitch
1952-53	Ch. Blanchy	1997	G. Ruault
1954	H.R. Barton	1998	J.G. Prats
1955	Ch. Blanchy	1999	G. Ruault
1956	L.M. Ravet de Marbaix	2000	O. Michel
1958	F. Laws Johnson	2001	A.J.W. Page

AUSTRALIA

OPEN CHAMPIONSHIP

1875–82	T. Stone	1980–81	C.J. Lumley
1882–1902	T. Horne	1982	C.J. Ronaldson
1903–09	*No known challenges*	1983	W.F. Davies
1910–31	W.T. Stone	1984–85	C.J. Ronaldson
1932–35	H.P. Finch	1986	L. Deuchar
1935–38	H.A. Finch	1987–88	W.F. Davies
1938–47	H.P. Finch	1989	G.J. Hyland
1948–49	A.W. Knight	1990	L. Deuchar
1950–51	*No known challenges*	1991	W.F. Davies
1952–54	R.W. Baker	1992	J.P. Snow
1955	J.S. Barnett	1993–94	R.L. Fahey
1956–58	R.W. Baker	1995	F.J. Filippelli
1959–67	*No known challenges*	1996–98	R.L. Fahey
1968–76	B. Toates	1999	C.J. Bray
1977–78	C.J. Ronaldson	2000	R.L. Fahey
1979	B. Toates		

MELBOURNE: GOLD AND SILVER RACKET COMPETITION

	Gold Racket	Silver Racket		Gold Racket	Silver Racket
1882	J.B. Box	F.R. Murphy	1930	R.C. Todhunter	K. Tolhurst
1883	J.B. Box	T.A. Quirk	1931	K. Tolhurst	H.S. Forrest
1884	J.B. Box	R. Travers	1932	K. Tolhurst	F. Strachan
1885	J.B. Box	J.N. Webster	1933	G.L. Patterson	R.C. Todhunter
1886	J.B. Box	C.W. Butler	1934	K. Tolhurst	G.L. Patterson
1887	J.B. Box	R. Cornish	1935	G.L. Patterson	R.A. Henderson
1888	J.B. Box	R. Cornish	1936	G.L. Patterson	R.A. Henderson
1889	J.B. Box	R. Cornish	1937	K. Tolhurst	Julian Smith Jr
1890	J.B. Box	C.C. Malleson	1938	W.H. Vestey	*unknown*
1891	J.B. Box	W.T. Coldham	1952	R.H. Searby	M.H. Searby
1892	J.B. Box	W.T. Coldham	1956	Hon. M.G.L. Bruce	S.H. Barstow
1893	J.B. Box	J.F. Strachan	1964	M.H. Searby	S.H. Barstow
1894	J.B. Box	W. Travers	1965	R.H. Searby	M.H. Searby
1895	J.F. Strachan	J.B. Box	1966	R.H. Searby	M.H. Searby
1896	W. Travers	H.J. Hill	1967	J.P. Drummond	R.H. Searby
1897	W. Travers	J.B. Box	1968	G.G. Hiller	R.S. Allen
1898	H.J. Hill	J.B. Box	1969	G.G. Hiller	D.G.D. Yencken
1899	J.B. Box	F.G. Travers	1970	G.G. Hiller	G.E. Limb
1900	H.J. Hill	R. Cornish	1971	G.G. Hiller	G.E. Limb
1901	T.A. Quirk	J.F. Strachan	1972	G.G. Hiller	R.H. Searby
1902	T.A. Quirk	C.H. Mollison	1973	G.G. Hiller	A.K. Heard
1903	C.H. Mollison	T.A. Quirk	1974	A.K. Heard	G.E. Limb
1904	C.H. Mollison	T.A. Quirk	1975	G.G. Hiller	A.K. Heard
1905	H.J. Hill	C.H. Mollison	1976	A.K. Heard	R.M. Cowper
1906	C.H. Mollison	T.A. Quirk	1977	A.K. Heard	R.M. Cowper
1907	T.A. Quirk	C.H. Mollison	1978	R.M. Cowper	G.E. Limb
1908	C.H. Mollison	T.A. Quirk	1979	A.K. Heard	R.M. Cowper
1909	C.H. Mollison	T.A. Quirk	1980	R.M. Cowper	E.W. Cockram
1910	C.H. Mollison	E. Maxwell	1981	E.W. Cockram	R.M. Cowper
1911	C.H. Mollison	C.T. Butler	1982	E.W. Cockram	R.M. Cowper
1912	W.D. Gibbs	Lord Denman	1983	E.W. Cockram	R.M. Cowper
1913	W.D. Gibbs	C.H. Mollison	1984	M.J. Happell	E.W. Cockram
1914	C.H. Mollison	T.A. Quirk	1985	E.W. Cockram	M.J. Happell
1915	C.H. Mollison	W.R. Clarke	1986	E.W. Cockram	M.J. Happell
1916	C.H. Mollison	T.A. Quirke	1987	M.J. Happell	E.W. Cockram
1917	C.H. Mollison	T.A. Quirk	1988	M.J. Happell	E.W. Cockram
1918	C.H. Mollison	H.R. Flack	1989	E.W. Cockram	C.M. Sievers
1919	C.H. Mollison	H.R. Flack	1990	C.M. Sievers	E.W. Cockram
1920	C.H. Mollison	H.R. Flack	1991	C.M. Sievers	V. Eke
1921	C.T. Butler	C.H. Mollison	1992	M.J. Happell	C.M. Sievers
1922	C.T. Butler	A.O. Henty	1993	M.J. Happell	C.M. Sievers
1923	C.H. Mollison	D.C. George	1994	M.J. Happell	C.M. Sievers
1924	C.T. Butler	D.C. George	1995	M.J. Happell	R. Dery
1925	C.T. Butler	A.O. Henty	1996	M.J. Happell	C.M. Sievers
1926	A.O. Henty	E.C. Dyason	1997	M.J. Happell	C.M. Sievers
1927	K. Tolhurst	E.C. Dyason	1998	M.J. Happell	C.M. Sievers
1928	J.L. Hudson	E.C. Dyason	1999	M.J. Happel	C.M. Sievers
1929	R.C. Todhunter	K. Tolhurst	2000	M.J. Happell	C.M. Sievers

HOBART CHAMPION RACQUET COMPETITION

1880	W.L. Dobson	1940–50	A.W. Knight
1881	A.L. Travers	1951–53	R.W. Baker
1882	C.W. Butler	1954–55	J.S. Barnett
1883–84	L. Travers	1956–58	R.W. Baker
1886	J. Macfarlane	1959	C.A.S. Page
1887–92	C.W. Butler	1960	A.W. Knight
1893	W. Travers	1961–63	C.A.S. Page
1895	K. Maxwell	1964	G.G. Hiller
1896	H.J. Hill	1965–66	R.W. Baker
1897	C.W. Butler	1967	J.S. Rogers
1898	H.J. Hill	1968–69	D.J. Martin
1899	F.A. Dodds	1970	D.A. Shepherd
1900	H.J. Hill	1971–72	D.J. Martin
1901	F.A. Dodds	1973	C.C.A. Butler
1902	C.W. Butler	1974–76	D.J. Martin
1903–10	E. Maxwell	1977–80	J.S. Wilkinson
1911	C.T. Butler	1981–84	G.G. Bradfield
1912–19	E. Maxwell	1985–87	A.P. Meares
1920–27	C.T. Butler	1988	G.G. Bradfield
1928	S.H. Bastow	1989	R.D. Edwards
1929	C.T. Butler	1990–97	G.G. Bradfield
1930	C.C. Boag	1998–99	P.J. Boyles
1931–32	C.T. Butler	2000	K. Booth
1933–39	C.C. Boag		

BALLARAT SILVER RACKET

1985	C.J. Ronaldson	1993	J.P. Snow
1986	G.J. Hyland	1994	B. McFarlane
1987	C.J. Ronaldson	1995	J.P. Snow
1988	L. Deuchar	1996	F.J. Filippelli
1989	J.P. Snow	1997	C.J. Bray
1990	F.J. Filippelli	1998	J.B.K. Howell
1991	C.J. Bray	1999	C.J. Bray
1992	J.P. Snow	2000	*no competition*

GOVERNOR'S CUP, HOBART

1975	F. Willis	1985	G.J. Hyland
1979	C.J. Ronaldson	1988	G.J. Hyland
1982	C.J. Ronaldson	1999	R.L. Fahey

ROMSEY OPEN

2000	R.L. Fahey

VICTORIAN OPEN SINGLES

Woolner Stone Memorial

1975–76	B. Toates	1989	G.J. Hyland
1977–78	C.J. Ronaldson	1990	F.J. Filippelli
1979	B. Toates	1991	M.J. Happell
1980	C.J. Lumley	1992	G.J. Hyland
1981	L. Deuchar	1993	M.J. Happell
1982	C.J. Lumley	1994	F.J. Filippelli
1983	E.W. Cockram	1995	R.L. Fahey
1984	M.J. Happell	1996	F.J. Filippelli
1985	G.J. Hyland	1997	R.L. Fahey
1986	L. Deuchar	1998	F.J. Filippelli
1987	P.G. Tabley	1999	S. Virgona
1988	L. Deuchar	2000–01	R.L. Fahey

RACKETS

WORLD SINGLES CHAMPIONSHIP

Eleven point games played in 1838, enclosed court used for first time in 1860

	Winner	Runner-up	Aggregate score	Venues
1820	Robert Mackay	*claimed*		
1825	Thomas Pittman	*claimed*		
1834	Thomas Pittman	*resigned*		
1834	John Pittman	*claimed*		
1838	John Lamb	John Pittman	8–4	Belvedere Gardens
1840	John Lamb	*died – title vacant*		
1846	John Mitchell	J.C.M. Young	5–0	Birmingham and Bristol
1860	Francis Erwood	John Mitchell	8–1	Woolwich and Bristol
1862	W.H. Dyke	Francis Erwood	8–3	Woolwich and Prince's
1863	Sir William Hart-Dyke	*resigned*		
1863	Henry Gray	*claimed*		
1866	Henry Gray	*resigned*		
1866	William Gray	*claimed*		
1875	William Gray	*died*		
1876	H.B. Fairs	Joseph Gray	8-3	Prince's and Rugby
1878	H.B. Fairs	*died*		
1878	Joseph Gray	*claimed*		
1887	Peter Latham	Joseph Gray	7–4	Rugby and Manchester
1888	Peter Latham	Walter Gray	6–3	Queen's and Charterhouse
1891	Peter Latham	George Standing	5–0	Queen's and Prince's
1897	Peter Latham	George Standing	6–3	Queen's and New York
1902	Peter Latham	Gilbert Browne	5–0	Queen's and Prince's
1902	Peter Latham	*resigned*		
1903	J. Jamsetji	Gilbert Browne	6–2	Queen's and Prince's
1911	Charles Williams	J. Jamsetji	5–0	Queen's and Prince's
1913	Jock Soutar	Charles Williams	6–4	Queen's and Philadelphia
1922	Jock Soutar	Charles Williams	7–4	Philadelphia and New York
1927	Jock Soutar	William Standing	8–1	Philadelphia and New York
1929	Charles Williams	Jock Soutar	7–3	Philadelphia and Chicago
1935	Charles Williams	*died*		
1937	David Milford	Norbert Setzler	7–4	New York and Queen's
1946	David Milford	*resigned*		
1947	Jim Dear	Kenneth Chantler	8–1	Montreal and Queen's
1948	Jim Dear	John Pawle	8–4	Queen's
1951	Jim Dear	John Pawle	8–2	Queen's
1954	Geoffrey Atkins	Jim Dear	6–5	Queen's
1963	Geoffrey Atkins	James Leonard	6–1	Queen's
1964	Geoffrey Atkins	Charles Swallow	7–5	Queen's
1967	Geoffrey Atkins	James Leonard	7–2	Chicago and Queen's
1970	Geoffrey Atkins	Charles Swallow	6–3	Chicago and Queen's
1972	William Surtees	Howard Angus	5–4	Queen's and Chicago

table continues

381

	Winner	Runner-up	Aggregate score	Venues
1973	Howard Angus	William Surtees	5–1	Chicago and Queen's
1975	William Surtees	Howard Angus	5–1	Chicago and Queen's
1977	William Surtees	Howard Angus	5–0	Chicago and Queen's
1979	William Surtees	Willie Boone	5–0	New York and Queen's
1981	John Prenn	William Surtees	6–4	New York and Queen's
1984	Willie Boone	John Prenn	7–2	Montreal and Queen's
1986	John Prenn	Willie Boone	8–6	New York and Queen's
1988	James Male	Willie Boone	6–1	Chicago and Queen's
1991	James Male	Shannon Hazell	6–2	Chicago and Queen's
1993	James Male	Neil Smith	6–5	Philadelphia and Queen's
1995	James Male	Neil Smith	6–2	Chicago and Queen's
1999	Neil Smith	James Male	4–2	Chicago
				(James Male forfeited second leg through injury)
2001	James Male	Neil Smith	6–1	New York and St Paul's

WORLD DOUBLES CHAMPIONSHIP

	Winners	Runners-up	Aggregate score	Venues
1990	James Male and John Prenn	Shannon Hazell and Neil Smith	8–5	Manchester and Queen's
1992	Shannon Hazell and Neil Smith	Willie Boone and John Prenn	7–3	Clifton and Queen's
1993	Shannon Hazell and Neil Smith	James Male and John Prenn	7–7 166 to 160 pts	New York and Queen's
1996	Shannon Hazell and Neil Smith	James Male and John Prenn	5–0	New York and Philadelphia
1998	Shannon Hazell and Neil Smith	Willie Boone and Peter Brake	7–6	Clifton and New York
2001	James Male and Mark Hue Williams	Shannon Hazell and Neil Smith	5–0	Philadelphia and St Pauls

UNITED KINGDOM

THE SHEPHERD CUP *(Challenge)*

From 1929 to 1975 the competition, for the Shepherd Cup, was a challenge event. In 1971 an Open Invitation Tournament for the Louis Roederer Trophy was initiated as an annual open event, but it was not the British Open. In 1975 H.R. Angus agreed to relinquish the British Open championship in order that the Open Invitation event could become the annual British Open championship, which it did from 1975 onwards.

	Winner	Runner-up			Winner	Runner-up	
1929	J.C.F. Simpson	C.R. Read	5–1	1959	J.R. Thompson	R.M.K. Gracey	3–1
1930	J.C.F. Simpson	C.R. Read	5–0	1960	J.P. Dear	J.R. Thompson	7–4
1932	Lord Aberdare	J.C.F. Simpson	8–2	1961	G.W.T. Atkins	*claimed*	
1933	I. Akers-Douglas	Lord Aberdare	4–0 (retired)	1967	J.W. Leonard	C.J. Swallow	7–4
1934	A.G. Cooper	I. Akers-Douglas	7–4	1970	C.J. Swallow	J.W. Leonard	7–4
1936	D.S. Milford	A.G. Cooper	8–3		*C.J. Swallow resigned title*		
1946	J.P. Dear	P. Kershaw	8–1	1970	M.G.M. Smith	C.T.M. Pugh	*walkover*
1951	J.P. Dear	J.H. Pawle	8–2	1971	H.R. Angus	M.G.M. Smith	6–2
1954	G.W.T. Atkins	J.P. Dear	6–4	1975	*H.R. Angus relinquished challenge title*		

OPEN SINGLES CHAMPIONSHIP

	Winner	Runner-up			Winner	Runner-up	
1975	H.R. Angus	W.J.C. Surtees	4–1	1988	J.S. Male	N.P.A. Smith	4–0
1976	H.R. Angus	J.A.N. Prenn	4–1	1989	J.S. Male	N.P.A. Smith	4–2
1977	J.A.N. Prenn	W.R. Boone	4–1	1990	N.P.A. Smith	W.R. Boone	4–0
1978	H.R. Angus	W.R. Boone	4–1	1991	J.S. Male	N.P.A. Smith	4–1
1979	W.R. Boone	J.A.N. Prenn	4–1	1992	S.M. Hazell	W.R. Boone	4–2
1980	J.A.N. Prenn	W.R. Boone	4–2	1993	N.P.A. Smith	S.M. Hazell	4–0
1981	J.A.N. Prenn	W.R. Boone	4–0	1994	N.P.A. Smith	R. Owen-Browne	4–3
1982	J.A.N. Prenn	W.R. Boone	4–2	1995	W.R. Boone	N.P.A. Smith	4–0
1983	J.A.N. Prenn	W.R. Boone	4–1	1996	J.S. Male	N.P.A. Smith	4–0
1984	W.R. Boone	R.S. Crawley	4–0	1997	W.R. Boone	M.G.N. Windows	4–1
1985	J.A.N. Prenn	W.R. Boone	4–1	1998	W.R. Boone	T.N. Sawrey-Cookson	4–0
1986	W.R. Boone	J.A.N. Prenn	4–2	1999	N.P.A. Smith	W.R. Boone	4–3
1987	J.S. Male	N.P.A. Smith	4–1	2000	J.S. Male	P. Brake	4–2

OPEN INVITATION TOURNAMENT
Louis Roederer Trophy

	Winner	Runner-up			Winner	Runner-up	
1971	M.G.M. Smith	C.T.M. Pugh	walkover	1973	H.R. Angus	M.G.M. Smith	3–2
1971	H.R. Angus	R.M.K. Gracey	3–1	1974	W.J.C. Surtees	H.R. Angus	3–1
1972	H.R. Angus	M.G.M. Smith	3–1				

OPEN DOUBLES CHAMPIONSHIP

	Winners	Runners-up	
1981	W.R. Boone and R.S. Crawley	C.J. Hue Williams and J.A.N. Prenn	4–0
1982	W.R. Boone and R.S. Crawley	C.J. Hue Williams and J.A.N. Prenn	4–0
1983	W.R. Boone and R.S. Crawley	M.W. Nicholls and P.C. Nicholls	4–1
1984	W.R. Boone and R.S. Crawley	J.A.N. Prenn and J.S. Male	4–0
1985	W.R. Boone and R.S. Crawley	J.A.N. Prenn and J.S. Male	4–3
1986	J.A.N. Prenn and J.S. Male	W.R. Boone and R.S. Crawley	4–1
1987	J.A.N. Prenn and J.S. Male	W.R. Boone and R.S. Crawley	4–3
1988	J.A.N. Prenn and J.S. Male	W.R. Boone and R.S. Crawley	4–2
1989	J.A.N. Prenn and J.S. Male	N.P.A. Smith and S.M. Hazell	4–2
1990	J.A.N. Prenn and J.S. Male	N.P.A. Smith and S.M. Hazell	4–1
1991	N.P.A. Smith and S.M. Hazell	J.A.N. Prenn and J.S. Male	4–3
1992	N.P.A. Smith and S.M. Hazell	J.A.N. Prenn and W.R. Boone	4–1
1993	J.A.N. Prenn and J.S. Male	W.R. Boone and N.P.A. Smith	4–0
1994	W.R. Boone and T.B. Cockroft	J.A.N. Prenn and R. Owen-Browne	4–1
1995	W.R. Boone and T.B. Cockroft	N.P.A. Smith and P. Brake	4–3
1996	W.R. Boone and T.B. Cockroft	J.S. Male and J.A.N. Prenn	walkover
1997	W.R. Boone and P. Brake	T.B. Cockroft and R. Owen-Browne	4–1
1998	J.S. Male and C.M. Hue Williams	N.P.A. Smith and S.M. Hazell	4–1
1999	J.S. Male and C.M. Hue Williams	J.J.S. Larken and T.N. Sawrey-Cookson	4–0
2000	J.S. Male and C.M. Hue Williams	G.W. Barker and A.J. Robinson	4–2

AMATEUR SINGLES CHAMPIONSHIP

	Winner	Runner-up			Winner	Runner-up	
1888	C.D. Buxton	E.M. Hadow	3–0	1951	D.S. Milford	G.W.T. Atkins	3–2
1889	E.M. Butler	C.D. Buxton	3–2	1952	G.W.T. Atkins	M.C. Cowdrey	3–0
1890	P. Ashworth	Capt. W. C. Hedley	3–0	1953	G.W.T. Atkins	D.S. Milford	3–2
1891	H. Philipson	P. Ashworth	3–2	1954	J.R. Thompson	D.S. Milford	3–1
1892	F. Dames-Longworth	H. Philipson	3–0	1955	J.R. Thompson	D.S. Milford	3–2
1893	F. Dames-Longworth	H.K. Foster	3–1	1956	G.W.T. Atkins	J.R. Thompson	3–1
1894	H.K. Foster	F. Dames-Longworth	3–1	1957	J.R. Thompson	M.R. Coulman	3–2
1895	H.K. Foster	G.F. Vernon	3–1	1958	J.R. Thompson	R.M.K. Gracey	3–0
1896	H.K. Foster	E.H. Miles	3–0	1959	J.R. Thompson	J.M.G. Tildesley	3–2
1897	H.K. Foster	P. Ashworth	3–2	1960	G.W.T. Atkins	J.R. Thompson	3–0
1898	H.K. Foster	W.L. Foster	3–0	1961	J.W. Leonard	R.M.K. Gracey	3–0
1899	H.K. Foster	E.H. Miles	3–0	1962	J.W. Leonard	G.W.T. Atkins	3–2
1900	H.K. Foster	P. Ashworth	3–0	1963	G.W.T. Atkins	J.W. Leonard	3–2
1901	F. Dames-Longworth	J. Howard	3–1	1964	C.J. Swallow	G.W.T. Atkins	3–2
1902	E.H. Miles	F. Dames-Longworth	3–1	1965	J.W. Leonard	M.S. Connell	3–1
1903	E.M. Baerlein	E.H. Miles	3–2	1966	C.J. Swallow	J.W. Leonard	3–1
1904	H.K. Foster	E.M. Baerlein	3–0	1967	J.W. Leonard	C.T.M. Pugh	3–2
1905	E.M. Baerlein	E.H. Miles	3–0	1968	C.J. Swallow	R.M.K. Gracey	3–0
1906	Maj. S.H. Sheppard	P. Ashworth	3–1	1969	C J. Swallow	J.W. Leonard	3–0
1907	E.B. Noel	B.S. Foster	3–2	1970	M.G.M. Smith	C.T.M. Pugh	3–1
1908	E.M. Baerlein	E.B. Noel	3–1	1971	M.G.M. Smith	H.R. Angus	3–2
1909	E.M. Baerlein	H. Brougham	3–1	1972	H.R.Angus	M.G.M. Smith	3–1
1910	E M. Baerlein	P. Ashworth	3–0	1973	H.R. Angus	M.G.M. Smith	3–1
1911	E.M. Baerlein	H.A. Denison	3–0	1974	H.R. Angus	C.J. Hue Williams	3–1
1912	B.S. Foster	G.G. Kershaw	3–1	1975	H.R. Angus	D.M. Norman	3–1
1913	B.S. Foster	H.W. Leatham	3–0	1976	W.R. Boone	J.A.N. Prenn	3–2
1914	H.W. Leatham	E.M. Baerlein	3–2	1977	C.J. Hue Williams	W.R. Boone	3–0
1920	E.M. Baerlein	Hon. C.N. Bruce	3–1	1978	W.R. Boone	J.A.N. Prenn	3–2
1921	E.M. Baerlein	Hon. C. N. Bruce	3–0	1979	J.A.N. Prenn	W.R. Boone	3–0
1922	Hon. C.N. Bruce	E.M. Baerlein	3–0	1980	J.A.N. Prenn	W.R. Boone	3–0
1923	E.M. Baerlein	Hon. C.N. Bruce	3–1	1981	W.R. Boone	J.A.N. Prenn	3–2
1924	Dr H.W. Leatham	Capt. T.O. Jameson	3–2	1982	J.A.N. Prenn	W.R. Boone	3–2
1925	C.C. Pell (USA)	Dr H.W. Leatham	3–0	1983	J.A.N. Prenn	W.R. Boone	3–0
1926	J.C.F. Simpson	Dr H.W. Leatham	3–2	1984	W.R. Boone	M.W. Nicholls	3–0
1927	J.C.F. Simpson	Hon. C.N. Bruce	3–2	1985 *Jan*	W.R. Boone	J.A.N. Prenn	3–2
1928	J.C.F. Simpson	Hon. C.N. Bruce	3–0	1985 *Dec*	J.S. Male	W.R. Boone	3–0
1929	C.S. Crawley	H.D. Hake	3–0	1986	J.S. Male	W.R. Boone	3–0
1930	D.S. Milford	I. Akers-Douglas	3–0	1987	W.R. Boone	M.W. Nicholls	3–0
1931	Lord Aberdare	I. Akers-Douglas	3–0	1988	W.R. Boone	J.A.N. Prenn	3–1
1932	I. Akers-Douglas	J.C.F. Simpson	3–1	1988	J.S. Male	W.R. Boone	3–0
1933	I. Akers-Douglas	C.S. Crawley	3–1	1989	W.R. Boone	J.A.N. Prenn	3–0
1934	I. Akers-Douglas	A.M. Hedley	3–0	1990	J.S. Male	W.R. Boone	3–1
1935	D.S. Milford	I. Akers-Douglas	3–1	1991	J.A.N. Prenn	W.R. Boone	3–0
1936	D.S. Milford	J.H. Pawle	3–1	1992	J.S. Male	W.R. Boone	3–1
1937	D.S. Milford	R.C. Riseley	3–0	1993	W.R. Boone	J.A.N. Prenn	3–1
1938	D.S. Milford	I. Akers-Douglas	3–0	1994	J.S. Male	W.R. Boone	3–1
1939	P. Kershaw	R.A.A. Holt	3–0	1995	J.S. Male	W.R. Boone	3–0
1946	J.H. Pawle	I. Akers-Douglas	3–1	1996	J.S. Male	W.R. Boone	3–1
1947	J.H. Pawle	D.S. Milford	3–2	1997	J.S. Male	G.W. Barker	3–0
1948	J.H. Pawle	D.S. Milford	3–2	1998	J.S. Male	W.R. Boone	3–0
1949	J.H. Pawle	D.S. Milford	3–2	1999	J.S. Male	A.J. Robinson	3–1
1950	D.S. Milford	G.H.G. Doggart	3–0	2000	J.S. Male	G.W. Barker	3–0

AMATEUR DOUBLES CHAMPIONSHIP

1890	P. Ashworth and Capt. W.C. Hedley	1947	R.A.A. Holt and Maj. A.R. Taylor
1891	P. Ashworth and E.L. Metcalfe	1948	D.S. Milford and J.R. Thompson
1892	E.M. Butler and M.C. Kemp	1949	R.A.A. Holt and Maj. A.R. Taylor
1893	F.H. Browning and H.K. Foster	1950–52	D.S. Milford and J.R. Thompson
1894	H.K. Foster and C.S.C.F. Ridgeway	1953	P. Kershaw and G.W.T. Atkins
1895	F. Dames-Longworth and F.H. Browning	1954–59	D.S. Milford and J.R. Thompson
1896–97	H.K. Foster and P. Ashworth	1960	C.J. Swallow and J.M.G. Tildesley
1898	H.K. Foster and W.L. Foster	1961–62	G.W.T. Atkins and P. Kershaw
1899–1900	H.K. Foster and P. Ashworth	1963	J.W. Leonard and C.J. Swallow
1901	F. Dames-Longworth and V.H. Pennell	1964–65	R.M.K. Gracey and M.G.M. Smith
1902	E.M. Baerlein and E.H. Miles	1966	J.R. Thompson and C.T.M. Pugh
1903	H.K. Foster and B.S. Foster	1967–68	J.W. Leonard and C.J. Hue Williams
1904–05	E.M. Baerlein and E.H. Miles	1969–71	R.M.K. Gracey and M.G.M. Smith
1906	E.H. Miles and F. Dames-Longworth	1972–73	H.R. Angus and C.J. Hue Williams
1907	W.L. Foster and B.S. Foster	1974	G.W.T. Atkins and C.J. Hue Williams
1908	F. Dames-Longworth and V.H. Pennell	1975–77	W.R. Boone and C.T.M. Pugh
1909	E.M. Baerlein and P. Ashworth	1978–79	H.R. Angus and A.G. Milne
1910–11	B.S. Foster and Hon. C.N. Bruce	1980–84	W.R. Boone and R.S. Crawley
1912	H.W. Leatham and H.A. Denison	1985	J.A.N. Prenn and C.J. Hue Williams
1913	B.S. Foster and H. Brougham	1986	W.R. Boone and R.S. Crawley
1914 & 1920	E.M. Baerlein and G.G. Kershaw	1987	J.S. Male and R. Owen-Browne
1921	Hon. C.N. Bruce and Dr H.W. Leatham	1988	J.A.N. Prenn and J.S. Male
1922–23	J.C.F. Simpson and R.C.O. Williams	1989	J.A.N. Prenn and J.S. Male
1924–27	Hon. C.N. Bruce and Dr H.W. Leatham	1990	J.A.N. Prenn and J.S. Male
1928	Hon. C.N. Bruce and A.C. Raphael	1991	J.A.N. Prenn and J.S. Male
1929	J.C.F. Simpson and R.C.O. Williams	1992	W.R. Boone and T.B. Cockroft
1930	Lord Aberdare and Dr H.W. Leatham	1993	J.A.N. Prenn and J.S. Male
1931	J.C.F. Simpson and C.S. Crawley	1994	W.R. Boone and T.B. Cockroft
1932–33	K.A. Wagg and I. Akers-Douglas	1995	J.A.N Prenn and J.S. Male
1934	Lord Aberdare and P.W. Kemp-Welch	1996	W.R. Boone and T.B. Cockroft
1935	K.A. Wagg and I. Akers-Douglas	1997	T.B. Cockroft and R. Owen-Browne
1936–37	C.S. Crawley and J.C.F. Simpson	1998	W.R. Boone and J.S. Male
1938	D.S. Milford and P.M. Whitehouse	1999	G.W. Barker and A.J. Robinson
1939 & 1946	C.S. Crawley and J.H. Pawle	2000	J.S. Male and C.M. Hue Williams

PROFESSIONAL SINGLES CHAMPIONSHIP
Scott-Chad Cup

	Winner	Runner-up			Winner	Runner-up	
1931	C.R. Read			1988	N.P.A. Smith	S.M. Hazell	3–0
1932	A.G. Cooper			1989	N.P.A. Smith	S.M. Hazell	3–2
1946	J.P. Dear			1990	S.M. Hazell	N.P.A. Smith	3–2
In 1979 it was played as a knock-out competition for the first time				1991	S.M. Hazell	N.P.A. Smith	3–0
1979	N.A.R. Cripps	T.S. Whatley	3–0	1992	N.P.A. Smith	S.M. Hazell	3–0
1980	T.S. Whatley	N.A.R. Cripps	3–1	1993	N.P.A. Smith	S.M. Hazell	3–0
1981	N.A.R. Cripps	T.S. Whatley	3–1	1994	P. Brake	N.A.R. Cripps	3–0
1982	S.M. Hazell	N.A.R. Cripps	3–1	1995	P. Brake	N.P.A. Smith	3–2
1983	N.A.R. Cripps	S.M. Hazell	3–2	1996	N.P.A. Smith	D.J. Makey	3–0
1984	S.M. Hazell	N.A.R. Cripps	3–0	1997	P. Brake	D.J. Makey	3–0
1985	N.P.A. Smith	S. Tulley	3–2	1998	N.P.A. Smith	P. Brake	3–1
1986	N.P.A. Smith	N.A.R. Cripps	3–0	1999	T.N. Sawrey-Cookson	M.V. Hubbard	3–0
1987	N.P.A. Smith	S.M. Hazell	3–0	2000	T.N. Sawrey-Cookson	M.V. Hubbard	3–0

PUBLIC SCHOOLS CHAMPIONSHIP

Played at Prince's 1868–86, Lord's 1887 and Queen's since 1888 except in 1941, when the final was played at Wellington

	Winner	Runner-up	
1868	Eton (C.J. Ottaway and W.F. Tritton)	Cheltenham (J.J. Read and A.T. Myers)	4-3
1869	Eton (C.J. Ottaway and J.P. Rodger)	Rugby (S.K. Gwyer and H.W. Gardner)	4-0
1870	Rugby (H.W. Gardner and T.S. Pearson)	Eton (J.P. Rodger and F.C. Ricardo)	4-2
1871	Harrow (G.A. Webbe and A.A. Hadow)	Eton (F.C. Ricardo and A.W. Ridley)	4-3
1872	Harrow (G.A. Webbe and A.A. Hadow)	Eton (E.O. Wilkinson and W.W. Whitmore)	4-1
1873	Harrow (P.F. Hadow and F.D. Leyland)	Rugby (J.J. Barrow and J. Harding)	4-0
1874	Harrow (F.D. Leyland and C.W.M. Kemp)	Winchester (H.J.B. Hollings and H.R. Webbe)	4-0
1875	Eton (J. Oswald and D. Lane)	Winchester (H.R. Webbe and A.L. Ellis)	4-1
1876	Harrow (H.E. Meek and L.K. Jarvis)	Eton (Hon. I.F.W. Bligh and V.A. Butler)	4-1
1877	Eton (C.A.C. Ponsonby and Hon. I.F.W. Bligh)	Marlborough (G.M. Butterworth and F.M. Lucas)	4-1
1878	Eton (C.A.C. Ponsonby and J.D. Cobbold)	Harrow (H.F. de Paravicini and M.C. Kemp)	4-0
1879	Harrow (M.C. Kemp and Hon. F.R. de Moleyns)	Rugby (C.F.H. Leslie and W.G. Stutfield)	4-0
1880	Harrow (M.C. Kemp and E.M. Hadow)	Eton (P. St. L. Grenfell and J.C.B. Eastwood)	4-2
1881	Harrow (E.M. Hadow and A.F. Kemp)	Marlborough (A.W. Martyn and H.M. Leaf)	4-1
1882	Eton (R.H. Pemberton and A.C. Richards)	Harrow (H.E. Crawley and C.D. Buxton)	4-2
1883	Harrow (H.E. Crawley and C.D. Buxton)	Eton (R.H. Pemberton and H. Phillipson)	4-2
1884	Harrow (E.M. Butler and C.D. Buxton)	Eton (H. Philipson and J.H.B. Noble)	4-3
1885	Harrow (E.M. Butler and E. Crawley)	Eton (H. Philipson and H.W. Forster)	4-3
1886	Harrow (E. Crawley and N.T. Holmes)	Haileybury(J.D. Campbell and H.M. Walters)	4-2
1887	Harrow (P. Ashworth and R.D. Cheales)	Charterhouse (H.L. Meyer and R. Nicholson)	4-1
1888	Charterhouse (E.C. Streatfeild and W. Shelmerdine)	Harrow (R.D. Cheales and E.W.F. Castleman)	4-2
1889	Winchester (E.J. Neve and T.B. Case)	Charterhouse (W. Shelmerdine and F.S. Cokayne)	4-2
1890	Harrow (A.H.M. Butler and W.F.G. Wyndham	Wellington (G.J. Mordaunt and R.H. Raphael)	4-3
1891	Wellington (G.J. Mordaunt and R.H. Raphael)	Malvern (H.K. Foster and W.L. Foster)	4-2
1892	Malvern (H.K. Foster and W.L. Foster)	Harrow (B.N. Bosworth-Smith and F.G.H. Clayton)	4-2
1893	Charterhouse (E. Garnett and V.H. Pennell)	Eton (P.W. Cobbold and H. Harben)	4-3
1894	Charterhouse (V.H. Pennell and E. Garnett)	Malvern (C.J. Burnup and H.H. Marriott)	4-2
1895	Harrow (J.H. Stogdon and A.S. Crawley)	Clifton (R.O. de Gex and A.H.C. Kearsey)	4-0
1896	Rugby (W.E. Wilson-Johnston and G.T. Hawes)	Eton (H.C.B. Underdown and E.A. Biedermann)	4-3
1897	Harrow (L.F. Andrewes and W.F.A. Rattigan)	Winchester (E.B. Noel and R.A. Williams)	4-3
1898	Harrow (W.F.A. Rattigan and L.F. Andrewes)	Eton (E.M. Baerlein and J.E. Tomkinson)	4-2
1899	Eton (S. MacNaghten and I.A. de la Rue)	Harrow (F.B. Wilson and S.J.G. Hoare)	4-1
1900	Malvern (B.S. Foster and W.H.B. Evans)	Rugby (S.C. Blackwood and O. Fleischmann)	4-0
1901	Marlborough (A.J. Graham and L.E. Gillett)	Haileybury (S.M. Toyne and P.F. Reid)	4-0
1902	Harrow (G.A. Phelips and C. Browning)	Rugby (K.M. Agnew and J.V. Nesbitt)	4-2
1903	Harrow (G.A. Phelips and L.M. MacLean)	Rugby (K.M. Agnew and K. Powell)	4-2
1904	Winchester (Hon. C.N. Bruce and E.L. Wright)	Malvern (G.N. Foster and A.P. Day)	4-0
1905	Eton (J.J. Astor and M.W. Bovill)	Wellington (H. Brougham and T. Hone)	4-1
1906	Charterhouse (C.V.L. Hooman and R.M. Garnett)	Wellington (H. Brougham and E.C. Harrison)	4-1
1907	Wellington (H. Brougham and E.C. Harrison)	Malvern (M.K. Foster and F.T. Mann)	4-1
1908	Malvern (M.K. Foster and N.J.A. Foster)	Rugby (C.F.B. Simpson and C.C. Watson)	4-1
1909	Charterhouse (H.A. Denison and H.W. Leatham)	Eton (V. Bulkeley-Johnson and J.E. Craigie)	4-1
1910	Charterhouse (H.W. Leatham and H.A. Denison)	Eton (E.L. Bury and Hon. J.N. Manners)	4-0
1911	Rugby (C.F.B. Simpson and W.H. Clarke)	Winchester (L. de O. Tollemache and D.F. McConnel)	4-3
1912	Charterhouse (G.A. Wright and C.B. Leatham)	Wellington (E.G. Bartlett and W.G. Grenville Grey)	4-0
1913	Wellington (E.G. Bartlett and F.A. Carnegy)	Haileybury (D.H. Hake and L.F. Marson)	4-0

table continues

	Winner	*Runner-up*	
1914	Charterhouse (L.D.B. Monier-Williams and J.H. Strachan)	Wellington (E.A. Simson and C.P. Hancock)	4–3
1919	Marlborough (G.S. Butler and G.W.F. Haslehust)	Malvern (C.G.W. Robson and N.E. Partridge)	4–1
1920	Malvern (C.G.W. Robson and J.A. Deed)	Eton (H.P. Guinness and R. Aird)	4–1
1921	Wellington (P.N. Durlacher and L. Lees)	Eton (R. Aird and H.D. Sheldon)	4–1
1922	Eton (G.S. Incledon-Webber and O.C. Smith-Bingham)	Radley (F.C. Dawnay and A.E. Blair)	4–2
1923	Rugby (D.S. Milford and G.M. Goodbody)	Radley (F.C. Dawnay and A.E. Blair)	4–2
1924	Rugby (D.S. Milford and E.F. Longrigg)	Eton (C.J. Child and T.A. Pilkington)	4–2
1925	Harrow (A.C.Raphael and N.M. Ford)	Eton (C.J. Child and T.A. Pilkington)	4–3
1926	Wellington (R.C. Dobson and J. Powell)	Harrow (N.M. Ford and A.M. Crawley)	4–3
1927	Eton (K.A. Wagg and I. Akers-Douglas)	Harrow (R.H. Anstruther-Gough-Calthorpe and G.L. Raphael)	4–0
1928	Eton (I. Akers-Douglas and I. A. de Lyle)	Winchester (P.J. Brett and W.D.D. Evans)	4–3
1929	Winchester (N. McCaskie and R.H. Priestley)	Haileybury (E.N. Evans and R.W. Bulmore)	4–0
1930	Radley (P.I. Van der Gucht and W.H. Vestey)	Eton (R. Grant and J. de P. Whitaker)	4–1
1931	Harrow (R. Pulbrook and J.M.F. Lightly)	Eton (A. M. Hedley and J.C. Atkinson-Clark)	4–2
1932	Harrow (R. Pulbrook and J.H. Pawle)	Rugby (R.A. Gray and R.F. Lumb)	4–2
1933	Rugby (R.A. Gray and R.F. Lumb)	Harrow (R. Pulbrook and J.H. Pawle)	4–2
1934	Rugby (R.F. Lumb and P. Kershaw)	Haileybury (W.M. Robertson and F.R.E. Malden)	4–2
1935	Winchester (J.T. Faber and A.B. Kingsley)	Marlborough (P.M. Whitehouse and J.D.L. Dickson)	4–2
1936	Malvern (P.D. Manners and N.W. Beeson)	Clifton (W.E. Brassington and S.G. Greenbury)	4–0
1937	Malvern (P.D. Manners and N.W. Beeson	Tonbridge (J.R. Thompson and P. Pettman)	4–3
1938	Rugby (A. Kershaw and J.D.L. Repard)	Malvern (P.D. Manners and D. Chalk)	4–2
1939	Rugby (J.D.L. Repard and W.H.D. Dunnett)	Winchester (A.R. Taylor and H.E.W. Bowyer)	4–0
1940	Haileybury (J.K. Drinkall and A. Fairbairn)	Rugby (L.G.H. Hingley and P.M. Dagnall)	4–1
1941	Haileybury (J.K. Drinkall and A. Fairbairn)	Clifton (R.J. Potter and L.J. Waugh)	4–0
1942	*no competition*		
1943	Winchester (G.H.G. Doggart and J.B. Thursfield)	Harrow (I.N. Mitchell and J.G. Hogg)	4–2
1944	Winchester (H.E. Webb and G.H.J. Myrtle)	Eton (A.J.H. Ward and J.R. Greenwood)	4–2
1945	Winchester (H.E. Webb and G.H.J. Myrtle)	Eton (J.A.R. Clench and W.H.R. Brooks)	4–1
1946	Wellington (C.B. Haycraft and J.E.L. Ainslie)	Harrow (G.R. Simmonds and J.A. Glynne-Percy)	4–1
1947	Harrow (G.R. Simmonds and R.K.F.C. Treherne-Thomas)	Eton (R.F.H. Ward and W.J. Collins)	4–2
1948	Harrow (D.W. Taylor and T.A.M. Pigott)	Wellington (A.H. Swift and R.L. Lees)	4–3
1949	Winchester (P.M. Welsh and M.R. Coulman)	Eton (I.C. de Sales la Terriere and A.C.D. Ingleby-Mackenzie)	4–3
1950	Winchester (M.R. Coulman and A.D. Myrtle)	Harrow (R.L.O. Bridgeman and R.J. McAlpine)	4–2
1951	Winchester (M.R. Coulman and A.D. Myrtle)	Tonbridge (M.C. Cowdrey and J.F. Campbell)	4–2
1952	Rugby (D.R.W. Harrison and J.G.H. Hogben)	Wellington(P. de Mesquita and M.W. Bolton)	4–2
1953	Winchester (R.T.C. Whatmore and D.B.D. Lowe)	Radley (E.R. Dexter and I.A.K. Dipple)	4–3
1954	Harrow (C.A. Strang and R.B. Bloomfield)	Marlborough (N.R.C. Marr and P.H.R. Anderson)	4–2
1955	Eton (C.T.M. Pugh and Lord Chelsea)	Winchester (C.N. Copeman and Hon. M.M. Mitchell-Thompson)	4–1
1956	Charterhouse (C.J. Swallow and J.J. Carless)	Tonbridge (M.S. Connell and M.R.V. Clinch)	4–2
1957	Tonbridge (M.S. Connell and P.D. Rylands)	Marlborough (C.P. Pyemont and N.C. Harris)	4–1
1958	Eton (J.W. Leonard and D.M. Norman)	Winchester (P.J.L. Wright and Nawab of Pataudi)	4–1
1959	Winchester (Nawab of Pataudi and C.E.M. Snell)	Eton (D.M. Norman and R.M. Bailey)	4–3
1960	Marlborough (A.J. Price and M.G. Griffith)	Winchester (C.E.M. Snell and P.B. Hay)	4–2
1961	Eton (G.P.D. Milne and B.A. Fitzgerald)	Marlborough (M.G. Griffith and J. Hopper)	4–2
1962	Marlborough (M.G. Griffith and J. Hopper)	Winchester (H.R. Angus and C.J.H. Green)	4–3

table continues

	Winner	*Runner-up*	
1963	Eton (R.A. Pilkington and M.D.T. Faber)	Winchester (H.R. Angus and C.L. Sunter)	4–1
1964	Eton (M.D.T. Faber and G.W. Pilkington)	Tonbridge (T.F. Tyler and A.H.V. Monteuuis)	4–3
1965	Rugby (W.J.C. Surtees and A.M.A. Hankey)	Eton (G.W. Pilkington and A.R. Bonsor)	4–3
1966	Malvern (P.F.C. Begg and P. D'A. Mander)	Radley (J.K. Rogers and B.M. Osborne)	4–0
1967	Eton (Lord Richard Wellesley and M.J.J. Faber)	Harrow (R.N. Readman and R.S. Crawley)	4–3
1968	Eton (M.J.J. Faber and W.R. Boone)	Rugby (S.R. Miller and J.C.A. Leslie)	4–0
1969	Eton (M.J.J. Faber and A.G. Milne)	Harrow (C.H. Braithwaite and G.R.J. McDonald)	4–0
1970	Eton (R.W. Drysdale and N.H.P. Bacon)	Rugby (T.H. Weatherill and J.H.M. Griffiths)	4–0
1971	Harrow (M. Thatcher and J.A.N. Prenn)	Clifton (J.P. Willcocks and D.G. Parsons)	4–2
1972	Winchester (A.C. Lovell and P.G. Seabrook)	Haileybury (J.E. Dawes and R.F. Hollington)	4–0
1973	Tonbridge (N.B.S. Hawkins and C.S. Cowdrey)	Malvern (J.G. Hughes and M.W. Nicholls)	4–1
1974	Malvern (M.W. Nicholls and P.C. Nicholls)	Eton (T.M. Brudenell and D.M. Lindsay)	4–2
1975	Malvern (P.C. Nicholls and M.A. Tang)	Harrow (A.C.S. Piggott and P. Greig)	4–0
1976	Marlborough (D.K. Watson and M.N.P. Mockridge)	Malvern (P.C. Nicholls and M.A. Tang)	4–3
1977	Malvern (P.J. Rosser and A.J.B. McDonald)	Marlborough (D.K. Watson and C.F. Worlidge)	4–3
1978	Haileybury (R.G.P. Ellis and P. Wallis)	Harrow (D.J.G. Thomas and M.J.L. Paul)	4–1
1979	Harrow (D.J.G. Thomas and M.J.L. Paul)	Eton (D.J.C. Faber and A.D. Pease)	4–1
1980	Wellington (J.H.C. Mallinson and R.A.C. Mallinson)	Marlborough (A.J. Naylor and M.R.C. Swallow)	4–0
1981	Tonbridge (G.R. Cowdrey and P.H. Reiss)	Clifton (P.B. Morris and T.R.V. Robins)	4–2
1982	Radley (J.S. Male and J.P. Snow)	Tonbridge (G.R. Cowdrey and A.M. Spurling)	4–0
1983	Tonbridge (A.M. Spurling and R. Owen-Browne)	Eton (A.C.B. Giddins and M.H. Brooks)	4–1
1984	Harrow (D.G. Dick and S. O'N Segrave)	Wellington (D.S.C. Mallinson and A.H. Gordon)	4–1
1985	Tonbridge (R. Owen-Browne and S.M.S. Davies)	Eton (P. Baily and M.C. Small)	4–0
1986	Tonbridge (J.I. Longley and J.A.G. Waters)	Clifton (G.J. Palmer and D.B. White)	4–0
1987	Tonbridge (J.I. Longley and J.L. Nance)	Marlborough (A.J. Robinson and G.W. Barker)	4–2
1988	Marlborough (A.J. Robinson and G.W. Barker)	Tonbridge (R.D. Gill and D.R. Penfold)	4–0
1989	Marlborough (T.P.W. Barker and J.J. Hey)	Radley (L.E. Danby and M.J. Lowrey)	4–0
1990	Clifton (M.G.N. Windows and J.A. Crane)	Eton (A.J. Smith-Bingham and J.J.S. Larken)	4–2
1991	Clifton (M.G.N. Windows and J.A. Crane)	Eton (A.J. Smith-Bingham and J.J.S. Larken)	4–2
1992	Winchester (N.R. Hall and M. Segal)	Marlborough (S. Gidoomal and T.C. Stewart-Liberty)	4–3
1993	Haileybury (R.E. Walker and D.A. Cruickshank)	Rugby (R.D. Carter and H.L. Green)	4–3
1994	Rugby (R.D. Carter and C.J.C. Robards)	Haileybury (R.E. Walker and D.A. Cruickshank)	4–2
1995	Rugby (R.D. Carter and R.J.A. Hicks)	Eton (N.A. Bailey and J.P.C. Wigan)	4–2
1996	Eton (N.A. Bailey and J.P.C. Wigan)	Winchester (E.D.C. Craig and H. Lloyd Owen)	4–0
1997	Eton (G.J. Smith-Bingham and H.J.H. Loudon)	Harrow (A.T.R. Titchener-Barrett and C.J.R. Wilson)	4–1
1998	Tonbridge (D.D. Cherry and J.W.R. Parker)	Harrow (A.T.R Titchener-Barrett and C.J.R Wilson)	4–2
1999	Harrow (R.J. Wilcox and T.G. Dunbar)	Tonbridge (J.W.R. Parker and N.G.H. Hutton)	4–1
2000	Harrow (T.G. Dunbar and O. Craven)	Cheltenham (G. Tyndall and M. Stout)	4–0

PUBLIC SCHOOLS SINGLES CHAMPIONSHIP

H.K. Foster Cup
1951–54 on handicap, 1955 open competition

	Winner	Runner-up
1951	A.D. Myrtle (Winchester)	M.D. Scott (Winchester)
1952	M.D. Scott (Winchester)	R.H.B. Neame (Harrow)
1953	T.L. Mesquita (Wellington)	N.R.C. Marr (Marlborough)
1954	R.B. Bloomfield (Harrow)	R.J.L. Sidley (Harrow)
1955	J.G. Tildesley (Rugby)	R.M.K. Gracey (Tonbridge)
1956	C.J. Swallow (Charterhouse)	P.R. Chamberlain (Marlborough)
1957	P.D. Rylands (Tonbridge)	J.W. Leonard (Eton)
1958	J.W. Leonard (Eton)	D.M. Norman (Eton)
1959	J.L. Cutherbertson (Eton)	J.W.T. Wilcox (Malvern)
1960	G.P.D. Milne (Eton)	J.W.T. Wilcox (Malvern)
1961	G.P.D. Milne (Eton)	M.G. Griffith (Marlborough)
1962	M.G. Griffith (Marlborough)	J. Hopper (Marlborough)
1963	H.R. Angus (Winchester)	R.P. Walker (Malvern)
1964	G.B. Trentham (Wellington)	A.H.V. Monteuuis (Tonbridge)
1965	A.H.V. Monteuuis (Tonbridge)	J.M.M. Hooper (Charterhouse)
1966	W.J.C. Surtees (Rugby)	J.K. Rogers (Radley)
1967	R.S. Crawley (Harrow)	M.J.J. Faber (Eton)
1968 *Jan*	M.J.J. Faber (Eton)	C.J.M. Symons (Clifton)
1968 *Dec*	M.J.J. Faber (Eton)	C.H. Braithwaite (Harrow)
1969	C.N. Hurst-Brown (Wellington)	R.W. Drysdale (Eton)
1970	R.W. Drysdale (Eton)	J.P. Willcocks (Clifton)
1971	M. Thatcher (Harrow)	J.H.M. Griffiths (Rugby)
1972	D.G. Parsons (Clifton)	J.E. Dawes (Haileybury)
1973	M.W. Nicholls (Malvern)	R.F. Hollington (Haileybury)
1974	M.W. Nicholls (Malvern)	M.A. Szarf (Harrow)
1975	A.C.S. Pigott (Harrow)	P.C. Nicholls (Malvern)
1976	M.N.P. Mockridge (Marlborough)	P.J. Rosser (Malvern)
1977	R.G.P. Ellis (Haileybury)	J.C. Spurling (Tonbridge)
1978	R.G.P. Ellis (Haileybury)	D.J.G. Thomas (Harrow)
1979	R.G.P. Ellis (Haileybury)	T.R.V. Robins (Eton)
1980–81	J.S. Male (Radley)	P. Tichener (Malvern)
1982	J.P. Snow (Radley)	A.M. Spurling (Tonbridge)
1983	A.M. Spurling (Tonbridge)	A.C.B. Giddins (Eton)
1984	R. Owen-Browne (Tonbridge)	D.G. Dick (Harrow)
1985	J.I. Longley (Tonbridge)	R.C.H. Bruce (Wellington)
1986	J.I. Longley (Tonbridge)	A.J. Robinson (Marlborough)
1987	G.W. Barker (Marlborough)	A.J. Robinson (Marlborough)
1988	G.W. Barker (Marlborough)	A.C. Hiscock (Malvern)
1989–90	M.G.N. Windows (Clifton)	A.J. Smith-Bingham (Eton)
1991	C.B.J. Danby (Harrow)	H.St.J. Foster (Harrow)
1992	H.St.J. Foster (Harrow)	G. Rees (Clifton)
1993	R.D. Carter (Rugby)	E. Behn (Radley)
1994	R.D. Carter (Rugby)	D. Stall (Haileybury)
1995	N.A. Bailey (Eton)	G.J. Smith-Bingham (Eton)
1996	A.T.R. Titchener-Barrett (Harrow)	G.J. Smith-Bingham (Eton)
1997	A.T.R. Titchener-Barrett (Harrow)	D.D. Cherry (Tonbridge)
1998	J.W.R. Parker (Tonbridge)	E.P. Cazalet (Eton)
1999	T.G. Dunbar (Harrow)	G. Tyndall (Cheltenham)
2000	J. Stout (Cheltenham)	A. Coldicott (Cheltenham)

THE UNITED STATES

OPEN SINGLES CHAMPIONSHIP

Clarence Pell Racquet Cup

1938	R. Grant III
1940	K. Chantler
1941	R. Grant III
1947	R.A.A. Holt
1948	R. Grant III
1950	R. Grant III
1957	K. Chantler
1958	G.W.T. Atkins
1959	A.B. Johnson
1960	K. Chantler
1961	D.M. Norman
1962–63	J.P. Dear
1964	A.B. Johnson
1965	S.S. Cox
1966–67	C.T.M. Pugh
1968	G.W.T. Atkins
1969–70	G.H. Bostwick Jr
1971–79	W.J.C. Surtees
1980	J.A.N. Prenn
1981	W.R. Boone
1982	J.A.N. Prenn
1983	D.H. McLernon
1984–86	W.R. Boone
1987	S.M. Hazell
1988	W.R. Boone
1989–90	J.S. Male
1991–96	N.P.A. Smith
1997–98	R. Owen-Browne
1999	N.P.A. Smith
2000	J.S. Male
2001	J.J.S. Larken

OPEN DOUBLES CHAMPIONSHIP

The Bertolotti Cup

1976	W.J.C. Surtees and E.F. Ulmann
1977	W.J.C. Surtees and P.M.L. Hannen
1978	W.J.C. Surtees and G.P.D. Milne
1979	W.J.C. Surtees and E.F. Ulmann
1980	W.J.C. Surtees and J.A.N. Prenn
1981	G.P.D. Milne and C.J.H. Green
1982	R.A. Crawley and A. Crawley
1983	D.H. McLernon and M.R. McMaster
1984	D.M. Norman and W.R. Boone
1985	J.A.N. Prenn and J.S. Male
1986	C.J. Hue Williams and J.A.N. Prenn
1987	S.M. Hazell and N.E.C. Barham
1988	S.M. Hazell and C.M. Hue Williams
1989	S.M. Hazell and N.P.A. Smith
1990	S.M. Hazell and N.P.A. Smith
1991	N.P.A. Smith and J. Cashman
1992	N.P.A. Smith and J. Burke
1993	N.P.A. Smith and D.G. Anderson
1994	N.P.A. Smith and W. Bristowe
1995	R. Owen-Browne and S. Tulley
1996	J.A.N. Prenn and J.S. Male
1997	N.P.A. Smith and P. Brake
1998	C.M. Hue Williams and M.G.N. Windows
1999	J. Beaumont and G. Devereux
2000	J. Beaumont and G. Devereux
2001	J.J.S. Larken and T.N. Sawrey-Cookson

AMATEUR SINGLES CHAMPIONSHIP

1890–91	B.S. de Garmendia	1911–12	R. Fincke	1947	J.R. Leonard	1980	W.R. Boone
1892	J.S. Tooker	1913–14	L. Waterbury	1948–51	R. Grant III	1981	D.H. McLernon
1893–94	B.S. de Garmendia	1915	C.C. Pell	1952	S.W. Pearson	1982	W.J.C. Surtees
1895	J.S. Tooker	1916	S.G. Mortimer	1953	R. Grant III	1983	W.R. Boone
1896–97	B.S. de Garmendia	1917–22	C.C. Pell	1954–56	G.W.T. Atkins	1984–85	D.H. McLernon
1898	F.F. Rolland	1923	S.G. Mortimer	1957	C.B. Pearson	1986	W.R. Boone
1899	Q.A. Shaw Jr	1924–25	C.C. Pell	1958	C.C. Pell Jr	1987	N.E.C. Barham
1900	E.H. Miles	1926	S.G. Mortimer	1959–60	G.W.T. Atkins	1988	D.H. McLernon
1901	Q.A. Shaw Jr	1927–28	C.C. Pell	1961–63	D.M. Norman	1989	W.R. Boone
1902	C.H. Mackay	1929	H.D. Sheldon	1964	P.B. Read	1990	W. Maltby
1903	P. Whitney	1930	S.G. Mortimer	1965	S.S. Cox	1991–95	W.R. Boone
1904	G.H. Brooke	1931–33	C.C. Pell	1966–67	D.M. Norman	1996–97	R. Owen-Browne
1905	L. Waterbury	1934	E.M. Edwards	1968	J.W. Leonard	1998	J.J.S. Larken
1906	P.D. Houghton	1935	H.D. Sheldon	1969–70	G.W.T. Atkins	1999	J.A.N. Prenn
1907	R. Fincke	1936	E.M. Edwards	1971–72	W.J.C. Surtees	2000	J.S. Male
1908	Q.A. Shaw	1937–39	R. Grant III	1973	H.R. Angus	2001	J.J.S. Larken
1909	H.F. McCormick	1940	W. Ingersoll	1974–79	W.J.C. Surtees		
1910	Q.A. Shaw	1941–46	R. Grant III				

AMATEUR DOUBLES CHAMPIONSHIP

1899	Q.A. Shaw, Jr. and H.H. Hunnewell Jr		1953	D.S. Milford and J.R. Thompson
1900	L.M. Stockton and G.R. Fearing		1954–55	G.W.T. Atkins and W. Wood Prince
1901	Payne Whitney and Q.A. Shaw Jr		1956–57	S.W. Pearson and C.B. Pearson
1902	H.D. Scott and G.H. Brooke		1958	G.W.T. Atkins and K.A. Wagg
1903	H.D. Scott and R.K. Cassatt		1959	C.C. Pell Jr and C.B. Pearson
1904	Q.A. Shaw Jr and Matthew Bartlett		1960	C.T.M. Pugh and R.M. Bailey
1905–06	H.D. Scott and G.R. Fearing Jr		1961	R.L.O. Bridgeman and J.A.R. Clench
1907	Reginald Fincke and R.D. Wrenn		1962	D.M. Norman and R.M. Bailey
1908	H.D. Scott and G.R. Fearing Jr		1963	C.J. Swallow and M.R. Coulman
1909	Q.A. Shaw Jr and P.D. Haughtonx		1964	S.S. Cox and W. Lewis
1910	Lawrence Waterbury and Reginald Fincke		1965	C.H. Pickwoad and A.J. Coote
1911	H.D. Scott and G.R. Fearing Jr		1966	M. Sales and R. Turner
1912	Q.A. Shaw and G.R. Fearing Jr.		1967–69	G.W.T. Atkins and S.S. Cox
1913	H.D. Scott and P.D. Haughton		1970	D.H. McLernon and M. Sales
1914	J.W. Wear and D.F. Davis		1971	W.J.C. Surtees and C.J. Hue Williams
1915	C.C. Pell and S.G. Mortimer		1972–73	W.J.C. Surtees and R. Lightfine
1916	Lawrence Waterbury and J.C. Waterbury		1974	D.H. McLernon and J.J. Wagg
1917	George H. Brooke and J.W. Wear		1975	W.J.C. Surtees and R. Lightfine
1920	Jay Gould and J.W. Wear		1976	D.H. McLernon and C.H. Pickwoad
1921–25	C.C. Pell and S.G. Mortimer		1977	W.J.C. Surtees and G.P.D. Milne
1926	R.A. Gardner and H.A. Linn		1978–79	W.J.C. Surtees and E.F. Ulmann
1927	C.C. Pell and S.G. Mortimer		1980	W.R. Boone and R.A. Crawley
1928	Hon. C.N. Bruce and J.C.F. Simpson		1981	D.H. McLernon and M. McMaster
1929	C.C. Pell and S.G. Mortimer		1982	J.A.N. Prenn and C.T.M. Pugh
1930	Lord Aberdare and Dr H.W. Leatham		1983	W.R. Boone and C.T.M. Pugh
1931	C.C. Pell and S.G. Mortimer		1984	D.H. McLernon and M. McMaster
1932	S.W. Pearson and W.C. Wright		1985	W.J.C. Surtees and E.F. Ulmann
1933	W. Palmer Dixon and H.N. Rawlins Jr		1986	W.R. Boone and V. Cazalet
1934	H.D. Sheldon and J.W. Brooks		1987	N.E.C. Barham and R.E. Wood II
1935–36	J.R. Leonard and M.C. Kirkbride		1988	D.H. McLernon and D.H. Hamlen
1937–39	Robert Grant III and C.C. Pell Jr		1989	E.F. Ulmann and W.R. Boone
1940	J.R. Leonard and M.C. Kirkbride		1990	W. Maltby and P.E. de Svastich
1941	Robert Grant III and C.C. Pell Jr		1991–94	E.F. Ulmann and W.R. Boone
1946	Robert Grant III and C.C. Pell Jr		1995–96	R. Owen-Browne and K. Nemec
1947	R.A.A. Holt and A.R. Taylor		1997	R. Owen-Browne and S.M.S. Davies
1948	J.R. Leonard and M.C. Kirkbride		1998–99	W. Bristowe and J.J.S. Larken
1949–50	Robert Grant, III and C.C. Pell Jr		2000	J.A.N. Prenn and J.S. Male
1951	R.A.A. Holt and K.A. Wagg		2001	J.J.S. Larken and J.A.N. Prenn
1952	K.A. Wagg and J.A. Rolland			

Canada

AMATEUR SINGLES CHAMPIONSHIP

1896	F.F. Rolland	1950–53	R. Grant III
1897	B.S. de Garmendia	1954–56	G.W.T. Atkins
1898	Q.A. Shaw	1957	C.C. Pell Jr
1899	F.F. Rolland	1958	G.W.T. Atkins
1900	E.H. Miles	1959	C.B. Pearson
1901–02	F.F. Rolland	1960	G.W.T. Atkins
1903	W.R. Miller	1961	R.M. Bailey
1904–05	F.F. Rolland	1962	D.M. Norman
1906	E. Hewitt	1963	M.S. Connell
1907	R.E. MacDougall	1964	J.A. Rolland
1908–09	F.F. Rolland	1965	S.S. Cox
1910–11	R.E. MacDougall	1966	C.T.M. Pugh
1912	F.F. Rolland	1967	D.M. Norman
1913	E. Greenshields	1968	G.W.T. Atkins
1914	C.C. Pell	1969	D.M. Norman
1915	H.M. Smith	1970–72	D.H. McLernon
1920	A.S. Cassils	1973–75	W.J.C. Surtees
1921–22	C.C. Pell	1976	D.H. McLernon
1923	J. Gould	1977	W.J.C. Surtees
1924–27	C.C. Pell	1978	W.R. Boone
1928	Hon. C.N. Bruce	1979	J.A.N. Prenn
1929	A.S. Cassils	1980	W.R. Boone
1930	Lord Aberdare	1981–86	J.A.N. Prenn
1931	W. Palmer Dixon	1987–91	J.S. Male
1932–33	Sir John Child	1992	J.A.N. Prenn
1934	H.D. Sheldon	1993	B.J. Sambrook
1935	C.C. Pell	1994	W.R. Boone
1936	H.D. Sheldon	1995	R. Owen-Browne
1937–39	R. Grant III	1996	T.B. Cockroft
1946	J.R. Leonard	1997	R. Owen-Browne
1947	R. Grant III	1998–99	T.B. Cockroft
1948–49	J.R. Leonard	2000	M.G.N. Windows

AMATEUR DOUBLES CHAMPIONSHIP

1920	A. Wilson and H.M. Smith	1960	G.W.T. Atkins and K.A. Wagg
1921	S.G. Mortimer and F.T. Frelinghuysen	1961–62	R.M. Bailey and D.M. Norman
1922	C.C. Pell and S.G. Mortimer	1963	M.R. Coulman and C.J. Swallow
1923	Jay Gould and L. du P. Irving	1964	C.E. Pacaud and J.V. Kerrigan
1924	C.C. Pell and S.G. Mortimer	1965	C.H. Pickwoad and A.J. Coote
1925	J.C.F. Simpson and R.C.O. Williams	1966–67	T.E. Price and D.M. Norman
1926–27	C.C. Pell and A.L. Corey	1968	G.W.T. Atkins and J.A. Rolland
1928	C.C. Pell and S.G. Mortimer	1969–70	D.H. McLernon and M. Sales
1929	F.C. Dobell and S.H. Dobell	1971	W.J.C. Surtees and W. Finkenstaedt
1930	Lord Aberdare and Dr H.W. Leatham	1972	D.H. McLernon and M. Sales
1931	G.D. Huband and A.S. Cassils	1973	C.H. Pickwoad and J.W.S. Chapman
1932	A.R. Chipman and S.H. Dobell	1974	W.J.C. Surtees and R. Lightfine
1933–34	G.D. Huband and Sir John Child	1975–77	D.H. McLernon and C.H. Pickwoad
1935	J.R. Leonard and M.C. Kirkbride	1978–79	W.R. Boone and C.T.M. Pugh
1936	G.D. Huband and Sir John Child	1980	W.R. Boone and R.S. Crawley
1937–39	Robert Grant III and C.C. Pell Jr	1981	J.A.N. Prenn and C.J.H. Green
1946	S.H. Dobell and C.E. Pacaud	1982	J.A.N. Prenn and C. Hue Williams
1947	J.H. Pawle and G.S. Crawley	1983	W.R. Boone and R.S. Crawley
1948	J.R. Leonard and F.F. de Rham	1984	J.A.N. Prenn and A.N.W. Beeson
1949	J.R. Leonard and C.C. Pell Jr	1985	R.S. Crawley and A. Crawley
1950	C.C. Pell Jr and K.A. Wagg	1986	J.A.N. Prenn and C.M. Hue Williams
1951	J.R. Leonard and F.F. de Rham	1987	C.H. Pickwoad and D.H. McLernon
1952	Robert Grant III and J.A. Rolland	1988–91	J.S. Male and N.E.C. Barham
1953	D.S. Milford and J.R. Thompson	1992	T.B. Cockroft and S.M.S. Davis
1954–55	G.W.T. Atkins and K.A. Wagg	1993	D.H. McLernon and B.J. Sambrook
1956	C.C. Pell and F.F. de Rham	1994–98	T.B. Cockroft and R. Owen-Browne
1957	J.C. Cushing and C.E. Pacaud	1999	C.H. Pickwoad and J.A.N. Prenn
1958	G.W.T. Atkins and J.E. Price	2000	B.J. Sambrook and M.G.N. Windows
1959	J.A. Rolland and J.J. Wagg		

FURTHER READING

De la Paume au Tennis, Guy Bonhomme, 1991

History of Hampton Court, David Best

A History of Royal Tennis in Australia, Michael Garnett, 1985

Kultur Geschichte des Tennis, Heiner Gillmeister, 1990

Leamington Tennis Court, Charles Wade, 1996

The Racquet Club of Philadelphia, John McFadden, 1989

The Royal Game, L.St.J. Butler and P.J. Wordie (editors), 1989

Tennis: A Cut Above the Rest, Chris Ronaldson, 1985

Tennis and Oxford, Jeremy Potter, 1994

Tennis in Nederland 1500–1800, Cees de Bondt, 1993

Tennis. The Development of the European Ball Game, Roger Morgan, 1995

Two Centuries of Real Tennis, John Shneerson, 1997

The Winning Gallery, Allison Danzig, 1985

CONTRIBUTORS

The author and editor wish to thank the following contributors for giving such valuable help on the club section of the book:

Davis Anderson
John Aspinall

Stephen Baldock
Derek Barrett
Gerard Belliveau
Thierry Bernard-Tambour
The late John Bodden
Dick Brickley
John Burnett

Yves Carlier
Mike Carter
Rudolph Chelminski
Karl Cook
Norwood Cripps
Martin Crosby
Roger Crosby

Peter Dawes
Colin Dean
Mick Dean
Lachlan Deuchar
Mark Devine
Lawrie Doffman
Brian Dowling
John Duns

John Eaton
Jonathan Edwardes

John Gibbs
Michael Goodell
John Gundry

Andrew Hamilton
Jack Hickey
Jonathan Howell

Elihu Inselbuch

Tim Johnson

Andy Kinzler

Jean-Christophe Laprée
Martin Lloyd
Peter Luck-Hille

Jim MacLellan
Chris Marks
Sarah McGivern
Bill McLaughlin
John McNamara
Harry McVickar
Martin Mercer
John Miller

Ed Noll

Alan Oliver

Major Iain Park-Weir
Michael Parsons
Jenny Paterson
Haven Pell
Nick Ponsford
Jacques Pouyot
John Prenn

Edward Reid
Brian Rich
Steve Ronaldson
Phillip Rosser

Toby Sawrey-Cookson
Anthony Scratchley
Brian Sharp
Adrian Snow

John Trapp
John Thompson

Edward Ulmann

Charles Wade
Robert Wakely
Dennis Webster
Gerard Welker
Jim Wharton
Robert Wood

PHOTOGRAPHIC ACKNOWLEDGEMENTS

The author and publisher would like to thank the following for permission to reproduce their copyright photographs:

Hilary Brown	Mike Garnett	Jo Miller
John Burnett	Murray Glover	Celie Parker
Brian Dowling	Maynard Hall	Dave Penman
John Duns	Christopher Hurst	Nick Ponsford
Noel Edwards	Jones Photography	The Queen's Club
John Evans	AKG London/S. Domingie – M. Rabattie	Mike Roberts
Michael Freeman	George Mars	

All other photographs have been kindly lent by people from their private collections.

INDEX